100 YEARS

SIMON &
SCHUSTER

ALSO BY MO ROCCA

Mobituaries: Great Lives Worth Reliving
with Jonathan Greenberg

All the Presidents' Pets:
The Story of One Reporter Who Refused to Roll Over

Mo Rocca

and Jonathan Greenberg

Roctogenarians

Late in Life

Debuts, Comebacks, and Triumphs

SIMON & SCHUSTER

New York London Toronto Sydney New Delhi

100 YEARS
SIMON &
SCHUSTER

1230 Avenue of the Americas
New York, NY 10020

First Simon & Schuster hardcover edition June 2024

SIMON & SCHUSTER and colophon are registered trademarks of Simon & Schuster, LLC

Simon & Schuster: Celebrating 100 Years of Publishing in 2024

For information about special discounts for bulk purchases,
please contact Simon & Schuster Special Sales
at 1-866-506-1949 or business@simonandschuster.com.

The Simon & Schuster Speakers Bureau can bring authors to your live event.
For more information or to book an event, contact the Simon & Schuster Speakers Bureau
at 1-866-248-3049 or visit our website at www.simonspeakers.com.

Manufactured in the United States of America

1   3   5   7   9   10   8   6   4   2

Library of Congress Cataloging-in-Publication Data is available on file.

ISBN 978-1-6680-5250-1
ISBN 978-1-6680-5252-5 (ebook)

Contents

Contents

Contents

Introduction

In the summer of 2015, I was in Chicago taping an appearance on NPR's comedy quiz show *Wait Wait . . . Don't Tell Me!* By that point I'd been a regular panelist on the show for over a decade, so I was used to all sorts of big-name special guests coming on to gab with us. I mean, who could top Dick Van Dyke when he actually sang the little-known lyrics to *The Dick Van Dyke Show* theme for us? We'd had presidents, Supreme Court justices, and tech titans on to answer completely absurd questions. (When Microsoft's then-CEO Steve Ballmer appeared, host Peter Sagal quizzed him on—you guessed it—lip balm.)

But this appearance was different. Instead of recording in the basement auditorium where we'd been doing the show for years, this episode was taping outdoors, in Millennium Park's Pritzker Pavilion, in front of thousands of fans—thousands of *young* fans, since the special guest was twenty-two-year-old hip-hop superstar Chance the Rapper. People were screaming. A few were trying to *climb onto the stage.* Much as I love our NPR audience, they don't typically show this kind of enthusiasm. Okay, for Neil deGrasse Tyson or Ina Garten they come close. But this was a whole other level of energy.

Chance the Rapper was charming, telling us about impersonating Michael Jackson at his kindergarten graduation. Pretty much every comment he made elicited a shriek, even when he talked about his grandmother and copped to being a "nice boy rapper." I did my best to play the role of the middle-aged dorky white guy who grew up on show tunes, a role that comes naturally to me. (When we talked about his writing process, I cited my own favorite rhyme of all time, from the musical *Funny Girl*: "Kid, my heart ain't made of marble / But your rhythm's really horrible.") Chance played ball and the audience seemed to enjoy it.

And then I asked Chance a question that I didn't intend seriously, at least not consciously: "Would you please give it to me straight? I'm forty-six. Is it too late for me to become a rapper?" The question itself got a laugh.

"No, I don't think so," Chance answered with a straight face. "Some people might say it's too *soon* for you to become a rapper." There was another big laugh, and the conversation moved on. Peter Sagal would go on to quiz Chance on "Saran the Wrapper."

But I was stopped dead by Chance's comment. In that moment, I realized that I had already begun thinking of my life as one of progressively fewer opportunities, of doors closing. I had accepted the conventional wisdom that the older I was getting, the fewer avenues would be open to me; that aging was a process solely of gradually diminishing capacities. Basically, though I wouldn't have admitted it even to myself, I saw myself as over the hill. Mind you, I was *forty-six*!

But Chance had flipped the script on me. Why *was* I too old to be a rapper? Okay, you're laughing. And the truth is, my beatboxing is really not where it should be. On the other hand, getting older was only going to *increase* the likelihood that I'd gain the life experience and wisdom and skillz (FYI, that's how the kids spell it) necessary for meaningful creative expression.

I wouldn't be able to write this if I'd been born fifty years earlier. Men born in the United States in 1919 lived on average to fifty-three. Considering I'm fifty-five right now, I wouldn't be able to write anything at all. But in 2024, if you're in your forties, fifties, or sixties and reasonably healthy, then—to quote one of my favorite lyrics from *Bye Bye Birdie*—there's such a lot of livin' to do. (Incidentally, *Bye Bye Birdie* starred the aforementioned Dick Van Dyke, who as of this writing is ninety-eight and still singing in a barbershop quartet.)

Don't take my word for it. According to renowned geriatrician Louise Aronson, author of *Elderhood: Redefining Aging, Transforming Medicine, Reimagining Life*, "We've added a couple of decades, essentially an entire generation, onto our lives, and we haven't kind of socio-culturally figured out how to handle that." Today turning one hundred is no big deal. The big question is what to do with all that extra time.

Fortunately, there are plenty of models from yesterday—and more and more each day—who came into their own at the stage of life when society would have had them packing it in. My coauthor, Jonathan Greenberg, and I call these individuals Roctogenarians.

Some of the people in this book were unknown before they broke through.

Introduction

Laura Ingalls Wilder published her first *Little House* book at sixty-five. A near-broke Harland David Sanders was just a year older when he hit the road with a bucket of the seasoning that would help make Colonel Sanders the face of a Kentucky-fried empire. Both were mere chicks compared to abstract expressionist artist Carmen Herrera. She was 101 when she had her first solo exhibition at a major museum. It took that long for the critics to catch up to her.

Some broke through early in life and kept getting noticed, peaking in their final chapters—a late-in-life capstone to a monumental life. Fittingly, architects are well represented in this group. Frank Lloyd Wright submitting his design for the Guggenheim at eighty-four is the ultimate mic drop. Rita Moreno is also in this category. One of Hollywood's first EGOTs, she's still got it in her nineties.

Others had unfinished business that needed settling. Brian May was an aspiring astrophysicist when his musical talent sent him shooting in an entirely different direction—and he became the superstar lead guitarist for Queen. But he never forgot his first love and at sixty went back to school to earn his PhD in astrophysics. Swimmer Diana Nyad managed to put her own dream aside for thirty years. But who was she kidding? She had to complete that swim from Cuba to Florida—and she did so at sixty-four.

One thing everyone in this book has in common: a belief that late life is no time to surrender. Perhaps no one epitomizes that like Mary Church Terrell, who was born just nine months after the Emancipation Proclamation to parents who had been enslaved. As a young woman, Terrell was a leader in the fight against the barbaric practice of lynching. In her middle age, she cofounded the NAACP. And at the age of eighty-six—when she had more than earned her rest—this veteran led sit-ins at a Washington, DC, lunch counter. The ensuing lawsuit resulted in the legal desegregation of the nation's capital.

Terrell was fighting not for herself but for the future. So was Samuel Whittemore. The seventy-eight-year-old patriot took up arms on the very first day of the American Revolutionary War, had his face blown off by a redcoat . . . and kept on fighting. No retirement for him. Or for Mr. Pickles the tortoise, who at ninety became a first-time father. Seriously, if you have kids at ninety, you cannot afford to retire. Mr. Pickles isn't the only one to find love late in life. Hello, Carol Channing. The woman famous for playing matchmaker Dolly Levi reconnected with a junior high school crush and, happy at last, married at eighty-two.

We're not trying to sugarcoat things here. There are inevitable challenges that come with aging, especially physical ones. How those challenges are handled makes the key—and inspiring—difference. Henri Matisse was in his seventies when the ravages of cancer made painting too difficult. But he didn't stop creating. Instead, he traded his paintbrush for a pair of scissors and began making his celebrated series of paper cut-outs. Describing one of his most exuberant paper creations, *The Parakeet and the Mermaid*, Matisse wrote, "As I am obliged to remain in bed because of my health, I made a little garden around me where I can walk. There are leaves, fruit, a bird. I am the parakeet. And I have found myself in the work."

May you, the reader, the future Roctogenarian, find yourself in these pages.

Fast-Food Legends

Colonel Sanders
& Clara Peller

Think of this book as a banquet. A sumptuous feast of stories for every taste. Most of them sweet (think Carol Channing's late-in-life marriage), some of them bitter (think Carol Channing's previous marriage). There's plenty of salty (think all that ocean water Diana Nyad swallowed swimming from Cuba to Key West) and even some sour (think the dismal childhoods of author Frank McCourt or pianist Ruth Slenczynska).

Do we need to include umami? Isn't that like the Pluto of tastes?

Well, in the world of fast food, we've come upon two different stories of late-life success, each remarkable in its own way. And so like any respectable caterers, we've decided to offer you a choice—chicken or beef (with apologies to our vegetarian readers).

Chicken: Harland David Sanders
began his KFC empire at sixty-six

His name and image have made him a figure of American legend, almost of folklore. At some point late in his life, Kentucky Fried Chicken's Colonel Sanders, a white-haired, white-goateed southern gentleman in a white linen suit, became more than just a spokesman for deep-fried take-out chicken and entered a kind of pop-culture pantheon, keeping company with figures like Paul Bunyan, Betty Crocker, and Mickey Mouse, characters who have cut loose from their original contexts and taken up residence in the collective American imagination. Except that Harland Sanders was a real person—and a fairly ordinary one at that.

For most of his working life, Sanders was the owner of a single roadside restaurant in the small town of Corbin, Kentucky. It was not until he was sixty-six that, faced with a collapsing business, he actively undertook the venture that would cause customers across the continent to greedily lick their greasy, well-seasoned fingers in a desperate effort to prolong a thoroughly satisfying chicken dinner. At what was retirement age for many people, Sanders, with only his $105 monthly

Social Security check for income, built a business empire that would forever alter the restaurant industry—and would make the Colonel himself an American icon and a millionaire many times over.

It may be no surprise to learn that Harland Sanders came from humble beginnings. He grew up on an Indiana farm; his father died when he was small. He began helping the family by cooking for his younger siblings when he was only seven. Harland quit school in the seventh grade and worked at all kinds of odd jobs throughout his youth, including part-time midwife. He was already thirty-nine years old when he opened a Shell station in Corbin and began serving chicken and biscuits to travelers as a way of generating extra income. It was at this Corbin gas station-turned-eatery that he perfected the recipe later marketed as eleven herbs and spices and developed the rapid pressure-frying technique that millions would come to love. The chicken was good, the word spread, and Sanders soon earned a mention in a travel guide by Duncan Hines (also a real person, by the way). After years of struggling to make ends meet, Sanders found himself the owner of a successful business.

Sanders Court and Café, as it was called, was still merely a single restaurant when its owner's famous "Colonel" persona was born. What happened was that the restaurant's popularity led the governor, the wonderfully named Ruby Laffoon, to bestow on Sanders the honorary title of Kentucky Colonel. (No, it was not awarded for military service; there was no Great Poultry War in which Sanders, wielding a blood-soaked cleaver, distinguished himself for uncommon valor.) The title of "Kentucky Colonel" actually derives from the state militia that served in the War of 1812. But in the nineteenth century, the designation evolved from a military rank into a purely ceremonial one. In the 1920s, a society of Kentucky Colonels was formed, and Governor Laffoon, who had a taste for public relations, began to bestow the title upon movie stars like Bing Crosby, Fred Astaire, and Shirley Temple as a way of drawing national attention and tourism to the state. (Subsequent honorees included Winston Churchill, Pope John Paul II, and Phyllis Diller.)

According to John Ed Pearce, one of Sanders's biographers, one day Harland's barber, while trimming his customer's mustache and goatee, suggested that the chicken virtuoso embrace his ceremonial title by dressing the part, with a tailored linen suit and a black string tie made from grosgrain ribbon. Sanders, around sixty at this point, liked the idea, and the character of Colonel Sanders was born. As Pearce rhapsodizes:

> *Before, he had been just Harland Sanders. Now, he began to think of himself as Colonel Sanders. And Colonel Sanders would be, in subtle and then major ways, a person different from Harland. He would be able to do things Harland had wanted to do but had never done, be things Harland had never been. In time, Harland would become submerged in the identity of the Colonel.*

As James Gatz of North Dakota became the Great Gatsby, as Bruce Wayne became Batman, as Garth Brooks became Chris Gaines, so Harland was reborn as Colonel Sanders. But it wasn't long after this self-reinvention that his thriving business found itself in trouble. In the early 1950s, a new highway was built through southern Kentucky, diverting the steady stream of traffic that was the lifeblood for Sanders's roadside eatery. Sales plummeted, and by 1956, the entire operation was in danger. At sixty-six, the Colonel needed to find a brand-new way to earn a living. (A similar thing happened to Norman Bates and his motel, but Sanders responded much more constructively.)

A few years before, Sanders had already experimented with franchising, providing his secret recipe and technique to a Salt Lake City–area restaurant owner in exchange for a regular fee. It was actually this initial franchisee, Pete Harman, who first used the name "Kentucky Fried Chicken"—a phrase invented by his sign painter, who thought it conjured warm feelings of southern hospitality. The chicken proved to be as finger-lickin' tasty in Utah as it was in Kentucky, and a few other restaurants also began to license the recipe, paying Sanders four cents for every chicken they sold.

Colonel Sanders
steering his way to a
fried chicken empire.
Courtesy of KFC

The Colonel gambled that franchising on a wider scale could sustain him and his wife financially. He closed his restaurant, selling it at auction for a loss, and began to drive around Kentucky with two pressure cookers and buckets of seasonings in the back of his car. (In the biopic, this would be a montage.) He would size up any restaurant he passed, and if it seemed a potential customer, he'd offer to make a meal for the staff, gambling on the quality of his own product. If, after the meal, the employees were still sucking the schmaltz off their fingers, he'd stay on as guest chef for a few days to win over the customers. Then he'd negotiate a deal to license the recipe and the technique. This itinerant lifestyle meant that Sanders was driving hours on end and often sleeping in his car—not easy for anyone, let alone a man in his late sixties who was by now suffering from arthritis. And despite all these efforts, after two years working as essentially a traveling chicken salesman, Sanders had acquired only five franchises.

But then suddenly, the gamble paid off. Sanders started gaining more customers. Soon the restaurant owners were coming to him asking to license his recipe. He and his wife were able to run their business from their home in Shelbyville, Kentucky, where they would mix, pack, and ship the blend of spices that they still kept secret, lest a competitor get hold of it. At the time, the fast-food market was dominated by the hamburger—notably McDonald's—but it turned out there was room for an avian alternative. By the Colonel's seventieth birthday, Kentucky Fried Chicken had four hundred outlets, and by his seventy-fourth, the number was somewhere around nine hundred, which included restaurants in Canada, Jamaica, England, Mexico, and the United Kingdom. By then he had patented the pressure-frying method that was essential to his success, and trademarked the slogan "finger lickin' good."

With the stunning success of the franchising strategy, Sanders was able to sell Kentucky Fried Chicken to the businessman (and later governor) John Y. Brown Jr. for $2 million in 1964. He stayed on as a consultant and member of the board, earning a yearly salary well above his Social Security allowance. The new owners saw the value of his Kentucky Colonel persona, and featured him in commercials and TV spots. Harland Sanders now enjoyed his seventies and eighties playing the character, Colonel Sanders, that he'd created. (According to another of his biographers, Josh Ozersky, for the last twenty years of his life Sanders never wore anything other than his white suit in public.)

A *New Yorker* profile in 1970 noted that the newfound wealth seemed unimportant to Sanders: "He and his wife, Claudia, live comfortably but modestly—by millionaires' standards, at least—in a two-story, ten-room house in Shelbyville, Kentucky, a small town thirty miles east of Louisville."

Sanders also spent these years protecting the reputation of the brand he'd created, suing franchises when the original recipe was not being followed and publicly decrying the poor quality of the "crispy" chicken marketed in 1978. He also became a spokesman for the value of working late in life, rejecting the very idea of retirement. In 1971, when he testified before a congressional subcommittee on the aged, he cited biblical precedent for his own work habits: "I told them that in the Garden of Eden God didn't tell Adam that he should work just to retirement age. He said in Genesis 3:19 a man should work 'till thou return unto the ground.'"

Not surprisingly, he cited diet as a factor in his longevity; surprisingly, that diet didn't center on chicken. In 1976, he told the *New York Times* he was on a "no-aging diet" that included a can of sardines every morning. In that same interview, he explained why he didn't drink wine: "Wine tastes like gasoline, and now that I read about all the arsenic in California wines, I'm glad I don't drink it. I have 14 more years to go to finish the century and I want to take care of myself so I make it." Apparently he had not read about fellow Roctogenarian and vintner Mark Grgich's triumph only months before, which *you'll* read about in the next chapter.

Sadly, Sanders lived only another four years, dying at ninety, on December 16, 1980. But before his burial, his body, dressed in his white linen double-breasted suit, lay in state in the Kentucky State Capitol in Frankfort so that satisfied customers from across the nation could pay their finger-lickin' respects.

Peanut: The World's Oldest Living Chicken

lived to 225 in chicken years

It was on Christmas morning 2023 that twenty-one-year-old Peanut the chicken died at home in Chelsea, Michigan, in the loving arms of her owner. "I realize she had a phenomenally long life for a chicken. I'm heartbroken nonetheless," Marsi Parker Darwin wrote.

"Phenomenally long" is no exaggeration. Chickens typically live five to ten years. According to one chicken-to-human years conversion calculator, Peanut's age in human years at death was an astonishing 225. (I'm suddenly picturing a production of *The Gin Game* not with Jessica Tandy and Hume Cronyn but starring Peanut the chicken and Mr. Pickles the tortoise, whom you'll read about later.)

That Peanut would break records was hardly preordained. Back in the spring of 2002, after her siblings had hatched, her egg remained in the nest. After a couple of days, Darwin decided to chuck the cold-to-the-touch egg into the pond behind her house. But just as she was about to release it, she heard a cheep. She peeled the shell back herself and discovered inside a "sad, wet waddled up mess," tiny and brown. Darwin named her Peanut.

Peanut's own biological mother rejected her, so Darwin raised Peanut as a "house chicken" for the first few years. "The [other] chickens didn't particularly care for her. They would peck at her." Darwin fed her a special diet of blueberries and yogurt.

A spokeswoman for the Michigan Allied Poultry Industries attributed Peanut's longevity to the attention given her by the Darwin family. "It is clear that she has received great housing, considerable attention and decreased stress, which has likely contributed to her life span. Peanut is an inspiration to us all."

Still, Peanut's final year was a turbulent one. After the *Guinness Book of World Records* had certified Peanut as a record holder, she suffered two losses. On Halloween, Millie, her fifteen-year-old daughter, died. And then on December 7, Benny, Peanut's boyfriend, believed to be somewhere between twelve and fifteen, died. (Yes, Peanut the chicken was a cougar.)

"I spent the night of the 23rd holding Peanut, and on Christmas Eve, exhausted, I took her to bed with me, wrapped in a soft blanket, and held her close to my chest," Darwin wrote. "I could feel her little head resting on my shoulder as she had done for years, and around 5 a.m. her neck relaxed into mine, and I knew she had died peacefully in her sleep, her final gift to me."

Beef: Clara Peller

became wildly famous for a TV commercial at eighty-one

In the 1980s, an innovative Chicago-based advertising man named Joe Sedelmaier began reinventing the TV commercial. After three decades, Americans had built up a strong immunity to ads, going into a kind of sleep mode during commercial breaks. Sedelmaier wanted to break through this stupor so that we, and our children, and our children's children, would once again become eager consumers willing to accept whatever ludicrous claims large corporations made on behalf of their products.

To do this, Sedelmaier replaced slick professional actors with inexperienced and slightly oddball real people. Then he filmed them in an off-kilter style that borrowed from the cinematic vocabularies of Buster Keaton and German expressionism. These commercials, such as the "Fast Talking Man" ads he did for FedEx, got viewers to pay attention again, and often became more memorable than the bland family-hour fare they interrupted. The most famous of Sedelmaier's ads was the 1984 spot for Wendy's that featured the famous slogan "Where's the beef?" The woman who spoke this line was one of Sedelmaier's ordinary people, probably his greatest discovery—an eighty-one-year-old newcomer to the acting profession named Clara Peller. The thirty-second spot made her, for a short time, ubiquitous.

We actually don't know exactly how old Clara Peller was when she achieved late-life fame, because we don't know exactly when she was born. Her children report that she was born in tsarist Russia on August 4, probably in 1902, but she never obtained a birth certificate. (I personally love that Wikipedia lists her birthplace as "Imperial Russia.") She came to the U.S. as a child, the youngest of eight in her family, and grew up in Chicago. When a marriage to a jeweler ended in divorce, she supported herself and her children for thirty-five years as a manicurist

Eighty-one-year-old Clara Peller went searching for beef . . . and made a whole lotta bread for Wendy's.

and beautician. And it was as a manicurist that she got her first break as an actor: Sedelmaier wanted a nail stylist for a bit part in another commercial, and when Clara was sent in to meet him, he was delighted by the rough, throaty voice that came from the gentle four-foot-ten Jewish woman standing before him. (1984 was a good year for breakout stars under five feet tall. One of my other favorites was Olympic gold medalist Mary Lou Retton, who was an inch shorter than Peller.) Sedelmaier cast Clara in a few commercials in the early 1980s and then put her in the landmark Wendy's spot that would almost overnight become a minor classic of Reagan-era pop culture. At the time she was—again, best estimate—eighty-one years old.

The ad features three diminutive, slightly deaf old ladies staring dubiously at a tiny fast-food cheeseburger that is dwarfed by an enormous fluffy sesame seed bun. They make various comments about the size of the bun before Peller barks out her signature query. A polite voice-over then informs us, "Wendy's Single has more beef than the Whopper or Big Mac."

It's hard to know exactly why this moment captured the country's fancy. Of course there was the surprise of this voice—really a snarl—coming out of this woman. (One reporter wrote of Peller that she "looks like 'Whistler's Mother' but talks like 'Tugboat Annie.'") The slightly skewed framing of the shot pulled you in. And the line itself captured the public's unhappiness with the bland and unsatisfying nature of the fast-food burgers they were paying for. Even more, it spoke to a general dissatisfaction with products that didn't live up to their billing, with false promises and continued disappointments. Clara's authentic growl was the perfect voice for this discontent.

The performance won her a Clio Award—those are the Oscars for commercials—for Female Performance in a Television Commercial. What's more, she was not only the star of the show but also, at least in part, the writer of the legendary line. Originally, the script called for Peller to ask, "Where's *all* the beef?" But she suffered from emphysema, and struggled to get the line out in one breath. So she shortened it to the three-word catchphrase that people across America would soon be happily mimicking around watercoolers and dinner tables.

Sidenote: I've oftentimes wondered how the other two women in the commercial, Mildred Lane and Elizabeth Shaw, felt about Clara's breakout. When they first showed up to shoot the ad, did they assume this was an ensemble project, maybe even that one of *them* could end up claiming the Clio or at least getting nominated? How did this white octogenarian Destiny's Child react when their Beyoncé became a solo superstar? And yes, I know that Destiny's Child wasn't formed until six years later.

Wendy's was thrilled with the ad. It was such a success that the company's annual revenue soared by 31 percent—approximately $620 million—prompting Vice President Denny Lynch to quip, "With Clara we accomplished as much in five weeks as we did in fourteen and a half years." It secured their place as a strong number three in the nation's fast-food hamburger stakes, behind, well, the Big Mac and the Whopper. Peller herself earned only what is called "scale," an actor's contractual minimum, for her work. In 1984, that was $317.40 per day. She did, however, make a follow-up commercial that presumably gave her a beefy raise. As Peller herself put it, "I made some money, which is nice for an older person, but Wendy's made millions because of me." The money she earned, Clara later said, would go to braces and college tuition for her grandchildren.

The hit commercial not only garnered Clara additional commercial work and bit parts in feature films, it put her on the talk-show circuit with Bryant Gumbel and on late-night TV. The *Philadelphia Inquirer* reported the sudden appearance of "Clara Peller fan clubs, look-alike and sound-alike contests, and Clara Peller T-shirts." She appeared on *Saturday Night Live*. She served as official timekeeper for the Battle Royal at *Wrestlemania 2* (won by André the Giant, of course). She recorded a "Where's the Beef" single with a Nashville DJ named Coyote McCloud. There was even a Where's the Beef? board game that involved *four* spitfire seniors racing around a restaurant looking for hidden beef . . . and at this point, it's starting to make me feel really uncomfortable.

Maybe most famously, Democratic presidential candidate Walter Mondale helped himself to secure the party's nomination when he quoted Clara's line in a primary debate with the handsome Gary Hart, whom voters evidently suspected of being something of an empty bun.

Peller's honeymoon with Wendy's came to an end after she upset her corporate overlord by doing a commercial for Prego Plus spaghetti sauce. In it, she enthusiastically declares, "I found it . . . I finally found it." (You can watch all of these old commercials on YouTube, but you have to watch a different commercial first. Such is our world today.) Prego was of course riffing on the Wendy's ad, suggesting that the missing beef had turned up in their sauce. Naturally Wendy's objected. A spokesman quoted in the *Los Angeles Times* sniffed, "Clara can only find the beef at one place: Wendy's. If she is finding the beef at Wendy's and in the spaghetti sauce and somewhere else, it gets very confusing." Dropping Clara turned out to be a bad decision for the burger giant, which saw their sales decline when Clara's ad campaign went off the air. (Wendy's really did overreact. The Prego ad was a dud. It was inartfully shot. And the very words "I found it"—limp, with no *r* sounds—didn't allow Clara to growl. No wonder it got ignored at the Clios.)

The breakup with Wendy's didn't faze Clara, who became an icon for late bloomers everywhere. Indeed, her late-life burst of celebrity seemed to augur a new willingness among the public to enjoy senior citizen stars. Suddenly, gray-haired goddesses were everywhere: Angela Lansbury's debut in *Murder, She Wrote*, the surprise hit movie *Cocoon*, the appearance of Bette Davis, then seventy-seven, on the cover of *People*. As America reelected the oldest president ever to hold the office (sorry, Mondale), elderly was *in*. And while a few senior advocacy groups found the "Where's the beef?" ad to be offensive, calling it a caricature of the aged, Clara found their objections to be more bun than beef. "They should be happy that people are working," she said.

Up until the end of her life, Clara seemed to think that her late-life stardom was no big deal. "What difference is it how old you are?" she said. "Age is just a number.

And if you're well enough, you can do things in your older age. And if you're not, you probably weren't any good when you were young." Age wasn't even a number when Clara eventually passed away, in 1987, since she had no birth certificate. But she was old, and unapologetically so. As the advertising executive Joe Sedelmaier intended, her authenticity as an old woman is what allowed her to connect so strongly with viewers. Marlene, her daughter, put it this way: "The remarkable thing about her really was that she was an old person. She acted generally like an older person—except when she hit the work."

OLD MONEY: Warren Buffett

Ninety-three-year-old Warren Buffett may be the greatest investor of all time, with a net worth of $106 billion as of 2023. He may also be the planet's happiest billionaire.

Nicknamed the Oracle of Omaha, he got his start in business at age six, selling chewing gum in his Nebraska neighborhood. At seven, his grandfather, who owned a grocery store, sold him six Cokes for a quarter. He sold them to kids in the neighborhood for a nickel each, for a cool 20 percent profit. He had a pinball machine business, a car polishing business, a loyalty program stamp business. "I was just having fun doing these businesses," he told Jane Pauley in 2017, "and buying stocks with the money I earned."

By age eleven, he'd started his lifetime of investing, making his first stock purchase (three shares of Cities Service at $38 apiece). After that, he was off and earning, with a net worth of $1 million by the time he was thirty. But Buffett has generated over 90 percent of his wealth since he turned sixty-five. It's thanks to something he's referred to as the Methuselah Technique—a combination of a long life and a stable and successful investment return. The longer he lives, the more those smart investments compound, creating more money. As one book put it, "His skill is investing, but his secret is time."

Another inexplicable secret to his longevity? His diet. The man loves McDonald's and drinks at least five sodas a day. His rationale: "I checked the actuarial tables, and the lowest death rate is among six-year-olds. So I decided to eat like a six-year-old. It's the safest course I can take."

His advice to young people on investing also sounds like a pretty good recipe for a life of contentment: "You need emotional stability. You need to be able to detach yourself from fear or greed. You've got to be able to come to your own opinions. But you don't need a lot of brains."

Like Fine Wine

Mike Grgich

Mike Grgich

an immigrant who made great wine till 100

I first learned that wine needs to be aged when I was a kid, and I learned it from Orson Welles. Welles used to do commercials for Paul Masson wine in the late 1970s, famously concluding each spot with a stentorian tagline from the great vintner M. Masson himself: "We will sell no wine before its time." Even then it bothered me that "wine" and "time" don't exactly rhyme. ("Riunite on ice, that's nice!" *That* was an ad that rhymed.) This was, incidentally, also my first introduction to Welles. Years later I was surprised to learn that the paunchy pitchman for cheap hooch was also one of the most accomplished theater, radio, and film directors in American history. But *Citizen Kane*, *The War of the Worlds*, and Welles's storied 1936 all-Black production of *Macbeth* didn't matter to me then; at that point, those Paul Masson commercials were more than enough to secure Welles a star on the Hollywood Walk of Fame. "We will sell no wine before its time" was second only to "Calgon, take me away!" as the great commercial mantra of my preadolescence. (Exactly why commercials for down-market jug wines were airing during reruns of *Gilligan's Island* and *Bewitched* is a mystery I still haven't properly reckoned with.) For now, the main point is that it was through Welles's resonant baritone that I learned that wine is our most durable cultural symbol of things that get better with age.

If you ask a vintner exactly *why* wine gets better with age, you're going to get a long answer that involves oxidation and tannins. Simply put, as wines age, the primary flavors from the grapes start to mellow and recede, allowing you to taste a more complex range of flavors underneath the fruit notes that dominate the taste of a younger wine. As a child I may have loved to drink Welch's grape juice from a wine glass, but even I couldn't convince myself that I detected "tertiary" notes.

In wine expert Anne Krebiehl's account, the chemical transformation sounds practically religious:

Once age allows fruit flavors to subside, a magical new world of flavor opens up. Cabernet Sauvignon and Merlot become suggestive of dried tobacco leaf and cigar box. Syrah develops smoky, visceral notes of cured meat and violets. Nebbiolo and Sangiovese become heady with lifted notes of sour cherry and rose. Riesling and Chenin Blancs can seem like chamomile tincture, while Pinot Noir attains an aura of fallen leaves, earth and undergrowth.

Well, just as some wines mellow and deepen as they get older, so do some winemakers. Mike Grgich was an immigrant who fled communism during the Cold War with his life savings sewn into the sole of his shoe. He was also instrumental in putting American wine on the world map. When he died, in December 2023, at age one hundred, he was celebrated for helping establish Napa Valley as one of the planet's premier wine regions.

Miljenko Grgich was born in 1923 in a village on the coast of Croatia, which was then part of the new nation of Yugoslavia. He was the youngest of eleven children born to poor farmers. The family produced its own wine, and Mike claimed to have transitioned directly from drinking breast milk to drinking wine at the age of two. (This was a matter of necessity. According to his *New York Times* obituary, "The local water supply was not considered safe to drink, so the custom was to blend it with wine for wine's antiseptic properties.") As a boy, one of Mike's chores was to crush the grapes for the family wine with his feet like a medieval monk. So, yes, he literally grew up steeped in wine. When Yugoslavia came under communist rule at the end of World War II, Mike realized that his future was limited, and although he studied business in college in Zagreb, a career as a bookkeeper promised little excitement. But then he discovered that the University of Zagreb had a program in viticulture (grape growing) and enology (wine making). Vistas began to open.

One of Grgich's professors (we're not sure whether he was a viticulturist or an enologist) had just returned from a sabbatical studying wine in Napa Valley,

A perfectly aged eighty-three-year-old Mike Grgich at his winery in Napa in 2006.

Jorgen Gulliksen/Napa Valley Register/ZUMA Press

California, and the students were eager to hear about his trip. But this was communist Yugoslavia, where any student could be an informant, and praising anything Western could get you in trouble with the government, so the professor initially kept silent. Finally, however, the students prevailed on him to speak. He leaned in, as if confiding a secret, and whispered two words: "*California . . . Paradise.*" With that piece of wisdom, Mike resolved that he would, one way or another, cross the Iron Curtain and build a career as a winemaker in America.

Leaving the Soviet sphere of influence for a career in the West was not a simple thing in 1954. For Grgich, the escape route involved an advanced program studying plant genetics in West Germany. After intentionally overstaying his student visa, he found a way to emigrate to Vancouver, where he worked various odd jobs. His next break came when a nephew in the United States, a Catholic priest, secured a connection to the Chateau Souverain winery in California. (Back then, it was essential to have a French name if you wanted to be taken seriously in the wine world; as you'll see, that's part of this story.) Souverain provided the letter of employment Grgich needed for entry to the United States. In 1958, four years after leaving Yugoslavia, and with $32 to his name and the most rudimentary English skills, Grgich arrived on a Greyhound bus in the promised land of Napa Valley.

Grgich credits his next step forward to a meeting with the Russian-born André Tchelistcheff, called "America's most influential post-Prohibition winemaker" by Wikipedia. Tchelistcheff was a diminutive man who had been left for dead on a battlefield in Crimea during the Russian Civil War—his family actually held a funeral for him—but eventually made it to France, where he acquired the winemaking skills that he brought to California's Beaulieu Vineyard in 1938. (Again, everything was French.) Twenty years later, he was the leading figure in American wine making.

When the young immigrant Grgich showed up for their meeting, Tchelistcheff shocked him by speaking "perfect Croatian." He soon hired Grgich as a wine chemist at BV. Grgich credited his true education in enology to the nine years he spent working under Tchelistcheff. (Among Grgich's innovations at BV was the introduction of special filters to reduce the risk of spoilage.) But Grgich was ambitious, and wanted eventually to own his own winery, and so he moved on, first to Robert Mondavi, then to Chateau Montelena, whose owner, Jim Barrett, offered Grgich a stake in the business he was starting up.

Then came an episode that is quite possibly the most important event in the history of the American wine industry: a 1976 wine-tasting contest, now known to wine historians as the Judgment of Paris, that pitted America against France. The event was organized by Steven Spurrier, a British wine vendor based in Paris, who wanted to leverage the hype around the American bicentennial. His idea was a friendly competition between French and California wines. The tasting would be blind, much like the vaunted "Pepsi Challenge" of the same era—what I wouldn't have given to be asked to take a televised taste test!—except Spurrier chose the most esteemed oenophiles in France to evaluate the very best wine from two continents. So taken for granted was the superiority of French wine culture that no one thought it strange or unfair that all nine judges—winemakers, critics, restaurateurs—were French.

The tasting was held on May 24 at the InterContinental Hotel in Paris. There were two tastings, one for red wines, one for whites. First came the whites, which were exclusively Chardonnays—the six American wines from California, the four French from Burgundy. The nine judges tasted each wine and scored it on a 20-point scale. When the tasting was complete, and the results tallied, the entire wine universe, from Adelaide Hills, Australia, to the banks of the river Rhine, let out a collective shriek. Or maybe it was a collective gasp. Or it could have been a bitter, sardonic, existential laugh. In any case, they were surprised.

The panel of French wine experts had placed three American Chardonnays among their four highest-rated wines. Even more astoundingly, the winner, with a score of 132, was Mike Grgich's 1973 Chateau Montelena. The French 1973

Meursault Charmes Roulot was a fairly distant second, with 126.5 points. The results of the red wine tasting that followed were just as stunning, as the 1973 Cabernet Sauvignon from California's Stag's Leap Wine Cellars triumphed over the vaunted 1970 Bordeaux from Château Mouton Rothschild. Paul Masson, if you're wondering, was not among the wines chosen for the tasting.

The American victory was big news. If they had been tasting whiskey, we could call it "the shot heard round the world." If they had been tasting beer, we'd have called it "surprise draft picks." And if wine drinking were an Olympic sport—and, for the record, I think we should give that idea some real consideration—this would rival the Miracle on Ice of 1980 in the annals of our greatest upsets. Brash, young upstart America had claimed its place on the world stage—thanks in large part to a fifty-three-year-old immigrant from a tiny village in Croatia.

Initially, the French media tried to downplay the result, but it was covered by a journalist for *Time*, George Taber, who later wrote a book about the contest, and the word was out. As a publicity stunt, it backfired on the promoter Spurrier, at least in the short term; he was suspended from France's major wine-tasting tour for a year as punishment for bringing shame upon the nation's greatest wineries. (Seems appropriate that during the American bicentennial year, a Brit should get his comeuppance.)

But for American wines, it changed everything. No longer would California be thought of mainly as a maker of inexpensive wines. Warren Winiarski of Stag's Leap Wine Cellars, who produced the winning red wine, recalled how dramatically his business changed in the wake of the judgment. All of a sudden, he said, "Here we had a visible endorsement from [French wine] authorities. People were willing to listen who wouldn't listen before. We had people calling us to ask where they could get our wines, both from the trade and among consumers." California wine could now compete—and win—on the world stage.

Before the Judgment of Paris, Grgich pointed out, the United States was "a whiskey and beer country." After the Judgment, in the 1980s, the number of

California wineries tripled. Today the U.S. is a wine country. "For years, everybody in the world believed that only French soils could produce great wines," Grgich said in recalling the famous Judgment. (The qualities imparted to a wine by soil and climate are called "terroir.") "We shattered that myth. That was probably the most significant result of the Paris tasting. Our victory pumped new energy into the California wine industry, particularly in the Napa Valley." The age of domestic terroir-ism had arrived.

The victory not only slingshotted American wineries into the stratosphere but also emboldened other countries and regions to develop their own industries. As Grgich noted, "More wine is being consumed here and all around the world. Since the Paris tasting people have been planting grapes in Chile, Argentina, Australia, all around the world. That echo did spread around." (South American wines really are terrific. I've long thought someone should open a Chilean wine bar called Pinot Chez.)

Just as that fateful tasting in 1976 changed the direction of the global wine industry, so it also altered the arc of Grgich's career. He had produced the world's best Chardonnay, and it was time for him to strike out on his own. The very next year he founded a winery bankrolled, interestingly, by coffee money. His backer was Austin Hills, of Hills Bros. coffee.

At Grgich Hills Cellars—today known as Grgich Hills Estate—Mike continued to develop his craft, becoming known for more than just Chardonnay. One particular interest was Zinfandel, a fuller-bodied red wine, and over the years Grgich Hills Zinfandels have won many prizes. But Zinfandel captured Mike's interest for another reason.

For decades, the origins of the Zinfandel grape had been a mystery to wine historians and enthusiasts. Most wine grapes are known to originate in a particular country, even a particular region. But the Zinfandel, which had been widely grown in California since the gold rush, could not be traced beyond its first appearance in Long Island and New England in the 1820s. (Some speculation traced it to the

Austro-Hungarian imperial court; the name, we now know, comes from the Hungarian *tzinifándli*.) In the 1960s, however, Austin Goheen, a professor of viticulture at the University of California, Davis, recognized the similarities between Zinfandel and the Italian grape called Primitivo. People began to think that the origins were Italian. But then, in the 1980s, a major wine historian named Leon Adams put forth the hypothesis that both Zinfandel and Primitivo came from a Croatian grape called Plavac Mali.

As Mike Grgich became interested in the question, he was, for obvious reasons, partial to the theory of a Croatian origin. "It's the wine that when I came to America, first day I noticed it," he said. "I felt when I saw those grapes, I know. Those grapes must have been from Croatia." With other Zinfandel producers, Grgich began to advocate for research into the question. Soon Carole Meredith, a plant geneticist also at UC–Davis, undertook to settle the mystery of Zinfandel's origins once and for all.

By then Grgich was well known among wine people as the world's most famous Croatian-born vintner. Naturally, he knew his homeland better than Meredith did, and when she and her team traveled to Croatia to gather samples, he offered critical suggestions as to where to find different Croatian grapes. When Meredith and her team completed their research and tested the DNA of all their samples, it turned out that the origins of Zinfandel/Primitivo were indeed Croatian. (It wasn't the exact grape that Leon Adams had hypothesized, but it was a Croatian relative.)

Grgich took great pride in helping Meredith to discover that the Zinfandel grape—like Grgich himself—was a Croatian immigrant. The hunt for Zinfandel's origin was a way of bringing his wine business back home.

In fact, Grgich brought his business back home in an even more fundamental way. After the violent breakup of Yugoslavia in the early 1990s, Croatia achieved independence, but was suffering terribly from the human and economic toll of the war. By this point, Grgich was an elder statesman of Napa Valley, and his professional success had made him a leading figure in the Croatian diaspora. On a trip home to visit family, he secured an audience with Franjo Tudjman, the first president of the Republic of Croatia. Tudjman encouraged the winemaker to bring his skills back to Croatia, and Grgich, with his daughter, Violet Grgich, and nephew Ivo Jeramaz, established Grgić Vina, a winery on the Dalmatian coast. The winery is located in the town of Trstenik on the Pelješac peninsula, overlooking the Mediterranean Sea, about an hour's drive from Grgich's hometown of Desne. According to Jeramaz, their winery has lifted the quality of Croatian wine across the nation. "We went there to show them how the best wine can be made," he said. "Before . . . the wine quality was terrible. People used to drink wine made from sugar and water and old skins. Their bottles of wine were a dollar. Mike set his bottle at three dollars." Initially, even this price seemed steep, and Grgić Vina was exporting much of what they made. But as Croatia has moved forward—economically and oenophilically—it has caught up with Grgich. Today Grgić Vina can't meet the demand for its product.

Under Grgich's leadership, and into his tenth decade, his business continued to grow and change with the times. The winery went biodynamic in 2003 and shifted to solar power in 2006. Mike was elected to the Vintners Hall of Fame at the California campus of the Culinary Institute of America in 2008. In 2016, on his ninety-third birthday, he received a hand-signed letter from the Obamas. Two years later, he won the James Beard Award. Only in 2018, when he was ninety-five, did he turn the reins over to his daughter and nephew.

But in terms of honors, it's hard to beat this one: in 2013 the Smithsonian Institution included a bottle of that world-shaking 1973 Chateau Montelena Chardonnay in their exhibition of "101 Objects That Made America." There it kept company with such artifacts of American history as Thomas Jefferson's Bible, Abraham Lincoln's top hat, Marian Anderson's mink coat, Dorothy's red slippers, and Neil Armstrong's space suit.

His was a spectacular journey, from stomping grapes for lack of clean drinking water . . . to the pinnacle of the wine world. As Mike Grgich wrote in his own memoir, "In my life, I have had real miracles. They were between God and me, and when I was offered one, I accepted it with all of my heart and soul, with gratitude. Be on the watch for miracles in your own life."

————

Mike Grgich isn't the only winemaker to live a good long life. Robert Mondavi, who also helped bring worldwide attention to Napa's wines, lived until ninety-four. And Warren Winiarski, who produced the winning red wine at the Judgment of Paris, is, as of this writing, alive at ninety-five. I asked my friend Scott Ehrlich, whose family has been growing grapes in Napa Valley for twenty-five years, if there was a relationship between wine growing and life span. Here's what he told me:

> *I think there is a connection. Wine growing regions tend to have milder climates, without harsh winters or humid summers that can take a mental and physical toll. And they tend to also be areas where other fruits and vegetables thrive—leading to a healthy, balanced diet.*
>
> *But I think there's another reason that winemakers tend to live a long time. Their lives revolve around nature and the cycle of seasons. You realize you cannot control nature, you can only adapt. Nor can you rush things. You have to let Mother Nature run her course, and then do the best with what she's given you. You can do things in the vineyard and in the cellar to influence the end result, but ultimately you are at her mercy. When you come to peace with this, it's not only humbling, but also freeing.*

Cheese Old Enough to Vote
Like wine, cheese undergoes chemical changes as it ages, losing moisture and intensifying in flavor. While some cheeses, like burrata or chèvre, are best served as fresh as possible, others need to age to develop their flavors. Firmer cheeses like cheddar, Gruyère, and Manchego can be aged in a cave or cellar for several years. But the Methuselah of cheese is a little-known Italian number called Storico Ribelle, which can be aged up to eighteen years.

You're not going to find this stuff at the supermarket next to the string cheese. To get it, you need to trek into the Bergamo Alps in the north of Italy, by the banks of the Bitto River. There twelve producers make this cheese, and they follow precise specifications and techniques that have been in place since the days of Galileo and Titian. The milk used must have a balance of 80 percent cow and 20 percent goat. All the animals must graze on the grass of the valley called the Valtellina, and the goats must belong to a native breed called Orobica. During the summer, the cheesemakers set up shop on the mountainside in stone huts called *calèccs*. They milk the animals right in the fields so that the milk they use is as fresh as possible; they mix it in copper cauldrons heated by wood fires on-site. Rennet, a set of enzymes derived from the stomach of an unweaned calf, is added to curdle the milk, and then the curds are broken up with special tools until they're the size of a grain of rice. This is poured into a mold, pressurized, salted, and moved to a special hut for aging. Seventy days is the minimum, with temperature and humidity strictly regulated, but most of the cheese is aged much longer. Restaurants open their wheels at ten years, and a fifteen-year-old wheel sold in China for $6,400. Production is limited to three thousand wheels per year.

With a recipe this specific, of course, it's never easy, and when Bitto Storico was granted DOP status, trouble began. DOP stands for *denominazione di origine protetta* ("protected designation of origin"), and it's a certification granted by the government meant to guarantee high quality by ensuring that ingredients and production are local and follow strict guidelines. But what happened was that the government then broadened the permissible region of production, loosened the restrictions on the all-natural diet of the cows, and—throwing caution to the wind—eliminated the requirement of 20 percent goat's milk. The twelve original producers had a cow. A major cheese war erupted, which culminated in the original producers renaming their product Storico Ribelle (Historic Rebel), leaving the name Bitto Storico for the newcomers.

Meanwhile, there's a lot to be said for the convenience of individually wrapped processed string cheese. That stuff lasts forever.

50-Year-Old Noodle Soup

In the Ekkamai neighborhood of Bangkok, beloved of hipsters, foodies, and expats, you can find, nestled among the funky cafes and vintage clothing shops, a piping hot bowl of Thai beef noodle soup that might be older than you are. At a casual noodle shop called Wattana Panich, the owner, Nattapong Kaweeantawong, serves customers from the same enormous pot of soup that has been on the fire since his grandfather owned the place in the 1970s. (A 2019 National Public Radio story pegged the soup's age at forty-five, so at the time of this writing it's pushing fifty.) Unlike the cheesemakers of northern Italy, Kaweeantawong doesn't follow a precise recipe, mixing generous amounts of beef with various Chinese herbs, garlic, cinnamon, cilantro, and black pepper. But the key to the process is that every night he takes what's remaining, removes it from the enormous pot he uses, and, after cleaning the pot (phew), simmers the day's remainder overnight so that it will form the stock for the next day's batch of soup. Technically speaking, then, this same pot of soup has been cooking continuously since *Sanford and Son* battled *All in the Family* for the top spot in the Nielsen ratings. The fermentation, which is common in Asian food, adds a distinctive tang, and the marrow and fat give a rich flavor to the broth. If you can't get to Bangkok soon, don't worry; odds are the same soup will still be simmering at Wattana Panich for a long time to come.

"Bee Upchuck"

Aged honey doesn't develop more subtle and complex flavors the way that wines and cheeses can. But the amazing thing about honey is that it can last forever. It keeps indefinitely. That's right: like sugar, salt, and your Uncle Carl's political opinions, honey never changes. This is because honey is *hygroscopic*. That means that it contains very little moisture, and since bacteria and other contaminants can't thrive without water, they can't breed in honey. On top of this, honey also has a very high acid content, which kills off any microorganisms that do survive. And finally, the honeybees who make the honey do it by regurgitating nectar, collected from flowers, into their honeycombs, in the process adding a special enzyme that breaks down the sugars from the nectar into simpler molecules. This process creates hydrogen peroxide, which some chemists believe helps kill off the bacteria. In other words, what makes honey not only delicious but long-lasting is the fact that it's been through the digestive tract of an insect. (Beekeeper readers will notice that we refrained from calling honey "bee vomit," since the regurgitated nectar comes from the bee's crop, its "second stomach," rather than the primary stomach where food goes. So it's technically not vomit. But "upchuck" seems sufficiently generic and too good a word not to use.)

A safety note: even though honey can, in theory, last for centuries, you still need to keep it clean. If other substances get into your honey, they can spoil it. So store your honey in an airtight container and don't use the same knife that you use for your butter!

Tabasco Sauce

Named for the variety of pepper native to the Mexican state of Tabasco, Tabasco sauce actually hails from Avery Island, Louisiana, where in 1868 a man named Edmund McIlhenny began to produce it commercially from mashed chili peppers, salt, and cane vinegar. The peppers were grown, and the salt was mined, on Avery Island, in the Gulf of Mexico. However, a number of journalists investigating the question believe that McIlhenny actually got the recipe, or at least the seeds and the peppers, from plantation owner Maunsel White, who was already producing his own hot sauce in 1850. If you're asking yourself if that means what you think it means, yes: White enslaved over two hundred people. The debate whether White or McIlhenny created the sauce is, for many, a bit too hot to handle. You'll find it vigorously contested by the McIlhenny descendants, who, incidentally, still own the company that produces the hot sauce—although today the peppers are grown mainly in Central America. In any case, back in the 1870s, Edmund McIlhenny would age his sauce in stone containers for thirty days before bottling it, but as the business passed down through the family, they discovered that this sauce fared better with a little more time on the shelf. Today the hot red stuff is aged for three years in decommissioned white oak bourbon barrels, which, like wine barrels, impart additional notes of flavor during the fermentation process.

Pro tip: if you're ever stuck at a bar drinking a tasteless commercial light beer, ask the bartender to hand you the Tabasco. One dash spices up your watery brew, giving you a kind of downmarket Bloody Mary at no extra cost.

Cast-Iron Skillet

It's not only food that can grow better with age, it's also the equipment you use for preparing it. Although nonstick surfaces like Teflon became popular in the 1960s, hardcore foodies will be sure to tell you that a good cast-iron skillet will give you the same benefits and a whole lot more. Cast iron, which is an iron alloy made with at least 2 percent carbon, has been used in woks and other cookware in China since the Han dynasty. But the casting method invented by British ironmaster Abraham Darby in 1707 led to its popularity in the nineteenth century, where it had the added benefit of serving as an impromptu weapon when wielded by an aproned matron in a saloon fight. When you use a cast-iron pan, the fats and oils used in cooking will create a patina on the surface of the skillet that prevents other foods from sticking to it. Some serious home cooks claim that this patina gets glossier with every use. When helping said cooks to clean up after dinner, be careful not to scrub away the patina with soap or steel wool. That's a crime tantamount to erasing a fresco from a medieval church wall. Also dry the pan well so that it doesn't rust. (We want you to be invited back for dinner.) Your skillet should last a lifetime—and it will be on hand in case an old western-style melee breaks out in your kitchen.

Yixing Teapot
In the city of Yixing, about a two-and-a-half-hour drive west of Shanghai, you will find a teapot that gets better with age. This Chinese city of one and a quarter million people is filled with artisans who make gorgeous teapots of a burnished cinnabar color. (Think spicy red-orange.) These vessels are unglazed and unpainted, and their porous clay is reputed to absorb the flavor of the tea, deepening it with every use. The teapots are expensive, but aficionados will buy more than one, reserving each for a single variety—black, green, oolong, or pu'er, the fermented tea from the southwest province of Yunnan. Tea drinkers caution against washing these teapots with soap, advising that you simply rinse them out.

The magic of these Yixing teapots comes from the special clay they are made from, *zisha*, which contains kaolin, quartz, and mica, along with a high level of iron oxide. It needs to be mined from deep in the earth, dried in the sun, and pulverized into a powder before being mixed again with water in precise proportions. The sandy clay, when fired, has a stony texture. The art of crafting the teapots developed over a period of more than five hundred years, reaching its peak in the early Ming dynasty, when the Yixing teapots became essential items for upper-class families. To make them, artisans do not use a potter's wheel but instead meticulously pound and shape each piece by hand. It's a lot of pressure making one, after which you'll be ready to break out the Celestial Seasonings Sleepytime and curl up for a nap.

OLD COUNTRY: Willie Nelson

It might be hard to believe, but Willie Nelson didn't always look like Willie Nelson. Back when he was still trying to make it in Nashville as a singer-songwriter, he sported short hair and wore a suit and tie. (Watching 1962 Willie is as trippy as watching clean-cut George Carlin and Richard Pryor do stand-up around the same time.) He had a big early success when his song "Crazy" was recorded by Patsy Cline.

But Willie wasn't happy with the music he was making. He wanted to get on the road (again) and return to his home state of Texas. And that was where he became the real Willie Nelson. He grew out his red hair and braided it, donned a bandanna, and indulged in a bit of marijuana. He started making the music that, as he would explain it, brought hippies and rednecks together, a sound that would be called outlaw country. (RIP fellow outlaw Waylon Jennings, who died way too young, at sixty-four.)

When Willie released his hit album *Red Headed Stranger* in 1975, at age forty-one, the music critic for *Texas Monthly* deemed it so remarkable as to have redefined country music: "What Nelson has done is simply unclassifiable; it is the only record I have ever heard that strikes me as otherworldly. . . . The world that Nelson has created is so seductive that you want to linger there indefinitely."

In the decades since, he's recorded thousands of songs and done about one hundred live shows a year, all the while championing causes and raising money for his organization Farm Aid.

Somehow, the older Willie Nelson gets, the more music he makes—he has produced over thirty-six albums since 2000, and not just country. He's recorded gospel and bluegrass and jazz, plus the standards once performed by his favorite singer, Frank Sinatra. As he once said: "A song doesn't get old. It doesn't age. If it was good a hundred years ago, it's still good today."

As he sang on the single "Last Man Standing" (released on the eve of his eighty-fifth birthday), "I don't wanna be the last man standing / On second thought maybe I do."

The Players

Estelle Getty,
Rita Moreno
& Morgan Freeman

Estelle Getty: The Golden Girl

made her prime-time TV debut at sixty-two

"After fifty years in the business, I'm an overnight success."

That was how Estelle Getty, with characteristic wit, described her sudden celebrity at age sixty-two. Getty was one of the stars of *The Golden Girls*, the popular Miami-set sitcom about the lives of four older single women—a series that incidentally introduced the word "lanai" to the general public. The show, which premiered in 1985 and ran for seven seasons, featured Getty in her debut TV role, playing the eighty-year-old widow Sophia Petrillo. As the relative newcomer to the screen, Getty shared top billing with established and beloved stars Bea Arthur, Rue McClanahan, and Betty White—and she more than held her own while trading one-liners with those other dynamos. At the time of life when most women in Hollywood are being pushed offscreen, Getty was stepping into the limelight for the first time.

The Golden Girls began as a comic sketch, a short parody of the popular but violent cop show *Miami Vice*. That sketch, part of a hastily produced special created to promote NBC's upcoming slate of fall shows, was called *Miami Nice*, and it featured NBC stars Doris Roberts and Selma Diamond as two Florida retirees. (In the bit, the hilarious Diamond describes Miami as a paradise of "Coppertone and corned beef, mink coats, cha-cha lessons . . .") It was intended to be forgotten as soon as the fall season launched. But the top brass at the network fell in love with the concept of a family-friendly Miami show to serve as a counterweight to their tough-guy police drama, and they brought in producer Susan Harris, the creator of the hit comedies *Soap* and *Benson*, to develop the premise.

Building a sitcom around an all-female, postmenopausal ensemble defied pretty much all the rules for prime-time programming. One would think that the only thing to get lower ratings would be a cinema verité documentary chronicling the psychoanalysis of French intellectuals in real time. Yet the show, in the words of writer Marc Cherry, became "the model for any female ensemble show" on television, from *Designing Women* to *Sex and the City* to *Girls*. (The show's writers, for their part, went on to absurd levels of success in the early 2000s: Cherry created *Desperate Housewives*; Mitch Hurwitz created *Arrested Development*; Christopher Lloyd created *Modern Family*.) *Golden Girls* debuted in 1985 atop the Nielsen ratings and enjoyed an impressive run as the centerpiece of NBC's popular Saturday night lineup.

The key to the show's appeal was its portrayal of four distinctively drawn unmarried older women enjoying full lives, including sex lives. It focused mainly on their relationships with each other, not with men, although it was not shy about portraying the fact that they *had* relationships with men. Interviewed for a twentieth-anniversary oral history of the series, director Terry Hughes described the show as "like watching a bunch of naughty grannies. A whole generation recognized their own grandmothers on that screen." To which producer Susan Harris added, "They especially loved Estelle. Here was a woman talking back to her daughter and giving her so much grief."

With her salty humor and sharp delivery, Getty had a knack for stealing scenes. The character Sophia had suffered a minor stroke, with the effect of lowering her inhibitions; the premise gave Getty license to blurt out all kinds of off-color quips that seemed all the funnier coming from a character in her eighties. The role earned Estelle an Emmy and a Golden Globe. To win the Golden Globe in 1986, she had to beat out her three costars, all of whom were also nominees. The show had cornered the market on senior female talent.

But while the plain-speaking Sicilian grandma Sophia Petrillo may have seemed the role Estelle was born for, getting there had been a long and circuitous journey. Like thousands, maybe millions, of girls, Estelle had dreamed of being a movie star since she was little. Born on New York City's Lower East Side in 1923 to Charles and Sarah Scher, Polish Jewish immigrants, Estelle was called "Etty" because that's how her older sister originally pronounced her name. Charles owned a business repairing glass for cars and trucks; the family's living quarters were in the same building

Golden Girls star Estelle Getty, discovered in her sixties.
DMI/The LIFE Picture Collection/Shutterstock

as his shop. But his business was healthy enough that he could afford to take the family out on Fridays to movies or the theater. The joy of attending those performances is what gave birth to Estelle's desire to take to the stage.

As she wrote in her memoir, "My father inadvertently introduced me to the arts. I was four years old when he took the family across town to the Academy of Music, where we saw a movie and five acts of vaudeville. I was stunned. I had found my world. My life changed that day. . . . That day, I realized I belonged with the people up on the stage."

Like many immigrant parents—like many parents, period—the Schers didn't love the idea of their daughter pursuing an acting career. They hadn't labored and saved so that she could pursue the unattainable fantasy of becoming a Hollywood starlet. Estelle recalls her mother remarking dismissively, "You're so beautiful you think you can be an actress?" And, with comments like that, it's no wonder that the diminutive Estelle doubted her looks. So, believing she was not fit to achieve stardom as a gorgeous ingenue, she did what any other young actress would do—she turned to stand-up comedy. For two summers, she delivered cornball zingers at a Catskills resort, bussing and waiting tables the rest of the week. Alas, no big-time talent scout strolled into the dining room and made her a star.

But she persisted in her quest to see her name in lights. At age twenty-three, she married Arthur Gettleman—she later shortened Gettleman to Getty for the stage—and the young couple moved to Oakland Gardens in Queens, where they raised their two sons. Over the following decades, Estelle worked as a secretary to help support the family, but she also auditioned, sometimes landing small parts. And she continued going to the theater, attending as many shows as she could manage, simply because she loved the theater. She passed up promotions at work because she feared that too much responsibility would prevent her from slipping out of the office to audition. She sent her sons to sleepaway camp so she could be free to do summer stock.

"I acted wherever I could," she recounted. "Regional theater, summer stock, dinner theater, experimental theater, Kabuki theater, children's theater." The venues were so tiny that she could only laugh about them. "I've worked houses where you couldn't even go backstage—there *was* no backstage. If you had to exit a scene, and enter later on the other side of the stage, you had to leave the theater, walk around the block, and come back in through the other entrance."

By 1976, Estelle's sons were grown, and she was able to give her full attention to acting. She was in her fifties now, and unlikely to be cast in lead roles. So she found work playing mothers. As she wrote, she played "Irish mothers, Jewish mothers, Italian mothers, southern mothers, New England mothers, mothers in plays by Neil Simon and Arthur Miller and Tennessee Williams. I've played mother to everyone but Attila the Hun." (For the record, we don't know who Attila's mother was, but it's a safe bet she's the one who called him "Hun." How's that for a cornball zinger?)

Estelle was now forty-five years into her acting career. And still there was no breakout role. Then, in 1978, she saw an unheralded small play called *International Stud*, written by, and starring, a young playwright named Harvey Fierstein. It was bold in its tender yet unapologetic depiction of gay themes. It was also produced on a shoestring budget, initially running for two weeks off-off-Broadway. (If another "off-" were possible, it would have added that one too.) The producers managed to

44

secure an off-Broadway opening, where the play enjoyed a longer run of seventy-two performances. Estelle loved it. After the curtain, she made her way backstage to tell the playwright. She and Harvey became friends. Then she asked him to write a part for her.

Estelle claims that she made the request as a joke but that Fierstein took it seriously. When it came time to write *Widows and Children First!*, the final segment of the three-act *Torch Song Trilogy*, of which *International Stud* had been the first installment, he created the character of Mrs. Beckoff, the protagonist's mother, with Getty expressly in mind. "I knew that if I put the right lines in her mouth she could rip their hearts out," he later recounted. When the trilogy opened in 1981, Getty threw herself into the role. And she not only played a mother, she became something of a maternal presence for the other actors. "She was the only one in the cast that had a job . . . and could afford to buy dinner . . . and had a car . . . and a real life," Fierstein recalled. Although Estelle lived a fairly vanilla, straight, middle-class life in Queens, she wasn't fazed in the least by gay culture, and she relished her role as a surrogate mother to the cast and crew.

Torch Song Trilogy caught on. From off-Broadway it went to Broadway, opening at the Little Theatre on 44th Street. Then it became a sensation. Looking back, Fierstein believes that Estelle's performance "changed a lot of lives." By dramatizing the emotional struggles between young gay people and their parents with power and compassion, it opened a space for communication and understanding. Said Fierstein, "I know that there were gay people who came in with their parents to the theater barely able to look at each other and left with their arms around each other."

It wasn't only Estelle's acting that made a difference in people's lives. She took up the fight against AIDS as a cause, becoming an early advocate for those suffering from the illness, and a beloved ally of the gay community. Her son Barry remarked, "A lot of creative people that she really knew and loved had suffered with this [disease], and it really broke her heart." Among those she lost to AIDS were her *Torch*

Song costar Court Miller and her nephew Steven Scher. Fierstein said that "Estelle became every gay person's mother." Later, when Estelle was a TV star, gay bars across the country would flip the channel over to *Golden Girls* on Saturday night so customers could cheer her on.

It was the success of *Torch Song Trilogy*—the Broadway run was followed by a four-year national tour—that put Getty in position to read for the role of Sophia Petrillo. She wasn't much past sixty, and had to convince the producers, and eventually TV audiences, that she was the octogenarian mother of Bea Arthur's Dorothy. To age her up by twenty years, Estelle's agent gave her a baggy dress and old-fashioned kid gloves to wear, and insisted that she powder her hair white. The performance worked. Not only did she land the part, but to this day people still have trouble believing that Bea Arthur was actually *older* than Estelle. (If you're keeping score at home, when the show premiered, Estelle was sixty-two, both Bea Arthur and Betty White were sixty-three, and Rue McClanahan was fifty-one.)

In the first episode of *Golden Girls*, more people saw Getty perform than had seen her in an entire lifetime's worth of stage work. Suddenly, improbably, after years and years of mostly tiny parts in mostly small plays performed in front of thin crowds, she was one of the most beloved actresses in America.

The transition from stage to screen wasn't without its difficulties. There were rivalries among the all-star cast of leading ladies, who often found themselves competing for awards and recognition. (All four eventually won Emmys.) And Estelle had to learn to calibrate her timing for the TV camera instead of the live audience. As she was learning, she developed a serious case of stage fright. She would forget her lines or flub them. She tried various tricks, including hypnosis, to calm her anxiety. Eventually the producers resorted to leaving prompts on different props, or even using cue cards. Yet audiences never seemed to notice. Sophia continued to score the laugh lines, and Estelle's popularity kept climbing. At one point, her Q score (a measure of both recognizability and likability) was the highest ever recorded.

Getty said she always attempted to ground the comedy in Sophia's character, and her interpretation of the character was rooted in empathy. As she told one interviewer, "I really like that lady. I play her with all the love I can." The on-screen relationship with Bea Arthur added to the appeal. Audiences just couldn't get enough of the pint-sized Sophia (four foot eleven) bossing around her towering daughter Dorothy (five ten). For Arthur, it was a comic pairing "absolutely made in heaven."

And then there was the appeal of communal living. *Golden Girls* showed older women living happily as a quartet, serving as each other's source of company and friendship. For Estelle, who had moved to Los Angeles to pursue film and TV roles and was living apart from her husband, Arthur, this kind of nontraditional family was radical in its own way. "I've always felt that loneliness, not age, is the real killer. . . . It all goes back to the Noah's Ark syndrome . . . the notion that people have to go through life two by two."

Finally, the show stood out for its willingness to tell the truth about older women's lives. "I think *The Golden Girls* in this respect has been tremendously liberating for America's elderly," Getty wrote. "There they are on television, older women who aren't afraid to admit they still want, like to talk about, and enjoy having sex. It let older women say, 'Thank God I'm not the only one.' "

Playing Sophia Petrillo led to more high-profile roles for Getty. She now had as much acting work as she could handle—often still playing mothers. She played mother to Cher, to Sylvester Stallone, to Barry Manilow—and grandmother to Stuart Little. But by 2001, she had to retire. She was feeling the effects of Lewy body dementia, a progressive brain disease related to Alzheimer's. The disease may have contributed to her forgetting lines on set, and it eventually took her life in 2008, at eighty-four.

Estelle Getty's passing marked the end of a remarkable late-career renaissance. Many actors slog away at odd jobs, while they audition for every bit part or commercial, hoping for some opportunity just to get noticed. Some persist for years. A few persist for a decade. Eventually, most people move on. But Getty kept taking those unsung roles for nearly fifty years, never calling it quits. To quote once more her friend and collaborator Harvey Fierstein, "It's not just that she believed in her dream and made it come true. . . . She had her marriage and raised her children, and then was able to take this dream that was sitting in the drawer—and it was finally *time.*"

———

PS: As a measure of how perceptions of age have changed just in the last forty years, consider that the fictional characters of the *Sex and the City* spin-off *And Just Like That . . .*—Carrie (fifty-five), Miranda (fifty-four), and Charlotte (fifty-four)—are actually older than *The Golden Girls'* Rose (fifty-five), Dorothy (fifty-three), and Blanche (early fifties) were when each series began.

Rita Moreno: Ageless
the EGOT who's still got it in her nineties

Confession: I prefer profiling older actors and luminaries over younger buzzy talents. Angie Dickinson, veteran late-night comedy producer Peter Lassally, hockey legend Bobby Orr—those are the kinds of interviews that have stayed with me. (Part of it is that I'm an old soul myself, perhaps because my parents were older when they had me. I'm glad I was born in 1969. But my second choice—I've really worked this out—would have been 1888. If we run into each other in an airport, I'll be happy to explain.) Older people just have more to say. More experience,

opposite page:
Rita Moreno and Morgan Freeman,
costars on the classic 1970s PBS series
The Electric Company.
Photofest

48

more wisdom, more stories. They're more likely to say what they actually think, less afraid of what others think of them.

So I leapt at the chance to interview Rita Moreno in 2013. Not long before, her memoir had come out, detailing her groundbreaking career. She also happened to be my first TV memory. She was part of the ensemble of PBS's *Electric Company*. The opening credits to the show thrilled me. They kicked off with an ultra-brassy Moreno roaring, "Hey, you guuuuuuys!" There was nothing "children's TV" about the sequence. With all due respect, *Sesame Street* was the slow lane. *The Electric Company* was more my speed.

Our piece would be the television companion to her written memoir: a look back, a valedictory, a chance for Moreno to set the record straight before clocking out for good.

As for the shoot plan, I was going to meet Rita on the stage of northern California's Berkeley Repertory Theater, where she had performed in years past, and chat on camera for just a bit. The theater wasn't far from where she lived and where I would later conduct the longer sit-down interview. We were going to be on our feet for this first portion, so I knew to keep it brief, maybe ten minutes. A woman of her age could stand for only so long, my producer and I figured.

Then Rita waltzed in from the back of the house, through the theater, and onto the stage. And before I knew it, she was teaching me a couple of the steps she danced in her Oscar-winning turn as Anita in *West Side Story*. My producer on that piece, Alan, turned to me afterward and said incredulously, "She's eighty-one." I was so swept up (and focused on getting the steps right) that I had forgotten. She seemed like a woman twenty years younger.

It became apparent only years later that her memoir wasn't so much a retrospective as it was a reintroduction—a reminder to the world that Rita is still here. Since our interview, she starred for three seasons as the zany matriarch in the Norman Lear–produced reboot of *One Day at a Time*. She played a dramatic role (a different one this time) in Steven Spielberg's 2021 *West Side Story*, for which she also served as executive producer. She was part of the star-studded ensemble in the 2023 blockbuster *80 for Brady*. She received a lifetime achievement Peabody Award. And those are just the highlights.

"Crazy. Who knew? And here I am now at ninety-two," she told me one day by phone. When I asked if she had expected her eighties and early nineties to turn out the way they had, she said, "Not in the least. First of all, I don't think I expected to even be here." And yet this stretch has been as busy as any stretch in an already legendary career.

Eighty-seven years ago, when she was five, Rita and her mother migrated from Puerto Rico to an overcrowded Bronx New York apartment, most of their belongings inside shopping bags. Rosita Dolores Alverío, as she was called then, was soon taking dance lessons and performing in clubs. Then, as she began to set her sights on a show business career, an agent told her she needed to change her name. His suggestion, "Orchid Montenegro," was a bit outlandish. Instead she chose the name Rita, after one of her idols, Rita Hayworth.

But when it came to style, she modeled herself on another star, Elizabeth Taylor. As Moreno told me during our 2013 interview, "I did my eyebrows like her. I did my hair like her. I wore a waist cincher because she has this wasp waist. I did everything I could. And when I did meet Mr. Louis B. Mayer"—the chief of MGM—"the first thing he said was, 'Look at that, she looks like a Spanish Elizabeth Taylor.'" He signed her on the spot.

But in Hollywood she found she was consistently cast as a certain kind of character . . . with a certain kind of accent, whether it was to play a Tahitian in *Pagan Love Song* or a Thai woman in *The King and I*. She called it "the universal ethnic accent." "I don't have to be embarrassed anymore," she reflected. "It's funny now. It was horrible then, but it is funny."

In 1954, an editor at *Life* magazine spotted her and put her on the cover, where she was in turn spotted by Marlon Brando. They began a tumultuous eight-year affair. As a lover, Brando lived up to his reputation. In her memoir, Rita wrote, "To say that he was a great lover, sensual, generous, delightfully inventive, would be gravely understating what he did not only to my body but for my soul." (That's a pretty good review.)

But her obsessive relationship with Brando was volatile, with constant fights and infidelity. And then one day, the King, Elvis Presley, came calling, enlisting his manager, Colonel Tom Parker, as a matchmaker. "I loved it. I loved every bloody moment," she told me, recalling how jealous it made Brando. (Elvis, it turned out, was not nearly as passionate. But she wasn't going to let Brando know that.) Eventually she and Brando rekindled their romance. Yet his inveterate womanizing eventually got to be too much. One morning, alone in Brando's house, she tried to kill herself. "I couldn't stand my going back to him every single time after all those humiliations. And I was obsessed. I just wanted to get rid of that self-hatred. I detested myself."

Brando's assistant found her and got her to the hospital. The affair was over. Months later—in a head-spinning reversal of fortune—she won an Oscar for her role as Anita in 1961's original *West Side Story* movie. The role made Rita the first Latina to win an Oscar. But that's not the only reason it's near and dear to her heart. As opposed to so many of the roles she'd played in Hollywood, Anita was a Latina "who had a sense of herself, a sense of dignity. And I had to portray that. And it felt really good."

Many more awards followed. In fact, Moreno is one of just nineteen people who have won what's now called a competitive EGOT—which stands for Emmy, Grammy, Oscar, and Tony.

Sidebar: As a twelve-year-old, I was obsessed with a 1981 commercial she did. She's in front of a full-length mirror, in a sequined gown, an ermine stole draped over her, as the voice-over breathlessly announces, "Rita Moreno, you're the only actress who's won an Oscar, Emmy, Tony, Grammy. You always look terrific. And that smile! What's your secret?" Her secret was Pepsodent toothpaste. *However*, a fact check reveals that at that point, Rita was the *second* actress to achieve EGOT status: Helen Hayes had beat her by seven months with a Grammy. Still, if you get all four, I think they should call it the Full Moreno, if only because she looked so damn good in that Pepsodent commercial.

In 1965, she married Leonard Gordon, a cardiologist. They remained together for forty-five years, until his death in 2010. (Another sidebar: When I sat down with Debbie Reynolds, earlier in 2013, she bemoaned all her own bad marriages. "Marriage and movie stars don't seem to work out," she told me. "The only ones that made it married a doctor." Makes me wonder if being married to a cardiologist for so long is one reason Rita's still so healthy.)

In 1971, Rita would begin her run on *The Electric Company*, which costarred a then-unknown Morgan Freeman. (More on that in the following essay.) Her work on the show netted her the *G* in her EGOT; she was a featured performer on an album based on the show. And over the next decade, she completed the Full Moreno. The *T* came in 1975 for her role as Googie Gomez in the Terrence McNally farce *The Ritz*. The *E* followed in 1977 with her guest appearances on *The Muppet Show*. (Her performance of the song "Fever," with Animal on drums, is not to be missed.)

The 1970s were a busy time for Rita. She was in her forties. And then, as often happens, especially with actresses, her career became gradually quieter over the next few decades. In 1997, at sixty-five, a role as a nun trained as a psychologist on HBO's *Oz* brought her renewed attention. But it wasn't until she was in her eighties that she was back with "Hey, you guuuuuuys"–level energy. In our recent phone conversation I asked how she sees the world in her nineties: "Almost everything is funny all the time at this age. You can use that as a chapter heading."

She found a twin of sorts in Norman Lear when they began working on the reboot of *One Day at a Time*, when Moreno was eighty-six—and playing the show's no-holds-barred Cuban American abuelita—and executive producer Lear was ninety-four. "It was as though we knew each other from another time, because we hit it off so quickly and so deeply," she told me.

They knew and loved the same old songs from the great American songbook. They shared values on social issues. But what struck me was the bond she described over humor—and not exactly an understated brand of humor. "About three or four months into the filming," she said, "I get a call from [Norman] at eleven at night, and he says, 'Rita, I have an idea.' And I said, 'Wow, it must be good, at this hour of the night.' Anyway, he says, 'You are going to have my love child.' And I'm staring at the phone like it has a life of its own. And I said, 'What the f–k are you talking about?' He says, 'Well, don't you think that would get some attention?' And I said, 'Boy, would it ever.'"

Now, this had nothing to do with a plotline on the series. It was just a silly joke between the two friends, something to crack each other up. The joke became long-running. They would FaceTime each other to catch up on the status of their imaginary love child, whom they named Moishe.

"We were like two gremlins. We were very mischievous." She also described Norman as a "pixie" in our conversation. Hearing her recall how much they laughed together—and barely able to contain herself as she reminisced—made *me* feel younger just listening.

"We laughed at each other. I mean, knee-slapping fun stuff. He thought I was just hilarious in *One Day at a Time*. When Norman would laugh at my antics, I glowed. I absolutely glowed. This is a man who had seen everybody do comedy for him all his life."

Of course, she doesn't get up laughing every day. I include the following story because it underlines the reality of aging—and also how Rita's outlook and resilience are such mitigating factors:

When she moved out of the beautiful house she'd lived in for almost twenty years and into a condo in 2023, it hit her much harder than she'd expected.

"I went through a bout of terrible and profound loneliness. And it really, really got to me. I lost my appetite. It was a brand-new feeling. And it was scary. My daughter was really kind of worried. I was deeply lonely. And then it finally oc-curred to me. I don't know how to make friends."

She had long-standing girlfriends, she says, but now she was in a new place. Plus she'd stopped driving three years before. So she would have to build a new circle. She decided she had to make the first move.

"I was at the local supermarket, and there was a lady [shopping] there who I'd seen a number of times, who always gave me the sweetest smile. And finally, one day I said to her, 'What is your name?' And she told me her name. And I said, 'Would you like to have lunch with me?' And she said, 'What?' And I said, 'You have such a lovely face. I would like to get to know you.' And she said, 'Why, yes, I would like that very much.' And so we made a date for that Sunday. We met at one of the local bistros. And we sat down and looked at the menu, and then she said to me, 'I just need to know something. Do you always go around picking up older women?' And I said, 'No. Really, no.'

"But it was my clumsy way of trying to make contact with someone near my age. And having realized that that was my problem, that that loneliness didn't have to be. So she's now a friend."

When we spoke, Rita said she didn't have anything currently lined up for work. She was just coming off a very big year with *80 for Brady* and her role as Abuelita Toretto—the grandmother of Vin Diesel's character—in *Fast X*. A sequel is in the works. I wouldn't be surprised if she ends up back behind the wheel.

"I think [my energy] kind of astonishes people. They say, 'Ninety-two-year-old people don't behave as you do.' At least that's what *they* think. It's not true. There are tons of us around."

Morgan Freeman: The Voice

became a Hollywood heavyweight in his sixties

One nice thing about getting older is that you get to play God. At least you do if you're Morgan Freeman. Unless you somehow missed out on the entirety of American popular culture in the last thirty years, you know Freeman as the voice of God. He is the perfect embodiment of the wisdom, dignity, and moral authority that we expect to hear coming down from Heaven—qualities, by the way, that usually come with advancing age. You might remember that Freeman actually played God in the 2003 Jim Carrey vehicle *Bruce Almighty*. But it's not just this one role that makes us associate Freeman's screen presence with the power and gravitas of the Omnipotent.

The depth and resonance and elegance of Freeman's voice are qualities that he worked hard to cultivate, and they are a large part of the reason that he seems such a natural fit to play not only God but other figures of wisdom and authority, like Nelson Mandela in *Invictus*, the president of the United States in *Angel Has Fallen*, or the narrator in, well . . . just about anything. As he told one reporter who asked about his penchant for wise and solemn roles, "Maybe I just gravitate towards gravitas." Of course, it's not only Freeman's voice that makes him right for these parts; the full range of his talent as an actor is crucial to carrying them off. But it's also true that these are not parts that would generally fall to a man in his thirties or forties. In the youth-oriented culture of Hollywood, Freeman made his age into an asset.

Freeman has been acting almost his whole life. He started with elementary school assemblies (I'm picturing him as all three Wise Men in his Christmas pageant), winning a drama award in a statewide competition at age thirteen. But his ascent to superstardom is almost entirely the result of his achievements in playing senior citizens. He didn't make his feature film debut until he was over forty, when he played a prisoner held in solitary confinement in the 1980 film *Brubaker*. He didn't receive his first Oscar nomination—one of five that he's earned to date—until age fifty, when he snagged the honor for his performance in the well-reviewed but little-watched crime drama *Street Smart*. He only became a household name at fifty-two, with the unexpected hit *Driving Miss Daisy*, where he played a sixty-year-old chauffeur (the director worried that he might be too young for the role) while also starring that year in the Civil War drama *Glory*. And, although we think of him as a mainstay of Hollywood awards ceremonies, he didn't win his first Oscar, for Best Supporting Actor, until he was sixty-seven. (Freeman is not, however, the oldest person to win that award. That distinction goes to Christopher Plummer, who won at eighty-two, followed by another voice of God, George Burns, who won at eighty.) Since Freeman turned sixty, he's made something like eighty movies, and that doesn't include the many feature films, documentaries, and commercials that feature his voice-over work.

Here's how another acting legend, Helen Mirren, put it in presenting Freeman with the American Film Institute's Lifetime Achievement Award in 2011:

> *Lord Byron wrote, "Years steal fire from the mind, as vigor from the limb, and life's enchanted cup but sparkles near the brim." . . . Bullshit. Whoever said that has clearly not watched the forty-plus films Morgan has made since he exploded onto the scene in 1989 at the age of fifty-two. Sure, at times, he's played God, he's been the voice of God, or he's chauffeured around a woman older than God. But that overlooks the sexiest and most fun part of Morgan Freeman. In movie after movie this AARP member has proven beyond a shadow of a doubt that he can kick some serious ass.*

Mirren was right to call out Lord Byron. With all due respect, the guy died at thirty-six.

Freeman, who will turn eighty-seven in 2024, is often asked about what life is like for an older actor. In one 2017 interview, as he was promoting his film *Going in Style*—where he starred alongside eighty-four-year-old Michael Caine and eighty-three-year-old Alan Arkin—he was asked for advice that he could offer to "older actors who say they're struggling to get hired." Freeman was candid . . . and funny. "I can't speak to that," he said. "I don't know anything about the struggle of being an older actor. I know about the struggle of being a younger actor."

It's true. Freeman was so busy in his sixties and seventies playing wizened con men, veteran spies, worldly wise doctors, blind sorcerers, Nubian sheiks, chief justices, global power brokers, and Batman's business manager that his greatest professional struggle was probably deciding which parts he had to turn down. But it's also true that his road to success was neither smooth nor straight.

Freeman set out on that road in 1959, after a stint in the Air Force. At the age of twenty-two, he headed to Hollywood to chase his dreams, like many a young actor. "I was going to be an actor or a bum," he said. Roles for young Black men were much scarcer than they are now, and Freeman seemed to be destined for bumhood. But he persisted. He studied acting at Los Angeles City College—he credits his teachers there with helping him cultivate the vocal style and cadence that became so famous—and began to develop his talent as a dancer.

Throughout his struggles, Freeman held to his principles. He was fired from a job with the San Francisco Opera when he refused to play a Native American stereotype. He walked out of an audition for a commercial when the script featured a part called "The Jew." He refused roles in blaxploitation films that he considered degrading. In 1968, he finally scored his first Broadway role, in a successful all-Black production of *Hello, Dolly!* that starred Pearl Bailey and Cab Calloway. But steady work remained hard to come by.

Then, in 1971, Freeman landed a role alongside Rita Moreno on *The Electric Company*, a new educational show airing on PBS, produced by the Children's Television Workshop, the same creative force that had launched *Sesame Street* two years earlier. With its unmistakable early-seventies style, fast-paced comedy, and colorful costuming, the show mixed instruction in phonics with comedy sketches penned by sharp-witted writers who would go on to contribute to *M*A*S*H* and *Everybody Loves Raymond*. (These included Amy Ephron, sister of Nora and Delia, and the marvelously talented Christopher Cerf.) The show aimed to continue where *Sesame Street* left off, teaching reading skills to grade-school students who had aged out of Ernie and Bert.

Freeman played a variety of roles, but the most prominent was Easy Reader, a bell-bottomed urban hipster who sashayed through city streets with his Afro and sunglasses, declaring "Right on!" and pausing to sound out everything from sandwich boards to graffiti to storefront signage. I can still hear the theme song, with its Herbie Mann–style jazzy flute and its bass line popping underneath the lyrics: "Easy Reader, that's my name / Readin', readin', that's my game." It was a fun role, and steady work. Freeman figured he might do the show for a couple of years and then find something else.

But while the steady paycheck was welcome, the regular work took a toll. "Five years," he told the *New York Times* years later. "I liked the first two." Morgan would walk down the street and be greeted by shouts of "Easy Reader!" and yet no one knew who Morgan Freeman was. He had greater ambitions, and didn't want to be seen as Easy Reader for the rest of his life. Each year that he returned to *The Electric Company*, he vowed it would be his last. It was a genuine struggle. "I could hardly stand to get up in the morning and go to work. I was drinking. That was part of the whole success syndrome and part of the whole frustration of being trapped by greed and insecurity—the actor's constant bane." When the show was canceled, he found himself relieved. "If that show had kept going, I might still be there," he later reflected.

For all that, Freeman acknowledged that *The Electric Company* was "a good show," with "a really good ensemble company." And his costar Moreno served as a lifeline. Unlike Freeman, she had already experienced the heights of stardom. With a daughter at home, she was transitioning to a career that had a more manageable pace as she entered midlife. He was still looking to climb the ladder, aspiring to bigger and more challenging roles. They were on opposite trajectories, yet they formed a bond.

Moreno has spoken about Freeman in interviews over the years. She recalled urging him to take his responsibilities on the show more seriously. "We had a great chemistry together. Morgan, for a very short while, didn't want to be doing the show, and I played the mama and said, 'You can't keep coming in here late, because a lot of people are waiting.' He didn't say a thing—he's a very proud man—but from then on he came to work on time." But she also recognized the source of his discontent. "The work he did after he left the show was stunning," she raved. "No wonder he'd get impatient on our set sometimes. That man just wanted to go out and do some heavy acting."

"We were all doing what really amounted to burlesque," she said. All the while, she, like so many others, had no inkling of the extent of Freeman's talent: "Who knew? I knew this much, he was very funny and clever and very cool, but I had no idea he could do serious drama. I saw him after he left in [the musical] *The Gospel at Colonus* and I nearly wet my knickers." She called working with Freeman "the highlight of my time" on the show: "We would break each other up terribly. There are a couple episodes where you can see us trying desperately not to laugh."

In 1995, when she was awarded a star on the Hollywood Walk of Fame, Freeman did Moreno a big favor. A prominent celebrity—Moreno is too tactful to say who—was slated to host the ceremony but pulled out at the eleventh hour. "We called Morgan," she recalled, "and on his own dime, he flew from Mississippi to L.A. and did my emcee chores. I will never forget that generosity."

opposite page:
Still electric: eighty-two-year-old Rita Moreno and seventy-six-year-old Morgan Freeman at the 2013 Screen Actors Guild Awards.
Stefanie Keenan/Wireimage/Getty Images

Of course, both went on to have remarkable careers. In 2013, the Screen Actors Guild recognized Moreno with its Lifetime Achievement Award. She chose Freeman to present it to her. Moreno was so excited that she had to be bleeped. She and Freeman then stood side by side onstage and, in a throwback to their *Electric Company* days, together sounded out the syllables of "SAG-AFTRA" as they thanked the actors union.

A few years later, it was Freeman who was named to receive the honor. And naturally it was Moreno's time to return the favor of presenting the award. As she came out onstage to a standing and cheering crowd, she reminded the sea of actors, "It was five years ago on this very stage that my dear and beloved friend Morgan Freeman presented this same honor to me. Can you imagine? And it was my wish even then, because I love him so, that I could reciprocate. And, well, you know what? The stars aligned and here we are."

When Freeman stepped up to the mic, he was modest and succinct. He said his thank-yous, including to Moreno, before acknowledging the significance of the award: "This is beyond honor. This is a place in history." He struggled momentarily to pick up his statue—a 2008 car accident had left his left hand paralyzed—and Moreno offered her assistance. Freeman managed it himself. Moreno quipped to the crowd, "You have no idea how heavy these suckers are." She turned to her old friend and asked, "You ready?" "Yeah, baby," he answered, and they left the stage arm in arm.

OLD SPICE: Sophia Loren

In the 1965 film *Lady L*, Sophia Loren plays a gorgeous laundress in turn-of-the-century Paris who falls in love with a Corsican anarchist and a British aristocrat (stay with me here). The wrinkle to the movie (pun intended) is that thirty-year-old Loren dons old-age makeup to play her character at eighty, looking back on an eventful life. The movie was a flop. The public wasn't buying a prematurely aged Loren.

Loren grew up poor in Naples and was nicknamed "Little 'Sofia Stuzz-icadenti'"—"Toothpick"—for her skinny legs. But as she writes in her memoir, "As I was about to turn fifteen, I suddenly found myself living inside a curvy, glowing body, filled with life and promise."

But even after she won a beauty contest, a cameraman complained, "Her face is too short, her mouth is too big, and her nose is too long." Loren refused to change her appearance and went on to become a star of Italian cinema, crossing over to Hollywood and winning an Oscar. Later, she would be the one instructing camera operators in how best to light her face.

And let's talk about that face—and the whole Loren aura. She once said, "I think I have an interesting face, but I think it is the ensemble of the face, the body and the attitude that make me what I am."

Sidebar: Growing up, we had a book of *Life* magazine covers. I was utterly transfixed by the November 14, 1960, cover: Loren staring straight ahead, over the caption "TIGER-EYED TEMPTRESS." At Pyle Junior High, I tried to curry favor with one of the most popular girls (the real power brokers) by calling her a "Tiger-Eyed Temptress." It softened her a bit.

If getting older and beauty possibly fading were concerns for Loren, she has never acknowledged it, telling a reporter in 2020, "If you accept the aging process and live in the present, then you age gracefully."

She's done just that, returning to film in 2020's *The Life Ahead* at eighty-five and receiving rave reviews. The *Washington Post* declared Loren "one of our final links to cinema's Golden Age . . . simply magnificent, both physically and in terms of her craft."

Playing for Herself

Ruth Slenczynska

Ruth Slenczynska

the childhood prodigy who found joy in her nineties

On a February afternoon in 2022, the crowd packed into the Annville, Pennsylvania, auditorium eagerly awaited a concert pianist renowned not just for her talent but also for her age. Not more than four foot eight, the pianist was greeted by a warm wave of applause. She smiled broadly, squinting, took a bow, and then settled onto the bench. She didn't seem nervous in the least.

After all, at ninety-seven, Ruth Slenczynska had been performing for the public for more years than a piano has keys. And the concert was an occasion for loving friends and adoring fans to celebrate this marvel.

"You practice. And then you pray. . . . If you're lucky, things go well," Ruth later told me, with a humility that seemed unpracticed. But something much more than luck was at play as she gave herself over to Beethoven, Prokofiev, and Chopin.

"Where are you mentally during the recital?" I asked her.

"I go to a place I can't take anybody," Ruth said. "It's a place from where I get my music."

Ruth Slenczynska began going to that place not long after she was born, in Sacramento, California, on January 15, 1925. She learned to read music at three and played her first concert at four. Hailed (and billed) as one of the greatest child prodigies since Mozart—and yes, she was already playing Mozart by then, and Liszt and Beethoven too—she soon embarked on a European tour, making her debut in Berlin at six, followed by Paris at seven.

"The concert in Paris I remember mainly 'cause it was the first time I played with an orchestra," she said.

The conductor of that performance was the celebrated French pianist Alfred Cortot. She also learned from Austrian pianist and composer Artur Schnabel. But the connection with early twentieth-century classical music royalty that makes my head really spin? Ruth is the last living pupil of composer, conductor, and virtuoso pianist Sergei Rachmaninoff. Although the two were fifty-two years apart in age, they became friends.

When I interviewed her, she showed me a necklace she said she always wears, a gold chain with a blue pendant. "It's a Fabergé egg," she chirped, a gift from Rachmaninoff himself. He gave it to her after she filled in for him at a concert when she was nine years old. (Not a typo. Ruth subbed for Rachmaninoff when she was nine.) "I've had it next to me all this time."

As a child, Ruth became known for her expert technique. A *New York Times* review from November 1933 noted that "her grasp of purely technical matters would have been the envy of older and more practiced pianists." But she was also praised for the maturity of her phrasing, as a pianist with "phenomenal gifts." (It seems, though, that young Ruth was not reading her reviews. "Well, I didn't know anything about it," she said. "I just did what I was told. I was an obedient kid.")

You could think of Ruth Slenczynska as the Shirley Temple of classical music. Parents wanted their children to be just like Ruth. Some people even called her a "miracle child." It's a moniker Ruth waved off: "Every child is a miracle." When I countered that she was an awesomely talented one, she insisted, "No. If I were talented, I wouldn't have had to work so hard."

Working hard is putting it mildly. Ruth's success onstage came at an unconscionable cost: near-constant abuse by her Polish immigrant father, Josef Slenczynski, a violinist frustrated by his own limited success. "He wanted for me to be the greatest pianist in the world," she said. "He would have been a great violinist, I suppose, but he was injured in the war, couldn't play the violin."

Josef observed his daughter's musical gift when she was just sixteen months old. He had tried teaching Ruth the violin, but she kept gravitating to the piano.

opposite page:
Five-year-old prodigy Ruth Slenczynska
playing for the world in 1930.
Associated Press

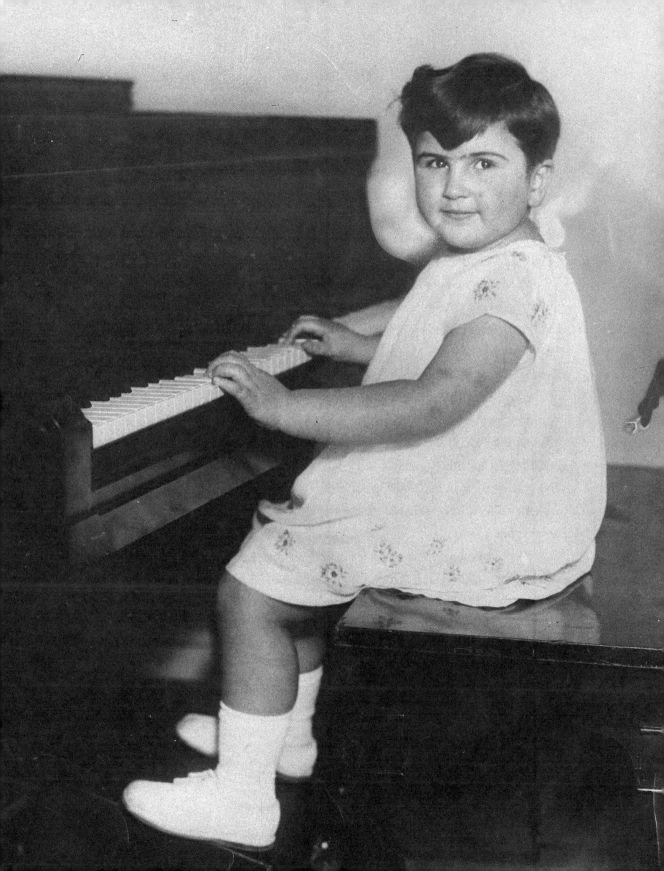

Josef seized on this discovery and effectively canceled her childhood before it even began. By the time she was three, her father had Ruth on a strict schedule of up to nine hours of practice every day. "My father was on top of me all the time to work, work, work, work." Even before breakfast, she had to play all of Chopin's études.

"I would be practicing and hearing from the street my sisters as they were playing with other kids," she told me plaintively, as if she were still a little girl desperate to go outdoors. "I wanted to be one of those kids who played."

But there were harsh consequences if she deviated from the regimen dictated by her father. "If I didn't practice, I was chased around the apartment with a stick, my father's 'magic stick.' I didn't like that kind of life. I didn't want that." She said her father mocked her, even denied her food, if she failed to play a passage correctly. (As for her mother, Ruth wrote that she was afraid to interfere—ultimately "meek and resigned" to his treatment of their daughter.)

Josef didn't limit his abuse to rehearsal. After Ruth's debut in Berlin, a concert-goer brought a doll to the stage for the then-six-year-old pianist. "Just as I was reaching out for this wonderful little doll," she recalled, "my father came onstage and pushed the doll back into the audience and said, 'Weg mit die puppe. Away with the doll.' He had trained me to keep away from dolls. And he didn't want a doll to interrupt my studies."

In Paris, she found solace in her working relationship with Rachmaninoff. The two had their own "secret language." "He spoke French to me. And I could answer in French. And we spoke French just well enough so that I knew my father couldn't follow what we said," she told me with a sense of mischief that almost made me forget the cruel context.

As Ruth entered adolescence, she began to push back. And by fifteen, she'd had enough. She quit playing and enrolled at the University of California at Berkeley to study psychology. Not long afterward, she left home, severing all ties with her father. The two never reconciled.

In 1944, Ruth married fellow student George Born. They divorced nine years later. By then, Ruth had begun teaching piano. "I had to do something to support myself." It was while she was teaching at College of Our Lady of Mercy in Burlingame, California, that she was invited by a concert organizer to return to the stage. She was hesitant. "He said, 'Would you like to play at the Carmel Bach festival?' And I said, 'I don't think I can. I used to play concerts. But I don't think that I have enough talent to play concerts. I think that I'm just a teacher.'"

Of course she was more than "just a teacher." And so at the age of twenty-six—young by any other measure but for Ruth already a lifetime—she made her way back onstage. This time it was on her own terms.

"How did your relationship with playing change?" I asked.

"Well, it just grew," she said. "I kept playing bigger and better."

Playing piano went from being a means of survival to something she began to enjoy. She started traveling the world again, touring with Arthur Fiedler and the Boston Pops. She recorded ten LPs for Decca and appeared on television, once in an episode of *This Is Your Life*. And in 1957 she wrote a searing memoir, *Forbidden Childhood*. (The dust jacket was co-designed by a then-little-known Andy Warhol.)

Over the decades she played for several U.S. presidents—including John F. Kennedy, Jimmy Carter, and Ronald Reagan—and *with* Harry Truman. "We played the slow movement of a Mozart sonata. I thought he played very musically," Ruth recalled. "He was a warm, personable individual. Not president of the United States."

But her greatest satisfaction seemed to derive from teaching. In 1964, she became Artist-in-Residence at Southern Illinois University at Edwardsville. That's where she met political science professor James Kerr.

"How much did your life change when you met your second husband?" I asked.

"Well, it changed completely," she said. "I became a real person. I'd marry him again, all over again."

Kerr gave her a much simpler last name (her joke), and he was an exceptional cook, a nice bonus since Ruth was either practicing or teaching most of the day. He had told Ruth that a person should always marry their best friend. Ruth and James were married—and best friends—for thirty-four years, until his death in 2001.

After Kerr's passing, Ruth kept teaching—in New York City, then in Taiwan for a year—and performing. One of her mentees—and she had hundreds by this point—was Shelly Moorman-Stahlman, a music professor at Pennsylvania's Lebanon Valley College. Dr. Moorman-Stahlman became a friend, and in 2020, Ruth, then ninety-five, moved in with her and her husband, Randy Stahlman. It was at their home that I met Ruth in 2022.

"She believes that you don't look back, you gain from the past, but you're always looking forward," Shelly told me then. "And I think that [has been] her secret to success in so many ways." Looking back was always complicated for Ruth. Shelly said that the first year Ruth lived with them, the family decided to carve a jack-o'-lantern for Halloween.

"And she never had experienced that before. And she loved sitting at the table and she would make up names for this jack-o'-lantern." Shelly and Randy also took Ruth driving through Hershey to see the lights at Christmastime. "Some things like that that she had not done before . . . simple things that you and I take for granted that she had not had the time to experience as a child, and then maybe had not had the time to experience as an adult." Shelly told me that Ruth took in these experiences with a kind of "childhood innocence," a sense of wonder.

I was the one filled with wonder sitting next to Ruth at her home piano as she played Chopin's Waltz in C-sharp minor, op. 64, no. 2. To think that she was seven years old when she first played it. And here I sat with her ninety years later. This time she volunteered to play it.

It was that same year, 2022, that Ruth, at ninety-seven, released her first album in sixty-six years, *My Life in Music*. "I thought I was retired," she shrugged. But she was still growing. "Nobody's a real pianist till they're past sixty. . . . It takes that long before you get there, before you have control, before you can do what you want to with your hands." As for what she's imparting to the audience now when

Ninety-seven-year-old Ruth Slenczynska playing for herself (and lucky me!) in 2022.

Michelle Kessel

she plays pieces she played as a child: "The notes are the same. But the story is different."

As of this writing, Ruth is ninety-nine and officially retired from performing and recording albums. Shelly told me by email that Ruth "still enjoys going to concerts, listening to recordings, giving a lesson to an occasional student, and reading immensely. However, at ninety-nine, she also enjoys watching birds and the animals in the yard (you may remember that she had a rocking chair by our bay window where she loves to sit and read), teaching French to my two-year-old grandson and holding the new two-month-old grandson. Ruth is a great inspiration to all."

I do remember that rocking chair by the window. That was my last sight of Ruth as the crew and I left that March day. She was looking out at the birds. And seemed perfectly at peace.

OLD CHESTNUT: Rockin' Around the Christmas Tree

I n 1958 the *Atlanta Journal-Constitution* wrote of Brenda Lee's voice that it was "full, strong and husky and she uses it to cajole, coax and caress until your heart turns emotional flip-flops." By then the thirteen-year-old Brenda was an old pro. Linda, her older sister, would later recall, "When she was about two years old, she could hear a song once on the radio and then whistle the tune perfectly. And sing all the lyrics, too. She did it so easily."

Lee became a major pop recording artist, with hits like "I'm Sorry" and "I Want to Be Wanted." The Beatles opened for her in Hamburg in 1962. She's among the four musical acts that charted the most singles in the 1960s, the other three being Elvis Presley, Ray Charles, and the Beatles (who ended up making it pretty big after those days in Hamburg).

But it's a rockabilly Christmas song that Lee recorded back when she was thirteen that would cement her musical legacy. "Rockin' Around the Christmas Tree" was not a hit when it was first released, though as she told *Rolling Stone* in 2018, "When we recorded 'Rockin',' I knew it was magical." The song gradually grew in popularity over the decades, with a major bump in 1990 when it was featured in the movie *Home Alone*. In a 2015 interview, Lee was candid about the song that had become her signature, even if it had never been a chart-topper: "It's extended my career. You get to a certain age in this industry and you're not as hot as you once were. It's meant to be that way . . ."

And so, in 2023, it was a Christmas miracle of sorts for Brenda Lee when "Rockin' Around the Christmas Tree," propelled by TikTok, finally hit No. 1 on the Billboard Hot 100 chart, sixty-five years after it was released. (In other words, the song itself is eligible for Social Security.) Lee, at seventy-eight, became the oldest living person to achieve a No. 1 song in the U.S., surpassing the previous record holder, sixty-two-year-old Louis Armstrong for "Hello, Dolly!" in 1964. Little Miss Dynamite, as Lee was nicknamed early on, still knows how to make some noise.

The Writers

Laura Ingalls Wilder,

Frank McCourt

& Peter Mark Roget

Laura Ingalls Wilder:
Literary Frontierswoman

began publishing the Little House
book series at sixty-five

Chances are, you know something about the life of Laura Ingalls Wilder. If, like sixty million other people, you once enjoyed the *Little House* books—*Little House in the Big Woods, Little House on the Prairie,* and six others—some of the details of her early life on the frontier are bound to have stayed with you: the doll she plays with that's made from a corncob wrapped in a rag, her sister Mary's blindness, the terrifying swarm of locusts that destroys a year's crops, or the touching bond between Charles ("Pa") Ingalls and the young daughter he called "Half-pint." First published in the 1930s, the books have become beloved children's classics, and they paint an indelible picture of frontier life in the later nineteenth century in the wake of the Homestead Act, when the federal government gave away 160 acres to any citizen or would-be citizen willing to cultivate it.

Before we get too far into the story of Wilder and her books: the *Little House* TV series is its own wonderful creation, family TV at its finest, thanks to the vision of the late Michael Landon. There's a good reason that it's been in continuous reruns since it first aired in the 1970s and 80s. Viewership skyrocketed during the pandemic. (The episode "The Wisdom of Solomon," guest-starring Todd Bridges before he costarred on *Diff'rent Strokes*, is a must-see. Plus any episode where Alison Arngrim's Nellie terrorizes Walnut Grove.) But the series was only loosely based on the books. We're focusing on Wilder and her books here. We thank all Bonnetheads in advance for their understanding in this matter.

Seen through the nostalgic lens of reminiscence, Laura Ingalls Wilder's childhood, for all the dangers and struggles, appears bathed in a kind of gauzy golden light. Pa Ingalls repeatedly builds his family a home, works the land, then gets restless, pulls up stakes, and sets off for another territory and another new start. If you read the whole series, you'll also remember the heroism of the young Almanzo Wilder during the "long winter" as he braves a weeks-long blizzard to secure food for the imperiled people of his town. The books, which were written for children, break off when Laura, at eighteen, marries Almanzo and leaves her parents to start her own life and her own family in her own little house.

But Laura Ingalls Wilder didn't publish *Little House in the Big Woods* until she was sixty-five. So what happened in the intervening years? And how did the heroine of the books become the beloved author who, many years later, told these charming stories?

For both Laura and her husband, Almanzo Wilder, the years in between childhood and the publication of the *Little House* series were not the happily-ever-after ending that readers of the books might like to imagine. In fact, between 1885, when Laura married Almanzo, and 1911, when she began to write a column for a local agricultural publication, her life was primarily one of poverty. According to the writer Judith Thurman, the early years of her marriage were "much more harrowing than her parents' experience as pioneers on the frontier." During these years, their second child, a boy, died after twelve days; Almanzo contracted diphtheria, which left him partially paralyzed; a fire accidentally started by their daughter, Rose, burned their South Dakota house to the ground; drought destroyed their crops. They struggled to support themselves, moving from South Dakota to Minnesota to Florida to South Dakota again to Missouri. Even when they finally settled in southern Missouri, they only scraped by. As Thurman relates, "Rose grew up as really the child of refugees, laughed at by the girls in school for her bare feet and her shabby clothes." These were hardly happy golden years.

Eventually the Wilders did settle down and buy a small farm in the Ozarks, and attained a level of security. But when Rose graduated from high school at the top of her class, they lacked the money to send her to college, and so she trained instead to be a telegraph operator.

Still, Laura Ingalls Wilder continued writing. When she was forty-four, a paper of hers, "The Small Farm Home," was delivered at something called the Missouri Home Makers' Conference. John Francis Case, an editor with an agricultural magazine called the *Missouri Ruralist*, heard it and invited her to submit it to his publication. It wasn't exactly the *Atlantic Monthly* or the *Saturday Evening Post*, but it was a real magazine, and Laura's reach began to extend. Case soon hired "Mrs. A. J. Wilder" to write a regular column on domestic matters—the business of running a small farm. Titles like "Good Times on the Farm" and "My Apple Orchard" give a sense of her subject matter. Cutting-edge it was not.

In the meantime, her daughter Rose's telegraphy skills secured her jobs at hotels, first in Kansas City and then in San Francisco. In San Francisco, she married a man named Claire Gillette Lane, and to make a living, the two sold real estate, among other things. Eventually Rose turned to journalism, first working freelance with limited success, in time landing an editorial assistant position with the *San Francisco Bulletin*.

Rose encouraged Laura to write as well. Sometime around 1914, she advised her to dig up some reminiscences that Laura had sent to her own mother, Caroline, and see if she might get them published. Rose urged Laura to adopt a plain, direct style in preparing them for publication: "Just think you are writing a diary that no one anywhere will ever see." (It's hard to think of better advice to a writer who might not be sure of her own voice.) Rose understood the emotional appeal of her mother's stories of the American West of the 1870s and 1880s; in one letter to Laura, she writes of "Indians and forests and half a continent practically untouched by the white race" just a generation earlier. As Rose saw it, her mother's stories of pioneer life were part of a great American epic, in which the whole continent was destined to be settled by European immigrants. (Of course, this belief in what historians call Manifest Destiny relied on denying the claims of the indigenous peoples already living there.) Laura visited Rose in San Francisco for several months in 1915, and during her stay they likely discussed the idea of Laura writing an autobiography or memoir.

Yet Laura's life story would remain unwritten for another fifteen years.

Laura did continue to write for the *Missouri Ruralist*, and soon was made editor of the "Farm Home" section. Her columns about farm life would prove good preparation for her later career as the author of children's books. They not only helped her cultivate a clear and graceful style but also stirred up poignant memories from her childhood. And they provided some useful extra income.

Then came 1929. The stock market crash devastated Laura and Almanzo's modest savings. And although Laura told her daughter that she was more interested in recognition or "prestige" than in money, it was almost certainly out of financial need—at least in part—that she put aside her reservations about writing and began to set her story down on paper.

There were also deeper motives at work. Mary, Laura's sister, had died in 1928, her mother, Caroline, in 1924. According to biographer Pamela Smith Hill, "After the deaths of Mary and her mother, [Laura] became much more conscious of her own mortality, and probably realized that if she wanted to set down her stories, this was the time."

For many people, the threat of mortality brings a recognition that, unless we set our memories down or someone else does, they will perish with us. We don't need to be celebrities or heads of state to believe that there is something special about our own lives, our own childhoods, our own memories, that makes them worth preserving. This is even more true when we see our lives as bound up with great historical movements. In Laura Wilder's case, she was aware that her experiences as a little girl represented a distinct moment in American history, one that was in fact already gone. "I realized that I had seen and lived it all—all the successive phases of the frontier," she later said, "first the frontiersman then the pioneer, then the farmers and the towns. Then I understood that in my own life I represented a whole period of American history." (It was 1890 when the Bureau of the Census announced the closing of the frontier. I'm picturing a guy in a coonskin cap with a musket showing up in the Oklahoma Territory only to find a "Frontier Closed" sign, then slinking off in disappointment.)

In 1930, Laura began writing. Rose was by now a well-known journalist, publishing in some of America's leading magazines, and the author of a biography of Herbert Hoover. (She had been sending her parents money for some time.) She was also connected in the literary world; her friends included bestselling novelist Sinclair Lewis and his then-wife, Dorothy Thompson, an international journalist who would become famous for her reporting on the rise of Nazism in Germany. Rose was indispensable to her mother's book, serving as typist, editor, agent, and publicist.

Laura completed a memoir, *Pioneer Girl*, that was aimed at the adult readers she was used to writing for. Caroline Fraser, author of the Pulitzer Prize–winning biography *Prairie Fires: The American Dreams of Laura Ingalls Wilder*, describes the work as "flatter and less emotional than the fiction," noting that its "frank, sometimes rueful self-portrait allows us to see the hard reality of poverty on the Great Plains." It lacked the warm, sentimental glow of the later *Little House* books. Perhaps because America was now in the midst of the Great Depression, publishers rejected it.

Somewhere along the line, however, an editor suggested recasting the narrative as a novel aimed at children eight to twelve years old. Laura, again in collaboration with Rose, rewrote her story. (How much Rose shaped the final product is debated among scholars.) The first-person "I" of *Pioneer Girl* became the "Laura" of the *Little House* books. The language was simplified, and some of the darker material removed. Laura always acknowledged that her books contained truth but "not the whole truth," and that a children's book had no room for episodes like a stay in Iowa that found Ma and Pa forced to hire out their girls as domestic workers to a hotel, or the family's middle-of-the-night flight from debt collectors.

Rewriting her story for children was the right decision. This time Wilder found a buyer—Virginia Kirkus, head of a new children's division at Harper & Bros. One December afternoon, Kirkus went to tea at the Biltmore Hotel in New York with an editor from Knopf. That editor had liked Wilder's manuscript but couldn't publish it herself, since Knopf was getting out of the children's book business. So she passed it along to Kirkus.

That evening, Kirkus boarded the train back to her home in Westport, Connecticut. She settled into her car and began reading. Kirkus herself was living what she called "a fairly rugged life" in Westport; her house lacked electricity and other modern conveniences, and so, she later said, her imagination rapidly transported her to the old Wisconsin woods of sixty years past. As the sun sank below the horizon, she continued to read, so absorbed in the story and the characters that she passed her stop. She later described the appeal of the book, which seemed a perfect fit for the new austerity of the Depression: "The real magic was in the telling. One felt that one was listening, not reading. And picture after picture—still vivid today, more than twenty years later—flashed before my inward eye. I knew Laura—and the older Laura who was telling her story. Here was the book no depression could stop."

Harper bought the book. And so, at age sixty-five, with a hard life of labor and disappointment behind her, Laura Ingalls Wilder published *Little House in the Big Woods*. On April 24, 1932, the *New York Times Book Review* gave it a single long paragraph under the heading "Books for Children." The reviewer praised the novel's "refreshingly genuine and lifelike quality," noting that the story was "full of incidents and accounts of daily doings that boys and girls will enjoy." She cited the "memories of pioneer life described with zest and humor," and concluded by saying, "The characters are very much alive and the portrait of Laura's father, especially, is drawn with loving care and reality." The book was a success.

With the book's healthy sales, the idea of not only a sequel but a series—what we might today call a franchise—took hold. In the thirties, multivolume novels weren't written for children, but Wilder saw no reason why they couldn't be.

Eighty-four-year-old Laura Ingalls Wilder
enjoying prosperity in 1951
after a life of hardship.
Laura Ingalls Wilder Memorial Society

She had enough material for several more books.

Over the next eleven years, Wilder would write seven more books, concluding with *These Happy Golden Years* at age seventy-six. After a life of hardship, she had finally achieved prosperity, as the burgeoning royalties made her a wealthy woman. A good portion of her own happy golden years were now spent responding to the letters she got from readers, students, and teachers, praising her book—sharing their thoughts, describing their own personal stories. The books would go on to sell sixty million copies in many languages. Rose, meanwhile, became a fierce critic of Franklin D. Roosevelt—criticizing the New Deal, urging the U.S. to stay out of World War II, and denouncing Social Security as a Ponzi scheme. Her suspicion of government bordering on paranoia, she grew her own food to protest World War II rations. (Today she's regarded by some as one of the "mothers of libertarianism," along with Ayn Rand.) She also seems to have plagiarized material from her mother's drafts for her own fiction. If her life were a TV series, it would air much later than *Little House* did, probably on FX.

Laura died in 1957, three days after her ninetieth birthday. The years after her death saw the posthumous publication of a ninth book in the series, *The First Four Years*, describing Laura's early years with Almanzo, and in 2014 the South Dakota State Historical Society published *Pioneer Girl*, eighty years after its composition. There were controversies, too. The enormous success of the books and the 1970s

TV series led, inevitably, to commercialization that some readers decried. Others lamented the ways that they thought Rose's political views slanted the narrative. And increasing numbers of readers balked at the stereotyped and sometimes dehumanizing representations of Black and Native Americans. (Louise Erdrich's *The Birchbark House* offers a more generous and accurate representation of indigenous culture, telling the story of a seven-year-old Ojibwe girl growing up in the Lake Superior region in the mid-nineteenth century.) Yet the *Little House* books remain both a treasured document of the frontier experience and an inspiration to late-life authors everywhere who might wonder if their childhood is worth writing about.

———

A final note: Even those who may not care for the *Little House* TV series will concede that the theme music, by David Rose, is terrific. When I profiled former *Little House* star Melissa Gilbert for *CBS Sunday Morning*, she told me that the same composer also wrote the iconic "The Stripper" music. (You'll know it when you hear it.) If Walnut Grove had its own strip clubs, Laura wisely cut them out of her narrative when she reimagined the stories for children.

Frank McCourt:
The Miserable Irish Childhood

a first-time author and best-selling memoirist at sixty-six

With some writers, there's no point in paraphrasing. You just need to let them speak for themselves, in their own words. Here's the writer Frank McCourt, near the beginning of his 1996 memoir, *Angela's Ashes*:

The Writers

When I look back on my childhood I wonder how I survived at all. It was, of course, a miserable childhood: the happy childhood is hardly worth your while. Worse than the ordinary miserable childhood is the miserable Irish childhood, and worse yet is the miserable Irish Catholic childhood.

People everywhere brag and whimper about the woes of their early years, but nothing can compare with the Irish version: the poverty; the shiftless loquacious alcoholic father; the pious defeated mother moaning by the fire; pompous priests; bullying schoolmasters; the English and the terrible things they did to us for eight hundred long years.

McCourt knows that this is a story we've heard before, or that we think we've heard before, whether in other books, old movies, or just sitting in a bar with a friend or relative. But familiar as the story may seem, McCourt, in these few simple sentences, gives us the sense that this is still a voice we want to hear more from—a voice whose compassion and humor and sidelong manner of looking at life will turn out to be wholly original.

For most of his life, McCourt would not set his story down on paper. He had a moving tale to tell and he possessed the literary gifts with which to tell it, but he didn't believe it was something anyone would want to hear. And so he waited until he was sixty-six to publish the book that would be called "the publishing industry's Cinderella story of the decade."

Once he did publish, this unassuming retired high school English teacher became, overnight, a literary celebrity. On its release, *Angela's Ashes* was adored by both critics and everyday readers. It topped the bestseller list for a solid two years. It sold four million hardcover copies and was translated into twenty languages. It won the National Book Award and the Pulitzer Prize. It led to interviews with countless newspapers, appearances on the *Today Show* and *Late Night with Conan O'Brien*, speaking engagements, commencement addresses, sequels, movies, documentaries,

a Broadway musical, a children's book, scholarly studies, and, for a while, a Frank McCourt museum in Limerick.

All of this happened after McCourt had started collecting Social Security.

As McCourt himself once told a reporter, "F. Scott Fitzgerald said there are no second acts in American lives. I think I've proven him wrong. . . . And all because I refused to settle for a one-act existence."

McCourt was actually born in New York City, in Bedford-Stuyvesant, to poor Irish immigrants, in 1930. In his colorful style, he described his conception as "a knee-trembler—the act itself done up against a wall." But the Depression was so bad in the U.S. that his parents, Malachy and Angela McCourt, made the choice to reverse-emigrate, returning to Ireland when Frank was four. Life there was no easier, and after failed efforts at finding work in Belfast and Dublin, the family settled in Angela's native Limerick. From there it was the childhood McCourt describes: poverty, alcoholism, depression; mean-spirited priests and schoolmasters; the illness and deaths of two little siblings; and the assumption, by Frank, of bread-winning duties at age thirteen when the alcoholic Malachy abandoned the family. This is the childhood that would make the man. (If you haven't yet read *Angela's Ashes*, make sure you have an extra blanket and hot cup of tea on hand when you do. The description of the inescapable dampness, the mustiness—really the *dankness*— of life in Limerick will chill you to the bone.)

The path from telegram delivery boy at age thirteen to bestselling author at sixty-six was a winding one. At nineteen, McCourt scraped together his savings and boarded a ship for New York City. He worked as a bellhop at the Biltmore Hotel, then as a meatpacker. During the Korean War he was drafted—he was a native U.S.

opposite page:
Sixty-six-year-old Frank McCourt
giving off that newly minted
bestseller glow in 1996.
Isolde Ohlbaum/laif/Redux

citizen, after all; coming home, he attended New York University on the GI Bill, where he studied English while working nights in a warehouse. That training allowed him to make a career for himself as an English teacher. He worked at a series of New York public high schools, many of them technical-vocational, often teaching immigrant children who came not from Ireland but from Latin America and the Caribbean. In 1972, he landed at Stuyvesant High, one of New York's most selective "specialized" schools, where he educated college-bound teenagers for another fifteen years. Over these years he married and divorced twice, and had a daughter.

Throughout his thirty-year career as a teacher, McCourt always nurtured literary ambitions, but whether because of modesty or a lack of confidence or an underlying sense of shame about the poverty from which he came, he never pursued a writing career. Something drove him, in the late 1960s, to return to school and earn a master's in English, and he began a PhD at Trinity College, Dublin. But after only eighteen months, he packed it in and returned once more to the U.S. At one point he attempted a memoir, but he found his own prose too heavily influenced by James Joyce and put the pages aside, deeming them mannered.

McCourt kept literary company, though, hanging out with successful Irish American New York City journalists like Pete Hamill and Jimmy Breslin in Greenwich Village's famed Lion's Head bar; he even cowrote and acted in an off-Broadway show, *A Couple of Blaguards*, with his brother Malachy, who owned a pub on Third Avenue and worked sporadically in movies. He published what he later described as "a few pieces in *The Village Voice*, *Newsday*, and a defunct magazine in Dublin." Yet despite all this, a fundamental modesty held him back. McCourt was never willing to call himself a writer, or even a writing teacher. In *Teacher Man*, his third book, he wrote: "I can never bring myself to say I teach creative writing or poetry or literature, especially since I am always learning myself. Instead I say I conduct a course."

What McCourt would later acknowledge was that in teaching others to write, he was also teaching himself. He didn't fully realize it, but his long years of teaching were a gestation period, during which he slowly discovered in himself the creative talents that would come to fruition in *Angela's Ashes*. In the classroom, he indulged his gifts as a storyteller and a raconteur, gifts he believes he inherited from Irish culture and specifically from his father. He developed these talents, he said, out of necessity—it was a means of survival in the classroom when faced with a roomful of American teenagers with seven-minute attention spans. (Yes, seven minutes seems like an eternity in the age of TikTok.) And so, even though colleagues advised him to keep a strict professional demeanor and share nothing of his private life with his students, he did just the opposite. He told them about his life, his childhood, the characters from Limerick. His personal stories were really all he had. And as he would rehearse these stories to the kids, he gradually gave them dramatic shape. The students listened. They told him he should write a book.

Yet he didn't. He made notes here and there, but that was it. There was always a reason not to write the book, or at least a pretext. His teaching was demanding, and he lacked the time he needed to sit down and write. Or, he worried that airing all the dirty laundry would embarrass his mother, who comes off in his book as a human but flawed character. (During one stretch, she sleeps with a cousin in order to provide a roof over her children's heads.) He later said that he just didn't believe that his own humble story of an impoverished Irish childhood was worthy of being read by others: "I didn't know you could write about yourself. . . . Nobody told us in school. The masters always made us write about noble topics like the Battle of Kinsale or the Siege of Limerick or that dirty rotten bastard Cromwell."

He then added, disclosing what was more likely the real reason, "Besides, I would've been ashamed to write about the way I grew up."

McCourt grew older. After his mother, Angela, died in 1981, he could no longer plead that he was protecting her feelings. After he retired from Stuyvesant in 1987, he could no longer plead a lack of time. As a *New York Times* profile said, as his sixties loomed, "Frank McCourt knew that the point of permanent regret was approaching." In his own words, "There was an accumulation of material in my drawer, and in '94 I had to get it out of my system. It was seared into my memory, festering and gestating. If I hadn't finished it, I would've died howling with despair."

McCourt credited his third wife, Ellen Frey, with providing the final push that he needed. They married in 1994. And while Ellen gave him encouragement, his four-year-old granddaughter, Chiara, gave him his voice. One day, listening to her talk, he realized that her simple child's language had the directness and vitality that he was seeking. So finally, at the age of sixty-four, with no more excuses, Frank Mc-Court began writing down what happened to him as a boy. By the end of 1995 he'd finished a draft. *Angela's Ashes* was published in 1996.

Yet although the book was lauded by critics and adored by readers, there was one place on the globe where it didn't go over so well: Limerick. It's been said—by the novelist Thomas Wolfe and many after him—that the first-time writer can't go home again. To tell the truth about where you come from is to burn your bridges as you leave. You can't convey your life story honestly and authentically if you're worried about protecting the feelings of your family and your neighbors.

The people of Limerick were outraged by McCourt's unflattering portrait of their city, and insisted there was more to their town than misery and squalor. They accused McCourt of dishonoring the dead, of playing to stereotypes, of exaggerating or even fabricating details. A local journalist named Gerry Hannan, himself too young to remember the years of McCourt's childhood, styled himself as Limerick's champion, compiling lists of errors and inaccuracies in McCourt's book and confronting the author live onstage during an Irish TV appearance. Photos of an apparently well-fed Angela McCourt surfaced, and old-timers recalled the spacious green lawn of the house where the family had lived. McCourt, for his own part, insisted on the truth of his story, in spite of whatever incidental details his memory might have failed to capture perfectly.

But in the long run, the people of Limerick came around. The anger cooled and the pride emerged. In 2011, the Limerick artist Una Heaton established the Frank McCourt Museum in the Leamy House, an 1840s Tudor-style building that was the site of the grade school McCourt had attended in the 1930s. The museum eventually closed, but the town now honored him. His papers are housed in Glucksman Library at the University of Limerick, and in 2013 the university created an endowed professorship in his name, the Frank McCourt Chair of Creative Writing.

As McCourt followed up *Angela's Ashes* with *'Tis* in 1999 and *Teacher Man* in 2005, his fame continued to grow. He passed away from cancer in 2009 at seventy-eight. That same year, the City of New York established Frank McCourt High School of Writing Journalism and Literature on the Upper West Side.

As McCourt put it, "All I had was this story. It took me two years and all my life to write it."

Peter Mark Roget: Finding Just the Words

*published his famous book of
synonyms at seventy-three*

There are books and there are books. Frank McCourt, as he considered his remaining years, felt a need to set his life story down in words, and wrote one of the most emotionally gripping memoirs of his era. Laura Ingalls Wilder also became a famous author in her sixties, writing a series of children's stories that became enduring documents of the American experience. *Angela's Ashes* and the *Little House* series are very different kinds of books, but at their core they're both human stories, drawn from real life, chronicling the struggles and triumphs of their authors' childhoods. Peter Mark Roget was another famous writer who waited until late life to complete the book he had been planning to write for decades. But when his time came to look back, take stock, and sum up all he had to say, he had no interest in telling his own life narrative. He was interested in making lists.

Roget's Thesaurus is basically a collection of lists: a list of lists. It's a list of words, and after each word is a list of synonyms—you know, substitutes, replacements, alternatives. It's handy to have at your elbow if you're writing and trying not to sound repetitive every time you need to mention a subject like, say, old age. Or at least it *was* handy before you could click on a tab on your screen called "Thesaurus." Some writers love consulting a thesaurus and some hate it, since the synonyms, if chosen carelessly, can sound a little off—clunky, wooden, stiff, artificial. The poet Sylvia Plath called herself "Roget's strumpet" for her overreliance on the book. "Strumpet," by the way, is a pitch-perfect choice. It wouldn't have sounded the same if she'd said, "Roget's harlot," "Roget's wench," or "Roget's ho."

Now, a thesaurus—the word is Latin for "treasury" or "treasure chest"—is a reference book. You rarely read reference books straight through. You dip into them, in search of a particular piece of information. That's you. If you read *Mobituaries*, then you know that *I* spent whole afternoons of my childhood lying on my stomach on the family room floor, poring over the 1974 *World Book Encyclopedia*. The glossy stock and gilded page ends made me feel like I was leafing through a holy text. And don't get me started on the wonder of almanacs. Scrunched-up type on thin pages bearing lists of Oscar winners, state birds, vice presidents, and world capitals, *all in one place*? My best friend Mario's mother worked at the World Bank. I kid you not, each year we were practically breathless waiting for her to bring home the *World Bank GDP Annual Report* so that we could see how the ranking of different countries' economies had changed. Malaysia, up three spots. Paraguay, down four! The only thing that could have made it more exciting was if Casey Kasem had been on hand to narrate.

Because Roget gave his name to the thesaurus, he'll always have a home in the reference section, like Noah Webster, John Bartlett, and Melvil Dewey. (Don't look them up; just think about it.) But Roget didn't really *invent* the thesaurus. That honor is usually given to a French priest named Gabriel Girard, who in 1718 wrote a book listing 295 concepts and providing synonyms for each one. (The 1700s also saw publication of Diderot's *Encyclopédie* and Samuel Johnson's *Dictionary of the English Language*; there was suddenly a lot more knowledge out there, and people needed to organize it.) After Girard's book was translated into English—how exactly do you translate a book of synonyms, by the way?—a Welsh-born woman named Hester Lynch Thrale Piozzi tried her hand at the genre. Piozzi was a close friend of Samuel Johnson and the novelist Frances Burney. In 1794, she published *British Synonymy; or, an Attempt at Regulating the Choice of Words in Familiar Conversation*. So Roget didn't invent the thesaurus, but he improved it—you know, enhanced it, developed it, took it to another level.

Peter Mark Roget was born on January 18, 1779, in London, to a Swiss father and a British mother. His father died when Peter was only four, and his maternal uncle, Sir Samuel Romilly, served as a surrogate father. (Sir Romilly himself has a noble place in history: a member of Parliament, he fought to abolish the slave trade.) Between Peter's father's death and his mother's subsequent depression, his childhood was not easy. Depression ran in his family, and he suffered from it.

By the age of eight, Peter was already making lists. Maybe this had something to do with the losses he'd experienced; among his first lists was one titled "Dates of Death," cataloging when various friends and family members had passed away. He also assembled verbal inventories on less morbid topics, such as "Parts of the Body" and things "In the Garden." It's been speculated that the boy may have had Asperger's syndrome or obsessive-compulsive disorder. Many people—including Joshua Kendall, who wrote a biography of Roget in 2008—describe his proclivity for list-making as a "coping mechanism." I like to think of him as a neat freak of the intellect, someone who liked to keep all his ideas and concepts in their proper place. His lists offered a way of imposing order on a chaotic jumble of a world.

As it happens, Roget was also brilliant, and he began studying medicine at the University of Edinburgh at fourteen. By nineteen he was a practicing physician. With some help from his uncle's connections, he was soon launched on a successful career, landing a position as personal physician to a former prime minister, William Petty.

Perhaps because Roget was very new to the practice of health care, Petty died a year later. I guess that's what happens when you entrust your personal health to the Doogie Howser of the nineteenth century. (Really at this point "Doogie Howser" should be accepted as a synonym for prodigy.) So Roget took a job in Manchester, where, among other things, he helped to establish a medical school. Kendall stresses that the poverty and grime of the city upset him and that he began work on the *Thesaurus* during his evenings, as an emotional response to the disorder of his surroundings. He was twenty-six when he began this project of gathering lists of words and their synonyms.

What's interesting here is that Roget did not think of the book as precisely a list of synonyms. It was more like what Kendall calls "a reverse dictionary." Instead of looking up a word to find the definition, you would look up a definition or concept to find a word. Roget listed a thousand concepts—exactly a thousand, since the number satisfied his taste for symmetry—and they weren't ordered alphabetically. Like the Swedish taxonomist Linnaeus, whom he admired (again, see *Mobituaries*), or Melvil Dewey, for that matter, he created a system of classification with broad categories—"Abstract Relations," "Space," "Matter"—that served as headers under which more specific concepts could be arranged. What we now call a thesaurus was actually just the *index* to his original book—an alphabetized list of the terms inside.

We don't know why Roget set it aside. Kendall, who examined a newly discovered manuscript of the book-length 1805 work, believes that Roget was composing it only for private use, not for publication, and that he considered it complete. In any case, he soon returned to London, where he went on to a successful career as a physician. He was elected to Britain's leading medical association, the Royal Society of Physicians, and later served as its secretary. As a medical practitioner, he is reported to have been cold and clinical, lacking in a sense of humor or a bedside manner. Still, he built himself a reputation as a lecturer on anatomy and physiology. He also invented a new kind of slide rule and wrote articles for the *Encyclopædia Britannica* (first published in 1768). As I mentioned, he was no dope. Is it any surprise that he was also an excellent chess player?

But his life remained punctuated by loss and sadness. In 1818, his aunt, Lady Anne Romilly, died at age forty-five, and his beloved uncle Samuel was so distraught that he cut his own neck with a shaving razor. Roget attended to him in his dying moments, calling for a surgeon to attempt to sew up the wound, and held him as he gave up his last breath.

Life went on. In 1824, he married Mary Taylor Hobson, and the next year he published his most important medical paper, "Explanation of an Optical Deception in the Appearance of the Spokes of a Wheel Seen Through Vertical Apertures." (This part is actually quite interesting, so don't skip ahead.) In his research, he had determined that the eye can still see an image momentarily even after the object leaves the field of vision. If another, slightly dissimilar image is produced in immediate succession, the brain perceives motion. This discovery, of course, underlies the science behind movies. For this reason, Will H. Hays, the first chairman of the Motion Picture Producers and Distributors of America—he's the guy who took all the sex out of the movies for over thirty years—later credited Roget as the inventor of motion pictures.

Roget's life had yet more heartbreak. In 1833, after only eight years of marriage and now with two young children, his wife, Mary, died of cancer. But he continued practicing medicine. He formally retired at age sixty-one, but stayed on as a secretary of the Royal Society.

It's believed that what turned him back to his lexicographical labor was the re-release, in 1849, of Piozzi's *British Synonymy*. (Piozzi had died back in 1821.) Roget believed he could do better. He thought the book disorganized, and set out to give his *Thesaurus* a more understandable, logical flow. By this time, too, Roget, who was no longer publishing and lecturing, had fallen off the A-list of British academics. So in part, the *Thesaurus* was his attempt to be taken seriously by Britain's intellectual elite again. But it was also a return to unfinished business. Sometimes there are just tasks that need to be completed before you can relax and tell yourself that your work is really done.

At age sixty-nine, forty-three years after he first began gathering synonyms, Roget returned to his grand project. The full title of the first edition, brought out in 1852, when he was seventy-three, was *Thesaurus of English Words and Phrases, Classified and Arranged So As to Facilitate the Expression of Ideas and Assist in Literary Composition.* It was a success, a smash, a triumph, a hit, a boffo debut. The *Westminster Review* raved that the book was worthy of being read straight through, stating, "Roget will rank with Samuel Johnson as a literary instrument-maker of the first class." Perhaps contributing to the strong reception was the fact that Roget knew how to edit. The authors of previous synonym books had instructed people in how to use each word. Roget simply provided a list of similar words, streamlining the entire volume.

When the book's success became evident, Roget negotiated to earn two-thirds of the profits from its sales. And so his oddball hobby amassed him a substantial fortune late in life. An American edition soon was published. The U.S. puritanical temperament being what it is, "vulgar" words were eliminated by the editor. Fortunately, today we have Urban Dictionary.

Roget continued for seventeen years to add and refine; the book went through twenty-eight editions in his lifetime alone. He was still working when he died, in 1869, at age ninety. He had aged gracefully, his memory and mental powers intact. Writing all those lists couldn't have hurt.

The book that he had begun so many years before, for his own personal use, has gone on to sell upward of forty million copies. It's hard to imagine that that wouldn't make even Roget happy. It may have taken him decades to complete, but, hey, sometimes finding the right words takes a really long time.

opposite page: Peter Mark Roget, circa 1865, looking dignified (also: courtly, stately, majestic, august).
Public Domain/National Library of Medicine

The Readers

The Readers

they learned to read in their eighties and later

Even if you never turn your life experiences into a bestselling book, setting down your story in words is a relatively common ambition for people as they enter retirement. For other people, the years of rest and leisure are best spent reading. One of the great pleasures of recent years for me has been observing the great pleasure my own mother, in her nineties, has taken in reading so many English-language classics for the first time, books that she wasn't exposed to growing up in Colombia. *Alice Adams* and *The Magnificent Ambersons*, by Booth Tarkington; Henry James's *The Portrait of a Lady* and *Washington Square*. Books by Jane Austen and Edith Wharton. I'm pretty sure she saw herself in Francie Nolan—and that tree—in Betty Smith's *A Tree Grows in Brooklyn*.

But what if you never learned to read at all? It's a situation more common than you might think: 21 percent of adults in the United States lack the skills needed to perform "tasks that require comparing and contrasting information, paraphrasing, or making low-level inferences"—what the Department of Education defines as basic literacy. For many of these people, as they struggle to survive in a world that expects us all to read, achieving basic literacy has remained a steadfast goal, the one and only item on a bucket list. But because we associate learning to read with early childhood, taking up the challenge in old age demands a special kind of courage and determination.

The great Brazilian educator Paulo Freire believed that addressing illiteracy was key to creating a more just and equitable society. He himself learned to read relatively late, primarily, he said, because of poverty brought on by the Great Depression; it's hard to focus on reading when you're constantly hungry. When he began his career, in the 1940s, literacy was still a requirement to vote in Brazil. (In the U.S., Jim Crow–era literacy tests were not banned until passage of the Voting Rights Act in 1965.) Freire worked with farmers, fishermen, indigenous peoples, and other disenfranchised groups to eliminate adult illiteracy in order to give people a stronger voice in their society.

Kimani Ng'ang'a Maruge already had a strong voice. A Kenyan citizen who grew up poor, he fought against British colonial rule in the 1950s, but he never learned to read. Born sometime around 1920, he was in his early eighties when the government passed a law providing free universal education. Maruge decided to enroll in the local elementary school in Eldoret, near his village in western Kenya. He was turned away several times, told that school was for children, but he persisted. On the first day of classes in 2004, he showed up again. "We found him in school in shorts, and a pullover and a shirt of the same color of the school uniform," said the school's headmistress. He began to attend class. That made him, according to the *Guinness Book of World Records*, the oldest person on record to begin elementary school. Incidentally, he was attending the same school as two of his thirty grandchildren, who were in more advanced grades.

He was a fast learner. According to *Guinness*, "It was reported that Ng'ang'a passed his first end-of-term exams with straight A's in English, Swahili and math, making him among the top five students in the class." By second grade, he'd been named "head boy," a student leadership role in the British educational system. In 2005, he flew to New York to address the United Nations on the importance of primary education. He also became an advocate for HIV/AIDS treatment and prevention. When asked about his goals for his American trip, he didn't mess around: "I would also like to marry a rich American woman to bring back money for my children. There's no point marrying a poor woman because I'm also poor." Maruge continued his education through episodes of political violence and personal health problems. He passed away in 2009, at an estimated age of eighty-nine.

As advanced in age as he was, Maruge was but a child when compared to Mary Hardway Walker. As with Maruge, we have no record of Mary's birthday, but she claimed to have been born in or about 1848, to enslaved parents in Union Springs,

Alabama. After Emancipation, she worked at various jobs, cooking, cleaning, child-care. In 1917, around the age of sixty-nine—late life for most people, but really just middle age for Mary—she moved with her family to Chattanooga. At some point (we don't have a date), she moved to a retirement residence in a high-rise on Market Street, where she met a woman named Helen Kelly. Kelly volunteered with a group called CALM, the Chattanooga Area Literacy Movement, which held classes in the building. According to Chattanooga's WRCB-TV, in 1963, reportedly past the age of 110, having outlived her husband and all three of her children, Mary began attending classes twice a week for an hour. There she learned basic math skills, and she learned to read and write. She passed away in 1969, around the age of 121.

The achievement understandably earned her various honors. U.S. presidents recognized her. The city of Chattanooga named her twice as its Ambassador of Goodwill and bestowed upon her its key to the city. (Cities still do that, you know, but more and more are switching to key cards.) They also renamed her retirement facility after her and erected a historical marker at the corner of Wilcox Boulevard and Greenwood Drive in her memory. Today a Mary Walker Foundation promotes Black literacy, and a children's book, *The Oldest Student: How Mary Walker Learned to Read*, written by Rita Lorraine Hubbard and illustrated by Oge Mora, helps others learn to read as well.

Finally, my CBS colleague Steve Hartman profiled a remarkable man named Charles Edwin Bray Sr. Ed was a World War II veteran who fought in the Battle of Normandy and earned two Purple Hearts and a Bronze Star. Steve interviewed him back in 2013. When they first met, Ed was eighty-nine and couldn't read.

"The toughest thing that ever happened to me in my life was not being able to read," he told Steve. This, mind you, from a man who had lived through the Dust Bowl, stormed Omaha Beach, and took a bullet in the knee in order to help liberate Europe.

For years, his wife would help him compensate, until she died in 2009. At his job, where he worked refueling planes at an Air Force base, a coworker would give him a hand when there was paperwork to be completed. He had tried several times to learn, but frustration would set in, and he'd give up. But the old soldier remained determined to win this final battle. "I want to read one book," he said. "I don't care if it's about Mickey Mouse. I want to read one book before I die."

On the recommendation of a friend, he sat down with Tobi Thompson, a professor of education at Oklahoma's Northeastern State University. Regular chats gave way to work with flash cards, and then, as Ed described it, "everything started clicking." Soon enough, Ed read his first book. It wasn't about Mickey Mouse but another great American—George Washington. It was a third-grade-level biography. "It gave me goosebumps and it still does. It still does," said Dr. Thompson.

When a local paper interviewed him a couple of years later, he told them, "Reading changed my life completely." And he had found a novel way to keep improving his skills—karaoke. Keeping up with the familiar words made for great reading practice as well as a fun night out. He also started giving motivational talks at schools, stressing the value of reading. Or as he put it, much more colorfully, "Get in there and learn, baby. Now! 'Cause you ain't going to learn in that pine box."

It turns out that Ed had a good amount of reading time left in his life. He died in May of 2023 at age one hundred, not long after he'd been inducted into the Centenarians of Oklahoma Hall of Fame.

Methuselah

"Methus'lah lived 900 years . . ."

With all due respect to lyricist Ira Gershwin, Methuselah lived 969 years, at least according to the Bible. (The character who sang that lyric in the 1935 opera *Porgy and Bess* warned us that the things we read in the Bible "ain't necessarily so," but that's an argument for another time.)

When it comes to biblical patriarchs, Methuselah doesn't have nearly the profile of Abraham or Noah. He didn't found a nation or save man- and animal kind. In fact, he's only mentioned in a few brief verses in Genesis. We learn about Methuselah's genealogy—his father, Enoch, and his son Lamech and some other unnamed sons and daughters. We find out that "all the days of Methuselah were nine hundred sixty-nine years; and he died." And that's it for Methuselah. We don't get any additional details about his life. The main takeaway is the guy was old.

But so were a lot of these biblical figures. Adam, the man who started all the begetting, lived to 930. Noah clocked out at 950. (At some point, these biblical ages go down dramatically. It's never exactly clear why. Abraham lives a mere 175 years; Moses, 120.) For whatever reason, Methuselah holds the record when it comes to oldness. Is his name a clue? Some have said Methuselah translates to "his death shall bring." Was this referring to the Great Flood, which happened after Methuselah's death?

Or is it possible that 969 was a mistranslation? A 1913 *Chicago Tribune* article headlined "Methuselah a Youngster" notes that "scientific research abroad" has reduced Methuselah's age to an unremarkable seventy-eight and three-quarters, theorizing that lunar cycles were previously used to determine the length of years, which would change many biblical ages.

Even so, Methuselah remains a byword for longevity—and not just for people. There's Methuselah, the world's oldest aquarium fish (believed to be around 101), and a 4,855-year-old bristlecone pine tree in California named Methuselah. There are Methuselah dogs and Methuselah genes that scientists believe are a factor in longevity.

He may have played a bit part in the Bible, but Methuselah's legacy is secure. When it comes to aging to the extreme, he really set the gold, or should I say gray, standard.

The Changemaker

Mary Church Terrell

Mary Church Terrell

led sit-ins at Washington, DC, lunch
counters in her late eighties

In our collective memory, the civil rights movement was a movement of the young. Martin Luther King Jr. was only thirty-four when he delivered his historic "I Have a Dream" speech at the March on Washington. John Lewis was just twenty-five when he led six hundred marchers across the Edmund Pettus Bridge in Selma, Alabama. Many of the original Freedom Riders were still teenagers when they set out to desegregate bus terminals in the South. And, tragically, Andrew Goodman, James Chaney, and Michael Schwerner were twenty, twenty-one, and twenty-four when they were murdered by Klansmen while seeking to register Black voters in Mississippi.

But idealism, sacrifice, and physical courage do not belong only to the young. Less celebrated, but just as essential, were the contributions of the movement's senior leaders, who brought to the cause not only their high ideals and ardent passion but also their hard work and years of experience. At a time in life when they could have been forgiven for receding into the background, they stepped forward—battling for a better world, one that even under the best of circumstances they would barely be able to enjoy themselves.

Among the most respected and almost certainly the eldest was Mary Church Terrell. Born during the Civil War, Terrell had already spent a lifetime as an activist when she led the fight to integrate the lunch counters of Washington, DC. When the Supreme Court finally ruled in her favor, she was eighty-nine.

She was born Mary Church in September 1863, nine months after the Emancipation Proclamation, to former slaves who had attained freedom and prospered in Memphis. (Her father, a real estate investor, is sometimes credited as the nation's first Black millionaire.) She attended Oberlin College, earned a BA in Classics, then stayed on to earn her master's, making her—along with her classmate Anna Julia

Cooper—one of the first Black women in the United States to earn a higher degree. She soon started teaching Latin at a Black high school in Washington, DC, where she met and married Robert Terrell, a graduate of Harvard and Howard Law School. She also traveled in Europe for two years, learning French, German, and Italian.

Then, in 1892, Mary was spurred to a life of activism by a group of murders that took place in Memphis. These brutal killings have become known as the People's Grocery Lynchings.

The murders were provoked by the simple act of opening a grocery store. Thomas Moss, a Black man, opened a shop in a mixed-race neighborhood of Memphis called the Curve. A white man named William Barrett, who owned a nearby market, began to think that the competition was hurting his business. In early March 1892, Barrett, accompanied by a group of armed men, entered Moss's store. Gunshots were exchanged; thirteen Black men were arrested. In the following days, forty more Black people from the neighborhood were rounded up, allegedly part of a conspiracy. They were held at the Shelby County Jail. On March 9, a white mob stormed the jail and dragged away Moss and two of his employees, Will Stewart and Calvin McDowell. The gruesome lynching that followed was described in agonizing detail by reporters, and the story made the front page of the *New York Times*.

The pioneering journalist Ida B. Wells, a Memphis resident who had known Moss, wrote a series of articles about the lynching in her newspaper, *The Memphis Free Speech and Headlight*. In response to these articles, a white mob attacked and destroyed the newspaper's offices. Wells left Memphis for the safety of New York, where she continued to wage a public campaign against lynching.

Terrell was living in DC, but she'd been raised in Memphis and had known Moss since childhood. She joined Wells in the anti-lynching cause. Although only twenty-eight, she reached out to the nation's most important Black leader, Frederick Douglass, then seventy-four, and enlisted his help in asking President Benjamin Harrison to make a public statement condemning the practice of lynching.

Douglass secured an audience with Harrison and brought Terrell with him to the White House so that she could make her appeal.

Harrison expressed his revulsion at the slaughter, but he wouldn't commit to a public statement. The issue was too politically sensitive to confront during an election year. Harrison went on to lose the November election to Democrat Grover Cleveland; the next month, as a lame duck, he condemned lynchings in his State of the Union, calling them "a reproach to a community where they occur." He added, "So far as they can be made the subject of Federal jurisdiction, the strongest repressive legislation is demanded."

Alas, the pronouncements of lame ducks carry little force, and the terror of lynching persisted for decades. In these years, Terrell became a key ally of Wells in her ongoing efforts to eradicate the practice. Among Terrell's contributions was an important 1904 essay, "Lynching from a Negro's Point of View," that challenged the prevalent notion among whites that lynching was a response to rape. Terrell instead explained that alleged rape was "simply the pretext" for anti-Black violence.

She embraced a life of activism, cofounding the Colored Women's League of Washington in 1892 and, in 1909, the National Association for the Advancement of Colored People (NAACP), which would become the most influential civil rights organization of the twentieth century. She worked equally hard for women's rights, picketing Woodrow Wilson's White House in the cause of women's suffrage and urging the U.S. Senate to take up the Equal Rights Amendment. She was also a mother to two daughters, as well as three children who died as newborns. (Terrell publicly stated that she believed they could have lived if she had been granted the access to incubators afforded white women.)

Terrell's career as an activist in the late nineteenth and early twentieth centuries secured her a place in the history books, where she is discussed alongside Wells, W. E. B. DuBois, and other Black leaders of the era. As she aged, she ceded her leadership role to others, although she remained engaged—writing to Franklin Delano Roosevelt, for example, to urge him to integrate the armed forces. But then in 1949, when she was eighty-five, she was pulled back into the center of America's struggle for racial justice.

Even though it was home to the federal government, Washington, DC, in the 1940s was in many ways a southern town. Restaurants, hotels, and other public accommodations were segregated by race. Senator Theodore Bilbo of Mississippi, who controlled the Senate's Committee on the District of Columbia and was informally known as "the Mayor of Washington," was a white supremacist. I'm not using that term loosely. Bilbo was a member of the KKK and wrote a book called *Take Your Choice: Separation or Mongrelization*. He filibustered anti-lynching legislation. He used his power to suppress Black votes and enforce a climate of Jim Crow however he could. After learning about Marcus Garvey's (voluntary) "back to Africa" movement, he proposed deporting all Black Americans to Africa, along with First Lady Eleanor Roosevelt, who he said could serve as their queen.

For progressives, the fact that the nation's capital was subject to Jim Crow was unconscionable. The city naturally held special significance for all Americans and was supposed to represent the best of what the nation stood for. The existence of racist policies in Washington was thus a blight on the entire country. As the NAACP would later argue in its efforts to integrate the city, "The District of Columbia symbolizes American democracy."

But in the late 1940s came a minor breakthrough. A Howard University Law School librarian named A. Mercer Daniel discovered that two Reconstruction-era laws, passed by a now-defunct legislative body governing the District, had actually made segregation in DC restaurants illegal. These laws, passed back in 1872 and 1873, were part of a wave of legislation enacted during Reconstruction that aimed to dismantle the legal structure of white supremacy.

The first law, introduced by Frederick Douglass's son Lewis, was most directly relevant to the question of segregation. It stated that no restaurant keeper or hotelkeeper could refuse to serve customers on the basis of "race, color or previous condition of servitude."

Yet Jim Crow had taken hold nonetheless. In the late nineteenth century, the Supreme Court began to narrow its interpretation of the "Reconstruction amendments"—the Thirteenth, Fourteenth, and Fifteenth—passed in the wake of the Civil War. A series of rulings by the southern-dominated court culminated in the infamous decision of 1896, *Plessy v. Ferguson*, which gave states permission to discriminate under the spurious doctrine of "separate but equal."

After *Plessy*, Jim Crow set in across the South, even in Washington—most notably during the presidency of Woodrow Wilson, the first southern president since Andrew Johnson. Despite the hopes of some Black leaders (including DuBois, who offered him conditional support), Wilson filled his cabinet with other southerners and effectively segregated the federal government. The old laws from the 1870s went unenforced and were soon forgotten.

Under FDR things got slightly better. Government-run cafeterias and eating places were integrated, and the city's public parks and recreational areas were open to all. Roosevelt also took the significant step of barring discrimination in federal jobs. But he was in thrall to southern Democrats for his majority, and could only push so far—not far enough for most civil rights leaders. Only when Harry Truman came to power did more significant changes begin. A major victory came in 1948, when Truman's Executive Order 9981 integrated the military.

That same year, the old Reconstruction-era laws barring segregation in the capital came to the attention of a young woman named Annie Stein. Stein, born Annie Steckler, was the daughter of poor Jewish immigrants from Ukraine. As a college student, she had been stirred to activism by the 1931 prosecution of the Scottsboro Boys. (They were the nine Black teenagers whose lives were derailed after falsely being accused of raping two white women.) She spent the 1930s in Washington, fighting for labor rights and consumer rights.

Stein realized that these old laws could be used to end segregation in the capital. But to accomplish that goal, she would need to fight on two fronts—in the law courts, and in the court of public opinion. She created an organization called the Coordinating Committee for the Enforcement of the D.C. Anti-Discrimination Laws. (Not terribly catchy, but at least you know what it's all about.) Stein knew she was not the ideal person to head up the committee, and decided to serve as the organization's secretary. For a leader, she needed a figure of national stature. That's where Mary Church Terrell came in.

In the final days of 1948, Thomas Buchanan, a lawyer with a group called the Civil Rights Congress (CRC), wrote to Terrell about the recently unearthed laws, saying, "If such a law could be restored to full validity, it would mean a new Declaration of Rights for our colored population." The strategy was clear. Once public accommodations were integrated, equality in other areas of life—"schools, housing, hospitals, jobs, and recreation"—would follow.

Terrell hesitated. This was a cause she supported fully. But she was eighty-five years old. She had already fought many battles, winning some, losing more. There must have been younger people with more energy and more physical strength to lead this campaign. Surely her career had earned her the right to sit this one out.

Moreover, Washington was in the grip of Cold War politics. The House Un-American Activities Committee (HUAC) was persecuting socialists and communists, and Buchanan's group, the CRC, was a target. Annie Stein herself was a supporter of the socialist Henry A. Wallace, who had left the Democratic Party to run as a Progressive in 1948. Prominent Black leaders including W. E. B. DuBois and Paul Robeson were coming under fire for their expressions of sympathy for the Soviet Union. The civil rights community was itself split, as the more mainstream NAACP kept the CRC at arm's length, fearing it too would be tagged as pro-Soviet. Terrell knew that joining Annie Stein's campaign would subject her to accusations of un-American behavior.

opposite page: Lifelong civil rights activist Mary Church Terrell circa 1935.

National Museum of American History, Smithsonian Institution

But there were other factors in play. In 1946, Terrell, along with a white friend, had applied to join the Washington chapter of the American Association of University Women. Terrell had been rejected because she was Black. She had sued, and the case made its way through the courts. On June 13, 1949, a federal appeals court ruled against her, upholding the right of the local chapter of the AAUW to discriminate on the basis of race.

The indignity stirred Terrell's outrage. The next week she gave a public speech in which she declared, "The time comes in the life of a human being and in the life of a group of human beings when patience ceases to be a virtue and becomes an ugly, disgraceful vice."

She had run out of patience. She joined the battle to integrate the nation's capital.

On January 27, 1950, at eighty-six, she invited three friends, two of them Black and one white, to lunch with her at Thompson's Restaurant, a cafeteria on 14th Street and New York Avenue, NW, not far from the White House. They chose Thompson's for its convenience: it was just steps from the law offices of Terrell's lawyers, Joseph Forer and David Rein. Terrell's intention, of course, was to test the validity of the seventy-five-year-old statutes forbidding discrimination in public accommodations. And as she and her allies expected, the manager of Thompson's refused to serve her and the other Black members of her group.

Terrell and her allies now had to convince the District of Columbia to enforce its old and largely forgotten law. At first, Washington's Corporation Counsel—DC's closest equivalent to a district attorney—simply ignored Terrell's complaint. So she held a press conference, and when the newspapers picked up the story, the corporation's commissioners instructed their counsel to enforce the statute.

For technical reasons, a new complaint had to be filed. A month later, on February 28, Terrell gave a repeat performance at Thompson's. Once again, she invited a group of friends, Black and white, to join her for lunch. Once again, the manager denied her and her Black companions service, while agreeing to serve the white member of the group. This time, however, the prosecution went forward.

Now the fight against segregation in DC was part of a larger long-term plan by civil rights groups to use the courts to overthrow *Plessy* once and for all. As Terrell's case was waiting to be heard in municipal court, other cases testing the limits of Jim Crow were moving forward across the nation. In June 1950, the Supreme Court delivered a triple victory for the NAACP, which had backed plaintiffs in three cases—known in brief as *Henderson*, *Sweatt*, and *McLaurin*. With these rulings, SCOTUS banned racial discrimination in interstate train travel and in graduate school admissions. *Plessy* was not yet overturned, but its demise appeared close enough that Thurgood Marshall of the NAACP could declare, "The complete destruction of all enforced segregation is now in sight."

But on the heels of this national victory came a local defeat. On July 10, Judge Frank Myers of the DC Municipal Court of Appeals dismissed the charges against Thompson's, ruling against the District of Columbia (and Mary Terrell) on the grounds that the Reconstruction statutes were no longer valid.

The decision did not deter Terrell and her allies. But since the judge had dismissed the charges, Terrell was required to head back to Thompson's yet again—the third trip in six months. She gathered friends, entered the eatery, grabbed a tray, selected a lunch, and was denied service. New charges were filed against the cafeteria, and the lawyers got back to work.

As the case inched forward, Mary Terrell and Annie Stein continued to bring pressure on eating establishments through other means. One by one, the lunch counters of Washington's five-and-dimes—Kresge's, Hecht's, Murphy's—felt the pressure of picket lines and boycotts. Soldiers recently returned from Korea stood out front with signs reading, "I fought in Korea, but can't eat here!" The great dancer and singer Josephine Baker, a friend of Terrell's—and this woman had a professional network, let me tell you—came in from Paris and joined the cause, attempting to order a soda at Hecht's and joining the picket line when she was denied. The celebrity sighting earned Hecht's an embarrassing headline, and they soon reversed their policy.

At the same time, McCarthyism was raising new challenges. HUAC was turning its fire on civil rights leaders. Terrell was not and had never been a communist—in fact, she was a lifelong Republican, having served as president of the DC Women's Republican League. Yet she was accused in a HUAC report of being a "fellow traveler."

The civil rights workers countered with their own invocation of the Cold War. America's stark failures in racial justice, they maintained, weakened its global stature as a champion of freedom. As long as the Russians could point to the fact that Black Americans remained second-class citizens, any rhetoric hailing the United States as the land of the free would ring hollow. Ending segregation, they argued, was essential to the struggle against communism.

Justice may be blind, but she can also be agonizingly slow. It was not until May 1951 that an appeals court finally ruled on Judge Myers's decision to invalidate the old anti-discrimination laws. The appeals court reversed his ruling, proclaiming the Reconstruction laws valid—a major victory for Terrell.

A few weeks later, at a meeting of the Coordinating Committee, Mary gave a public speech, rallying her supporters and urging enforcement of the statutes. She also took the occasion to lambaste HUAC for the hypocrisy of attacking civil rights leaders while finding nothing un-American in racism. Mary, now a hale eighty-seven, stressed that she was getting on in years. "I am no longer 'Sweet Sixteen,'" she said, "and I would like to live long enough to see the law enforced." If it hadn't been clear before, it was clear by now. She was not fighting this battle for herself; she was fighting for the future.

Now it was Thompson's turn to appeal, and the case proceeded up to the federal appellate court. In the meantime, an election year arrived. In 1952, Terrell declared that she was switching political parties to support the Democrats because of their commitment to civil rights. The position of the Republican nominee, General Dwight D. Eisenhower, was equivocal, as he proposed leaving decisions to the states. Besides, Terrell was grateful to Truman for his commitment to the cause—she praised him as the country's strongest president on racial justice since Lincoln.

Eisenhower defeated Adlai Stevenson handily in November and was inaugurated in January 1953. How the civil rights agenda would progress with him in the White House was uncertain. But history was not sitting back and waiting. On January 22, just two days after the inauguration, a ruling came down from the U.S. Court of Appeals in *District of Columbia v. John R. Thompson Co.* It was another reversal: 5–4 in favor of Thompson's. The judges had ruled that the 1872 laws were not valid.

The final appeal would be heard by the United States Supreme Court.

Civil rights cases had been filling the court's docket for several years now, and the justices welcomed the opportunity to reconsider institutionalized segregation in many areas of life. That spring, instead of putting the Thompson's cafeteria case on the docket for the coming fall, they agreed to hear it immediately—leaving both sets of lawyers a mere three weeks to prepare to argue their cases in the highest court of the land.

Arguments began on April 30. The lawyer for Thompson's was Ringgold Hart, whose real expertise, according to historian Joan Quigley, was in taxes and zoning laws. Hart had intended to focus his remarks on the legitimacy of the long-unenforced statutes, not the constitutionality of segregation. But the justices were skeptical of his initial arguments, and as the day wore on, Hart abandoned that position, falling back instead on the claim that restaurants have a fundamental freedom to do business with whomever they please. Citing precedents from the *Plessy* era—and completely ignoring the court's own recent rulings in *Henderson*, *Sweatt*, and *McLaurin*—Hart seemed unaware that the justices in recent years had been moving rapidly to the left on civil rights. By arguing that racial discrimination was a business's fundamental right, he was digging himself a deeper and deeper hole.

After the arguments concluded and the justices convened privately, all but one were prepared to end segregation in Washington, DC. Only the Kentuckian Stanley Reed hesitated. Although he had ruled in favor of integration in recent cases, in private he still worried about the social implications of an integrated capital: "Why—why this means that a nigra can walk into the restaurant at the Mayflower Hotel and sit down to eat at the table right next to Mrs. Reed!" he reportedly said. But in discussions, even Reed came around, and the decision was unanimous.

On June 8, Justice William O. Douglas announced the reversal of the appellate court decision. The old laws had never been repealed and still held. Segregation in Washington, DC, was illegal. And although the ruling, which applied to matters of municipal governance, did not invalidate *Plessy v. Ferguson,* it showed that Jim Crow's days were numbered. Next spring, the court would again rule unanimously as it banned public school segregation in the landmark case *Brown v. Board of Education.*

Mary and her allies were overjoyed. She was flooded with telegrams congratulating her; *Ebony* magazine wrote to arrange a photo shoot at Frederick Douglass's old DC home. Mary's face appeared on the cover of the *Washington Post* and the *Afro,* Baltimore's Black newspaper. Headlines celebrated the end of segregation for the people of Washington, DC.

Three days later, Mary returned to Thompson's for a fourth visit, with the same lunch dates who had accompanied her during her first trip five years before. She was dressed to the nines, her biographer tells us, in a striking sea-blue dress and a red hat. Reporters, photographers, and ordinary residents crowded the scene. The restaurant's manager, Harding Balance, graciously carried the eighty-nine-year-old legend's tray for her, bearing a bowl of soup, a slice of cake, and a cup of coffee. Far away, at a Young Republicans event at Mount Rushmore, South Dakota, President Eisenhower hailed the decision as a victory for freedom.

It had been sixty-one years since the lynching of Terrell's friend Tommie Moss, fifty-seven years since the *Plessy* ruling had legitimized Jim Crow. With her eighties coming to a close, Terrell could at long last declare victory. "I will be 90 on the 23rd of September," she said, "and will die happy that children of my group will not grow up thinking they are inferior because they are deprived of rights which children of other racial groups enjoy."

Mary Church Terrell made it to her ninetieth birthday, dying ten months later, on July 24, 1954.

. . . And Other Late-in-Life Activists

Norman Rockwell Before 1964, Norman Rockwell was an artist beloved for the scenes of American life he painted, most notably for the *Saturday Evening Post*, where his art had appeared for almost fifty years. But on January 14 of that year, weeks before Rockwell turned seventy, his painting *The Problem We All Live With* was published as the centerfold in *Look* magazine. Stark and stylized, the painting depicts Ruby Bridges, a six-year-old Black girl, walking to her elementary school in New Orleans, surrounded by federal marshals and past a slur graffitied on the wall. (She was the first Black student at the school.) The painting represented a major shift for Rockwell, who had left the *Post* the previous year when they wouldn't allow him the freedom to say what he wanted with his art about the civil rights movement. After the painting was published, Rockwell was inundated with hate mail. But no matter. As critic Tom Carson wrote in *Vox*, "One of the minor marvels of the '60s was that the period made Rockwell happier than he'd ever been. The hippies he came to dote on had a word for it: liberation."

Ben Franklin The Papa Smurf of the Founding Fathers, Franklin was at seventy the oldest signer of the Declaration of Independence, edging out Stephen Hopkins of Rhode Island by a year. It was an audacious act. When Franklin put quill to parchment, he was signing his death warrant. Later in 1776, he sailed for Paris, on a mission to win the backing of the French for the Patriot cause. As charming as he was courageous, America's first diplomat proved a sensation with the court of Louis XVI. (It wasn't just his intellect; his fur cap was a major statement piece.) Much to John Adams's chagrin, Franklin was there for more than eight years. But Franklin understood that diplomacy was a slow seduction. (Big John Adams fan here, but he was not among our more seductive Founding Fathers.) The money and arms Franklin helped secure ensured the survival of the infant American republic. By 1787, he was back in Philly, and at eighty-one became the oldest signer of the Constitution. Like any true radical, he was in it for the long haul.

Jane Goodall

When Jane Goodall was just a year old, her father gave her a stuffed chimpanzee named Jubilee instead of a teddy bear. Friends worried that Jubilee would scare the little girl. Instead the stuffed animal inspired young Jane. At twenty-six, Goodall ventured to what is now Gombe Stream National Park in Tanzania to immerse herself in the little-understood society of chimpanzees. Despite her lack of college education (her family couldn't afford it), her observation that chimpanzees make and use tools changed our understanding of our closest living relatives—and by extension what it means to be human. She further observed that the animals had individual personalities. Goodall later shifted her focus to conservation, tirelessly advocating for the protection of animal habitats. "The least I can do is speak out for those who cannot speak for themselves," she has said. Eighty-nine years later, Jubilee and Jane Goodall are still together, still making a difference. (PS: To support Goodall's work, you can buy your own Jubilee plush through the Jane Goodall Institute website.)

Sue Kunitomi Embrey

In December 1969, twenty-six years after her release, Sue Kunitomi Embrey returned to Manzanar in eastern California, the site of a camp where she and her family had been incarcerated after the bombing of Pearl Harbor by Japan during World War II. (Manzanar was one of ten camps that forcibly detained over 120,000 people of Japanese descent, most of them American citizens.) Sue's widowed mother had been forced to sell the family's grocery store in L.A.'s Little Tokyo. Her brother had volunteered to help build the camp, to try to make their new living quarters as civilized as possible. Sue herself was nineteen when they arrived. She worked in the camp's camouflage net factory, then as a reporter and managing editor at the *Manzanar Free Press*. Learning to ask questions and demand answers prepared her well for life as an activist. After her '69 pilgrimage, she began speaking publicly about her life at the camp. She soon became the co-chair of the committee that organized the annual pilgrimage, and she led the campaign to designate Manzanar as a national historic site. Embrey was sixty-nine in 1992, when President George H. W. Bush signed the bill establishing the park. She never stopped speaking about and developing the site for future learning. She was eighty-three and confined to a hospital bed when she participated by phone in the 2006 pilgrimage. She died two weeks later.

Jimmy Carter

In 1952, twenty-eight-year-old navy lieutenant James Earl Carter Jr. interviewed with Admiral Hyman Rickover for the opportunity of a lifetime: to join the navy's fledgling nuclear submarine program. At the end of the interview, Rickover asked about Carter's time at the U.S. Naval Academy: "Did you always do your best?" Taken aback, Carter answered, "No, sir, I didn't always do my best." Rickover replied "Why not?" and walked out of the room.

Rickover's words and mentorship (Carter was accepted into the program) had a profound effect. Carter would strive to do his very best in the years that followed—as a husband and father, as governor of Georgia, and in the White House.

Jimmy Carter's presidency is not typically considered successful. There was the Iran hostage crisis, endless lines for gas, and his infamous "malaise speech" (during which he never actually uttered the word "malaise"). There was the "killer rabbit" that attacked his fishing boat. (Look it up, but be advised: it was probably a nutria, not a rabbit.) Voters turned Carter out of office after one term.

In his Farewell Address to the nation, Carter noted, "I will lay down my official responsibilities in this office—to take up once more the only title in our democracy superior to that of president, the title of citizen."

And in the four-plus decades since then, Jimmy Carter has proved to be an extraordinary citizen. He established the Carter Center, an institution dedicated to conflict resolution and public health. He's worked with Habitat for Humanity to build thousands of houses. For his tireless efforts to promote democracy and human rights, he won the Nobel Peace Prize in 2002. And he taught Sunday school. (A Baptist, he renounced his ties to the Southern Baptist Convention in 2000 because of its "rigid" views on women.) It was profoundly moving—and not at all surprising—to see the ninety-nine-year-old former president, himself ailing, at the funeral of his wife and partner of seventy-seven years, Rosalynn Carter. The likely final public act of his life.

As the longest-living president in U.S. history, there's no question that Carter has done his best with his time on earth. Admiral Rickover would surely attest.

Old Soldiers Never Die, They Just Reenlist

Samuel Whittemore,

John L. Burns

& Goda

"Old soldiers never die—they just fade away." So said General Douglas MacArthur in a speech before a joint session of Congress in April 1951, just days after being relieved of his command in Asia by President Harry Truman, after MacArthur publicly disagreed with the president over the handling of the war in Korea. (The phrase was actually taken from an old song—as MacArthur called it, a "popular barrack ballad.")

MacArthur was a World War II hero, still beloved by a vast swath of the American public, and his military career was over. He was seventy-one . . . about the age that some soldiers are just getting their second—or is it third or fourth?—wind.

Samuel Whittemore

fought in the Revolutionary War at seventy-eight

The oldest colonial soldier to fight in the American War of Independence saw combat on the very first day of battle. On the fateful morning of April 19, 1775, the day of the Battles of Lexington and Concord, Captain Samuel Whittemore was a spry seventy-eight and, in the words of the nineteenth-century historian Lucius Robinson Paige, "vigorous in body and mind." Indeed, he was vigorous enough to take out (by which I mean kill) somewhere between one and three British redcoats before being shot in the face, stabbed in the head, and left to die.

The night before the battle, British Lt. Colonel Francis Smith, acting on orders of Governor Thomas Gage of Massachusetts, had begun to advance roughly seven hundred troops from Boston to the town of Lexington, with instructions to "seize and destroy all artillery, ammunition, provisions, tents, small arms, and all military stores whatever" under control of the patriots. The rumor was that the Brits were also coming after Samuel Adams and John Hancock, leaders in the resistance to British policies. But then a certain plucky silversmith named Paul Revere got wind of the British plan and made a midnight ride, alerting the American colonists, including Adams and Hancock, to the British advance. In the predawn hours of the nineteenth, the minutemen (colonial militiamen ready at a moment's notice, hence the name) gathered on Lexington Common and awaited the British force. Paige writes that "in spite of the expostulations of his family," Whittemore "repaired to the post of danger."

Whittemore had been born long before there was any talk of independence in the Massachusetts Bay Colony, way back in 1696, in Charlestown, a town just north of Boston on a peninsula where the Mystic and Charles Rivers converge. In the military conflict called King George's War, he served as a member of the British Royal Dragoons . . . and can I just interject, if I had to serve in any military unit at any point in history, I'd give the Royal Dragoons serious consideration for the name alone. It would probably come down to the Royal Dragoons or the Praetorian Guard. (And if you're wondering, the name "dragoon" comes from the weapon of the original dragoons, a firearm that seemed to spit fire like a dragon.) Anyway, King George's War was fought between the British and the French in northeastern North America from 1744 to 1748; Whittemore, already well into middle age, took part in a key British offensive that captured the French fort of Louisbourg, on the rocky coastline of Cape Breton in Nova Scotia. Alas, to the dismay of many of the Massachusetts soldiers who'd fought, the British returned the fort to France at the end of the war in exchange for Madras—the colony of Madras, in India, some eight thousand miles away. (It's not clear if the French threw in some shirts to sweeten the deal.)

Whittemore lived in the village of Menotomy, on a farm bordering the Menotomy River, and in a different era his life might have been as, well, monotonous as the gentle current of that unremarkable waterway. Today his farm would be part of Arlington, Massachusetts. Back then it was all part of the town of Cambridge. In any case, the aging captain apparently didn't see quite enough musket fire during King George's War, so he sallied forth into battle a second time some ten years later in the French and Indian War (1754–1763), a territorial dispute between the British, the French, and the Native Americans. Then fifty-eight, Whittemore must have experienced a little déjà vu as he again took part in the British capture of Fort Louisbourg. (Honestly, I'm starting to feel bad for little Fort Louie. For his sake, the British and the French should have brought in a mediator and agreed to joint custody.)

Whittemore was active in politics as an American patriot. As one historian has pointed out, many years before he was shot in the face at the outbreak of the Revolutionary War, "he had been entrusted by his fellow townspeople with important duties whereby he helped shape the coming revolution on the local level." As anti-British sentiment began to rise after the passage of the notorious Stamp Act of 1765—and here I'm going to assume you were paying attention in sixth-grade history class, because I don't have the space to explain the details of the Stamp Act—he became a leader in Cambridge politics, crafting the town's response to various unpopular British policies.

In 1768, he served as a delegate to the Massachusetts Committee of Convention, in which representatives from different towns throughout the state gathered to coordinate a response to the imminent arrival of British troops. (Unfortunately, Whittemore never attended; the people of Cambridge seem to have been so disorganized that they only held their election after the convention had concluded.) But the mere fact that he was willing to serve in this capacity—which was, strictly speaking, not sanctioned by the British government—tells us that he was weary of British rule. In 1772, Whittemore, now seventy-six, was elected to the Cambridge Committee on Correspondence, where he joined representatives from other towns in coordinating resistance to the Tea Act. You probably remember the part of the story where they chuck the tea into the harbor.

It was no surprise, then, that when 1775 rolled around, Whittemore was firmly committed to the cause of independence. What *is* striking is that he would risk his life in battle at this age. For insight, I asked retired General Wesley Clark, who spent thirty-four years in the army and later served as the Supreme Allied Commander Europe of NATO, if the story of Samuel Whittemore surprised him. He answered with this remembrance of his service in Vietnam, where he was injured in 1970, when he was twenty-five:

> *I awoke in the hospital outside Saigon the day after I'd been wounded. I looked around the ward at the other young men, wounded and bandaged. I looked at the bandages on my hand, leg, and shoulder—and I just knew I was now part of the fraternity of the committed. They were my brothers. We'd given blood. We'd survived. We'd never forget. We'd never be quite the same. I stayed with the army for another thirty years.*

The general continued: "When you've deliberately and with purpose put your life on the line, especially if you've been wounded, you're forever changed. It's initiation into a cause, the convictions underscored by sacrifice, it is the purpose-driven life—and you keep on giving because it's who we are at our deepest levels."

In other words, the general wasn't the least bit surprised by this story: "I find that for many of us the commitments, the passions, the what-would-you-risk-your-life-for motivation that drove us forward as young people deepens and intensifies with age!"

And so, although Samuel Whittemore was now seventy-eight, no longer the "large, athletic man, of strong constitution" he had been in his prime, and although his children begged him not to head out to confront the redcoats, he wouldn't be deterred. (It's worth noting here that Clint Eastwood was also seventy-eight when, confronted by those neighborhood punks in the 2008 film *Gran Torino*, he growled, "Get off my lawn"—basically what Whittemore was saying to the redcoats with his musket. And how great would Eastwood be in the Samuel Whittemore biopic?)

Whittemore's actions on April 19 are described in his 1793 obituary (which slightly overstates his age) from the *Columbian Centinel*, an influential Boston newspaper of the time:

Old Soldiers Never Die, They Just Reenlist

When the British troops marched to Lexington, he was 81 years of age, and one of the first on the parade; he was armed with a gun and a horse-pistol. After an animated exhortation to the collected militia to the exercise of bravery, and courage, he exclaimed, "If I can only be the instrument of killing one of my country's foes, I shall die in peace." The prayer of this venerable old man was heard; for on the return of the [British] troops, he lay behind a stone wall, and discharging his gun a soldier immediately fell; he then discharged his pistol, and killed another; at which instant a bullet struck his face, and shot away part of his cheek bone; on which, a number of the [British] soldiers ran up to the wall, and gorged their malice on his wounded head. They were heard to exclaim, "We have killed the old rebel." About four hours after, he was found in a mangled situation; his head was covered with blood from the wounds of the bayonets, which were six or eight; but providentially none penetrated so far as to destroy him.

A mangled situation, indeed. A chunk of his face was gone, and his head had been sliced with bayonets. The good people of Menotomy who ran to his aid must have assumed that his chances of survival were slim. At a nearby tavern, a doctor did what he could to treat and dress the wounds. Astonishingly, Whittemore not only pulled through but lived another eighteen years, dying in February 1793 at the age of ninety-six, just before George Washington's second inauguration.

The *Centinel* obituary praised him for his "manly and moral virtues," and noted his impressive tally of 185 descendants. (Yes, he was a lover *and* a fighter.) Most of all, his longevity allowed him "to see the complete overthrow of his enemies, and his country enjoy all the blessings of peace and independence."

Now I need to add a little footnote here. You'll recall that I described Whittemore as the oldest *colonial* combatant in the Revolutionary War. That's because there was actually a soldier who was even older, a Frenchman, Jean Thurel, who fought with the colonists at Yorktown at age eighty-three. His story is lower down.

John L. Burns

fought in the Civil War at seventy

Maybe it's something in the American character. Maybe, as General Wesley Clark said, it's something in the nature of a soldier. But the same fighting spirit that compelled Samuel Whittemore to take up arms for American independence at age seventy-eight seems to have been present fourscore and eight years later at the Battle of Gettysburg, in the service of freedom, in the person of John L. Burns.

A monument to John Burns stands on McPherson Ridge, on the west side of Gettysburg. It was dedicated on the fortieth anniversary of the battle by a Pennsylvania chapter of the Sons of Union Veterans. Burns is the only civilian known to have fought in what may well be the most important military battle ever waged on American soil. The Union victory, achieved at enormous human cost, decisively turned the tide of the Civil War, rebuffing Confederate General Robert E. Lee's attempt to invade the North. Burns, seventy, was not supposed to be fighting; he had already been rejected for service because of his advanced age. But when the Confederate army marched into his hometown, he grabbed a musket off his front porch and ventured out to join the fray.

Burns was born in Burlington, New Jersey, in 1793, the same year Samuel Whittemore died. You can almost imagine the ghost of old Captain Whittemore departing his scarred body and entering the newborn Burns as he came into the world. As a young man, Burns served in the War of 1812 and fought in the Battle of Lundy's Lane, in which Canadian troops held off an American invasion at Niagara Falls, Ontario. (Yes, the U.S. invaded our neighbors back then.) Apparently the young soldier acquired a taste for battle, because when the U.S. invaded Mexico in 1846—see, we did it again—he tried to enlist a second time, but was deemed too old. When the Civil War broke out, he tried yet again, with no better luck.

So in 1863, Burns and his wife were living in Gettysburg, where he was serving as a constable. The job was something of a sinecure, given to the old man to afford him a living. In late June, a week before the Battle of Gettysburg itself, the Confederate general Jubal Early, true to his name, came through town ahead of schedule. His men laid waste to a bridge, some railroads, and some telegraph lines. The elderly Burns, deeply loyal to the Union, apparently put up enough of a stink that the rebel soldiers jailed him for resistance. But General Early did not stick around, and when he pulled out, Burns resumed his duties as constable and arrested the Confederate soldiers who, for whatever reason, had stayed behind.

All of this, however, was just a prelude to the battle itself. For that event, we need the language of a real nineteenth-century narrator. B. D. Beyea was a contemporary whose account of Burns's role in the battle has become a key source for historians. We pick him up on the fateful day of July 1, 1863, as the two armies converge on Gettysburg. I like to read the words to myself while trying to channel the timbre and cadence of the great David McCullough:

The rebels came on. Old Burns kept his eye on the lookout until he saw the Stars and Stripes coming in, carried by our brave boys. This was more than the old fellow could stand. His patriotism got the better of his age and infirmity. Grabbing his musket, he started out. The old lady hallooed to him, "Burns, where are you going?" "Oh," says Burns, "I am going out to see what is going on."

Reports have it that he sauntered out onto the battlefield, tracked down Major Thomas Chamberlin of the 150th Pennsylvania Infantry, and asked to fight alongside his men. Under any conditions, Chamberlin would probably have been skeptical about putting a septuagenarian in the line of fire, but Burns's clothing seems to have made his appearance on the battlefield seem downright surreal. The writer Bret Harte actually recorded Burns's appearance in a poem ("John Burns of Gettysburg") published the next year. According to Harte, Burns "wore an ancient long buff vest, / Yellow as saffron," underneath "a bright blue coat, with a rolling

collar, / And large gilt buttons,— size of a dollar,— / With tails that the country-folk called 'swaller.'" (A swallowtail coat is a formal coat with long, tapered tails.) And the entire outfit was topped off with "a broad-brimmed, bell-crowned hat, / White as the locks on which it sat." Burns was also carrying a flintlock musket and powder horn (a container for gunpowder) that would have been several decades out of date.

Chamberlin must have been dumbstruck at this bizarre apparition, and all he could do was fob Burns off on his superior, Colonel Langhorne Wister. We don't know Wister's reasoning, but perhaps he told himself that every able body would be needed, and he sent Burns to join a unit from Wisconsin that was fighting in the woods. At least there, under cover of the foliage, the old man would have a bit more protection both from enemy fire and the harsh July sun.

Burns eagerly hooked up with what became known as the Iron Brigade, a unit of Wisconsin, Indiana, and Michigan infantrymen so gritty and determined that General George McClellan reputedly said that "they must be made of iron." Given the limitations of his age, Burns served mainly as a sharpshooter. (He had replaced his musket with a modern Enfield rifle acquired from a wounded soldier.) The historical record seems pretty solid in claiming that he killed three Confederates, including a charging officer whom Burns shot off his horse. One member of the Iron Brigade, Private Chauncey Hitchcock, is reported to have said of Burns, "He was true blue and grit to the backbone, firing from an advanced position in our line."

Although the Union army was ultimately victorious, at one point the battle turned and the Northerners were pushed back. The white-haired sharpshooter was wounded in the arm, leg, and chest. One shot hit him in the belt buckle, saving him from a particularly nasty fate. Ultimately, his fellow soldiers had no choice but to

opposite page: "Old Hero of Gettysburg"
John L. Burns, who fought for the Union at
age seventy, on his porch in 1863.
Brady's National Photographic Portrait Galleries/Library of Congress

leave him behind on the battlefield. "Down I went, and the whole rebel army ran over me," he later recalled.

Burns was savvy enough to bury his remaining ammunition on the battlefield, and when he was captured by the Confederate army, he could pretend he was a noncombatant. Noncombatants were not supposed to be getting mixed up in the fighting, and by the rules of engagement could be put to death, but Burns was spared, perhaps due to his age. He seems to have convinced his captors that he was searching for his wife on the battlefield when he was caught in cross fire. Again, our source B. D. Beyea gives us an account:

> *The Confederate captors asked him, "Old man, what are you doing here?" Burns eventually replied, "I will tell you. My old woman's health is very poor, and I was over across the country to get a girl to help her; and, coming back, before I knew where I was, I had got right into this fix, and here I am."*

The Southern doctors treated his wounds, and left him with a blanket; he claims to have spent the night of July 1 on the battlefield. The next morning some local citizens found him and brought him to a residence outside of town, where he was allowed to recuperate until strong enough to return to his own home. By that point, of course, the three horrific days of bloodshed at Gettysburg had passed, General Lee was in retreat, and, down in Vicksburg, Mississippi, Ulysses Grant had forced the Confederates to surrender. The war was far from over, but the Union now decisively held the upper hand.

As for the old man Burns, back in Washington, DC, the famed photographer Matthew Brady heard about his exploits and sent Timothy H. O'Sullivan to photograph him. (Brady, according to the Library of Congress, often acted as "more of a project manager" who supervised a "corps of traveling photographers.") The subsequent photo of Burns sitting on the front porch of his cottage, looking every inch the badass Methodist described by contemporaries, only added to the legend.

When Abraham Lincoln arrived in November to dedicate the Soldiers' National Cemetery and deliver his famous address, he asked to meet with Burns.

With newspapermen gathered around them, the Great Emancipator thanked the old soldier for his patriotism and courage and invited Burns to accompany him that evening to a service at the Gettysburg Presbyterian Church. The aged veteran walked with the president from the home of lawyer David Wills, where Lincoln was staying, down Baltimore Street to the church, where a series of speeches and tributes would be delivered. (Lincoln had already given his great address that afternoon.) Reports are that, with all the speeches, the evening ran long. The president ducked out early to catch his train back to Washington, while Burns probably dozed a bit in the pews.

Burns seemed to revel in his late-life fame, and some residents of Gettysburg found that he was becoming self-important and even a bit obnoxious. But no one could deny his courage or his patriotism in venturing into battle during his eighth decade of life. Sadly, Burns ended life with an undiagnosed cognitive ailment, likely dementia. One time he was found wandering in New York City and sent back home. He died at the age of seventy-eight and was buried in Evergreen Cemetery.

Yoda

at 900 mentored Luke Skywalker

Samuel Whittemore was nearly seventy-eight when he picked up his musket one last time to fight in the Revolutionary War. John Burns was seventy when, with calm but brazen determination, he strode off his front porch to join the Battle of Gettysburg. Impressive as those men's achievements are, they were whipper-snappers when compared to another veteran warrior, who came out of retirement to share his martial wisdom with a young soldier in the midst of a history-making war of independence—at age *900*.

I'm talking, of course, about Yoda.

Even if you're just a casual *Star Wars* fan, you probably remember the scene in *The Empire Strikes Back* where Luke Skywalker crashes his fighter plane on a swampy planet in his search for the master who will train him to become a Jedi Knight. You probably also remember that George Lucas and the other writers throw us all a curveball when they reveal that the fabled warrior Luke seeks is not a towering specimen of physical strength but a two-foot-tall wrinkly green puppet that resembles an Indonesian pygmy tarsier (a small primate with giant eyes) with a few strands of Albert Einstein's DNA spliced into his genome. (Special effects designer Stuart Freeborn drew on Einstein's image, especially the wrinkles around his eyes, in creating Yoda's look.) You may very well remember his penchant for speaking in riddles and apothegms, usually with an inverted grammar that adds an air of profundity. ("Named must your fear be before banish it you can.") Finally, if you remember anything at all of the three super confusing prequels that came out in the early 2000s, you might recall some fun footage of Yoda doing Simone Biles–style leaps and flips as he wields his lightsaber in duels with white-haired bad guys and wizards (who are usually played by accomplished British Shakespeareans seeking a late-career paycheck).

Now, if you want a truly comprehensive bio of this old wizened Jedi Master, you're probably going to have to dig deep into all nine movies, as well as the comic books, the spin-off streaming series, the Reddit boards, the YouTube channels, and—my favorite source—the fandom site called Wookieepedia. But I'm going to leave that to the *Star Wars* junkies, and give you just a thumbnail sketch.

Yoda was born in 896 BBY. That stands for "before the Battle of Yavin," which is when Luke Skywalker blew up the Death Star. Like Luke, Yoda comes from a remote corner of the galaxy, and, like Luke, he found his mentor when he crashed his spaceship on a foggy, swampy planet rife with slithery things. He was trained by a couple of Jedi Masters you've probably never heard of: first a snake-like creature with four human arms and a 1950s-style space-alien head named N'Kata Del

Gormo (which also, coincidentally, is the name of a lovely *pensione* in Florence), and then a female warrior named Fae Coven, who looks like a cat in a housecoat standing on her hind legs. He built his own lightsaber, became a Jedi Master before he turned one hundred, led the Jedi High Council, and opened an academy for young Jedi in training. Apparently he battled some evil Jedi witches at one point. He led an army of clones against Count Dooku's army of droids. And around 19 BBY, after failing to stop Emperor Palpatine (aka Darth Sidious) from taking over the galaxy, he went into exile back on his swampy planet, named Dagobah. That's where Luke Skywalker found him. He mentored Luke to become a Jedi, after which he breathed a deep sigh and "became one with the force," which is Jedi-speak for dying.

As an old soldier, Yoda has a very different spirit from the rough-edged, gritty, determined American types epitomized by heroes Samuel Whittemore and John L. Burns. What makes him so beloved to *Star Wars* fans is not so much his tough-as-nails courage and stubborn defiance of old age but his enormous wisdom and experience. We sense from our first on-screen encounter with Yoda that he is possessed of vast knowledge of the history of the galaxy, and of the workings of the force—all the invisible, spiritual influences in the universe that guide and constrain us. His age and experience give him supreme patience and an awareness that everything always belongs in a broader context. The Jedi are modeled on the Japanese samurai, and Yoda's worldview is vaguely Buddhist—Buddhist by way of Hollywood, of course. He is perfectly in control of his passions, sensitive to any disturbance in the force, and always keen to the youthful follies of Jedi Knights in training. And, let's face it, when you're 900 years old with the placid temperament of a Japanese koi pond, everyone and their little brother looks like a rash and excitable young warrior.

At the same time, Yoda's diminutive stature cuts against the grain of the modern stereotype of the warrior as a roided-up WWE brawler. George Lucas has explained that in his original conception of *Star Wars*, he imagined that Obi-Wan

Kenobi would train Luke, and when he decided to kill off Obi-Wan, he realized he needed a new Jedi Master—"an uber-Jedi Master"—for the sequel. (Actor Alec Guinness actually lobbied for his own character to be killed. As he later revealed, "What I didn't tell Lucas was that I just couldn't go on speaking those bloody awful, banal lines. I'd had enough of the mumbo jumbo.") But Lucas didn't want another version of the white-haired Guinness, so when he had to invent a new character, he zagged.

Lucas notes that myths and folktales often deploy a seemingly incidental or insignificant character to furnish the hero with critical guidance or wisdom. He wanted Yoda to seem insignificant in this way, "like a frog" in a fairy tale, before being revealed as the most powerful Jedi in the universe.

Yoda's size and his, well . . . *froggishness* make him, as Lucas said, "attractive but strange." He looks wise and worthy of reverence, but also kind of cute, not unlike a Muppet. In fact, Lucas's first casting choice for the voice was Jim Henson, who voiced Kermit the Frog. Henson declined, but recommended his longtime collaborator Frank Oz, who of course made the voice of Yoda famous, even if he does sometimes sound uncannily like Bert from *Sesame Street*.

Inventing this small, quiet, patient former space gladiator created another unforeseen problem. When the *Star Wars* franchise continued to grow, Lucas had to go back in time and show little Yoda as a daunting warrior engaged in hand-to-hand combat with human figures many times his size. Lucas called this decision a big risk, since there was a good chance that it could look "ludicrous." He credits the animators and actor Frank Oz for pulling it off. Even if you're not a *Star Wars* aficionado, the results are delightful. The mere sight of the small robed creature moving about, whether walking slowly and deliberately while leaning on his cane or leaping and spinning through cavernous sets in the fury of battle, has something of the sublime charm of Kermit pedaling a bicycle in the first Muppet movie. He manages to be both amusing and convincing at the same time.

In the end, though, what's most special about Yoda is less his prowess in

A fresh-faced 900-year-old Yoda in *The Empire Strikes Back*.
AJ Pics/Alamy

battle than our sense of his vast experience, which stretches back into the mists of *Star Wars* pre-history. He knows more about the history of this universe than the most in-the-weeds, Comicon-attending, fanfic-writing *Star Wars* junkie. He probably knows more than George Lucas himself. For many, the real allure of the *Star Wars* movies was the way that they hinted at legends and lore that could never be recovered or revealed, narrative pathways stretching off endlessly in any and all directions. It's the seductive promise of stories yet untold, and fans of all different ages have tried to chart and map every inch of this imaginative territory.

Yoda, in his old age, is a singular, living archive. Just as an elderly relative can suddenly surprise us with a remarkable incident from their youth that we've never heard before—maybe even something about their wartime service—so Yoda embodies the principle that among the aged there are always more tales to be told. With his slow, patient, ruminative manner, Yoda helps us understand how much we don't know, and he leaves us with a sense of wonder.

One More Veteran Veteran: Jean Thurel

fought at Yorktown at eighty-three

An 1807 edition of a journal called the *American Register* contains an obituary of a Frenchman known as "the oldest soldier in Europe," Jean Thurel, who died at the age of 108. Thurel's life spanned three centuries, from the reign of France's Sun King, Louis XIV, to that of Napoleon. A fusilier (a *fusil* is a kind of musket), he was born in Burgundy in 1698, joined the regiment of Touraine at age eighteen, fought in four wars, and finally called it quits in 1792 after seventy-five years of vigorous fusiliering. The injuries and losses he sustained in this long career include "a musket ball in the neck at the Siege of Kehl" (1733, War of Polish Succession), "seven sabre wounds . . . on his head at the Battle of Minden" (Seven Years' War, 1759), and the death of three of his brothers at the Battle of Fontenoy (War of Austrian Succession, 1745). At age eighty-three, he served France in support of the American colonies at Yorktown, making him even older than Samuel Whittemore was at Lexington. The only man ever to receive the Médaillon des Deux Épées three times—it's awarded after twenty-four years of service—he was honored by both Louis XVI and, seventeen years later, Napoleon. The notice in the *American Register* concludes, "To the moment of his death he preserved his senses and judgment; and, until his last illness, which was but for a few days, he enjoyed good health."

OLD GLORY: "The Star-Spangled Banner"

It's played at baseball games, fireworks shows, and every time an American wins gold at the Olympics. But when it comes to being our official anthem, "The Star-Spangled Banner" is actually a late bloomer.

As you probably remember from grade school—at least I hope you do—"The Star-Spangled Banner" was written by Francis Scott Key two years into the War of 1812. A lawyer, Key witnessed the British bombardment of Baltimore's Fort McHenry and was so inspired by seeing the American flag waving after the smoke cleared, he jotted down a poem.

Originally titled "Defense of Fort M'Henry," Key's stanzas were set to a popular tune that had come over from England, considered by some to be a drinking song. This new song hit almost immediately. The *Baltimore Patriot & Evening Advertiser* called it a "beautiful and animating effusion" destined "long to outlive the impulse which produced it." In releasing the sheet music version, a publisher changed the title to "The Star-Spangled Banner."

There were detractors early on, though. In 1889, John Philip Sousa told a reporter, "We ought not to adopt as our national air the work of a foreigner. The words of the 'Star-Spangled Banner' are American, but the music is English." Others complained that the song was too militaristic and too hard to sing. There were also claims of racism that continue to this day: Francis Scott Key was a slave owner and the third verse of the song declared, "No refuge could save the hireling and slave / From the terror of flight or the gloom of the grave."

It wasn't until 1930 that the House of Representatives took up the matter of the song's status. Two sopranos were brought in to prove that the song could be easily sung. The stunt must've helped, because the House passed the measure to make it the national anthem, with President Herbert Hoover signing the bill into law on March 3, 1931. "The Star-Spangled Banner" was official.

In 1968, Frank Sinatra called the anthem a "terrible piece of music," adding that "if you took a poll among singers, it would lose a hundred to nothing." Even so, he sang it on opening day at Dodger Stadium in 1977. (He went up on the lyrics, which probably made him hate it even more.) Sinatra thought "America the Beautiful" should be our anthem. I don't disagree. But revered or reviled, the song endures—not unlike that flag at Fort McHenry.

It Could Happen to You

to You

Late in Life Marriage,

Parenthood

& Coming Out

Most of the people you've been reading about so far spent their golden years doing something new or unusual or impressive in the public world. They wrote great works of literature. They fought in wars. They struggled against injustice.

But there's another group of people for whom the later years mean an occasion to do something new in their *personal* life—falling in love, for example, or having children. We sometimes talk about old age as a time when such major life opportunities have passed us by. But even though biology might favor youth or middle age as prime time for these experiences, there are always exceptions. Unlikely as it may seem, old age can be a time to finally connect with that old crush you've long carried a torch for, or to roll up your sleeves and start changing a new baby's diapers, or to come out of the closet in order to live life openly and authentically as yourself. It might sound a bit corny, but there's a truth in the old song: fairy tales can come true, it can happen to you—if you're young at heart.

Marriage

As we age, we naturally spend less of our life planning ahead, and more of it looking back—sometimes with pleasure, sometimes with regret, sometimes simply with the idle curiosity of wondering what if. Whether you've been happily married, happily single, or completely embittered and unfulfilled, old age can be a time to think back on a lost love, the proverbial one that got away. For most of us, an old romance from decades ago remains no more than a pleasant memory, maybe even a salutary reminder that we've made the right choices in life. Yet there's something uniquely uplifting in a story of someone who, in their final years, goes back to the past and reconnects with that long-lost love.

Carol Channing and Harry Kullijian

high school sweethearts married at eighty-two (her) and eighty-three (him)

In May 1998, the *New York Post* ran a headline designed to get you to click—provided, of course, you had a state-of-the-art high-speed 56K modem capable of connecting you to what was then commonly referred to as the World Wide Web. "SEX-STARVED CHANNING DEMANDS DIVORCE AT 77," blared the block letters from the newly digital tabloid. The *Washington Post*'s headline was only slightly more civil (and somewhat less grammatical): "Carol Channing, Unhappily Ever After End to 41-Year Marriage Stuns Friends."

In an irony that was not lost on journalists, Channing, that avatar of stamina, renowned for playing the eponymous matchmaker of the long-running Broadway hit musical *Hello, Dolly!* over five thousand times, was ending the run on her marriage. And a good thing, too. Her divorce filing, seeking a separation from Charles Lowe, her third husband and business manager, cited physical abuse, mismanagement of her money, and a neglect of husbandly duties—they'd had sex, she alleged, only twice in four decades. (Apparently both the matinee and the evening performance had failed to please the critics.)

Channing, whose singular voice managed somehow to be at once gravelly and kittenish, had become a star at twenty-eight playing the flapper Lorelei Lee in the Broadway adaptation of Anita Loos's *Gentlemen Prefer Blondes*. She reached new heights of renown in 1964 as Dolly Levi, returning to the signature role in a 1994 revival, still belting out "Dolly'll never go away again" at the age of seventy-six. But even though Dolly was sticking around, Carol was heading for the exits. "I was miserable," Channing said soon after her decision to divorce. "I was unhappy. And I didn't realize it wasn't my fault. But I'm going to survive. I'm going to live. I'm free." As it turned out, Lowe passed away before the divorce was final, and Channing was on her own.

One of the first things she did with her newfound independence was to write a memoir, *Just Lucky, I Guess*. In the course of telling her life story, Channing recalled her junior high school sweetheart in San Francisco, a boy named Harry Kullijian, writing fondly, "I was so in love with Harry I couldn't stop hugging him." They remained an item through high school, where Harry, enamored of Carol's performing talents, encouraged her to develop impressions of their teachers. But after graduation, Carol took her show on the road. She went on to Vermont's Bennington College. Kullijian stayed local, attending the University of San Francisco before serving in the military during World War II, where he earned three battle stars.

Sixty-four years later, a friend of Kullijian's named Mervin Morris, who was also still friendly with Channing, read her newly published memoir, with its sweet words about Harry. He encouraged his friend, who was recently widowed, to get in touch. Morris told Kullijian, "You've got to call Carol tomorrow, January 31. It's her birthday." Kullijian was surprised. "Call Carol?" he asked, "I thought she was dead."

Carol wasn't dead—nor were the embers of the teenage passion that she and Harry had shared at school dances during the Roosevelt administration. The octogenarian lovebirds were engaged in a matter of weeks, and a year later, in 2003, eighty-two-year-old Carol and eighty-three-year-old Harry tied the knot. The newlyweds lived the rest of their eighties together, reigniting the passion of first love that they had experienced back at Aptos Middle School. Now that's what you call a hit revival!

Suzanne Pleshette and Tom Poston

rekindled their romance at sixty-four
(her) and seventy-eight (him)

Carol Channing and Harry Kullijian got married seventy years after they first met. For TV sitcom stars Suzanne Pleshette and Tom Poston, romance moved along

Lovebirds Suzanne Pleshette and Tom Poston attending *The Producers* musical on their wedding day, May 11, 2001.
Henry McGee/Globe Photos/Zuma Press/Alamy

much more quickly. They took their vows a mere forty-two years after their first date.

The wedding, in May 2001, was Suzanne's third marriage and Tom's fourth—or fifth, depending on how you count, since he'd married one wife twice. (Hey, this is Hollywood, okay? Don't be so judgy.) For both of them, early-life mismatches had given way to long-term unions, and both of them were recently widowed. Pleshette had been married to her manager, Tommy Gallagher, for thirty-two years, while Poston had been wedded to Kay Hudson, a nurse, for the better part of thirty. When Gallagher died in 2000 after a long struggle with lung cancer, Poston, then seventy-eight, reached out to his old flame, then sixty-four, to express his sympathies. (Hudson had died in 1998.) It wasn't long before they headed to New York's Supreme Court in lower Manhattan to get hitched.

When they went on their first date, in 1959, it was a different world. Back then, both were starring on Broadway in a show called *The Golden Fleecing*, a moderately successful farce about U.S. naval officers in Venice trying to win big at roulette by using a new high-speed military computer. Poston played one of the naval officers, and Pleshette, only twenty-two—and a radiantly beautiful twenty-two, by the way—was Julie, described by *Time* as "the admiral's inevitably winsome daughter." (When did Suzanne Pleshette ever not steal the show? I'm convinced that if those birds hadn't killed her in the Hitchcock classic, Rod Taylor would have gotten back together with her and sent Tippi Hedren packing.)

Pleshette recalled their initial love connection much later in an interview with the Television Academy Foundation. She was not originally cast in *The Golden Fleecing*, and, as she remembered it, the production had already begun in Philadelphia with someone else in the lead. However, as the production prepared for its Broadway opening, there were problems:

> *They had already gone on the road with The Golden Fleecing, and they were very unhappy with the leading lady. So they called me and I flew in that night to Philadelphia, and Tom and I read together, and of course—perfect, you know! Abe [Burrows, the director] loved me. But they didn't want to tell [the female lead] that she was fired until they were ready to move on to Boston. So I was hidden in the hotel. I learned the lines and learned the blocking from sitting in the audience at night watching the play. And then . . . after the Saturday night performance they told [the female lead] she was not going to continue on, and I went on.*

Pleshette was so new to the show that she was still learning her lines during her first performances, and they had to hollow out part of the set so that the stage manager could feed her prompts. One evening, she got a call in her hotel room. It was Poston. As she recounted, "He said, 'Uh, do you want to come run the lines?' And I said, 'Well, I'm in my robe.' And he said, 'Well that'll be fine.'" She then added, with a smile and a little laugh, "Well it *was*—for him."

Despite the early sparks, however, the relationship didn't last. Suzanne and Tom briefly reconnected in 1964 after the demise of Pleshette's six-month marriage to Troy Donahue, but again they went their separate ways, and in 1968 both married the spouses who would be their partners for the next three decades. During those years, as their fans know, both acted in *The Bob Newhart Show*, where Pleshette costarred as Bob's wife, Emily, while Poston had an occasional role as a college roommate of Bob's. By that point, however, the past history made things awkward, and Pleshette preferred to keep her ex off the set. "I didn't like him," Pleshette later said. "I kept telling Bob, 'Get rid of him.'"

Yet, many years later, after the death of her beloved husband Gallagher, Pleshette welcomed the call from her long-ago boyfriend. As Poston told Ed Bark, the longtime TV critic for the *Dallas Morning News*, "We commiserated with each other and we ended up being married, and I'm as happy as I've ever been in my life." Pleshette seemed happy too. When Bark asked about her favorite TV and film roles, she quipped, "There are those porno films that Tom and I have been doing." Apparently things were still going strong for the reunited couple. The loving pair enjoyed wedded bliss for only six years, but they died within a year of each other, having lived out a happy final chapter that ensured they would exit this life with no regrets.

Parenthood

There's an obvious appeal to stories of late-life parenthood. To bring new life into the world or to raise a child after years of disappointment and missed chances reminds us that it's never too late to make a major change that can bring us happiness. And in spite of all the jokes about chasing after toddlers on bad knees or falling asleep while reading bedtime stories, a belated entrance into parenthood can be even more gratifying than becoming a mother or father when you're young: sometimes the delays and deferrals make reaching the destination all the more special.

Fatherhood: Mr. Pickles

first-time father at ninety

Many well-known stories of senior-citizen dads are more likely to elicit a groan or an eye roll than a hearty "mazel tov." In 2023, both Al Pacino, eighty-three, and Robert De Niro, seventy-nine, became fathers again; whatever they were serving at the *Godfather* reunion party must have had something special in it. And in July 2020, British business magnate and fraudster Bernie Ecclestone fathered a child at age eighty-nine with his forty-four-year-old-wife, Fabiana Flosi.

But there is a recent new father who has all of these rich old dads beat, and—even better—whose story can be placed squarely in the "heartwarming and adorable" file. That dad is named Mr. Pickles, and he is a radiated tortoise who lives at the Houston Zoo. In 2023, at the age of ninety, he became a first-time father.

The baby tortoises' mother is named Mrs. Pickles, although it's whispered in the back corridors of the reptile house that the two never formally tied the knot and are content to remain common-law spouses. To make things more scandalous, Mrs. P. is only fifty-three. When news of the tortoise babies first ran in the *New York Times*, one wag in the comments section wrote, "Mr. Pickles is old enough to be Mrs. Pickles' father. But then, who am I to judge?" The three offspring, named Dill, Gherkin, and Jalapeño, were hatched in February 2023, and the little creatures, with their brown-and-gold patterned shells, are exquisite. In their baby pictures they look almost like gemstones, with little turtlish legs poking out.

No good data exists on how long male radiated tortoises stay fertile. The creatures themselves can live 150 years, and so it's possible that the Pickleses might even give parenthood another go. With the staff of the Houston Zoo at their disposal, they have plenty of support—no need to hire a nanny.

The proud nonagenarian father is the oldest resident of the zoo, but what makes the births especially welcome is that the entire species is critically endangered,

Ninety-year-old first-time father Mr. Pickles, radiating pride with one of his offspring, at the Houston Zoo, March 22, 2023.

Mel Hodges/Houston Zoo

and it reproduces infrequently. Native to Madagascar, radiated tortoises are imperiled because of illegal collecting and poaching and because of changes to their natural habitat. If you're wondering why they're called radiated, it's because of the distinctive yellow-brown lines emanating from the center of each plate of the animal's carapace (the top part of the shell). Perhaps the most famous member of the species—at least prior to Mr. Pickles's headline-making virility—was Tu'i Malila, who was born (or, technically, hatched) in 1777. A story goes that he was picked up by the British explorer Captain James Cook and given as a gift to the royal family of Tonga, but historians doubt this account. However he got to Tonga, Tu'i Malila lived an incredible 188 years, dying in 1966.

As for Mr. Pickles, he was hatched in 1933 and spent his youth traveling Europe, not of his own volition, alas, but as the property of collectors. Eventually he made it to Houston, joining the zoo in 1987. He waited nine years to meet Mrs. Pickles, who arrived in 1996. But then again, he was in no hurry. Another quarter century passed before this good-looking chelonian couple got down to business.

It was in 2022 that a zookeeper observed Mrs. Pickles laying her eggs in the sand right around closing time. The soil in the zoo is not ideal for the eggs, so the zookeepers relocated them to the climate-controlled interior of the Reptile and Amphibian House, where they were monitored carefully. Five months later, the beautiful little trio of tortoises were hatched. Another *Times* reader, responding to the story, quoted a favorite song, "The only one for me is you, and you for me / So happy together." In case you're wondering, that's by the Turtles.

I think you know the moral of this story: slow and steady wins the race.

Motherhood: Sarah

first-time mother at ninety—and no epidural!

There's no denying that ninety, for both humans and reptiles, is an advanced age at which to assume the obligations of fatherhood. For motherhood, it's even more of a challenge, since the female body contains a limited supply of ova—whereas sperm are about as disposable as cardboard coffee sleeves from Starbucks. The modern record for age of motherhood is held by Erramatti Mangamma of Andhra Pradesh, in southeast India, who was seventy-three when she gave birth to twin daughters in 2019, helped along by in vitro fertilization and a donor egg. She and her husband, Raja Rao, who was eighty-two when their daughters were born, had been married (and childless) since 1962. Sadly, Rao died only a year after his daughters' birth; that of course is a risk that comes with taking on parenthood late in life. Said his widow, Ms. Mangamma, "He only had twelve months with his girls, but at least he tasted the joy of fatherhood before he died."

But compare Mangamma's seventy-three to the age of a famous woman who gave birth for the first time at ninety. That's Sarah (originally Sarai) of the Hebrew Bible, the wife of Abraham and the first of the biblical matriarchs. She was also Abraham's half sister, which is just a weird fact that they seem to always skate right past in Sunday school. (Think about that the next time someone tosses out the phrase "the biblical definition of marriage.") Anyway, the story goes that God promised to make Abraham the father of a great nation, but that Sarah could not conceive. In every translation of the Bible that I've seen, she's called "barren" (the original Hebrew is *aqar*), which always sounded kind of harsh to me—like she's being compared to a desert. Where is Roget when you need him?

The Bible tells us that Sarah was beautiful and kept her good looks well into her later years, not unlike Suzanne Pleshette. In Genesis 12, famine strikes the land of Canaan, so Abraham and Sarah head to Egypt. Because Sarah is such a "fair woman to look upon"—mind you, she's sixty-five at this point—Abraham is worried that the Egyptians will kill him off in order to claim Sarah for themselves. Sure enough, when they get to Egypt, Sarah is brought "into Pharaoh's house." But God sends some plagues, and the pharaoh sheepishly returns her to Abraham, saying he thought that she was Abraham's sister—which, to be fair, is how Abraham introduced her.

Flash forward ten to twelve years and we're back in Canaan. Still no baby for Abraham and Sarah. Because Sarah is unable to conceive, she gives her handmaid, Hagar, to Abraham so that he can beget a son. Eighty-six-year-old Abraham begets Ishmael with Hagar. (Begetting was a very popular activity back in the days of the Old Testament.) Maybe sending in a handmaid to bear a child in your stead seems a little unconventional, but it was the closest thing they had back then to IVF. Clearly Sarah is convinced that this is the only way her husband is going to perpetuate his line.

Now hit that fast-forward arrow on your remote once more. After another thirteen years, God appears and again promises to make Abraham "the father of a multitude of nations." Frankly, I'm just impressed that everyone is still alive. Abraham is ninety-nine; Sarah, ninety. God also promises to make Sarah a mother, whereupon Abraham "fell upon his face, and laughed, and said in his heart: 'Shall a child be born unto him that is a hundred years old? And shall Sarah, that is ninety years old, bear?'" But God's not goofing around. He generally doesn't goof around about stuff like this.

A few days later, three men show up at Abraham's tent. But—surprise!—they're not really men, they're angels, messengers of God. Sarah, who is ninety, remember, goes to prepare some food, but, standing outside the door of the tent, she overhears the men tell Abraham that she is going to have a child. If this were an episode of *Three's Company*, you would see Sarah doing a hammy take directly to the camera with her jaw hanging open in disbelief, or maybe loudly dropping her platter of Middle Eastern appetizers in shock. But the ancient scribes were a bit more restrained. Sarah's reaction, like Abraham's, is to laugh at this idea—she "laughed within herself," according to the King James Version. God, again not joking, asks her, "Is anything too hard for the Lord?"

Now, let's go a little deeper on this laughter thing for a moment, since I for one get very nervous when I read about these people laughing at God. (Laughing WITH Him is one thing; AT Him is asking for it.) At first it sounds like Abraham and Sarah laugh because they are skeptical. They're really old, and the idea of getting pregnant at ninety seems preposterous. But nine months later, when Isaac, their son, is born, Sarah says, "God has brought me laughter, and everyone who hears about this will laugh with me." (The name Isaac, or Yitzhak, means "he will laugh.") The laughter she's talking about now is the laughter that comes with the discovery, after something like seventy years of waiting, that you are finally a mother. It's a laughter of gratitude or celebration.

A final note here. The story of Sarah becoming a mother at ninety is such a good one that, when they decided to come out with a sequel to the Hebrew Bible, the writers of the Christian New Testament reused it. In the Gospel of Luke, chapter 1, there's a righteous man named Zacharias, who, like Abraham, gets visited by a messenger of God. This messenger, aka the angel Gabriel, tells Zacharias that Elizabeth, his wife, will bear him a son. Like Abraham, Zacharias is a little skeptical, since he's quite old, but Elizabeth becomes pregnant, and her son will grow up to become John the Baptist. And although the Gospels don't give an exact age for the proud parents, another ancient text, known as the Mandaean Book of John, describes Zacharias as ninety-nine and Elizabeth as eighty-eight.

In addition to being the mother of John the Baptist, Elizabeth was also the cousin of the Virgin Mary. According to Luke, while Elizabeth was pregnant, Mary also received a visit from Gabriel. You've probably heard of that visit—maybe even seen some paintings of it—because that's when Gabriel announces that Mary will bear a son. Apparently announcing unlikely pregnancies was part of Gabriel's job description. When Mary asks how that is possible, since she has never known a man, Gabriel mentions Elizabeth's pregnancy as proof that "with God nothing shall be impossible." And whether you're a religious person or not, there's no question that conceiving a child after years of trying can feel like a miracle.

Coming Out: Kenneth Felts

came out at ninety—then married at ninety-three

Not long ago I went to see Madonna in concert for the first time, at Barclays Center arena in Brooklyn. She came onstage two and three-quarter hours late. (This is the kind of late start we're *not* celebrating in this book.) Her fans have aged along with her, so you could feel the grumpiness setting in as it neared 11:00 p.m. on a Wednesday and she still had not appeared.

But all was forgiven (by me, at least) with her performance of her 1986 song "Live to Tell." It's always been one of my favorite Madonna songs. Madonna has said that the song was written about her relationship with her parents and the scars she carried with her. But during this tour she used it to pay tribute to the forty million (and counting) lives lost to HIV/AIDS. As she sang, faces of victims were projected onto giant hanging backdrops: artist Keith Haring . . . singer Freddie

Mercury . . . choreographer Alvin Ailey . . . their images Rushmore in scale. Madonna, suspended high off the ground inside of an illuminated box, floated around and among these screens as the images transitioned from single portraits into mosaics of smaller and yet smaller pictures, eventually including the faces of hundreds of the not-famous who perished, scorned by so much of society, sometimes by their own families. All at once, Barclays became a Hall of Remembrance, the enormity of the loss—and this wasn't long ago at all—newly devastating and outrageous. And knowing how Madonna had come up during the 1980s, when the epidemic first struck, and never waffled in her support of gay people, made it even more moving. The crowd fell silent.

Those lives—so many of them gay men—ended in their prime. People in their twenties and thirties dying in huge waves. (For more on what AIDS did to the Broadway community alone, you can listen to the "Death of a Dancer" *Mobituaries* podcast episode.) But the lyrics of the song (". . . hope I live to tell the secret. . ."), especially when I was a closeted teenager, have always evoked for me another kind of death that so many gay people throughout history have experienced—while still being alive in body.

To spend one's life suppressing something as fundamental as who you love is unbearably sad. How lucky (a word I generally shun) am I to live in a time when I don't have to live a lie. So much has changed on this score in just the last twenty years—we're talking tectonically. Thank goodness Kenneth Felts lived long enough to taste freedom.

In June of 2020, Felts, ninety, came out on Facebook. The story went viral (the good kind of viral), and he became something of a sensation. During the pandemic, a time when so many of us felt trapped, it was thrilling to watch someone break free. But this was hardly preordained. Just months before, Kenneth had voluntarily ended his chemo for Hodgkin's lymphoma. He was, for all intents and purposes, packing it in. Taking stock of the life that was ending, he started writing a memoir.

He was born in Kansas during the Depression in 1930 to a deeply religious family. There was no question in his mind that homosexuality was evil. Likewise no question that he had to keep his true desires secret when he realized at twelve years old that he was gay. (Twelve is also when I realized I was gay. I went off walking by myself along River Road in my hometown of Bethesda, Maryland, something weighing on my mind. What it was, I wasn't sure. I was walking through the pedestrian tunnel under a railroad bridge when it dawned on me that I was gay. I walked out the other side of the tunnel . . . and went home to watch TV. I think *Dynasty* was on that night.)

Kenneth graduated high school in 1948 and enlisted in the navy in 1950, at a time when being gay wasn't just illegal; the discovery was usually life-ruining. To even associate with another gay person was a risk. When he was twenty-seven, he took a job as an insurance investigator in Long Beach, California.

That's when he met Phillip Jones, who became his first true love. They had to be careful. "You had to stay apart in order to be together," Kenneth told CNN. Still, they eventually moved in together. Kenneth and Phillip were happy, which is what makes what happened next so sad. One day in church—Phillip sang in the choir—Kenneth was overcome with guilt about the "sin" the two were living. "I had to make a choice. Phillip lost in the battle," he said. "I determined then to go straight."

And so Kenneth left Phillip without even saying goodbye and returned to Kansas. He married a woman in Colorado in 1962, and they had a daughter in 1973, before divorcing in 1980. At that point he began combing through California phone books—wherever he could find them and in secret, of course—looking for Phillip. "Phillip Jones" being a common name, Kenneth's hopes were raised over and over—and disappointed each time he called to find it wasn't *his* Phillip.

In the mid-1990s, Rebecca, Kenneth's daughter, came out to him, unaware that her father was gay. He wasn't sympathetic. "It won't last six months," he told her. That remark is a painful reminder of the toll being closeted takes not just on you but on the people around you. When you're unforgiving with yourself, you're likely to be just as ungenerous with others. (Rebecca's relationship has not only lasted, she and her wife have two children together.)

Fast-forward to 2020. Kenneth's memoir writing forced a reckoning. "I got up to Phillip—it hit me so hard that here was this great love affair I'd had, and I walked away," Kenneth told Olivia Young of CBS News Colorado. It plunged him into a depression. Rebecca saw that her father was despairing. Eventually he opened up to her about Phillip. That's when, with her encouragement, he came out on social media at the age of ninety. The response was overwhelmingly positive. "Pretty soon I was doing interviews in Tokyo, in Berlin, in Paris, and everywhere wanted an interview of this old man who decided to get out of the closet and be a real person," Kenneth said. "My life has changed so much, from happy to die . . . to wanting so much to live."

"Rejection was always the greatest fear that I had," he said on Australian TV, "that if people found out I was gay, that would be the end of the relationship." Instead he formed bonds with people far and wide. A stranger from New Jersey offered to try to track down Phillip. Sadly, it turned out he'd died two years before. Kenneth also learned that Phillip had ended up having a long-term relationship.

"What that meant to me was that I was finally able to say goodbye, to accept that Phillip had forgiven me for leaving," Kenneth said through tears, "and that he had gone on and lived his life as a good life, and that freed me up to go ahead and start living my life again. I guess I'll never get over Phillip."

But he did. Johnny Hau, a much younger gay man living in Colorado, had been struggling with coming out. After he saw Kenneth's social media post, he reached out. The two met, began dating, and moved in together. And in July 2023, Kenneth, ninety-three, married Johnny, thirty-four.

For the wedding, the *New York Times* reported that Kenneth (now cancer-free) "donned a pink jacket over a purple button down shirt." Rebecca, his daughter, told the paper, "He used to be such a conservative dresser. Now he wears the loudest stuff." As he told the BBC (I told you Kenneth had gone viral), "I can wear the shirts I want, I can wear necklaces, I can get blue color in my hair. It's the freedom of doing without fear that somebody is going to disparage you for it. . . . It's freedom. Just plain old freedom."

OLD YELLER: Ethel Merman

"From the first my voice was easily identifiable. When I was a baby and people in the next room or down the street heard me, they'd say, 'That's Ethel.'"

As she acknowledged in her memoir, Ethel Merman's voice was distinctive from the start. Cole Porter said it was "like a brass band going by." Famed conductor Arturo Toscanini described it this way: "Hers is not a human voice. It's another instrument in the band." One reporter would later call her sound "the clarion call to Broadway."

Merman first charmed audiences with that brassy belt in the 1930 Gershwin musical *Girl Crazy*. During her show-stopping performance of "I Got Rhythm" she held a high C for a full sixteen bars. (She would later write, "It's been said that I can hold a note as long as the Chase National Bank.") That night, George Gershwin told her, "Don't ever let anybody give you a singing lesson. It'll ruin you."

As for technique, Merman explained it this way: "I just stand up and holler and hope that my voice holds out." That "hollering" would lead her to starring roles in classic musicals like *Anything Goes* and *Gypsy*. It was *Annie Get Your Gun* that gave Merman her signature song, "There's No Business Like Show Business," a mantra of sorts for the highs and lows of her career.

And no, not everything Merman did was successful, particularly her attempts at a movie career, though I did love her in the 1963 comedy *It's a Mad, Mad, Mad, Mad World*. (Come to think of it, how great would she have been as Susie Essman's mother in *Curb Your Enthusiasm*?) But as long as her voice kept going—and it did—there was no stopping her. She (in)famously released a disco album in 1979. And in 1982, at age seventy-three, Merman gave a concert at Carnegie Hall, with the *New York Times* noting, "She had the help of a body microphone, but there is a quality in the Merman voice that defies all amplification subtleties. Time has not withered it. It still cuts like an ax, and she flaunts its bravura excesses with relish."

The Widows

Madame Clicquot,
Mary Delany &
Myrlie Evers-Williams

Let's be honest. Even though a late-in-life marriage can be the perfect final chapter to a life well lived, *sometimes the exact opposite is true.* Sometimes new horizons don't really open up until a person is free of the bonds of marriage. That's the case with the first two stories here. (The third is much different.)

Marriage, for all the happiness it can bring, can also mean subordinating your own dreams to someone else's. And, even accounting for great progress in gender equality over the centuries, it's women who still do more of the subordinating than men. Which is why widowhood can sometimes be an example of addition by subtraction. For these women, widowhood is by definition a late-in-life debut, comeback, or triumph. 'Til death do you part? More like after death do you party.

Barbe-Nicole Ponsardin Clicquot

*founded a champagne empire as a
thirty-six-year-old widow*

Take Barbe-Nicole Ponsardin, the daughter of a French textile manufacturer, born in 1777. At twenty-one, she married François Clicquot, the son of another industrialist, in what was essentially an arranged marriage. After only six years of marriage, François suddenly died—maybe from typhoid, maybe from suicide. Whatever the cause, Madame Clicquot was left on her own, with a young daughter, at age twenty-seven.

Barbe-Nicole's inherited wealth was enough to ensure her and her daughter a comfortable life. But that wasn't the path she took. You see, Barbe-Nicole was aware that widowhood came with advantages in nineteenth-century France. In the words of her biographer, Tilar Mazzeo, widows were "the only women granted the social freedom to run their own affairs. Having lost their husbands, they could make their own decisions." And so, instead of going into mourning for years and years, the Veuve Clicquot (*veuve* means widow) decided to break out the bubbly. She went into the champagne business.

Barbe-Nicole's late husband had left her a failing wine business, but she believed she could reinvigorate it. She borrowed a huge sum from her father-in-law, then learned the art of wine making by apprenticing herself to a successful vintner. For several years, the business struggled. But when the Napoleonic Wars were drawing to a close, this enterprising widow took an enormous risk.

She knew that Russians enjoyed champagne. She also knew that with the end of the war, the Russian market would, after many years, reopen. Finally, she knew that all the other winemakers knew this too. So, in 1814, evading her own country's naval blockade, she smuggled her champagne to the Prussian port city of Königsberg (see the *Mobituaries* book for that city's dramatic history), which positioned her to get her product to St. Petersburg weeks ahead of her rivals. First impressions matter, and when Tsar Alexander I endorsed her brand, business exploded like—well, like the popped cork of a yellow-labeled Veuve Clicquot champagne bottle.

Getting the tsar treatment in Russia was just the beginning. (Sorry, I had to.) With a growing market came the need to scale up production, and, working with her cellar master, Madame Clicquot devised a new process, called riddling, or *remuage*, that eliminated the yeast in the wine. This made it less cloudy, better-tasting, and faster to produce. In other words, she basically created the clear, sparkling product we drink today to celebrate a late-in-life marriage or new baby. The widow went down in history as not only a famous vintner but a pathbreaking businesswoman.

Through all these years, she never remarried, although Mazzeo reports flirtations. I mean, an attractive, successful widow with the keys to France's best champagne cellar . . . something's bound to happen. Yet to have remarried would have meant, legally and socially, subordinating herself to a husband. That was a step that this widow clearly did not want to take. And so she remained a widow, and the name Veuve Clicquot became synonymous with fine champagne.

Toward the end of her life, Madame Clicquot summed up her acquired wisdom in a letter to a great-granddaughter. "The world is in perpetual motion, and we must invent the things of tomorrow," she wrote. "One must go before others, be determined and exacting, and let your intelligence direct your life. Act with audacity."

Mary Granville Pendarves Delany

began creating classic works of collage at seventy-two

Then there's the case of Mary Delany. Born in 1700 to a well-off, well-connected family in the southwest of England, Mary was given an unusually good education for a girl of her time. But when she was seventeen, her father's declining fortunes compelled him to marry her off, against her wishes. The groom was a sixty-year-old member of Parliament named Alexander Pendarves. "When I was led to the altar," Mary later wrote, "I wished from my soul I had been led, as Iphigenia was, to be sacrificed." (I told you she was well-educated.) "I lost all that makes life desirable—joy and peace of mind," she added. It turns out that Mary was more of a nurse than a wife to Pendarves, who drank heavily and suffered from gout. When he died, in 1725, we can assume her grief was shallow and short-lived. She might even have reached for a bottle of Veuve Clicquot had it been invented.

Patriarchal laws being what they were, Mary didn't inherit her husband's money. However, as a widow, she acquired the same social freedom that Barbe-Nicole Clicquot would enjoy decades later in France. Although financially dependent on relatives and friends, she had the leisure time to develop skills in gardening, drawing, needlework, and painting. Eventually she married again, this time willingly. The groom was a Dublin minister named Patrick Delany. This marriage lasted twenty-five years and was much happier. The Delanys traveled in literary circles—he was a close friend of the writer Jonathan Swift—and Mary tried her hand at writing a novel. She ended up outliving hubby number two, becoming, at sixty-eight, a widow once more.

This is where it really gets interesting. Mary now spent much of her time living at the estate of a close friend, the Duchess of Portland, who introduced her to the leading botanists of the age. These men were followers of Mister Taxonomy himself, Carl Linnaeus; taxonomic classification of plant species was an important part of the Enlightenment project of ordering the world's knowledge. Studying informally with them, Mary came to appreciate not only the visual beauty of different plants but also their intricate biology, the nature and function of their various parts.

This knowledge made it possible for her, at the age of seventy-two, to begin a series of collages that she referred to as "Paper Mosaiks." (Okay, so spelling wasn't her strong suit.) They were examples of what are now called works of decoupage—something like what Matisse, as you'll read later, was doing in *his* seventies, except Delany's collages were extraordinarily detailed. She created remarkably precise renderings of hundreds of different plant species by placing layer upon layer of colored paper fragments on a black background, until an image of the entire flower, with all its shadings, was complete. (Some slivers of paper were so fine, she used tweezers, which makes me think she would have been amazing playing the board game Operation.)

These weren't simply beautiful pictures—although they were that. What Mary did was to bring together her knowledge of plant structures with her creative talents. Like John James Audubon's *The Birds of America* several decades later, they were a fusion of science and art. In the words of a contemporary, the writer and printmaker William Gilpin, "These flowers have both the beauty of painting, and the exactness of botany." Over the next seventeen years, Mary produced 985 of these mosaics, ceasing only when her eyesight failed, shortly before her death, at age eighty-eight. This kind of collection was called a *florilegium* ("gathering of flowers") or a *hortus siccus* ("dry garden"), but Mary's particular portfolio is most often referred to as the *Flora Delanica* (Delany's Flowers). Those Linnaeans—they sure loved their Latin, didn't they?

On her death, Mary left a number of her works to the queen of England, who had taken an interest in them on a visit to the duchess. Most are now owned by the British Museum. Public interest in them surged in the 1980s after the Irish designer

Sybil Connolly created dinnerware for Tiffany & Co. based on them. And these exquisite collages are not only a remarkable fusion of art and science. They are a testament to the freedom and opportunity that widowhood can bring.

Myrlie Evers-Williams

*finally achieved justice for her
murdered husband at sixty-one*

Finally, let's consider the story of Myrlie Evers, the remarkably courageous widow of the civil rights leader Medgar Evers, who was assassinated in Jackson, Mississippi, in 1963 by a White Citizens' Councils member. At the time of the murder, Medgar was thirty-seven and Myrlie only thirty.

They married when Myrlie was eighteen. She had become an active partner in her husband's civil rights efforts, and when he was killed, she resolved to continue his work and bring his killer to justice.

Medgar Evers was a college graduate, a U.S. Army combat veteran, and the field secretary for the Mississippi NAACP. As a young man, his efforts to fight segregation had been met with multiple death threats. On the night of June 12, 1963, he came home from a meeting with an armload of NAACP T-shirts. As he carried them from his car to his home, a sniper, hiding in the bushes 150 feet away, shot him in the back. He made it to his doorstep but died in a hospital soon after. The gun was traced to a white supremacist named Byron De La Beckwith, who was arrested. The evidence to convict Beckwith was strong; his fingerprints were on the murder weapon. But in two separate trials, two separate juries—both of them all-male and all-white—deadlocked, and the Hinds County prosecutor dropped the charges.

Myrlie Evers could hardly see a way forward. She had just lost her husband of twelve years, and she had three small children. People do not get rich working for the NAACP, and she had debts to pay. She contemplated suicide, but her obligation to her children kept her going.

She moved the family to Claremont, California, received her degree from Pomona College, and began what would become a successful career in fundraising and public relations. She frequently gave talks for the NAACP. In 1970, she ran for Congress. Eventually she married a longshoreman and former activist, Walter Williams. But she always considered her first husband's murder to be unfinished business.

Twenty-six years after the murder, in 1989, a ray of hope broke through when a Jackson news reporter uncovered evidence of jury tampering. A state government agency called the Mississippi State Sovereignty Commission, created to fight desegregation efforts, had illegally provided Beckwith's lawyers with information about the jury pool. (The reporter, Jerry Mitchell, also unearthed evidence that helped to convict the killers in several other infamous civil rights–era murders, earning him the sobriquet "the South's Simon Wiesenthal.")

Reopening a case after nearly thirty years isn't so simple, especially in Mississippi. Evers-Williams lobbied the Hinds County prosecutor, who was reluctant to undertake a third trial. The file on the case was only three pages long, and a key piece of evidence, Beckwith's rifle, had gone missing. (It later turned up in the private collection of a Mississippi judge. Hmmmm.) The prosecutor also told Evers-Williams that there was no existing transcript from the original trial. This absence, he felt, would cancel out any hope of bringing Beckwith to justice.

But Evers-Williams—whom friends sometimes had chided for living in the past—had been saving a certified carbon copy of the transcript to pass on to her children. She had the entire record. Still, the defense raised objections to the legality of holding another trial after so many years. The question went to the Mississippi State Supreme Court, which took its time deciding the matter. Finally, in 1994, with Evers-Williams now sixty, the court ruled that the trial could go forward.

The trial took place in the same courtroom that had held the two previous

Myrlie Evers-Williams, who spent more than thirty years seeking justice for her slain husband, Medgar Evers.

Alcorn State University

trials, but this time there were new witnesses. Former Klansmen and associates of Beckwith's had changed in the intervening thirty years. Some had seen society evolve and no longer harbored hatred for Black Americans. Others were no longer afraid to tell the truth about what they had seen and heard. Still others, perhaps, wanted to go to the grave with a clean conscience. When it was time to take the stand, several witnesses testified that Beckwith had not only admitted to the murder but bragged about it.

The new evidence, heard by a racially diverse jury, made all the difference. On February 5, 1994, the jurors returned a guilty verdict, and Beckwith, then seventy-three, was sentenced to life in prison. Evers-Williams, sitting with her children, wept. She later said that she declared to her departed husband, "Medgar, I've gone the last mile of the way."

The Mississippi Supreme Court later upheld the decision. Beckwith died in a hospital in 2001, having been transferred there from prison for medical reasons.

Some years later, Myrlie Evers-Williams told an interviewer from the *New York Times Magazine* that she believed the trial had had a positive effect on Mississippi. She noted that a poll taken before the third trial showed that the public was against the reopening of the case but that afterward, the decision was strongly supported. As she said, "Mississippi has always been known as the poorest state and one filled with racism. I have watched Mississippi try to make progress, try to get accepted. Getting this verdict helped."

OLD NEWS: Mike Wallace

Legendary television journalist Mike Wallace was often asked over the years about when he would retire. To which he would respond, "When my toes turn up." Wallace had no intention of signing off before he had to.

Of course, television didn't exist when Myron Leon Wallace was born, in Brookline, Massachusetts, in 1918. He started in radio but moved over to TV in 1949, starring in a police drama called *Stand By for Crime*. In the years that followed, Wallace did it all—talk shows, game shows, commercials. But he became the Mike Wallace we knew and loved (and feared) with the 1956 interview talk show *Night Beat*, which he called "nosy, irreverent, often confrontational."

When *60 Minutes* premiered, Wallace was fifty and ready, though not everyone was ready for him. He perfected the art of the ambush. He told Ayatollah Khomeini (with the Wallace signature caveat, "forgive me") that Egyptian president Anwar Sadat had called him a lunatic. As Wallace himself put it, he walked "a fine line between sadism and intellectual curiosity." Whatever it was he was doing, it was thrilling to watch.

Sometimes he became the story. A $120 million libel suit brought by General William Westmoreland—eventually settled out of court—sent Wallace into a clinical depression. But still, he kept going. When he signed a new four-year contract with CBS News in 1997 at age seventy-nine, he declared, "Term limits are for politicians." To be fair, he wasn't the only *60 Minutes* correspondent of a certain age. The average age of the show's correspondents then was sixty-four (factoring in curmudgeon Andy Rooney, then seventy-eight).

By spring of 2006, Wallace decided to scale back, conceding that those toes were "beginning to curl a trifle." Yet a few months later, he was back on the air, interviewing Iranian president Mahmoud Ahmadinejad. The piece won him his twenty-first and final Emmy, at age eighty-nine.

What kept him going for so long? Wallace unapologetically loved his work more than anything else. He called interviewing newsmakers his "bliss." And he loved being on TV. As a former colleague of his put it to me, "Mike was never more alive than when he was watching himself on television."

Turning Loss into Gain

Henri Matisse,

Jorge Luis Borges

& Sam & Betsey Farber

Let's be candid. As we get older, what our bodies can do generally becomes more limited. (That's why you *must* keep stretching. If you can, you should be sitting on the floor, leaning forward in a straddle, as you read this.) But here's the good news: over time, our creative, emotional, and spiritual capacities—even our mental capacities—can blossom.

Yes, while muscles may give way, the imagination never atrophies. Here are three stories of remarkable individuals who, when faced with withering loss, flowered in entirely new ways.

Henri Matisse:
Trading a Paintbrush for Scissors
reinvented himself in his seventies

When World War II had ended and France had been liberated from German occupation, Pablo Picasso paid a visit to his old friend Henri Matisse, who was then living in Vence, an ancient Roman village in the hills above Nice on the Riviera. The two great artists had first met forty years earlier, in the Paris salon of the American writer Gertrude Stein. Over the first four decades of the century, their friendship had flourished, deepened by a strong but respectful feeling of rivalry; their lifelong relationship, which Matisse once described as a boxing match, motivated both of them to push back the frontiers of visual art further and further. (Think of the Beatles and the Beach Boys in the sixties, buying each other's albums, listening obsessively, then trying to surpass them in the studio.) Together these two giants of modern painting revolutionized the world of the visual arts, transforming the very idea of what an artwork could be.

However, as Picasso approached the residence of his old friend, he and his girlfriend Françoise Gilot, a painter, were more apprehensive than joyous. In early 1941, at the age of seventy-one, Matisse had been diagnosed with cancer of the intestine and had undergone a long, painful, and risky surgery to remove a tumor. When a postoperative infection set in, a second surgery followed. The surgeries saved the great painter's life but permanently damaged his abdominal wall, confining him to his wheelchair and his bed and subjecting him to excruciating pain, even when he slept. Digestive problems limited him to a diet of "pap and vegetable broth" for long stretches. He could not stand for any length of time at his easel, and moving easily about his studio was unthinkable. Age and illness had deprived one of the century's greatest painters of the ability to paint.

Yet what Picasso and Gilot discovered on their arrival in Vence stunned them. They found Matisse sitting upright in his bed, wielding an enormous pair of tailor's scissors with his right hand while manipulating a large sheet of colored paper with his left. Before their eyes, the paper was being transformed into a gorgeous series of opulent curves. Gilot later recalled the scene: "Delicately holding the piece that suited his purpose in his left hand, he wound it and turned it while his right hand skillfully cut the most unpredictable shapes. Women, vegetation, birds, dancers, bathers, starfish, abstractions—a complete world emerged from his hands, full of strength and vitality."

Far from surrendering to age and incapacity, Matisse had embarked upon a highly unlikely and completely marvelous final phase of his career, making what art critics and historians would come to know as his famous cut-outs. He had, for the most part, given up painting, trading his brushes and paints for scissors and paper. From the limitations imposed by his declining physical abilities, he had unlocked not merely a new method of making art but a new wellspring of creativity. It was almost as though he had been reborn. He had turned his loss into gain.

During these final years of his life—and the surgeries gave him another thirteen years of life—Matisse, working mainly in this new mode he called "painting with scissors," would produce some of his best-known works. These include *Icarus*, a stark, faceless black figure in free fall against a blue sky dotted with explosive bursts of yellow starlight; the *Blue Nudes*, a series of abstract blue-on-white female forms that achieve a remarkable sense of depth and motion; and *The Swimming Pool*, an immense composition that wrapped around his dining room—and has now been preserved at New York's Museum of Modern Art (MoMA)—depicting swimmers and divers along with splashing waves and a whimsical proliferation of marine life. (The story goes that Matisse had gone one day to his favorite pool in the south of France, but it was insufferably hot. He went home and declared, "I'm going to make my own pool." That's one way to do it!)

The cut-out method represented not just an accommodation to illness but a creative breakthrough. For the artist Annelies Nelck, who often sat as a model for Matisse in these late years, it appeared to offer a freer, more spontaneous relationship between the artist and his materials than painting or sculpture had. She described its virtues this way: "There is nothing to resist the passage of the scissors, nothing to demand the concentrated attention of painting or drawing, there are no juxtapositions or borders to be borne in mind. And the little creatures extracted from their element fall from the scissors in quivering spirals, and subside like those fragile organisms the sea leaves washed up on the sand."

While confined to his chair and his bed, Matisse continued to amaze his friends. On a later visit, Picasso and Gilot brought with them a magician to entertain the great artist, a typically grand gesture for the showman Picasso. Matisse responded to the magician's performance with a magical display of his own, nimbly cutting colored scraps that proved, when guided into their proper places, to be portraits of Picasso, Gilot, and the magician himself. "We were spellbound, in a state of suspended breathing," Gilot later told a biographer. "We sat there like stones, slowly emerging from a trance."

Now if you need a refresher course, Matisse is generally regarded as one of the greatest painters of European modernism. Together he and Picasso are credited with advancing the discoveries and innovations of the Impressionists and leading the great revolution in artistic style, technique, and taste that took place during the first decades of the twentieth century. Whether you walk into MoMA or your

local coffeehouse, you will see their influence everywhere. Not since the Renaissance had there been such a dramatic change in painting, sculpture, and all the visual arts.

Matisse was born on December 31, 1869, to a well-off family from northern France. As a young man, he seemed destined for a career as a lawyer. Curiously, it was a different medical crisis, a bout of appendicitis, that set him on his life's course as an artist. He was working as a law clerk in the city of Saint-Quentin when the illness and subsequent convalescence forced him to take time away from the office. His mother, with no other aim than helping her son find a hobby to fill his time, bought him paints and brushes, and so the young Matisse took up painting. But the hobby became a passion, and the passion a career. The late nineteenth century was, of course, an exciting time to be a painter in France, as artists like Cézanne, Monet, and Van Gogh were undertaking radical experiments in form and color, paint and light. Matisse rose to prominence quickly in this milieu and before long was a known figure in the Paris art world.

Around 1900 came Matisse's famous turn to fauvism—*fauve* is French for "beast," and the term, coined by a critic of the time, refers to the apparent wildness of Matisse's early style. (When his fauvist works came to Chicago in 1913, the art students there, apparently traditional in their tastes, held a mock trial and burned replicas of his work in protest.) One of many movements within the larger trend of modernism, fauvism emphasized the radical use of color. For Matisse and others of this school, color no longer needed to indicate a literal, realistic fidelity to nature. "When I put down a green, it doesn't mean grass; and when I put down a blue, it doesn't mean the sky," Matisse once remarked. And although the fauvist moment eventually passed, and Matisse settled into a comfortable position as one of the

opposite page:
Eighty-two-year-old Henri Matisse
at work on his cut-outs in 1952.
AFP via Getty Images

leading figures of modern art, he remained obsessed with the possibilities of color for the rest of his career.

Throughout the twenties and thirties he continued working in painting, drawing, and sculpture, even designing sets and costumes for the Ballets Russes, the French dance company founded by the Russian impresario Sergei Diaghilev. As he entered his sixties, however, it seemed (to some critics at least) that he was beginning to rest on his laurels. His biographer Hilary Spurling writes that the naysayers believed that the master was now content "turning out sexy pictures for rich men's Manhattan apartments and villas in the south of France." But Matisse's artistic temperament never let him stagnate creatively, and Pierre Matisse credited *The Pink Nude* of 1935 with revitalizing his father as a painter.

Then came a series of crises that would change everything.

In the early 1930s Matisse had hired a twenty-year-old Russian émigré, Lydia Delectorskaya, to help him in his studio. When Matisse's wife, Amélie, fell ill, Lydia became her caretaker and nurse. Soon Lydia was also modeling for Matisse—she is the subject of *The Pink Nude*. But even though both painter and model insisted all their lives that their relationship was platonic, Mme Matisse became jealous of the beautiful young Lydia. In 1939, after forty-one years of marriage, Amélie filed for divorce. This was also, of course, the eve of World War II. The next spring, Germany invaded France; in June, Paris fell. The occupation further separated Henri from Amélie and their children: she was in the suburbs of Paris, while he was at his studio in Nice, living under the Vichy regime. Then, at this dark and troubled moment, Matisse was diagnosed with cancer.

It was the cancer and subsequent surgeries that spurred Matisse to turn to his new technique of cutting paper, or decoupage. The method was not completely new to him. In the early 1930s, the American collector Albert C. Barnes commissioned him to paint a mural on an interior wall of his foundation in Lower Merion, Pennsylvania, outside Philadelphia. Matisse, who was then over sixty, resorted to cut-outs as a substitute for drawing in order to spare himself the physical effort of sketching out the huge figures he would eventually paint. At this point, decoupage was still just a labor-saving technical innovation, but the artist was already beginning to see that the method had aesthetic virtues all its own, and he would continue to use it occasionally throughout the thirties. But it was not until he could no longer paint that colored paper became his primary medium and oversized scissors his primary instrument.

Even this new technique required the aid of assistants, who painted the sheets of paper with which Matisse worked, then pinned, arranged, and rearranged the fragments that he had created, following his precise and demanding instructions. The pinholes visible in many of the cut-outs attest to the perfectionism of the artist, his restless search for the ideal arrangement of the shapes he had created. Indeed, the longtime *New York Times* art critic Holland Cotter sees "the pin holes, cut marks, layerings, tearings, and revisions" as signs not only of the exuberance that the art conveys but, underneath it, an artistic rigor. As he writes, "Matisse's softness comes out of toughness."

What was it about these late-career paper cut-outs that made them special? Critics tend to agree on certain qualities that make them so innovative and striking. Richard Lacayo of *Time* talks about their "beguiling lyricism" and "radical flatness." Biographer Hilary Spurling sees in the rapidity and spontaneity of their creation "a new world of decorations whose patterns corresponded to the inner movements of his mind." Holland Cotter comments on their "exceptionally direct appeal: color, line, beauty without reservation."

To put it a little more plainly, after the ordeal of his illness, Matisse returned in his late years to an almost childlike fascination with the basics of colors and shapes, and rediscovered a delight in the organic forms of nature—plants, animals, water—and of the human body. Illness seemed to have stripped away a complication, reducing his art to essential concerns.

Matisse insisted that these years were for him a kind of gift. To the painter Albert Marquet he wrote, "My terrible operation has completely rejuvenated and made a philosopher of me. I had so completely prepared for my exit from life, that it seems to me that I am in a second life." And so the cut-outs also constitute a summation of his career, and in them he freely references his earlier paintings, including his famous *Blue Nude* of 1907, which informed the series of *Blue Nude* collages and lithographs that he completed in the 1950s. "What I did before this illness, before this operation," he said, "always has the feeling of too much effort; before this, I always lived with my belt tightened. What I created afterwards represents me myself: free and detached."

The cut-outs became an essential part of Matisse's final, crowning achievement as an artist. During the recovery from his surgeries, Matisse had been cared for by a night nurse and aspiring artist named Monique Bourgeois. She later joined a Dominican order of nuns in Vence who ran a nursing home. By 1947 the nuns needed a chapel, and Monique, now Sister Jacques Marie, began the process of enlisting her former patient Matisse in the chapel's design. Soon Matisse, motivated in part by gratitude for the woman who helped restore him to health, in part by his own unrelenting ambition, began creating maquettes, or models, for stained glass windows. Naturally, he used colored paper.

It was an unlikely pairing. Matisse had never been a religious man, and he had a reputation for painting sensuous nudes. Most of the nuns, and the church in general, viewed his work with skepticism. But a twenty-seven-year-old monk named Louis-Bertrand Rayssiguier championed the great artist, and the project went forward.

In committing himself to create the windows, Matisse became interested in the chapel as a whole. He went on to design black-and-white wall murals and even the brightly colored chasubles and vestments that the priests would wear. He took a keen interest not only in the artworks per se but in the entire built environment. Wheeling himself around his studio in what he referred to as his "taxi-bed," Matisse pushed himself physically as well as creatively. By April 1950, he was choosing the glass samples for the chapel windows.

By the time the Chapelle du Rosaire, or Rosary Chapel, was inaugurated, it was June of 1951.

By this point the nuns who had been wary of the modern design of their chapel had been won over by its serene beauty, what Spurling calls "its consoling and contemplative calm." Sadly, Matisse, eighty-one, who had added heart and eye ailments to his existing struggles, could not attend the ceremony. Pierre, his son, represented him. But Matisse sent a short statement that attests not only to his devotion to the work of designing the chapel but to the entire unlikely proliferation of art that his final years produced: "This work has taken me four years of exclusive and diligent work, and it is the result of my entire working life. Despite all its imperfections I consider it to be my masterpiece."

Jorge Luis Borges: Vision without Sight

*turned from fiction to poetry when
faced with blindness in his sixties*

An obscure scholarly reference to a strange central Asian country leads a man to discover a vast fictional universe outlined in a secret encyclopedia; this invented world then ominously begins to supplant reality. Another man lies awake all night consumed by his own recollections, cursed with a perfect photographic memory that compels him to recall every detail of every day of his life, from the shapes of the clouds on a particular morning to the ripples made in a river by a raised oar on a long-ago evening. A third man, a minor and undistinguished poet, dedicates his life to an impossible project: writing a book that is identical, word for word, to Cervantes's masterpiece, *Don Quixote*.

These are some of the premises of the enchanting, perplexing, experimental works of short fiction written by the great Argentine writer Jorge Luis Borges, works that are so different from those of previous writers that he did not even call them "short stories" but rather *ficciones*—in English, simply "fictions." Dispensing with the stable formulas of plot and character central to the realistic short story, Borges's fictions sit at the crossroads of fable and philosophy, reworking popular genres like detective stories, science fiction, and folktales while exploring mind-bending intellectual puzzles and paradoxes. His playful intellect and willingness to break the rules made him probably the most important Spanish-language writer of the twentieth century, and an essential influence on the next generation of Spanish-language writers—those authors from across Mexico, the Caribbean, Central America, and South America whose ornate storytelling, magical realism, and lush, colorful post-modernism became known in the 1960s as the "Latin American boom."

But Borges, not unlike Henri Matisse, faced a truly existential challenge as he aged. Cancer and surgery took away Matisse's ability to paint; for Borges, it was blindness that threatened to extinguish his ability to write. For the great author, the loss of his vision was a particularly painful deprivation, since he drew his ideas and inspiration from books as much as from reality. Books, in fact, *were* his reality. "To me, reading has been a way of living," he admitted. "I think the only possible fate for me was a literary life. I can't think of myself in a bookless world. I need books. They mean everything to me." Literature was his lifeblood, his oxygen.

He was born Jorge Francisco Isidoro Luis Borges Acevedo in 1899 in Buenos Aires into a highly literate middle-class family. His father was a lawyer and psychology professor who studied the philosophy of William James (known as the father of American psychology); his father's mother was a Protestant Englishwoman with a scholarly interest in the Hebrew Bible. The Borges home was full of books, in both English and Spanish, and Jorge, or "Georgie," grew up bilingual, with an eclectic canon of influences ranging from Edgar Allan Poe and Arthur Conan Doyle to idealist philosophers like George Berkeley and Arthur Schopenhauer. The family spent Georgie's teenage years in Switzerland, and as a young man Borges lived in Spain for a stretch before returning to Argentina. His unique education and travel led him to draw creative inspiration from international sources and traditions: *Don*

Quixote, The Arabian Nights, Jewish mysticism, Icelandic sagas, Indian philosophy, Greek myth. The themes that emerged from this heterogeneous curriculum are high-end catnip for philosophy majors: infinity, mirrors, mysteries, labyrinths, libraries, dreams, memory. The mingling of fantasy and realism, the travel between alternate universes, the pleasure taken in what Borges called "useless and out-of-the-way erudition"—all of it opened up exciting possibilities for later writers in the Spanish-speaking world and beyond.

Even as a young man, Borges suffered eye problems as a result of a hereditary condition. His father had lost his sight before him, and his great-grandfather's eye surgeries had been documented in the pages of the British medical journal *The Lancet*. Borges described his own loss of vision as "a slow, summer twilight" with "nothing particularly pathetic or dramatic about it." But in his late fifties, the vision problems progressed to the point where he could effectively no longer read and write on his own.

Yet this was a man for whom reading and writing were everything. Even his day job immersed him in books; in 1955 he had been named director of the National Public Library in Buenos Aires. In his mind, he simply had no choice but to continue to write. As he told an audience at Dickinson College in the 1980s, "I keep on writing. What else can I do? You see, I am blind, I am old, I can't read—what else can I do but dream and write? Or dictate, rather, since I can't write by myself. My letters overlap."

In the face of this devastating loss, Borges maintained a fierce optimism. He even went so far as to call his loss of vision "a gift." "Blindness has not been for me a total misfortune," he said in a lecture, stressing that he did not want to be viewed "in a pathetic way." Blindness, he said, "should be seen as a way of life: one of the styles of living."

As Matisse, crippled by illness, gained a new way of making art, so Borges, grappling with blindness, developed a new way of creating literature. Specifically, he turned his attention from writing prose to writing poetry, a genre he had worked in as a young man but had abandoned in the 1930s as his *ficciones* established his literary reputation. As he put it, "Blindness made me take up the writing of poetry again." What's more, Borges's youthful poetry had been sprawling free verse written in the manner of Walt Whitman. But with the loss of his sight in his late fifties he turned instead to traditional poetic forms, like the sonnet, that make use of rhyme and meter.

The reason for this is straightforward. Poems that possess a consistent rhythm and regular rhyme scheme are much easier to remember than paragraphs of flowing prose. "Regular verse is, so to speak, portable," Borges said. "One can walk down the street or be riding the subway while composing and polishing a sonnet." In fact, what Borges says about another writer who struggled with failing vision, James Joyce, applies equally to himself: "Part of his vast work was executed in darkness: polishing the sentences in his memory, working at times for a whole day on a single phrase."

Because he worked on it in this way—measuring every line, every syllable—Borges's later poetry has a formal, classical rigor, and shares qualities with the Victorian English verse he had devoured in his father's library as a boy. In the words of his editor and translator Stephen Kessler, in the sonnets written after 1960, "Borges distills all the obsessive themes that pervade his other writings—the mirror, the labyrinth, the garden, the dream, the soldier, the hoodlum, history, oblivion, memory, ancestors, time, eternity, literary and philosophical forbears—into the gemlike form of fourteen tightly rhymed lines." At the same time, the vulnerability of the aging genius losing his sight adds an element of pathos, making the poetry "far more intimate and personal" than the prose he had written before.

Among the themes of this poetry was blindness itself. As the hyperliterate Borges well knew, the figure of the blind poet is a famous trope, going all the way back to Homer, who was reputed to be blind. As Borges writes, there is an ancient "friendship between poetry and blindness." In myth and legend, the loss of outer vision brings an accompanying growth of inner vision, so that the old, blind poet becomes a bard or a sage, blessed with a special wisdom and insight, what the great (and blind) English poet John Milton called "things invisible to mortal sight." For Borges, like many of the mystics and idealists whose writings fascinated him, the outer world was always simply a world of appearances, a veil covering deeper truths. In characteristically learned fashion, he invoked the example of the ancient Greek philosopher Democritus, who "tore his eyes out so that the spectacle of reality would not distract him."

Borges came to revere Milton as an example of "a man who overcomes blindness and does his work." Milton went blind in his forties and was forced to dictate his poetry—first to his friend Andrew Marvell, later to his daughters. In one of his most famous sonnets, "When I Consider How My Light Is Spent," Milton meditates on losing his vision in midlife, afraid that he will be unable to use his talent to serve God. In another sonnet, "Methought I Saw My Late Espoused Saint," he also discusses his blindness. (By "espoused saint," by the way, Milton means *his wife*. A pro tip for all you non-poets: that's a very flattering term to pull out of the top drawer for Valentine's Day.) In the poem, he recounts a dream in which his wife, who had recently died in childbirth, returned to him. But on waking, Milton realizes, painfully, that his vision was an illusion; wakefulness in fact reminds him that he can no longer see: "I waked, she fled, and day brought back my night."

One of Borges's most moving ruminations is found in a five-paragraph prose piece, "The Maker," written when blindness was just beginning to set in. Here he imagines the experience of Homer struggling to come to grips with his loss of the visible world. At first, Borges's Homer feels an overwhelming sense of diminishment:

Little by little, the beautiful world began to leave him; a persistent mist erased the lines of his hand, the night lost its multitude of stars, the ground beneath his step became uncertain. Everything grew distant and blurred. When he knew he was going blind, he cried out. . . . I shall no longer look upon the sky and its mythological dread, he felt, nor this face which the years will transform.

Suddenly something changes. One morning, Homer wakes up and experiences—"as one recognizes a tune or a voice"—an almost mystical insight: "that all this had already happened to him and that he had faced it with fear but also with joy, hope, and curiosity." Embracing his future, he hears what Borges calls a rumor, "a rumor of the *Odysseys* and the *Iliads* it was his destiny to sing and to leave resounding forever in mankind's hollow memory." It's a realization—a vision—of his future as a poet. This is what spurs him to joy, hope, and curiosity.

But can such feelings really arise from such a terrible deprivation as losing your sense of sight? In March 2023 another accomplished poet, Edward Hirsch, wrote about his own blindness. Like Borges, Hirsch talks about the importance of accepting his loss—being able to ask for help and accept it, to take up the hard work of adapting to a changed body, to find reward and even pleasure in overcoming new challenges. "My sister says there is nothing fun about going blind," Hirsch writes, "but I found the challenge exhilarating." It means, too, rethinking your role in life; for Hirsch, leaning on the arm of a hotel doorman makes him feel "like an aging prince."

Ultimately, Hirsch discovers in himself some of the same feelings that Borges imagined in Homer: joy, hope, and curiosity.

I once felt that I would rather die than go blind. Now I feel the opposite. Daily life has a renewed delight and vigor. I am learning new things constantly. The most ordinary tasks, like going to the post office, have become terrifically interesting. In terms of everyday life, I feel that I am finally in there, more mindful and alert, more fully present. I have chosen curiosity over despair.

I asked my friend Frank Bruni, a contributing Opinion columnist at the *New York Times* and a professor at Duke, what lessons he drew from the story of Borges. In October 2017 Frank awoke with the vision in his right eye gone. He had suffered a rare stroke that irreparably damaged one of his optic nerves. More ominously, there was a more than slim chance the same thing would happen to his other eye.

He wrote about the ensuing drama in his moving book *The Beauty of Dusk: On Vision Lost and Found*. Here's what he wrote me:

> Part of what I think Borges both appreciated and modeled—and what so many people with disabilities or with challenges along the lines of disabilities appreciate and model—is how nimble and elastic and adaptable we humans are, how a loss of function or even opportunities in one area can lead to a discovery of function and different opportunities in other areas if you have the right perspective, the right spirit, the right ingenuity. That's usually a big part of what's happening when people hit unexpected strides, flex unknown talents and rack up surprising accomplishments late in life. Once I adjusted to blindness in my right eye, to monocular vision and to some of the dislocations and impediments of that, I weirdly didn't feel diminished—in some ways, I felt fortified. I gained the reassurance that I could solve problems and forge alternate routes when I needed to. I don't read as quickly as I used to, but for the first time, I can listen to and focus on audiobooks, even at 1.6 or 1.8-times speed, and follow the narrative and retain the information as never before. And that sort of adaptability seemed to suffuse my life. I've an easier time being disappointed or annoyed by someone in my life—I shift focus to what I love about the person. I'm more accepting not only of their shortcomings but of my own and don't torture myself the way I used to. That's aging accelerated by hardship, and there's enormous gain in it.

Ultimately, the lesson that Borges drew from his blindness extended beyond the loss of vision to all the losses that we experience as we age: "When something ends, we must think that something begins."

———

In 2022, I profiled entertainment dynamo Sandy Duncan for *CBS Sunday Morning*. Back in 1972, when she was twenty-six, she lost sight in her left eye after an operation to remove a tumor from her brain. (Contrary to popular belief, Sandy does not have a glass eye.) The loss of sight in one eye meant the loss of depth perception; to this day she has to focus when she reaches for a glass of water. And yet it was *after* she'd lost her sight in one eye that she scored her greatest theatrical triumph, flying through the air as Peter Pan. "I'd fly into the wings and push off the light poles," she told me. "I mean, I was that daredevil. And loved it so much." You'd think it would be at least nerve-racking flying toward a wall when you don't know exactly where it is. But Sandy described the experience as the most joyful in her long career. "She just lets go of gravity, gracefully and gleefully," *New York Times* theater critic Walter Kerr wrote at the time, "and lets the mechanical equipment catch up as best it can."

Sam and Betsey Farber: A Gripping Story

revolutionized kitchen utensils in their retirement

They may not have revolutionized modern painting or transformed the nature of the short story, but Sam and Betsey Farber left a legacy that is, in its own way, just as enduring as a Matisse cut-out or a Borges sonnet. The Farbers were a kitchenware executive and an architect—well-respected in their fields, to be sure, but hardly figures of international acclaim. Yet when faced with a physical challenge later in life, they applied their creative talents in a surprising new direction. The result was a small, humble innovation that nonetheless opened new possibilities in the manufacture of everyday household products. The OXO Good Grips Swivel Peeler, which the Farbers launched in 1990, not only improved the lives of pie-baking grandmas and taken-for-granted sous-chefs everywhere but ushered in a new way of thinking about the entire field of industrial design.

In 1988, Sam and Betsey were recently married; it was a second marriage for both of them. He was sixty-three; she was in her early fifties. Successful professionals, they had their dream retirement all mapped out. The plan was to rent a house in the South of France, where they could spend time relaxing, cooking, and entertaining friends. It would be a storybook ending to two very full lives.

Sam had spent his life manufacturing kitchen products. His father, Louis, a Russian Jewish immigrant, had started Farber Brothers, known for making glassware and barware, in 1915. (Louis's brother Simon had founded Farberware, which made pots, pans, and other cookware—and still does.) Sam, after serving in World War II and earning a BA from Harvard, went to work for his father for a decade and a half. Then, in 1960, he struck out on his own and founded Copco, which specialized in cast-iron enamel-coated pots and pans. Twenty-two years later, when Sam cashed out and sold the company, he was looking forward to enjoying the fruits of his labors. In 1985, he married Betsey Wells Kriegsman, an architect with the celebrated firm of Skidmore, Owings & Merrill; together they planned their extended sojourn in Provence.

But there was another chapter to their story yet to be written. The legend goes that the happy couple had been living in France only a short time when Betsey, an amateur *pâtissière*, decided to make an apple tart. (And trust me, if you're a foodie, as Betsey was, and you're living in a country villa in the South of France, it's pretty much obligatory for you to attempt an apple tart.) She was peeling apples with an old peeler she'd found in the kitchen drawer. But her incipient arthritis was making the job painful. The old, flimsy peeler was inadequate and put too much strain on her joints. (Another version of this story has Betsey doing some gardening with a household scissors she'd found in the rental; they too had an inadequate grip that caused hand pain.)

Betsey reasoned that there had to be a better way. A problem like this should be right in her husband's wheelhouse. After all, hadn't he spent a career overseeing the design and manufacture of kitchen products? Together the Farbers took up the challenge of building a better peeler, with Betsey pulling out modeling clay to begin to experiment. What they recognized, right from the start, was that the problem was not in fact Betsey's arthritis but rather the design of the peeler. A simple utensil like a vegetable peeler should be easy to use for someone with mild arthritis. However, as Sam recalled, "Kitchen tools had always been terrible, and that's because manufacturers hadn't paid any attention to them. . . . In my twenty years in housewares, no one had done anything about gadgets."

The design problem extended well beyond peelers. "We decided we wanted to do something about the bad design throughout kitchen utensils," Sam later told an interviewer. "Why couldn't there be comfortable tools that are easy to use, not just for arthritis victims but for everybody?"

That night, Sam and Betsey hit the pause button on retirement and got back into the design business.

Sam called his old friend Davin Stowell back in the U.S. Stowell was president of Smart Design, a design consultancy. He had grown up outside of Corning, New York, and cut his teeth designing products for CorningWare. He'd established a reputation as an innovative and forward-looking thinker. He recalls that first conversation he had with Sam in 1988: "One night I'm in my office, it's 7:30 p.m., and I get a call from Sam. He's in France, where it's 1:30 in the morning, and he's incredibly excited." Farber was already envisioning a full line of kitchen tools, made for the comfort of aging chefs, or simply anyone who wanted their kitchen prep work to be a little less arduous. But Sam needed someone with Stowell's design expertise to help him realize this vision. The two men worked out the business arrangements and Stowell got to work.

Stowell did his homework. He consulted with the American Arthritis Foundation to find test subjects. He also brought in designer Patricia Moore, who had built a career understanding the needs of senior citizens. In her twenties, she had disguised herself as an old woman, latex mask and all, and traveled through North America obtaining a better understanding of the world through the eyes of the elderly. She later published a book about her experiences. John Farber, Sam's son and a lawyer by trade, was also part of the team.

Turning Loss into Gain

The key element of the new peeler was the handle. The designers and engineers at Smart Design experimented with foam prototypes, which they evaluated by asking their test subjects to try out various twists, turns, and squeezes. These test subjects included people of different ages, abilities, strengths, and hand sizes. After testing hundreds of variations, the designers concluded that the new handle would need to be fatter and wider than the usual products sold in the supermarket.

But before they could start manufacturing, they needed to find the right material. They settled on a substance called Santoprene. In the world of industrial chemistry, Santoprene is known as a thermoplastic elastomer. Think of it as the manufacturer's equivalent of Donny and Marie Osmond—but instead of a little bit country, a little bit rock 'n' roll . . . it's a little bit rubber, a little bit plastic. Now if you're not a chemistry nerd, feel free to jump ahead to the next paragraph, but if you don't mind a few multisyllabic jawbreakers, then bear with me. Santoprene worked largely because it has the look and texture that designers like about rubber. It's easy and comfortable to grip. Yet for manufacturing purposes, it also has some of the advantages of plastic. If you *really* want to get into the weeds, visit the website of the United States Plastics Corporation, which describes Santoprene as "fully dynamically vulcanized ethylene propylene diene monomer rubber in a thermoplastic matrix of polypropylene." In other words, the rubber is basically broken into particles and then encased in a plastic. Aren't you glad you asked?

According to the OXO people, the decision to use Santoprene was a minor breakthrough, since at the time thermoplastic elastomers were used mainly in the automobile world, or for things like gaskets and dishwasher seals. But it turned out to be a great choice for kitchen gadgets. It's soft and easy to grip; it doesn't get slippery when it gets wet; it can stand up to the stress of repeated runs through a hot dishwasher. And as for those signature rubber "fins" on the handle—those thin flaps that you're tempted to run your thumb along? They were put there mainly for cosmetic reasons, to entice consumers to pick up the tool. Sam got the idea from looking at the rubber grips on a bicycle handlebar.

Once the design was in place, the Farbers and Stowell still had to find a manufacturer. The clock was ticking: they planned to debut not only the now-famous peeler but fourteen other Santoprene-handled gizmos and gadgets at the 1990 Gourmet Products Show in San Francisco, a major kitchenware expo. But the thin fins, so appealing for aesthetic reasons, proved a challenge in manufacturing, and many companies turned down the Farbers. Finally they hit upon a Japanese company, Mitsuboshi Cutlery, a knife manufacturer founded in 1873. Its history included the manufacture of samurai swords. The company produced the OXO implements in time for the expo.

Stowell recalls that week in San Francisco. (Significantly, this was the same year Congress passed the Americans with Disabilities Act, which required that new buildings and environments be constructed to accommodate the needs and abilities of everyone.) Initially, interest was slow, since a high-end, high-priced peeler seemed to most buyers about as necessary as a gold-plated lawn mower. But Lechters, a national retail chain, took a chance. Sam Farber suggested a display of a bowl of carrots that would invite consumers to try out the peeler for themselves. The gimmick worked, and the peelers started to sell.

Within two years, the company was thriving, the product line was expanding, and it was time for Sam Farber to cash out again. The Farbers sold their new company to General Housewares Corporation for over $6 million. It continued to flourish, developing products for barbecuing, baking, gardening, and more. OXO is now a household name.

But for all of its financial success, the real story of the OXO Good Grips line wasn't just its popularity as a catalog of consumer products. It was the principle of what is now called universal or inclusive design. The idea behind universal design is that a product should serve as many potential users as possible. Patricia Moore— the designer/gerontologist who worked with Smart Design on creating the line— points out that before OXO, a gadget or household product made for someone with a condition like arthritis would be a high-priced specialty item. It would be produced in small numbers and available only through a medical catalog or a small niche supplier. It might also carry a stigma for the user, for whom it would be seen as a special accommodation. And the limited appeal of the product would limit the supply, raise the price, and prevent it from going mainstream.

What the Farbers realized is that a product designed for the needs of older consumers could still have broad mainstream appeal. They understood the value of a single product designed for all possible users, visually attractive, highly functional.

"People with disabilities are often incredible problem solvers—they notice or suffer the shortcomings of a product or environment, then adapt it to fit their specific needs," Katherine White, curator of design at The Henry Ford Museum of American Innovation in Dearborn, Michigan, told me. "Betsey Farber did just this—she struggled with deficient kitchen tools that exacerbated her arthritis and conceptualized a solution. But she and her husband Sam took it a few steps further: in moving beyond an individualized workaround, they created a line of products that addressed the needs of many."

In 1999, the Good Grips Swivel Peeler won the "Design of the Decade" award given jointly by *Business Week* and the Industrial Designers Society of America. Kristina Goodrich, who served as executive director of IDSA for seven years, framed the Farbers' accomplishment this way: "They have taken [the] spirit of concern for the consumer and universal access and applied it in one category after another. They have made a measurable improvement in the quality of little everyday things for everyone."

OXO products have garnered over one hundred design awards, and in 1994, the Farbers' Good Grips Swivel Peeler was given a permanent place in the collection of the Museum of Modern Art, where it keeps company with *The Swimming Pool*, Henri Matisse's great cut-out installation.

———

Of all the people who deserve an OXO Good Grips Swivel Peeler, it's hard to think of anyone more worthy than Beetle Bailey. Since September 4, 1950, the poor private has been peeling potatoes with a knife. (By 1989 he had already peeled over fifty thousand, according to someone with way too much time on his hands.) Dangerous work, since Beetle Bailey's eyes are always covered by his helmet. Here's hoping a compassionate cartoonist will take note and give the guy a better implement.

OLD ENGLISH: Judi Dench

Tell the truth: When did you first become aware of Judi Dench? Was it in 1995, when she played James Bond's boss M in *GoldenEye*? Or 1999, when she won an Oscar for eight minutes of playing Queen Elizabeth I in *Shakespeare in Love*?

Judi Dench may have been a revelation to American audiences in the 1990s, a sixtysomething who suddenly burst onto the scene. In reality, she had been dazzling British fans for decades. Her career in the theater goes back to 1957, when she played Ophelia at the Old Vic. Dench went on to play almost every female Shakespeare lead. She also played Sally Bowles in the original London production of *Cabaret*. In 1981, she was supposed to star in the original London company of *Cats*, but she snapped her Achilles tendon one week before the start of previews. (She played Old Deuteronomy in the much-maligned 2019 film adaptation.)

In 1988, Queen Elizabeth II made Dench a Dame Commander of the Order of the British Empire. Her career finally crossed the pond in a big way with those aforementioned films in the 1990s and suddenly she was everywhere, making movie after movie, piling up Oscar nominations. Her status as a national treasure in the UK was made complete when she topped the queen as Britain's most liked and respected person in a 2002 poll, but she's a global treasure, too.

Dench, who will turn ninety in 2024, has called "retirement" the rudest word in her dictionary. Even while dealing with age-related macular degeneration, which causes deteriorating eyesight, Dench has explained her path forward: "I've got to teach myself a new way of learning." Consider her a spiritual cousin to Jorge Luis Borges.

On the subject of poetry, if you'd like every hair on your body to stand on end, watch the video of Judi Dench spontaneously reciting Shakespeare's Sonnet 29 ("When, in disgrace with fortune and men's eyes . . .") for the marvelous Graham Norton on his talk show in 2023. It's yet another reminder of how spectacular this Dame is.

Ageless Architects

Frank Lloyd Wright,

I. M. Pei

& Yasmeen Lari

Google the phrase "20 under 20" and you'll find lists of promising young storytellers, Arab Americans, environmental activists, and tech entrepreneurs. Search "30 under 30" and up pop names of soon-to-be-famous realtors, news media professionals, and tech entrepreneurs. And swap in "40 under 40" and your magic little handheld device spits back rosters of up-and-coming advertisers, novelists, and tech entrepreneurs. (Whatever the age of the tech entrepreneur, they're sure to be wearing a hoodie.) The world today, it seems, is just bursting with rising stars, wunderkinds, budding phenoms, exciting new voices, and young talents poised to dominate the next decade.

Ours is a society that celebrates youth. As much as we call attention to the achievements of those who have done amazing and inspiring and ennobling things in their later decades, many careers simply favor the young. There just aren't many K-pop bands, TikTok influencers, or Olympic gymnasts who finally find their niche in their late seventies.

But there are exceptions. In certain lines of work, age and experience are helpful, even essential. Take wizards. I'm talking about the wizards you read about in fantasy novels, the kind with long beards who walk with staffs and wear cloaks, like Dumbledore or Gandalf. Now that's a job where seniority really means something. You're not going to find Gandalf scrubbing his graduation date from his CV, or Dumbledore sneaking off to the salon to dye his graying hair. No one ever caught Merlin ducking into the local clinic for a little Botox. Or what about the pope? You don't read many stories about that dashing young pope with a million-dollar smile, or some up-and-coming teen pope shaking things up in the Vatican. These are jobs that require the gravitas that comes with age.

The same goes for architects. Architects are more like wizards than Olympic gymnasts. Almost every great architect in history kept going in life, getting better with each passing year. Leonardo da Vinci (1452–1519) lived until sixty-seven, which might not sound super old today but was pretty advanced for the fifteenth century, when the leading causes of death included warfare, famine, plague, and sweating sickness. The great English architect Christopher Wren (1632–1723), who designed St. Paul's Cathedral and the Greenwich Royal Observatory, lived to age ninety. When he was in his sixties he designed the exquisite Wren Library at Trinity College, Cambridge, and redesigned Kensington Palace and Hampton Court.

Both were mere children compared to Mimar Sinan (1488–1588), the master architect of the Ottoman Empire, who lived to almost one hundred and served three sixteenth-century sultans, beginning with Suleiman the Magnificent. (Sidebar: How great would it be to go through life with a title like that, like the Russian empress Catherine the Great or the 2008 election breakout star Joe the Plumber?) Sinan designed over three hundred buildings; his masterwork, completed when he was eighty-six, was the Selimiye Mosque in Edirne, in western Turkey (near the present-day border of Greece and Bulgaria), whose magnificent dome rivals the Hagia Sophia in size. Three years after that, on the cusp of his tenth decade, he designed the Mehmed Pasha Sokolovic Bridge spanning the Drina River in Bosnia-Herzegovina. Having survived bombings in two world wars, the bridge is now a UNESCO World Heritage site.

The longevity—and extended productivity—of architects isn't just a phenomenon of the Renaissance era. It's even more noticeable today than it was five hundred years ago. The Canadian architect, writer, and professor Witold Rybczynski (eighty-one as of this writing) wrote an essay on this topic. According to Rybczynski, late starts—and late finishes—are more the norm than the exception among architects:

Architects have traditionally hit their stride in late middle age. Ludwig Mies van der Rohe was 62 when he started designing the Lake Shore Drive apartments, which became the model for all subsequent steel-and-glass towers; Le Corbusier was 63 when he built the marvelous chapel at Ronchamp, setting the architectural world on its ear; Louis Kahn was 64 when the Salk Institute was built; and Frank Gehry was 68 when he produced the Bilbao Guggenheim.

Ageless Architects

Rybczynski doesn't even mention the great Japanese architect Arata Isozaki, who died in 2022 at the age of ninety-one. In his eighties, he designed major works including the Qatar National Convention Centre (the sprawling steel beams on the exterior resemble trees—absolutely stunning) and Shanghai Symphony Hall, and won the prestigious Pritzker Architecture Prize in 2019, at eighty-seven.

And let's not forget these bad boys, still with us and still working: Rem Koolhaas (seventy-nine), Norman Foster (eighty-eight), and Frank Gehry (now ninety-five!). Just call them the Draft Pack.

So why is it that architects possess such remarkable longevity? Rybczynski offers a few theories. To start, it's a trade in which the creator is dependent on clients with a lot of money, and clients with a lot of money are more likely to hire someone with an established record of achievement. Are you really going to trust a thirty-year-old with $100 million to build your new corporate headquarters? And because world-class architects do not work alone but rely on teams of engineers, designers, assistants, and underlings, an older architect can be spared much of the grunt work that goes into the creation of a dazzling new skyscraper or museum or opera house.

Another Pritzker winner, Kevin Roche—a disciple of Ludwig Mies van der Rohe and a junior partner of Eero Saarinen—died in 2019, at the age of ninety-six. Among his many accomplishments were the designs for the expansion of New York's Metropolitan Museum of Art and the headquarters of the Ford Foundation. With Saarinen, he also created the famous TWA terminal at New York's Kennedy Airport and Dulles International Airport, perhaps best known as the setting of *Die Hard 2*. (So yes, if not for Roche, we may never have heard Bruce Willis exclaim "Yippee ki-yay.") Roche *never* retired. The only concession he made to age was scaling back to a four-day workweek at age ninety-five. In an interview given a few years before his death, he said that most people only retired because they found their work unfulfilling. "I am energized very much by what I am doing all the time, and very excited about it," he said. "And I think it's a great opportunity on two levels. One is to be able to make a contribution to the environment, and the other is to satisfy your creative desires—to create something, sculpturally or visually, that's attractive and interesting and beautiful."

And then there's Oscar Niemeyer, Brazil's greatest architect, designer of the bold modernist civic buildings in Brasília, who died in 2012 ten days before his 105th birthday. He designed Rio de Janeiro's Museum of Contemporary Art at age eighty-nine and continued to work up until the year of his death. In an interview for his one hundredth birthday, he told Carmen Stephan of *Spiegel International,* "I do the same things I did when I was 60, so I'm only 60. . . . You have to keep your mind alive, work, help others, laugh, cry and experience life intensively. It only lasts for a brief moment."

Here are three more master builders and the capstones that helped define them:

Frank Lloyd Wright

submitted design for New York's Guggenheim Museum at eighty-four

The life of Frank Lloyd Wright is truly an American epic, material for a 650-page biography, a two-part Ken Burns documentary, or a three-and-a-half-hour Oscar-winning feature film. Two of those, in fact, actually exist; the third was in development about ten years ago with Brad Pitt in the lead role but never made it to the screen. We're going to make do here with a few pages of brisk, sparkling prose.

Born in 1867, Wright grew up in a troubled family, studied engineering at the University of Wisconsin, then went to work for the great Chicago architect Louis Sullivan. He fell out with Sullivan but always regarded the man as his "lieber meister," or "beloved teacher." In his early career, Wright made an indelible mark on American architecture with his Prairie style of home design, epitomized by Chicago's Robie House, with its emphasis on strong horizontal lines, open floor plans, minimal ornamentation, and graceful integration with the natural surroundings.

In midlife came a series of sensational crises, the stuff of tabloid headlines. In 1909, Wright abandoned his wife and six children to run off to Germany with a married woman, Mamah Cheney. They returned to the United States, and Wright built the magnificent Wisconsin home to which he gave the Welsh name Taliesin. Three years later, an aggrieved worker went on a rampage, killing Mamah, her two children, and four others, and setting fire to the house. Then came a trip to Japan, a second fire at the rebuilt Taliesin, a second marriage, a second divorce, then a third marriage. By the 1930s, Wright's career was on the downswing as the high modernist International Style of Le Corbusier, Walter Gropius (founder of the Bauhaus Group), and Mies van der Rohe had superseded his organic forms. He was adjusting to the role of elder statesman as he and his wife invited students to come study with him at Taliesin. Now in his sixties, Wright appeared to be closing the book on one of the most celebrated careers in the history of American architecture.

But he was just getting started.

Wright was sixty-seven when, in 1935, Pittsburgh department store owner Edgar Kaufmann engaged him to build a weekend retreat for the family at Bear Run, a stream running through a forested ravine in the Allegheny Mountains of southwest Pennsylvania. The result, Fallingwater, is the most famous house of the twentieth century. Constructed literally on top of a waterfall, the residence is marvelously—seemingly miraculously—integrated into its natural surroundings, anchored in the rock of the ravine, with floors and terraces cantilevered out over the river and surrounding forest. It was immediately recognized as a monumental achievement, landing Wright on the cover of *Time* and earning him a solo show at MoMA.

Sidebar: Fallingwater is unforgettable. Go if you can. But I could never live there: 1) The water, which runs around and under it, is just one reason it's in need of almost constant repairs. 2) Wright didn't want shades on the windows. You're supposed to get up with the light. No, no, no, no, no. 3) Wherever you are in the house you can hear that water. Which made this visitor want to keep going to the bathroom. Hard to imagine sleeping eight hours straight, even with blackout shades.

His career reinvigorated, Wright developed his idea of the Usonian house, in which he applied his design principles to modest, affordable housing for middle-class families. The Usonian house would be, he wrote, "a companion to the horizon," practical, functional, and aesthetically pleasing in its simplicity and respect for the natural environment. Sixty were built, but their impact on the design of postwar American homes was immeasurable.

Into his seventies and eighties, Wright continued working, indefatigable. At seventy-two, he completed the breathtaking Johnson Wax Headquarters in Racine, Wisconsin. At eighty-six, he began to design the neo-Mayan ziggurat that is the Beth Sholom synagogue, outside of Philadelphia. At eighty-nine, he designed the Price Company Tower in Bartlesville, Oklahoma, his first and only skyscraper, which he described as "the tree that escaped a crowded forest." But the crowning achievement of his late career was the Solomon R. Guggenheim Museum, the only public building he ever created in New York City.

The history of this unique structure is itself a minor epic. In 1943, Solomon Guggenheim, a wealthy art collector whose family made their money in mining, commissioned Wright to create a permanent home for his collection of abstract art. At the time Wright was but seventy-six; the project would occupy him the rest of his days. Guggenheim and the museum's director, Hilla Rebay, gave Wright only one condition: "The building should be unlike any other museum in the world."

Wright took that to heart. At one point he boasted that his new creation would make the neighboring Metropolitan Museum of Art "look like a Protestant barn." (Self-confidence was never a problem.)

Wright had always kept aloof from New York, but he couldn't deny that the city was fast becoming the architectural center of the world. The dominant International Style had gained popularity after World War I. (If you want a shorthand definition, try the one from London's Tate museum: "mostly rectilinear, undecorated, asymmetrical, and white.") MoMA in 1939, the United Nations headquarters in 1948, the Seagram Building in 1958—whether constructed for art, politics, or business, sleek modernist buildings were transforming the look of the city.

Wright refused to be rendered obsolete by the next generation. (Philip Johnson—who worked until his death at age ninety-eight—once dissed Wright as "the greatest American architect of the nineteenth century.") Always partial to natural shapes and forms, Wright began with an old, unrealized design from the 1920s—a tourist attraction intended for a mountaintop in Maryland called the Gordon Strong Automobile Objective. For that project, he had sketched out a wide circular tower reminiscent of Pieter Bruegel's *The Tower of Babel*. The building was to feature panoramic views and a planetarium. It would be accessible by car—hence its name. The spiraling ramp that Wright had imagined for that site became key to the Guggenheim building, with people replacing the automobiles, and paintings replacing the natural scenery.

For a decade and a half, Wright had to maneuver around one obstacle after another. Solomon Guggenheim died in 1949, at which point the land for the museum had not even been acquired yet. Several sites were considered before the final location was determined and the real estate purchased. Rising prices for construction materials drove up the cost of the project. New York City's labyrinthine building codes were another challenge. When Wright and his team finally submitted their initial plans in 1952, they were found to be in violation of thirty-two different regulations. Changes, appeals, and requests for variances followed over the next four years. Construction didn't begin until August 1956. By that point, Wright had been through six sets of plans and 749 drawings. He was eighty-nine.

Just when it looked like things were moving forward, the art world itself revolted. Drawings and descriptions of the museum had appeared in the press, and many painters and sculptors were outraged at the swirling novelty Wright proposed. Clearly the outré design would overwhelm the artworks the museum intended to display. In an open letter to the director and trustees of the museum, twenty-one of the world's most distinguished living artists, including Willem de Kooning, Milton Avery, Robert Motherwell, and Seymour Lipton, took aim at the octogenarian architect. They wrote: "The basic concept of curvilinear slope for presentation of painting and sculpture indicates a callous disregard for the fundamental rectilinear frame of reference necessary for the adequate visual contemplation of works of art." Translation: when it came to exhibiting art, the old man didn't know what he was doing.

Wright was incensed. He shot back with his own public rebuke, haughtily asserting the place of architecture among the fine arts: "Dear Fellow Artists: I am sufficiently familiar with the incubus of habit that besets, if not befits, your minds to understand that you know too little of the nature of the mother art, architecture." These upstarts weren't going to tell the grand old man of architecture how to do his job.

The end result, of course, is now one of the most distinctive buildings in the city. The museum welcomes 1.3 million visitors a year. Facing Central Park, it fits the urban environment as gracefully as Fallingwater fits the forest of western Pennsylvania. Its signature ramp, curling outward as it ascends toward a domed skylight, lacks conventional galleries and radically transforms the way you move through a museum and experience its collection. When Hilla Rebay engaged Wright to create the museum, she told him she wanted "a temple of spirit, a monument." That is what he produced.

Ultimately, Wright did not live to see the opening of the museum, dying in April 1959 at age ninety-one after emergency surgery for an intestinal obstruction. But when it opened later that year, it appeared to many as the folly of a dotard. The famous urban planner Robert Moses called it "an inverted oatmeal dish and silo."

opposite page: The architect and his capstone: ninety-one-year-old Frank Lloyd Wright at the unfinished Guggenheim Museum, November 1958.
William H. Short © Solomon R. Guggenheim Foundation, New York

The *New York Times* called it "an indigestible hot cross bun." Even the famous architecture critic Lewis Mumford, who reviewed the new landmark for *The New Yorker*, agreed with the protesting artists that the building's success as an enormous work of sculpture came at the cost of its functionality as an exhibition space: "You may go to this building to see Kandinsky or Jackson Pollock; you remain to see Frank Lloyd Wright."

Yet for all his criticisms, Mumford didn't trash the building as other critics did. He remained amazed by the power of Wright's genius: "From the time you scrape your feet on the unmistakably Wright grating in the vestibule . . . you are under his enchantment." As for succeeding generations—Mumford's sons, if you will—they've come to see the museum not as the product of an old man's arrogance or folly but as the flowering of a talent that had, with time, grown confident, wise, and visionary.

In his review, Mumford paid tribute to the departed master. He stood in awe of the way that Wright's genius had reemerged in the final decades of his life, leading him to take on new challenges and break new ground when others would have wallowed in nostalgia for the good old days. Even if the Guggenheim had never been built, Mumford wrote, Wright's last years would still be a marvel:

> *One would still know him for the original artist that he was, the inexhaustible creator, whose formal structures and images, far from shrinking into a convention, were unfolding until the very moment of his death and were far more rich and free in the last third of his life than in his early years.*

I. M. Pei

rejuvenated the Louvre at seventy-five

While Frank Lloyd Wright put his name on the line to create a very new museum, another great architect, I. M. Pei, risked his reputation to reimagine a very old one. In doing so, he nearly became known as the man who ruined the Louvre.

Ageless Architects

I. M. Pei is familiar to many, since his vowel-heavy name shows up all the time in crossword puzzles—much like Etta James, Yoko Ono, and, increasingly these days, Issa Rae. But he's best known as one of the most accomplished architects of the late twentieth century. Since he lived for 102 years, Pei actually witnessed most of that century, as well as a healthy chunk of the twenty-first.

For the greater part of those 102 years, Pei was working—another ageless architect who continued to create wonderful things into his tenth decade. At age eighty-nine, he designed the Chinese Embassy to the United States; at ninety-one, the Museum of Islamic Art in Doha, Qatar. But just as the prolific Wright's last years are remembered for the Guggenheim, so Pei's last years will be known for his renovation of the Louvre. In both cases, a career-crowning project was surrounded by controversy; in both cases, the completed work is now seen as a striking affirmation of the principle that often it is the oldest people who have the boldest ideas.

Ieoh Ming Pei was born in China in 1917 to an established family that traced its roots to the Ming dynasty. His father moved the family to Shanghai when he was appointed to lead that city's branch of the Bank of China. Then, sadly, Pei's mother died of cancer when the boy was only thirteen. At eighteen, Pei, who had been an extremely diligent and serious student throughout his school years, chose to attend college in the United States. The reason? He'd enjoyed Bing Crosby movies like *College Humor*, and the campus high jinks looked like a lot of fun when compared to the rigorous and sober education he'd thus far received in China.

We don't have a record of Pei participating in any similar high jinks at the University of Pennsylvania, where he enrolled to study architecture. However, we do know that he was disappointed to find the Penn faculty more interested in the nineteenth-century Beaux Arts movement than European modernism. He transferred to MIT, where, in 1935, a brief visit from Le Corbusier became what he later called the most influential two days of his professional life. (He also drove to Wisconsin in 1938 to meet Frank Lloyd Wright, but after waiting for two hours gave up and returned to Boston.) In Boston, he met Eileen Loo, also a Chinese native and a Wellesley College student. They fell in love, married in 1942, and remained together until her death seventy-two years later.

Both Eileen and I. M.—and yes, friends called him I. M.—began graduate study at Harvard, she in landscape design, he in architecture. The Harvard Graduate School of Design was then home to the famous German modernist architect Walter Gropius, who helped Pei get a job as an assistant professor there. By his late thirties, the ambitious Pei had established his own firm. But his breakthrough came in 1964, when Jackie Kennedy chose him to design her late husband's presidential library. (She liked that he was born the same year as JFK and that at forty-seven, he was young—for an architect, at least.) Originally planned for a site in Cambridge, the library project ran into resistance from local residents. While the ultimate result was a critically admired complex of buildings in Dorchester, Pei was disappointed that his original vision, which included a glass pyramid truncated at the top to represent Kennedy's untimely death, had been compromised by politics.

Still, the project launched Pei into the upper echelon of American architects, and high-profile commissions followed. In 1968, Pei and his colleague Henry Cobb were engaged to build a skyscraper for the John Hancock Mutual Insurance Company, which wanted a headquarters that would literally overshadow the recently completed Prudential Tower, home to their rival. The final result is a striking, sleek tower of blue glass that is still the tallest building in New England. But for several years the tower was beset by troubles, as high winds fractured glass panes, which fell onto the street below. The fault eventually was determined to lie with the glass manufacturer, but it was a major setback for Pei and his firm.

Nonetheless, through his sixties, Pei continued to design some of the country's most important public buildings. With the East Building of the National Gallery of Art in Washington, DC, completed in 1978, and the West Wing of the Museum of Fine Arts in Boston, completed in 1981, his reputation as the go-to architect for renovating museums was, as it were, cemented.

Then came the Louvre controversy. In April 1981, France had elected François Mitterrand president, the first socialist to hold the office since the new constitution of 1958. In September, at his first press conference, Mitterrand announced plans for a massive renovation of the great museum.

An upgrade of some sort was long overdue. The building, created in 1204 as a fortress on the Seine, repurposed as a royal palace some two hundred years later, and converted into a public museum in 1793 during the French Revolution, was a total calamity as a modern exhibition space. It was hard to navigate, and people struggled to find the paintings they wanted to see. It lacked the basic facilities—bathrooms, cafeterias—needed to accommodate tourists, so when people felt the call of nature or just wanted to grab a quick croque monsieur or espresso, they often just left the building, never to return. Nor did it have anything like the complex infrastructure essential for the proper operation of a great modern museum: information kiosks, auditoriums, conference rooms, temperature-controlled storage spaces, workshops for restoring damaged paintings, and so on. One wing of the building was not even used as part of the museum, serving as a home to the Ministry of Finance. Visitors to the Louvre on average stayed ninety minutes, half the time they spent at New York's Met. As Pei himself said, "The Louvre did not work as a museum and the French knew it."

Everyone agreed there was a problem. No one agreed on how to fix it. But when Mitterrand came to power, he made the renovation a priority. Wasting no time, he handpicked Pei to head up the vast project—"the Grand Louvre," as it was called. In itself, the choice of a Chinese American architect was controversial for the renovation of this quintessentially French institution. And that was before Pei unveiled his plans.

The task before Pei was Herculean. He had to transform a narrow, eight-hundred-meter-long corridor of a museum into a space that would be bigger and airier yet more compact and walkable. A central entrance and lobby had to be created somehow. At the time, the wings of the building were separated by the Cour

Napoléon, or Napoleon Courtyard, a largely wasted outdoor space that served by day as a parking lot for the Finance Ministry bureaucrats and by night as a shadowy spot for furtive hookups. However, rather than build an addition *in* the courtyard, Pei decided to build *under* it, excavating two levels down, creating half a million square feet of usable space, while providing easy pedestrian access to all sides of the museum, shortening a typical museumgoer's walk from eight hundred meters to fifty.

Still, the new underground space would need a prominent, welcoming, and easily identifiable entrance point aboveground. For this challenge, Pei returned to a discarded design from years before—just as Frank Lloyd Wright had done with the Guggenheim. In Pei's case the resurrected concept was the glass pyramid he had originally intended for the Kennedy Library. Pei had always found the pyramid to be the most solid and stable of structures, and he proposed a 70.5-foot-high transparent structure made from 70 glass triangles and 603 glass diamond pieces set in a steel-and-aluminum frame. Glass of the utmost transparency was essential so the structure wouldn't block the views of the other façades of the museum.

A giant modernist all-glass pyramid set in the middle of a stately French neoclassical palace in the heart of Paris. Who could possibly object?

When Pei unveiled the plan before France's Committee on Historical Monuments in 1984, it met with a mixed response—of outrage and fury. One prominent architect called the pyramid "a gigantic, ruinous gadget." At the hearing, attacks came with such speed and venom that Pei's translator was literally shaking as she tried to give voice to his defense. The press was no better. France's leading newspaper, *Le Monde*, was particularly scathing:

> *You rub your eyes; you think you're dreaming; it seems that you've gone back to the era of castles for sale and Hollywood copies of the temple of Solomon, of Alexander, of Cleopatra. . . . It doesn't seem justified to treat the courtyard of the Louvre like a Disneyland annex or a rebirth of the defunct Luna Park.*

The Egyptian associations of the pyramid were seen as out of place. (Never mind that the nearby Place de la Concorde has boasted a seventy-five-foot-tall Egyptian obelisk since 1836.) Others said that Pei, as a Chinese American, lacked the necessary knowledge of French culture to be entrusted with the job. And there was a political element to the debate, as Mitterrand was accused by his political enemies of trying to put his stamp on the city in the way that Georges Pompidou had created the Centre Pompidou and Valery Giscard d'Estaing had created the Musée d'Orsay. One commentator, objecting to the fact that Mitterrand selected Pei without consulting committees or juries, called it an act of despotism.

As for Pei, he was, in the words of one journalist, "accused of defacing one of the world's great landmarks."

Yet Pei, backed by an unflinching Mitterrand, persisted. The next two years were spent—or "wasted," according to Pei—in convincing the media and the public of the merits of the plan. When the pyramid opened in 1989, Pei was seventy-one and his labor on the museum was not done. The stubborn bureaucrats in the Finance Ministry still had to be vacated from the north wing so that their extensive rabbit warren of offices could be gutted and proper galleries built. Additional underground spaces had yet to be completed. Air-conditioning was desperately needed for the Denon wing, home to the *Mona Lisa*, which grew notoriously hot during the summer. A planned pedestrian bridge across the Seine would unite the Left and Right Banks, finally freeing the Louvre from its origins as a fortress eight centuries before. It would be another four and a half years before the second phase of the Grand Louvre finally concluded.

But by November 1993, at the opening of the Grand Louvre, when Pei was seventy-five, the public and the press had come around. The museum's exhibition space had been doubled, its floor space tripled. Pei's controversial pyramid had already become iconic, second only to the *Mona Lisa* as a visual emblem of the museum itself. Today, in the words of its former director, Jean-Luc Martinez, "The Louvre is the only museum with a work of art as an entrance." (Martinez, for the record, was arrested in 2022 for money laundering, fraud, and trafficking in antiquities. But he's right about the entrance.) The new Richelieu wing allowed for an orderly display of the museum's collection of European paintings. Underground parking for cars and buses provided access for tourists. And France's minister of culture, Jacques Toubon—a member of the conservative RPR (Rassemblement pour la République) party—seemed delighted to endorse the project once championed by the socialist Mitterrand. Toubon called the Grand Louvre "an incontestable success," describing it as "a historic and cultural space without comparison in the world." He singled out the "exceptional quality of I. M. Pei's work." In recognition of his accomplishment, Pei was made an officer of the Legion of Honor.

Pei savored his triumph, even as he credited Mitterrand as the real visionary behind the project. "These have been the ten most exciting years of my life, thanks to the Louvre. The sad part is, of course, that it is coming to an end," he said, even as he must have been turning his full attention to a newer commission, the Rock & Roll Hall of Fame in Cleveland, which had broken ground the previous June. "In this case it was the challenge," Pei continued, "not only of the museum establishment but of the public, of Paris, of France. The responsibility was a very great one. We had to be sure we were right"—he paused, then added, with the confidence borne of a long and successful career—"and *are* right."

Today the Grand Louvre represents a nation that embraces change, not one that simply worships the grandeur of the past. The striking but elegant glass pyramid looks forward rather than back, recognizing the demands of the modern world, opening the former royal palace to a global public. The same can be said of the architect himself, who might have been content to take an easy victory lap with some ersatz classical additions but instead challenged France's cultural establishment to embrace a future full of possibility.

That abovementioned museum in Cleveland opened to much fanfare in 1995, when I. M. Pei was seventy-eight. But what he did at the Louvre was Pei at his boldest, his most iconoclastic, his most rock and roll.

Wonder of the architecture world I. M. Pei in front of his pyramid at the Louvre, 1989.

Yasmeen Lari

*began building sustainable housing
for the poor at age sixty-four*

Even as she was building glass towers, Yasmeen Lari was breaking glass ceilings.

Born in Punjab in 1941, Lari grew up near Lahore, traveled to England for school, and settled in Karachi, where, at the age of twenty-three, she opened an architectural firm with her husband, Suhail Zaheer Lari. That made her Pakistan's first professional female architect, a lone pioneer in a field dominated by men. During the forty-year career that followed, she designed major buildings in Karachi, including the Taj Mahal Hotel (1981), the Finance and Trade Center (1983–1989), the Pakistan State Oil House (1985–1991), and the ABN Amro Bank (2000)—structures that *Architects' Journal* called "postmodern landmarks of steel, cement and reflective glass." She was elected to the Royal Institute of British Architects (RIBA) in 1969, and served as president of the Institute of Architects, Pakistan, in 1978. She was forty-six when she was one of three architects featured, along with India's Balkrishna V. Doshi and Sri Lanka's Minnette de Silva, in a MoMA exhibition of modern South Asian architecture, *The Project of Independence: Architectures of Decolonization in South Asia, 1947–1985.*

But as Lari entered her sixties, she turned her back on the high-profile projects that had made her one of Pakistan's leading "starchitects." Formally retiring from the high-end corporate work that had earned her a very good living, she turned her attention to Heritage Foundation of Pakistan, a nonprofit organization she had founded with her husband twenty years earlier with the aim of preserving her country's rich and diverse cultural heritage. Among the buildings the Laris had successfully preserved was the Hindu Gymkhana of Karachi, built in 1925 in Mughal Revival style. It had been on the brink of demolition in 1984, before their intervention; it now serves as home to Pakistan's National Academy of Performing Arts.

They also conserved historic monuments at two UNESCO World Heritage sites—the Necropolis at Makli, an enormous funerary site built over four centuries, and Lahore Fort, a sixteenth-century citadel constructed during the Mughal Empire.

Then came the devastating 2005 Kashmir earthquake, the largest ever recorded in South Asia. Registering 7.6 on the Richter scale, the disaster left over eighty thousand dead and displaced five hundred thousand families. The catastrophe spurred Lari to completely reenvision her work as a builder.

Renouncing the creation of projects designed to serve the elite, she devoted herself instead to constructing basic living space for thousands of poor and displaced Pakistanis. In essence, she turned her back on the dominant values of her profession, in which the design of dazzling and expensive landmarks is the coin of the realm. She rethought her very identity and mission as an architect, including the kinds of buildings that she considered important, the kinds of materials she used, and the kinds of people with whom she collaborated.

Using "vernacular" or indigenous materials such as bamboo, lime, adobe, and mud, Lari began working with local communities, including Pakistan's most impoverished, to build low-tech houses that are affordable, sustainable, and disaster-resistant. In the twenty-first century, Pakistan has been hit by many natural disasters, including the 2022 floods that submerged a third of the country and affected 33 million people. With each one, the need to deploy climate-adaptive building practices has become all the more urgent. And with 55 million people living below the poverty line, Pakistan is acutely in need of safe, inexpensive housing built on a large scale. The work that Lari has focused on in her sixties and seventies—and now into her eighties—responds directly to these crises, placing both environmental justice and economic justice at the center of her mission.

Since her putative "retirement" twenty-plus years ago, Lari has, in partnership with the United Nations' International Organization for Migration, helped to build forty-three thousand eco-friendly and disaster-resistant shelters. According to the World Congress of Architects, this work has placed "Pakistan in the lead as

Yasmeen Lari, a "starchitect"
building sustainable housing for
Pakistan's most vulnerable.
Wikimedia Commons

[the nation with the] world's largest zero-carbon shelter program."
Lari herself, they point out, has
been "acknowledged as the largest
provider of houses for the poor."
Lari's motivation is simple. She
believes that architects, who have a central role in shaping our built environment,
have a special responsibility to be its stewards.

But what's maybe most radical about Lari's work is not the materials she de-
ploys or the plans that she designs or even the people she serves. It is the way that
she collaborates with and empowers the communities on whose behalf she works.
Lari insists that the construction of housing for hundreds of thousands of poor and
shelterless families must be undertaken as a massive collective operation. What she
calls "barefoot social architecture" aims, therefore, not only to leave a light carbon
footprint but also to cultivate an attitude of self-reliance among underprivileged
communities, especially women, by giving them an active role in the physical construction of their own homes and environments. The skills Lari teaches are not
hard to learn, and the materials she uses are not hard to come by. Her collaborative
work with communities not only gives people a roof over their heads but affords
them the dignity and pride of taking care of themselves.

To advance these goals, Lari draws on the understanding of traditional building methods that she developed in her conservation work. Volunteers and students
work with local communities to train people in the skills they need to build their
own homes in a process Lari calls "participatory design." "I treat these people as

partners, not as victims," she asserts. "Don't treat them as if they can't do things." She disdains the dominant model of Western disaster relief, in which money and experts flow into a region in response to a crisis but do little in the long term to help communities mitigate or respond to future disasters.

Lari's decision to turn her attention to the many instead of continuing to concentrate on the few was not completely unanticipated. Throughout her career, she'd worked on public housing projects whose design and construction were grounded in traditional Pakistani architecture and planning. Still, she says that her late-life dedication to barefoot social architecture required her to relinquish the great egotism that her profession cultivates and even demands. She had to go through "a period of unlearning" as she dispensed with elements of her Western training and attuned herself to the needs of her country's women and its poor.

Today she looks back on her corporate work with some chagrin. "What a terror I was when I designed these mammoth buildings," she said to one interviewer. "If something was a little bit out of line, well[,] it had to be demolished immediately. I was that bad, a control freak, as architects are supposed to be." Today, on the other hand, if "things are not quite straight when I work in an earthquake area, as long as basic elements are in place, it's OK." Indeed, she describes her current work as a kind of penance, or at least an effort to undo some of the harm that she might have caused while accepting big commissions from banks and fossil fuel companies: "At the time I enjoyed using expensive building materials such as large glass panels, polished granite and steel trusses. . . . Perhaps with my present work I am atoning for the damage I caused with my earlier projects."

Among Lari's most influential ideas has been her 2014 design of a chulha, a traditional clay stove. Her version, which added an air-regulation pipe and a chimney, reduces the toxic emissions of the traditional stove that often caused women to suffer ocular, cardiac, and respiratory ailments and disease. The design, which she calls a Pakistan Chulha Cookstove, decreases the risk of fire and of burns. Because it is elevated and mounted, it does not wash away during flooding; it is also significantly more energy-efficient than the traditional stove, making use of agri-cultural waste as fuel rather than newly cut firewood. By elevating the cooking area off the (often dirty) floor, it reduces the risk of bacterial contamination and disease among children and infants, and, further, relieves women of the need to sit on the ground while preparing food. Made of mud and lime plaster, Lari's cookstoves are cheap and easy to produce; with some basic instruction, residents can make them themselves. A 2021 news story estimated that fifty thousand had been produced.

This kind of work, serving women, the poor, and the planet, has, late in life, brought Lari a new wave of recognition, including a World Habitat Award (2018), the Jane Drew Prize for innovation in architecture (2020), and the RIBA Royal Gold Medal for a lifetime of achievement (2023).

In accepting the RIBA award, Lari, then eighty-two, took the opportunity to highlight what she sees as the proper goals for architecture and design work in the current century:

> *RIBA and the Award Committee have heralded a new direction for the profes-sion, encouraging all architects to focus not only on the privileged but also hu-manity at large that suffers from disparities, conflicts and climate change. There are innumerable opportunities to implement principles of circular economy, de-growth, transition design, [and] eco urbanism . . . to achieve climate resilience, sustainability and eco justice in the world.*

Today Yasmeen Lari, in spite of herself, has become a new kind of starchitect—less a Frank Lloyd Wright; more a Frank Lloyd Righteous.

OLD TOWN: St. Augustine, Florida

The pilgrims landed on Plymouth Rock in 1620. Jamestown was settled even earlier, in 1607. Yeah, so what? St. Augustine was established all the way back in 1565, which is why the Florida city calls itself the Oldest Continuously Occupied European Settlement in America. (I know it's a mouthful, but try singing it to the tune of the *Guys and Dolls* lyric "the oldest established permanent floating crap game in New York" and it sort of works.)

When Don Pedro Menéndez de Avilés arrived on the northeast coast of Florida in September of 1565, he claimed the land for the Spanish empire. There was even a Thanksgiving meal when Menendez and his crew reached land, celebrated with members of the Seloy tribe who were already living in the area.

It wasn't until after the Civil War that St. Augustine would really hit its heyday, thanks to Standard Oil founder and railroad tycoon Henry Flagler. Flagler thought St. Augustine could be a destination for wealthy northerners and decided to create a "Winter Newport." Given that he owned a railway company, he made sure St. Augustine was easily accessible. He also built several fancy hotels, including the Spanish Renaissance–style Ponce de León, decorated with Tiffany glass and wired for electricity by Thomas Edison himself. The *New York Times* declared in 1903, "There is no more interesting place in Florida than St. Augustine. . . . the picturesque beauty of the old city mingles with its modern gorgeousness in an enchanting manner." But eventually the wealthy would move on to Miami and Palm Beach.

St. Augustine has remained a tourist destination—just a more touristy one. In the summer of 1978, my family drove from Maryland to New Orleans, stopping in St. Augustine. I still remember seeing what was billed as America's oldest schoolhouse. Even cooler, the *original* Ripley's Believe It or Not Museum. It's where I was introduced to my first headless chicken, along with other animal and human oddities.

St. Augustine is now nearly 460 years old. And it still looks damn good. Old age seems to agree with it.

No Signs of Slowing Down

Ed Shadle

Ed Shadle

chased the world land speed record in his seventies

If you've ever been responsible for the care of an aging parent, you probably have had to broach The Conversation. No, I don't mean the birds and the bees—that's for teenagers. I mean something far more awkward. I mean giving up the keys to the car.

Here's how it goes. An elderly parent bangs up the side of their old Buick, or narrowly avoids a crash, or briefly nods off at the wheel. The adult children, who have been noticing for a while that the parent's driving isn't as steady as it used to be, gently suggest that it might be time to stop driving. But driving, from the first moment you acquire a license, is for so many a critical symbol of independence, and most seniors want to be able to take care of themselves, whether that means picking up groceries, visiting friends, or just leaving the house whenever they choose. To give up that independence is a step—usually an irreversible one—in subjecting yourself to the care of others and acknowledging the decline of your physical and mental powers. And so a struggle ensues, the parent becoming more dug-in and resistant to advice, the child becoming more frustrated and worried.

I think it's safe to say that no one ever had to have The Conversation with Ed Shadle. For Shadle, an Air Force veteran and retired IBM engineer, the later decades were all about driving, and driving fast. Instead of cruising through retirement at 12 miles an hour in an electric-powered golf cart, Shadle decided to hit the accelerator—on his one-of-a-kind, rocket-powered race car, and on life itself well into his seventies. We're talking speeds of triple digits, speeds that get measured in Mach numbers. In fact, Shadle's ambition was to travel faster than any human being had ever gone without leaving the surface of the planet. Assembling a team of test pilots and engineers, he dedicated his retirement years to breaking the land speed record, the highest velocity ever attained on earth.

For many boys of the Baby Boomer generation, cars were an object of love and fascination. Shadle and his contemporaries were the demographic that grew up reading hot rod magazines and building their own cars to run in the Soap Box Derby. Shadle, who was part Ojibwe, grew up in north-central Washington State with a father and uncle who loved amateur stock-car racing. "[They] would take me along in their jalopies ripping along on those dirt tracks at 60, 70 miles an hour," Shadle told an interviewer. "By the time I was a teenager, I was paying 50 cents to drag race all night at the local airport. I raced an old '49 Ford and a '51 Studebaker. Horribly dangerous, but if you did well, you'd drive around afterward picking up the chicks. The thrill kinda stuck from there."

And it wasn't just cars he enjoyed; he learned to fly, too. His father worked as a crop duster and would show off by doing barrel rolls over the family home. That only further inspired young Ed. This was the Sputnik era, when the U.S. government was pouring billions into aerospace and military technologies, and American can-do technology whizzes were seen as the best hope of the free world. Test pilots were major celebrities; astronauts were household names. The teenage Ed Shadle "wanted to be the next Chuck Yeager." (In October 1947 Yeager became the first human to fly at supersonic speed—in other words, faster than the speed of sound. As he reached a speed of 700 mph at an altitude of 43,000 feet, a sonic boom was heard across the Mojave Desert.)

At different times in his life, Shadle took up motorcycle racing and horse racing—anything, it seems, to satisfy the need: the need for speed. But things got serious in 1997, when a Royal Air Force fighter pilot named Andy Green became the first driver ever to break the sound barrier *on land*. Shadle, then in his mid-fifties, took it as a personal challenge. Green and his British team had shattered the old land speed record when they hit a top velocity of 763 miles per hour. Shadle, who had already taken up high-speed racing at the Bonneville Salt Flats in Utah, felt the rumblings of patriotism and decided it was time to bring the record home to the United States. In the 1960s, when jet engines were first attached to race cars, the sport had been something of a sensation, and was dominated by Americans such as Craig Breedlove and Art Arfons. But for the better part of two decades, Great Britain had ruled the roost. Shadle thought he could claim the world record for America once again.

A casual conversation on an airplane with Seattle-raised Boeing manager Keith Zanghi hatched an idea. What if they converted a fighter plane into a race car? But where do you get a fighter plane, much less at an affordable price? (This was in the days before eBay.) A search began, and, in a Maine junkyard, the men eventually located a 1956 Lockheed F-104 Starfighter, a single-engine fighter plane that had been used during the Cold War. From his time in the service, Shadle knew that the F-104 was "aerodynamically very efficient," just what he needed for the body of the car. They bought it for $25,000.

"It was a wreck," said Shadle. "It looked like it had been rolled down a mountain." Shadle spent another $3,000 to haul it out west, then put together a team to convert it into the fastest land vehicle ever. The battered fuselage was covered with graffiti and full of holes, but Shadle saw the potential. "Within that wreck you could see the image of what we were going to develop," he said. "[But] you had to have the vision."

With an all-volunteer crew that included Boeing engineers and ex-military people, Shadle and Zanghi began the long process of turning the husk of the plane into the vehicle that they hoped would travel 800 miles per hour on land. It took three years of what Shadle called "scrounging and tenacity and networking." Fund-raising wasn't easy; Shadle estimated that over the life of the project he invested a quarter of a million dollars of his own money. Both the time and the money were sacrifices, and Shadle admitted that his wife might have preferred to spend their money on a home with a view of Puget Sound and their retirement years enjoying the view.

But instead he decided to spend his golden years working on the high-tech hobby he grandly dubbed the North American Eagle Project. He and Zanghi initially imagined the process would take three or four years, but it took more than that just to build the car. They bought a J79 jet engine, manufactured by General Electric, that had been used on another plane; the engine consumes about ninety gallons of fuel per minute (okay, this isn't exactly a "green" hobby) and generates 42,000 horsepower. (That's ten times the horsepower of a typical train locomotive.) It exploded in early testing but was repaired. They deployed a special magnetic nonskid braking system that worked alongside parachutes to make sure that the rocket ship of a car could stop safely. They found a Los Angeles company that manufactured aluminum wheels for roller coasters. And with only one engine, the car was four tons lighter than the world-record-holding British ThrustSSC, which had twin engines. That weight difference, combined with the aerodynamic design of the plane, would be a key to the team's success.

As Shadle pursued the record, the years stretched into decades. Shadle aged out of his sixties into his seventies. But he not only stuck with the project; he remained in the driver's seat. "I just feel compelled to be the monkey in the seat to drive the beast," he said. "It is very difficult for me to allow anyone other than myself to take the risk in my place until it is a proven concept."

"I think his age was actually an advantage," Matt Anderson, curator of transportation at The Henry Ford Museum of American Innovation, told me. "Every land speed driver is literally racing the clock, but Shadle was simultaneously racing it in the metaphorical sense. He knew, as we all do, that he wouldn't live forever, so he was determined to keep pushing himself for as long as he was physically able."

As the team incrementally increased their speed over dozens of test runs, each effort provided new data on how the car held up over greater and greater speeds. They would then feed that data back into their computer models and use it to fine-tune the engineering on the machine. Those computer models, by the way, anticipated an eventual speed of 835 miles per hour.

It was an engineering project but also a creative one. Shadle described the field of land speed racing as "an engineer's playground." And in an age when hardly

Ed Shadle, fast and furious and having the time of his life.
Courtesy of Facebook

anyone even changes a spark plug by themselves, Shadle was a holdover, an inveterate tinkerer with a do-it-yourself mentality. "I like to think of it as a science project," he said of his efforts, adding that it requires not only technical know-how but also "a great deal of creativity."

When Shadle was in his midseventies, the project was still going strong. He and his team had reached the point where they needed a longer, better track. "The Alvord Desert in Oregon where we've done our testing is only around nine miles long, and when you're pushing up into the 500s and 600s and beyond, that's not long enough for the margin for error," Shadle said at the time. "It takes more than three miles just to stop at these rates of speed." So they chose Diamond Valley, in Eureka County, CA, a dry lake bed, "because of its smooth surface and remote location, which makes it easier to secure for long test runs." Diamond Valley was big enough, flat enough, and isolated enough to allow them to construct a sixteen-mile-long track. After the inevitable regulatory delays, they obtained a permit in December 2017, from the U.S. Bureau of Land Management.

Sadly, Shadle never had the chance to make that attempt. His last year of life instead was spent battling cancer. He died in September 2018, at seventy-seven. He had topped 500 mph in 2016. "It's not a bad ride, really," he said. "The faster you go, the smoother it gets. Once you get up to 400, it's very smooth."

It's a terrible cliché in the news business: "At 73, Nevada's longest-serving lunch lady shows no signs of slowing down"; "At 78, Bemidji, Minnesota's favorite barber, shows no signs of slowing down"; "At 92, Hollywood legend Mitzi Gaynor shows no signs of slowing down." And it's usually a load of bull. (Well, except in the case of Mitzi. She's unstoppable.)

For most people, old age is a time to slow down. Physically, we don't move as fast as we used to. Emotionally, we're no longer in such a hurry, and we're more able to take the time we need to appreciate a beautiful landscape or contemplate a weighty problem. Ed Shadle wasn't most people.

As Matt Anderson from The Henry Ford put it: "All racers have a 'never give up' attitude. (In fact, 'never give up' was the motto of racing driver Louis Chevrolet, namesake of GM's car brand.) But Ed Shadle truly lived that philosophy. At a time in life when others would've settled into a quiet retirement, Shadle was determined to set a land speed record. Of course, it would've been a happier Hollywood ending had he broken the record, but the fact that he never stopped trying is triumph enough in my mind."

———————

A sad postscript: Ed Shadle did eventually share the driving, with racer Jessi Combs, known as "the fastest woman on four wheels." She tragically crashed and died in the same vehicle in 2019, during a ride in which she set the women's world record of 523 mph.

OLD IRONSIDES: Jack LaLanne

Jack LaLanne was famous for saying, "I can't afford to die. It'll wreck my image." And the man did seem immortal.

Growing up in San Francisco, young Jack loved junk food. But at fifteen, he heard a lecture by a nutritionist and started lifting weights, using paint cans filled with cement. In 1936, he opened a health club in Oakland—some say the nation's first. This was an era when doctors had concerns about the health effects of weightlifting. As he later recalled, "People thought I was a charlatan and a nut."

In the 1950s, TV's *The Jack LaLanne Show* found an audience primarily of women. Dressed in his signature blue jumpsuit, LaLanne encouraged viewers to exercise with him (and Happy, his German shepherd) using household items like broomsticks and chairs. In 1960, *Sports Illustrated* called him an "athletic Moses leading women out of the waistland while finding along the way a promised land for himself."

LaLanne was a showman. At age forty, he swam the length of the Golden Gate Bridge underwater with 140 pounds of equipment (including two air tanks). At seventy, he towed seventy rowboats during a mile-long swim in Long Beach, California—while handcuffed. The feats might have continued even longer were it not for his wife, Elaine, who told the *Chicago Tribune*, "If Jack wants to pull off another water stunt for his 80th birthday, he can tow me across our bathtub."

In his nineties, LaLanne would start his day with two hours of exercise (one hour of weight training and one hour in the pool). When he died, at ninety-six, he was celebrated as the Founding Father of Fitness. In his eulogy, Arnold Schwarzenegger envisioned what was happening in heaven with the newest arrival: his friend Jack, he said, "has already told old Saint Peter that the wake-up call is going to be at six in the morning. And there will be thousands of push-ups."

"Older people don't feel old unless they're told they're old," LaLanne once said. "I can't say that a 96-year-old man can look like a 16-year-old boy. But with good eating habits, a good exercise program and a good attitude—he'll be the sexiest, healthiest 96-year-old around, and isn't that what counts?"

A Trifecta of Horse Stories

Michael Blowen,

Snowman

& John Henry

The term "front-runner" didn't originate in politics. "Homestretch" doesn't come from baseball. "Daily Double" wasn't coined by the folks at *Jeopardy!* They all began with horse racing. (Ditto "win, place, or show," which I always thought started as a Sondheim lyric in *Gypsy*.)

The same goes for "trifecta." It's when a bettor chooses the first three finishers in the correct order. We're using it here in the more colloquial sense to describe a group of three, in this case three stories of horses living out their final years in glory. Two of these horses accomplished astonishing physical feats at advanced ages. These horses pushed the limits of what their bodies might do, forcing us to reconsider what might be achieved by any creatures, human or animal, as they get older.

There's no win, place, or show here. These are all winners, hands down and across the board. (Yup, both of those come from horse racing, too.)

Michael Blowen and His Old Friends

retired at fifty-six to help retired horses

If the Great Resignation taught us anything, it's that a lot of people are weary of their jobs. Even people who appear successful and fulfilled can reach a point where they've had enough. Michael Blowen was someone like that. On the outside, he seemed to have a good gig. A longtime film critic for the *Boston Globe*, he was lucky enough to be paid to watch movies. His wife, Diane White, was a star columnist at the same paper. They lived in a nice neighborhood near Harvard Square, enjoyed a certain social status in town, and made a good living as journalists.

But Michael wasn't happy. He recalled the moment back in 1987 when reviewing movies got to be just too much: "They sent me to a movie called *Date with an Angel*. Emmanuelle Béart, who's a wonderful French actor, she had done [the French language film] *Manon of the Spring*, and she was terrific." But her first Hollywood film was a clumsily scripted high-concept rom-com. The premise: a cosmetics executive living in Beverly Hills wakes up to find that an angel with a broken wing has crash-landed in his swimming pool. "I had one of those *Network* moments," Blowen remembered, referring to the Sidney Lumet film of 1976. "I actually stood up at the screening and I said, 'I can't take this anymore.'"

Blowen's editor at the *Globe* wanted to keep him on, so he was moved to the stand-up comedy beat. But that wasn't any more gratifying. Blowen was slowly realizing that his real passion wasn't in the world of entertainment—at least not human entertainment. His real passion was the racetrack.

That's right, it wasn't horses, at least not yet. It was *betting on horses.* "I only liked horses because I liked to drink and gamble," he said. As a kid he was afraid of them and later on was puzzled as to why *Sports Illustrated* would put Triple Crown winner Secretariat on its cover instead of some baseball or football player. But when a *Globe* editor invited Blowen to go to Suffolk Downs—that was East Boston's old racetrack, located out past Logan Airport—he warmed to the idea of trying to pick the winners. "I liked the challenge of reading the racing form. It was like playing chess with yourself and trying to predict the future. I liked the betting part of it," he told me. He also liked the characters at the track, the lively conversation, the beer.

He soon found himself spending as much time at the track as in the newsroom—and eventually falling in love with the horses themselves. "I never got paid. I [mucked] stalls and I took care of the horses" in the wee hours of the morning, before heading off to his regular job. He was, he said, leading a double life.

When the *Globe* began looking to cut overhead and was offering buyouts to staff, Michael decided he wanted to make a change. A job offer had come in from a Kentucky-based organization dedicated to saving retired Thoroughbreds from slaughter and abuse. The idea of providing a better life for these racehorses in their homestretch promised exactly the change he needed.

But Michael still had to convince his wife, the reigning queen of Boston-area columnists, to trade the bookstores and cafes of Cambridge for the pastures and hay barns of Kentucky. (Back in 1984, Diane, a perennial winner, had been named columnist of the year by *Boston Magazine*. The high praise came with a low blow aimed at Michael: "Snow White—she's the queen of all the columnists," the magazine noted. "And all the rest of the columnists are dwarfs, especially her husband, Dopey.") It seemed a tough sell. Yet Diane, to Michael's surprise, agreed to the plan. And so, after more than two decades in the newspaper trade, it was time for Michael Blowen's second act. In 2001, he and Diane took their buyouts and headed south.

After a short spell at his new job, Michael, at age fifty-six, was ready to start his own farm, one that would be open to the public. Mind you, he had no real money and no backers. But he was determined. "I wanted to have a place of my own," he told me when I visited him in Kentucky for *CBS Sunday Morning*, "and I wanted to open it up for visitors." He reasoned that the public's admiration for these splendid creatures might help to support them in their golden years. "I knew the way people were around movie stars, and I thought of all these great horses as movie stars. And I thought, 'If you open it up and people can come see them, it could succeed.'" The idea for Old Friends Thoroughbred Retirement Farm was born.

Around this time, a terrible story shook the horse-racing world. A former Kentucky Derby champion, Ferdinand, had been sold for slaughter in Japan. Ferdinand had won the Derby in 1986. The following year he bested 1987 Derby winner Alysheba in a showdown of champions at the Breeders' Cup. He won Horse of the Year honors in 1987 and was retired to stud in 1989, at which point he ranked as the fifth-greatest money-winner of all time, one of the greatest Thoroughbreds of his era. But when Ferdinand's offspring didn't prove to be winners themselves, his stud value dropped. He was sold to an outfit in Japan looking to breed American-style champions. After six unsuccessful breeding seasons in Japan, he was sold again. A few years later, when journalist Barbara Bayer tried to track him down, she learned that he had been "disposed of."

The news hit Michael Blowen hard. "The idea that you could just toss 'em away like that was really grotesque. He was beautiful," Blowen recalled of Ferdinand. "[By] all accounts, just a marvelous horse. And he . . . he should've lived out his life that way. But it's the same thing with humans. . . . if you can't generate income you're vulnerable. And I don't care what you are, a horse, a human, or whatever it is. If you can't generate income you're in trouble."

From that point on, Michael dedicated his life to making sure that there was a better fate for the great champions who earn so much money for their breeders and bring so much joy to their fans but are no longer bringing home million-dollar purses.

Getting started was rough. Blowen, coming late in life to the horse business, speaking with a heavy Boston accent, seemed out of his element in the world of Kentucky Thoroughbreds. In the beginning, he recalls, "I would hear people. I would walk away and I could hear 'em in the background makin' fun of me." These days, however, no one's laughing. Old Friends is thriving. About twenty thousand visitors pay each year to meet the veteran racehorses—both the champions and the also-rans.

The farm sits on 270 acres in Georgetown, Kentucky, and offers exactly the kind of late-life care that befits these majestic creatures. When I visited, its senior residents included Alphabet Soup, winner of the Breeders' Cup in 1996. He spent most of his time hanging out with a donkey named Gorgeous George. A particular favorite of Michael's is Silver Charm, who won the Kentucky Derby and the Preakness in 1997. And in the next paddock is his former rival, Touch Gold, who won the Belmont the same year in a fierce comeback, denying Silver Charm the Triple Crown. Old Friends even boasted an actual movie star among its residents: Popcorn Deelites was only moderately successful on the racetrack, but enjoyed a second career as an actor, playing Seabiscuit in the Oscar-nominated film of that name. (As of this writing, of the abovementioned horses, only Silver Charm and Touch Gold are still with us.) I may have been most charmed by Little Silver Charm, a miniature horse and unofficial mascot of Old Friends who would make the perfect Sancho Panza to Michael Blowen's Don Quixote.

In all, the residents of the retirement community at Old Friends have earned

Michael Blowen and his favorite "old friend," Kentucky Derby and Preakness winner Silver Charm, in 2015.
Laura Battles/ OldFriendsequine.org

north of $240 million in prize money. Many have made millions more from their stud fees. It's often said that the value of a horse disappears the last time it crosses a finish line—or, for some of the stallions, the last time he walks out of the breeding shed. At Old Friends the exact opposite is true. For Blowen, whether you're a horse or a human being, when the hard work of earning a living is behind you, "that's where life begins."

And the horses have quite a life at Old Friends. For them, the farm is part assisted living community, part luxury spa. Dr. Bryan Waldridge, a veterinarian I met there, has for years tended to the animals, never charging a penny for his services. (He's just one of many volunteers who seem to view their service to the animals as a privilege.) And if these former champions are feeling any old-age aches and pains, they have equine massage therapists.

What's most special about Old Friends, Blowen told me, is that it's a place where majestic old horses can, after a life spent competing, "return to being themselves." Dr. Waldridge agreed, describing to me how so many new residents seemed confused by their new freedom: "You can see some of them go, 'What do I do now?'

They're looking around because their life at the track is really regimented." A competitive Thoroughbred does the same thing every day, getting worked out and fed on a regular schedule. But at Old Friends, "They just get to do what they want. I mean, these horses come out and roll in the mud, and, you know, they just . . . *frolic*, I guess is the best word for it."

These horses may not reminisce and swap stories of their glory days the way that human athletes do, but they do live out a kind of retirement that many of us can only envy. Raised to excel, to compete, and to win in the most competitive of arenas, these aged warriors get to spend their later years remembering *how* to frolic.

Old Friends has also allowed Michael Blowen to return to being himself. The man who stepped away from his career as a movie and comedy critic in his mid-fifties took a risk to make his dream a reality. The payout has been immeasurable.

"How many people in the United States of America can wake up every morning and say, 'This is great'?" he said with a sense of wonder. "The horses tell you to relax, just take it easy. Don't worry about it. Things will work out. And so far, so good."

———

A postscript: In January 2024 Michael Blowen, on the verge of seventy-seven, stepped down as president of Old Friends after identifying a worthy successor. Ultimately he loves the horses too much to risk a transition that's anything less than smooth for them. But Michael and Diane are staying in their home at the farm, where he'll greet the horses every morning as he has since 2003. He wouldn't have it any other way.

opposite page: Me hanging
out with Old Friends mascot
Little Silver Charm.
Michelle Kessel

When I spoke to him this time, he was working on his memoir, *Final Furlong*, which is also the name of the final leg of a horse race. "When kids accompany their parents to the farm," he said, "I always engage them by saying, 'I'll bet your parents tell you this is the best time of your lives.' . . . They nod in agreement. But that's totally a lie."

He said he told them that "every day, they tell you when to get up and when to go to bed, what to eat and when to eat it. Do this. Do that. When you get to be old and bald and toothless, you get to do whatever you want. That's why being old is so much better. It's like these horses," Michael continued. "The pressure on them to win the Kentucky Derby when they're three is incalculable, but now that they're like Silver Charm and they can't compete anymore, they relax and enjoy life. And no one tells them what to do. They tell *us*. That's why they're so happy."

Snowman: The Cinderella Horse

Horse of the Year at age eleven; rider competed internationally at eighty-one

Another creature who seemed destined for a sad end was an old plow horse, later named Snowman. On a cold, snowy February day in 1956, he was brought to a livestock auction in New Holland, Pennsylvania, Amish country. He had been born eight years earlier, on February 29, 1948—Leap Day. It was a day whose name would eventually prove auspicious. But in 1956, this gelding's owner had decided that he was no longer productive, and so he brought him to an auction that sold injured, skinny, and malnourished horses. Most of the buyers were from the meat industry. The horses they picked up would become feed for other animals, including dogs.

Yet on that fateful afternoon, the gray-white beast of burden received a remarkable reprieve. It was a horse's equivalent of the call from the governor that

Champion show jumper Snowman and owner Harry deLeyer; both defied the odds.

commutes the sentence of a death row convict. In this case, the miracle phone call came in the form of a handsome Dutch immigrant named Harry deLeyer.

DeLeyer was a riding instructor and young father who was seeking inexpensive horses for his students and children to learn on. On his way to the New Holland auction, Harry got a flat tire; by the time he arrived, the more vigorous horses had been purchased. The rest were being sold en masse to a slaughterhouse. But they were still on the lot, and Harry took a look around. The hapless plow horse (he had only one shoe) caught his eye, and, as he recalled it, they shared a meaningful look. "At the same time I looked at him, he looked down to me. Snowman and I clicked right away," a smiling Harry recalled many years later. (You can view this moment for yourself, as well as some terrific old film clips, in *Harry & Snowman*, an utterly charming 2016 documentary by Ron Davis.)

Having grown up on a farm in the Netherlands, Harry knew horses well, and he saw that this one appeared to be still sturdy. He was sixteen hands high, a healthy size. Harry especially liked his calm temperament, which would suit beginning riders at his school. As he said, "I remember seeing his eyes and thinking, 'This one seems nice and quiet. I'll give him a chance.'" Harry bought Snowman for eighty dollars. That small investment ended up paying out unimaginable dividends, as this unheralded workhorse turned into one of the most famous and successful show jumpers in history—all at an age well past the point where horses normally become champions. Harry would later turn down a blank check offer for Snowman from real estate developer Bert Firestone.

Snowman was not the first horse Harry had rescued; he had a history of rescuing both horses and human beings. Born in Sint-Oedenrode in 1927, Harry grew up on his family's farm. He learned to ride as a toddler and by seven was competing. Life changed dramatically when Hitler's army invaded in 1940. The school Harry attended was commandeered to intern Jews. Meanwhile Harry's father became active in the resistance, supplying the Allies with information about German positions. The family would shelter Jews beneath their cow barn, covering the entrance to the cellar with hay and manure. Refugees would stay with the deLeyers for a few days before moving on to their next stop, the ultimate destination being England.

As the tide turned and the Allies recaptured the Low Countries, the Germans retreated. But Allied bombing had knocked out many bridges, and the Germans, who had taken hundreds of Dutch horses for their own use, now abandoned those same horses in their flight. Harry recalls that hundreds, maybe thousands were abandoned by a river for days, starving. "All I wanted to do was save them poor horses," he said years later.

Perhaps witnessing the horrors of the war had an effect on Harry when he came across Snowman in New Holland more than a decade later. In any case, this was one horse he was able to save.

He brought him home to his converted two-acre chicken farm in St. James, Long Island. It was his four-year-old daughter, Harriet, who christened the animal "Snowman." But Harry had promised a neighbor, a chiropractor, that he would sell him the next worthy horse he acquired, and so he sold Snowman to the man for a modest profit. Yet from the moment that they had shared their first meaningful look, Harry had formed a bond with Snowman, and he was reluctant to let him go. So he and the chiropractor made a deal: if the doctor ever decided to sell the horse, he would sell him back to Harry.

Apparently Harry wasn't the only one who had already formed a bond. Not long after the sale, he came home one day to find Snowman back on his property. Assuming that his neighbor had neglected to close the gate, he returned him. But when Snowman came back a second time, Harry and his neighbor realized that this old plow horse had actually jumped the paddock fence. The solution seemed obvious—a higher fence. To everyone's surprise, Snowman jumped that, too. So they tied a rope to him, with a truck tire at the end of it, thinking it would allow him freedom to move about but keep him from escaping. Snowman jumped the fence, tire and all, and returned once more to Harry's stables. At that point, both men realized that Snowman belonged to Harry.

Of course, in leaping the neighbor's fence, Snowman had demonstrated special ability as a jumper. Harry was a capable rider; as a young man, he had been an alternate on the Dutch Olympic team that competed in London in 1948. In 1957, he finished fourth in the National Horse Show Championship. Initially, he had not thought of Snowman as a future jumper. "He didn't look anything like a jumper—he was very long in the body, he stumbled over the poles of a two-and-a-half to three-foot jump, he ran like he was drunk," he later remembered. But he began to work with him, training him to compete in shows.

Show jumping, especially in the 1950s, attracted a particular crowd—the same types who might go in for yachting, big-game hunting, and competitive hot-air ballooning. In 2016, I did a piece on show jumping for *60 Minutes Sports* and discovered that show jumping is for neither the faint of heart nor the light of wallet. My interviewees included Jennifer Gates (daughter of Bill), Georgina Bloomberg (daughter of Mike), and Jessica Springsteen (daughter of Bruce). All of them are accomplished equestrians. Springsteen was a silver medalist at the 2020 Summer Olympics. Over the years Georgina Bloomberg has broken more bones than a hockey player—and has gotten back on the horse each time. Suffice it to say, this is the kind of sport for which having family money helps.

Harry deLeyer taught riding at the Knox School for Girls, a tony boarding school on Long Island whose website to this day boasts of forty waterfront acres. (Today the school is coed.) The students at Knox came from the moneyed elite. In Harry's day they included Teddy Roosevelt's granddaughter and Francesca Hilton, Zsa Zsa Gabor's daughter. When Harry brought Snowman into the clubby world of show jumping, both of them were outsiders. Both horse and rider came from humble beginnings, and from lives of hard work. Harry's childhood on his family farm and Snowman's eight years pulling a plow had created two tough, determined, and resilient competitors. Their appearance in the show jumping world was regarded as a curiosity. When Snowman competed, his lack of credentials, and especially his bargain-basement eighty-dollar purchase price, became a story unto itself.

Yet Harry had been riding Snowman for only two years when the horse had a breakout season. In 1958, the ten-year-old competed at a small Long Island event, the Rice Farms Horse Show. He won that competition and every event he participated in for the rest of the year. Harry believed in him, and kept pushing him to participate in front of bigger crowds and against more prestigious—and younger—horses.

In June of that year, Snowman won the Sands Point Horse Show, defeating the two-time champ. Still there were detractors who thought it was a fluke. But then he won the Ox Ridge Charity Horse Show in Darien, Connecticut, qualifying him for the upcoming National Horse Show, held at Madison Square Garden. The odds were long. Snowman, you might say, had a snowball's chance.

It was a big year for the Madison Square Garden event, which was celebrating its Diamond Jubilee. The cover of *Sports Illustrated* featured Olympian Hugh Wiley, and the article inside recalled fondly that three-quarters of a century ago, "the first National was held in William Vanderbilt's horsecar barn on Madison Square." Snowman would be competing against the reigning (reining?) champion jumper McLain Street as well as the formidable Windsor Castle, who had recently been purchased for $50,000—making him, at the time, the most expensive horse ever. Yet Snowman's preternatural leaping ability and Harry's skill in guiding the animal swiftly over every obstacle proved an unbeatable combination. Together they defied the naysayers (neigh-sayers?) and took home the blue ribbon. By year's end, Snowman had won the unofficial triple crown of jumping, being named not only champion of the National Horse Show but also the American Horse Shows Association's Horse of the Year and the Professional Horseman's Association champion.

The astonishing run of victories brought recognition to the whole deLeyer family. Fame and a degree of fortune ensued. Snowman and Harry were featured in *Life*. They appeared on *To Tell the Truth* and Johnny Carson's slightly ungrammatical game show, *Who Do You Trust?* Snowman fan clubs popped up; parents would bring adoring kids out to Long Island for a chance to pet the champion horse, who took all the attention—yes—in stride. The unassuming ungulate toured Europe, managing the transport on ship and plane with his patented equine equanimity. He even scored an endorsement deal with Bulova. A magazine ad, available on eBay, shows a rather blasé Snowman surrounded by dozens of female riders in equestrian garb, all holding up their wrists to display their watches.

In 1959, Snowman again won top honors from the Professional Horseman's Association and the American Horse Shows Association. (Winning the AHSA's Horse of the Year twice had never been done before.) The accomplishment was all the more impressive given Snowman's age at this point, eleven.

Capitalizing on their unlikely celebrity, Snowman and Harry started performing exhibitions. They would demonstrate the sorts of jumps required in competition, but, as the same round of jumps over the same obstacles became stale, they developed a new trick—jumping over another horse. NBA fans are familiar with a famous moment at the 2000 Olympics when Toronto Raptors star Vince Carter leaped over the seven-foot-two French center Frédéric Weis to dunk a basketball. Now imagine that feat—but with horses. (If Harry and Snowman had done this in Central Park and put out a tip jar, they would have made a killing.)

After mastering that stunt, Harry set yet another goal, breaking the American record for the equine high jump (what equestrians call "puissance"). The powerful Snowman cleared seven feet, one inch, an American record that stood for a decade.

Snowman, however, was aging. In 1962, at age fourteen, he earned his final ribbon, a third-place finish. Harry wanted to remain competitive as a rider, so he moved onto younger horses when competing. But Snowman stayed in the public eye for the rest of the decade. In 1969, a gala retirement party was held for him in Madison Square Garden. Thousands of fans came to the arena to cheer on the quiet, steady champion one last time. Harry, his wife, Johanna, and all eight of their children were in attendance. At twenty-one, a horse is elderly and toward the end of its life; Snowman was still jumping. Draped in roses, he strode around the ring to the strains of "Auld Lang Syne" while the crowd gave him a standing ovation.

Throughout these years, Snowman was a member of the deLeyer family. He would pull them on a sleigh through the snow at Christmastime and accompany them to the beach in the summer, swimming out into Long Island Sound with three or four kids on his back. The kids would even stand up and dive off him into the water. The strong and patient Snowman seemed always to enjoy it, or at least to indulge the deLeyer children. (The home movies included in Ron Davis's documentary are irresistible.)

Snowman lived out his retirement on the deLeyer farm in Long Island. In 1974, at age twenty-six, his kidneys began to fail. The horse was in pain, and the family made the difficult decision to put down the beloved animal. Harry couldn't bear to be there for the euthanasia. But when Harry's children, accompanied by the veterinarian, tried to lead Snowman from his stable, the old fella wouldn't budge. Eventually, they called Harry to see if he could help. Snowman immediately followed Harry, the man who had saved his life almost twenty years earlier, the man he evidently wanted at his side in his final moments. Decades later, speaking about Snowman's death was still challenging for Harry. In his words, Snowman was more than a horse. He was a friend.

In 1992, Snowman was inducted into the Show Jumping Hall of Fame.

But Snowman wasn't the only one to do remarkable things in old age. As Harry got older, he seemed to take on the indomitable spirit of his favorite horse. He continued to compete in show jumping competitions, often against riders one-third his age. Someone gave him the moniker "Galloping Grandfather," which he embraced. Harry's mere entrance into any horse jumping contest made the show an instant event. He became the sport's preeminent ambassador. In these years, he told Dick Cavett, "My biggest thrill is to compete against the young people. I am against the boys and I still can keep up with them."

As Harriet, his daughter, says, Harry was no one-trick pony.

In 1979, twenty years after his feats with Snowman, Harry won the National Horse Show in his division again. He was fifty-two when he earned his third and final blue ribbon in the open jumper class. Even after that, the Galloping Grandfather continued to thrive on competition. At seventy-seven, he suffered a serious fall—from his hayloft—and broke his back. With steel rods in place, he made a recovery, and at eighty-one competed in the Washington International Horse Show. One critic called him "star of the class."

Harry passed away at the age of ninety-three, a legend in show jumping circles, famed for his own abilities as a rider, trainer, and teacher, but above all for the unexpected champion he had bought at auction some sixty-five years before.

John Henry: The Geriatric Marvel

left the competition in the dust at age nine

Racing is a young horse's game. Horses can live into their midtwenties or even to the age of thirty, but in the most famous and lucrative races, those that make up the American Triple Crown (the Kentucky Derby, the Preakness Stakes, and the Belmont Stakes), only three-year-olds are allowed to run. This is a tradition that was inherited from the British, whose own Triple Crown (the St. Leger, the Two Thousand Guineas, and the Epsom Derby) maintains the same rule. The oldest of these competitions, the St. Leger Stakes, started in 1776; we don't know why it was restricted to younger horses, but 250 years later, this arbitrary distinction is still in effect.

Horses actually get stronger after age three, usually reaching peak speed around four or four and a half. One reason that fans enjoy the Breeders' Cup Classic, held every fall, is that it provides a chance for top three-year-olds to compete against top four-year-olds, so that Derby winners can race against each other. But even four-year-olds are still young, and no horse older than five has ever won the Breeders'

Cup. Champions older than six are quite rare, and most horses retire before that age, in part due to the tremendous physical demands that the sport makes on its participants. Show jumpers like Snowman can push the age limit a bit, but among racehorses there is one "geriatric marvel"—to quote *Equus* magazine—who stands out above all the others, one indefatigable veteran who "convincingly proved that the race is not always to the youngest." That horse was John Henry.

John Henry's late-life accomplishments, which include seventeen Grade 1 victories over eight years of competition, are all the more remarkable given his inauspicious beginnings. (Grade 1 is the most competitive tier of races.) He was not quite as much of a no-name as Snowman, but he seemed to have very little going for him as a foal. (That's a horse that's less than a year old.)

For starters, he was born "back at the knee." In the world of horse breeding they say, "No legs, no horse," because the build and proportions of a horse, what breeders call its "conformation," are critical for success on the track. Conformation for a horse breeder is like design for an engineer: it makes high-end performance possible. And a horse born "back at the knee" is unlikely to give you high-end performance. This is a condition in which the horse's knee—technically, it's not really the knee but the carpus, but don't worry about that right now—is set behind the top of the foreleg due to the angle of what is called the cannon bone. Breeders don't like this condition: as the horse ages, it puts stress on the tendons and ligaments in the leg, causing arthritis and fractures of the carpal bones, among other potential injuries.

Beyond the problems with his conformation, John Henry was small; he grew to a height of only 15 hands and a weight of only 1,000 pounds—light for a male Thoroughbred. There were also questions about his temperament. He was named John Henry after the "steel-driving" Black American folk hero because as a yearling (a horse between one and two years old), he would knock over steel feed buckets and stamp them flat. And his pedigree was unimpressive; the word they use in the business is "obscure." His sire, Ole Bob Bowers, was a stallion too stubborn and temperamental to be successful on the track. His dam, Once Double, was described by Chris Lincoln of ESPN as "nondescript." Even John Henry's birthplace—Golden Chance Farm—was undistinguished; it had become a pig farm by the time he died. There was, however, more noble blood further back—on his mother's side, the legendary Man o' War. His father was descended from Princequillo, the grandsire of the incomparable Secretariat. But the championship blood seemed to have been pretty well diluted when John Henry was foaled, on a chilly March day in 1975.

The horse's early years did nothing to change expectations. As a yearling, he sold for a mere $1,100. He was gelded because of his intractable temperament and was sold four times by 1978. The final buyer was Sam Rubin, a first-time horse owner, who bought him sight unseen, and might have wondered if there was a lemon law for horses. (Rubin did not even know what a gelding was when he bought the horse.) At this point, any chance at greatness seemed surely to have passed; by the end of their third year, some of the greatest Thoroughbreds are already being put out to stud. John Henry, in contrast, had won only a single, relatively uncompetitive race.

Under Rubin, however, he began racing on turf rather than dirt, which seemed to bring out his strengths. In 1979, Rubin hired trainer Ron McAnally, and John Henry began to win, finishing first in six consecutive graded stakes, three of which were Grade 1 contests. When asked about the turnaround, McAnally said that the secret was to treat John Henry with kindness. The excitable horse had been treated poorly as a colt, and breaking him out of his angry disposition was key to harnessing his athleticism. Under McAnally, he developed, as *Equus* wrote, "from an average sprinter on dirt to the premier distance horse on grass." The next year, as a five-year-old, he earned a million dollars and was named champion turf male horse of the year.

It wasn't until age six, however, that this late bloomer began to make history. That year John Henry won eight of ten starts. The highlight of the racing season was the 1981 inaugural Arlington Million Stakes, a nationally televised event in which

John Henry took on the best horses from around the globe. It was the first race ever with a million-dollar purse—60 percent of which would go to the winner—and a chance to see whether this "little bay horse with the average body" could still win against the best of the best.

There were some bad omens. John Henry drew the outside post, a poor starting position. The turf was wet and boggy, and he had yet to show that he could win a major race on a soft track. Finally, he was no spring chicken at age six and, because he had run a full schedule that year, there was some thought that he might simply be worn out.

Nor did the race begin well for the old man. Coming into the homestretch, it was 40–1 longshot The Bart who led the field. But John Henry, ridden by legendary jockey Bill Shoemaker, showed astonishing determination, working his way through the field, slowly gaining on the leader. At the sixteenth pole—that's one-sixteenth of a mile from the finish—John Henry still trailed by a full length. Yet he kept coming.

To watch the final ten seconds of this forty-year-old race still carries something of the thrill it must have had for those who saw it live. John Henry charges on the outside, seemingly out of nowhere, passing two other horses as if they're standing still, chewing up ground with his full, graceful stride, pulling even with The Bart right at the line. It was a photo finish (yup, another term that originated with horse racing). The NBC broadcaster called it for The Bart but had to eat his words. The camera revealed that John Henry had nosed out the victory. "He's a tough little dude," Shoemaker later said. "The toughest little dude I ever rode in my life. He scraps, he fights, he don't give up." At year's end, John Henry was rewarded with Horse of the Year laurels, the first unanimous recipient of the award.

The champion continued to win the next year, but in 1983, owner Sam Rubin decided to transport him to Japan—partly out of vanity, to display the magnificent horse to his business associates in Asia. Later, Rubin admitted that this was a mistake due to his own "ego" and that he had been warned that John Henry was too old

Photo finish: Bill Shoemaker rides six-year-old John Henry
(on the outside) to victory in the 1981 Arlington Million Stakes.

Bettmann/Getty Images

for the thirty-hour trip. Indeed, he suffered muscle seizures and was unable to race for seven months. Bill Shoemaker, despite his admiration for the horse, left to ride other Thoroughbreds.

It seemed that a great career was winding down. But maybe the most remarkable part of John Henry's story was yet to come. In 1984, the late bloomer bloomed a second time.

By now he was nine, positively ancient by the standards of racehorses. *Sports Illustrated* called him "the grand old geezer of racing," while his Mexican groom, Jose Mercado, favored the simple "El Viejo." With Chris McCarron now his jockey, the old man won the Hollywood Invitational in May, and then once again took the Arlington Million, beating out Royal Heroine and Kentucky Derby champ Gato Del Sol, who was a third his age. "He's the greatest thing that's ever happened to horse racing," commented John Gosden, the trainer of Royal Heroine, who, like many of John Henry's opponents, was run down at the finish. "He's now beyond being a horse. If you're going to get beat, get beat by an institution."

Next came another win at the Turf Classic in Belmont, followed by the Ballantine's Scotch Classic. In this final race, John Henry again trailed late; he was in eighth place with one lap to go when he made his move. With a half lap to go, he had climbed to fifth. In the last half lap, that supernatural power seemed to burst forth once again. As the horses came down the stretch, announcer Dave Johnson was shouting, "John Henry, out on the far outside, and he's flying. Down the stretch they come. The Old Man, John Henry, takes command!" He blazed past the failing competition and won by nearly three lengths. He had equaled the track record.

The end of 1984 promised a special event, the inaugural Breeders' Cup Classic, created as a kind of end-of-the-year championship. Rubin was prepared to enter his great champion, but John Henry had strained a ligament in his Ballantine's run and had to sit it out. Nonetheless, he won Horse of the Year a second time.

Few horses have ever won Horse of the Year at age six, as John Henry did in 1981. Only two horses, Exterminator in 1922 and Kelso in 1964, won Horse of the

Year at age seven. John Henry's 1984 age-nine victory is a complete outlier. He was voted Racehorse of the Decade for the 1980s and was inducted into the National Thoroughbred Racing Hall of Fame in 1990.

John Henry retired at ten years old in 1985. He had run eighty-three races over seven years, amassing over $6.5 million in prize money, more than any other horse at that time. It was not only his longevity but also his character that in the end made him so beloved. What had been youthful intractability developed, as the great champion aged, into a preternatural determination, which seemed to give the horse great reserves of strength as he powered past his rivals in closing out his victories. He was such a phenomenon that in 1984, the year of his second Horse of the Year award, *People* magazine counted him among their "25 Most Intriguing People," alongside Mary Lou Retton and Bruce Springsteen, then on his *Born in the U.S.A.* tour.

Not bad for a geezer.

Sister Jean

I'm pretty sure no one had it on their bracket back in 2018 that the biggest star during that year's NCAA March Madness basketball tournament would be a ninety-eight-year-old Catholic nun. But Sister Jean Dolores Schmidt, the team chaplain for Loyola Chicago men's team, became a sensation, as her beloved Ramblers advanced to the Final Four for the first time since 1963.

As she cheered her team on from the sidelines, the media fell in love with Sister Jean, describing her as godmother to this Cinderella team. And while she is not a saint (yet), she has become an icon, her image printed on T-shirts, socks—even bobbleheads.

In reflecting on this time in her 2023 memoir, Sister Jean tried to understand why she became an object of fascination: "I think it starts with the fact that I'm so old. Let's face it, people love little old ladies! We're harmless, we're cheerful, and we've been through a few things."

Sister Jean has been through more than a few things. Born in San Francisco in 1919 at the end of the influenza pandemic, she lived through the Great Depression. She walked across the Golden Gate Bridge on the day it opened in 1937. Her religious calling came at age eight, when she met a teacher who belonged to the Sisters of Charity of the Blessed Virgin Mary and "never looked back." Sister Jean would later join the "BVM motherhouse," as she put it, and begin her career as an educator and a coach. "I love working with these young people. I think that's what kept my heart young—not my body young—but kept my heart young all these years."

Basketball has also always played an important role in her life—playing in high school, then with her fellow sisters after entering the convent. Her motto: "Worship, Work, Win."

Having turned 104 in August 2023, Sister Jean is still mentoring, inspiring, and praying with her players. As she told one interviewer, "I pray for the other team, perhaps not as hard."

Founding Fathers of Comedy

Carl Reiner,

Mel Brooks

& Norman Lear

W as ever a group of friends collectively responsible for more laughter in the world?

The three men, who became friends starting out in television in the 1950s, look today like something very close to the Founding Fathers of American comedy. Their combined body of work is monumental. They created, wrote, directed, produced, and starred in some of the funniest and most beloved movies and TV shows in history; they wrote sketches, plays, musicals, record albums, books—really just about any kind of comic form practiced in the history of human expression. Together their influence on the performing arts is so broad and so deep that any comprehensive account would read like a history of American entertainment itself.

You would need a small almanac to track the honors, awards, and recognition they've collectively earned: Emmys, Oscars, Grammys, Tonys, National Medals of Arts, Peabody Awards, Kennedy Center Honors, the Mark Twain Prize for American Humor, WGA Laurel Awards, Golden Globes, induction into the Television Academy Hall of Fame, handprints and footprints on Hollywood Boulevard, scores of lifetime achievement awards, and—as I know from researching this piece—enough delightful YouTube clips to keep you smiling for weeks on end.

All three men were born in the 1920s, before television, before the talkies, and all lived to be centenarians, give or take a rounding error. (Lear passed away at 101, during the writing of this book; Reiner in 2020, at ninety-eight; Brooks, the baby of the bunch, is going strong at ninety-seven.) All three were children of Jewish immigrants who took early inspiration from the films of the Marx Brothers and the Ritz Brothers (look them up), and from the radio shows of Jack Benny and George Burns. All three rose from these humble beginnings to the pinnacle of artistic and commercial success.

Members of the Greatest Generation, all three served in World War II as young men. Following their service, all three sustained, through a turbulent and often violent century, an old-fashioned and fiercely optimistic belief in the democratic promise of America as the land of the free—while working, on and off camera, to realize those aspects of this American promise that remained unfulfilled.

Their life stories are braided together like the strands of a loaf of challah. After the war, all three honorably discharged veterans pursued similar paths, writing comedy in New York City. Brooks and Reiner met on *Your Show of Shows*, the legendary Sid Caesar variety hour that, along with its successor, *Caesar's Hour*, put the borscht belt on prime time and launched a dream team of comedy writers. That star-studded roster included Reiner, Brooks, Mel Tolkin (later a head writer for *All in the Family*), Larry Gelbart (creator of *M*A*S*H*, writer of *Tootsie*), Neil Simon, his older brother, Danny Simon, and Woody Allen. (Life with Caesar is immortalized in Neil Simon's play *Laughter on the 23rd Floor* and the Brooks-produced film *My Favorite Year*.) Lear did not write for Caesar, but he did write sketches for Danny Thomas, Jerry Lewis, Martha Raye, and other variety show hosts, and he soon found himself traveling in the same circles as the other two.

Decade after decade, these three lords of laughter maintained a deep friendship as they moved, with the television industry itself, from New York to L.A. In the 1950s, they would spend summers together on Fire Island. In the 1980s, they would escape from Hollywood politics and business with their wives for group getaway weekends. In the 2010s, Brooks and Reiner, both widowers by now, would eat dinner together every evening at Reiner's house on Rodeo Drive, often joined by Lear. Usually those evenings would wind down with *Jeopardy!* and *Wheel of Fortune* or, even better, an old movie. They were partial to the films they grew up on: musicals, old comedies, war movies. As Reiner once said, "Any movie that has the line 'Secure the perimeter,' you know it's good."

Each of these heroes of hilarity, in his own distinctive way, also had a knack—more than a knack, a gift—for drawing on the ethnic Jewish comedy of their childhood and presenting it to America in a way that made the whole country a little more Jewish, and made Jews feel a lot more American. None of them was particularly observant, but they drew from their heritage an ethical commitment to broadening the nation's understanding of who belonged, and of what belonging really

Carl Reiner, Mel Brooks, and Norman Lear, packing nearly three hundred years of funny onto one stage, May 2017.
Jeff Kravitz/FilmMagic/Getty Images

meant. The comic vision of America they offered was one full of foreign words and varied accents, of unpredictable behavior that questioned the need for good taste, of families of all backgrounds and cultural styles that could struggle and squabble and still love each other.

Perhaps most inspiring of all is the fact that each of these men continued into his nineties with astonishing vitality and good cheer. What's impressive about their later decades is, yes, their continued creative activity—guest-starring roles, memoirs crammed with cornball jokes, producing projects that nurtured the careers of a younger generation—but also their robust engagement with the world: with work, with politics, with people, with friends and family. Put simply, Reiner, Brooks, and Lear truly seemed to love old age.

Maybe when you've enjoyed a long and successful life with relatively good health, it's easy to age gracefully. Still, for all three of these colossi of comedy, the later decades were never a time for fading away or doing less but rather an extended opportunity to savor the gift of life. And in interview after interview over the years, all three men who spent their careers making others laugh have said some version of what amounts to the same thing: their own laughter is what kept them young.

Carl Reiner

comedy's ringmaster, unleashing brilliance
all around him until age ninety-eight

Carl Reiner never seemed to mind second billing. His signature roles were that of the straight man, the second banana, the supporting actor. It was in such capacity that he shone as a performer on Sid Caesar's *Your Show of Shows*. And as a writer and director he tended, unlike his best friend, Mel Brooks, to shun the spotlight. Yet the challenges of playing the supporting role should not be underestimated. Praising Reiner as "the best straight man I've ever worked with," Sid Caesar pointed out that "most people still don't realize the importance of a straight man in comedy, or how difficult that role is." Norman Lear told me very much the same thing when I spoke to him after Carl's passing. "Carl had no need to be the principal in anything," he said. "A lot of comics do. So he could be very funny as a sidekick and a straight man. Mel will tell you himself, he needed to be up front. Carl was a champion from the side." And Brooks himself kvelled, "There was no better straight man in the world." Theirs was a partnership based on trust and confidence in each other: "While he deferred the punch lines to me, he knew me well enough to follow along and cross paths enough to set me up for more opportunities. He also knew he could throw me a complete curveball and I'd swing for the fences."

What is the art of the straight man? You know the old line about how Ginger Rogers had to do everything Fred Astaire did, only backward and in high heels? It's something like that. As Caesar said, "Carl had to make his timing my timing." Sometimes Reiner stood in for the audience as a voice of sanity while playing off against manic, eccentric characters. As a performer, he balanced the excess of comedians like Caesar and Brooks with artful understatement, registering their outrageousness with a slight change in tone or a subtle deadpan. And as a kind of onstage director, he managed the unpredictable ad-libbing, creating a structure for them to work within. As Brooks put it, "I would dig myself into a hole, and Carl would not let me climb out."

Reiner savored the role. "As second banana," he said, "I had a chance to do just about everything a performer can ever get to do. If it came off well, I got all the applause. If it didn't, the show was blamed." But his willingness to take second billing actually spoke to a fundamental modesty. When he won the Mark Twain Prize for American Humor, he disavowed any credit for his achievements, saying, "I'm standing here because Sid Caesar and Mel Brooks and Mary Tyler Moore and Dick Van Dyke and Steve Martin were in my life. That's the truth."

Born in the Bronx, Reiner was a teenager when his older brother encouraged him to take a WPA-sponsored acting course; he memorized Queen Gertrude's monologue from *Hamlet* (which he could still perform beautifully in his nineties), but he had yet to launch his career when, at twenty-one, he was drafted into the Air Force. He trained as a radio and teleprinter operator and eventually sailed for Hawaii across what he called "a decidedly non-pacific Pacific Ocean—a roiling sea that did not allow me to keep a single meal down during our long, long, long crossing." In Hawaii, as his unit was preparing to ship out for Iwo Jima, he was corralled into auditioning for the Special Services, the military's entertainment unit. He threw together some gags and impressions, and, as he told Conan O'Brien, "I killed." Instead of seeing combat in Iwo Jima, he spent the next two years touring the Pacific theater.

From that point forward, his fate was to make people laugh. His career began in earnest in 1950, when he was hired as a regular on *Your Show of Shows*. He began as an actor but soon "worked my way into the writers' room without a portfolio." Reiner felt that the pressure of creating new material every week, along with the brilliance of his fellow writers, made "the creative process much more exciting" than theater, where routines could grow familiar. You might say that if Norman Lear later made TV politically relevant, Reiner helped forge its dominant comic style. As James Poniewozik of the *New York Times* put it, "Reiner's acting and writing in television's early days . . . helped define what TV would become. It would be playful, experimental, fast-paced. It would be mouthy and expressive, a medium that blew your lapels back."

Helping to blow back those lapels was Brooks. Reiner was fond of recalling their first meeting: "I came in and didn't know who he was. But Mel was standing there doing a Jewish pirate, saying, 'You don't know how hard it is to set sail. It's $3.87 for a yard of sail cloth. I can't afford to pillage and plunder anymore.'"

It was also in the writers' room of *Your Show of Shows* that Reiner began the ad-lib with Brooks that would launch their next big thing. He came in one day and Brooks was sitting on the couch. In a moment of inspiration, Reiner pulled out a tape recorder and in the flat tone of a popular news show called *We the People* asked Brooks if it was true that he was present at Jesus's crucifixion. Brooks responded with a weary sigh, and then, in the Yiddish accent of an old Jewish relative, "Oh boy." The 2000 Year Old Man was born.

Soon they were doing what Reiner called "command performances" at parties, with Brooks dispensing the wisdom of his two millennia along with little-known historical anecdotes (his affair with Dolley Madison: "I dillied with Dolley") or the origin of the War of the Roses ("One day we woke up and all the roses in England were gone"). "We never went to a party that someone didn't ask," Reiner recalled.

Finally, George Burns told them that if they didn't record their shtick, he would steal it, and so they put it on vinyl. They worried, though, that it was too much inside humor, with no appeal to non-Jews. Then Cary Grant, who was headed to England for a trip, asked for twelve copies. When he returned, he reported that Britain's Queen Mother loved the record. "The biggest shiksa in the world," Reiner laughed. As usual, he shrugged off the credit. "I always knew if I threw a question to Mel he could come up with something. I learned a long time ago that if you can corner a genius comedy brain in panic, you're going to get something extraordinary."

What came next was the creation that Reiner always prized as his "greatest achievement," *The Dick Van Dyke Show*. Reiner scripted a season's worth of shows with himself in the lead as a TV writer coming home to his young family in the suburbs. It was to be called *Head of the Family*. This was the early sixties, when postmodern self-reference was all the rage, and Reiner's show was the first sitcom about a sitcom. But when the network balked at his performance in the pilot, he agreed to let someone else be the star. Johnny Carson was considered, but the producer Sheldon Leonard suggested Dick Van Dyke. Reiner recalled, "I said, 'Sheldon, I don't want to fail with the same material twice.' He said, 'You won't fail. I'll get a better actor to play you.'"

Reiner welcomed the idea of a better actor in the role he'd written for himself. "I went to New York and saw [Van Dyke] in *Bye Bye Birdie* and I saw the single most talented man I've ever seen in my life," he said. And despite the fact that Van Dyke was "a midwestern gentile," he fit perfectly into the role, making it his own. Reiner took the supporting part of showrunner Alan Brady. And, of course, he wrote and directed and produced. As Reiner said, he was always a busybody, what his mother called a washerwoman. Telling other people what to do came naturally.

The show was a surprise hit. Van Dyke recalled, "We were on against *Perry Como*, on Wednesday nights, and no one noticed. We always thought we were going to be canceled." But when they were given *The Beverly Hillbillies* as a lead-in, the show became a hit. It may not have been as transgressive as Norman Lear's *All in the Family* a few years later, but before TV's "rural purge"—the mass cancellation of rural-themed comedies—it stood out for its intelligence and wit. The attractive young leads gave off a Jack and Jackie Kennedy vibe, and although they slept in twin beds, per network standards, Reiner never hid the fact that "there was a sexual connection" between them. (Van Dyke commented that unlike on previous sitcoms, "you actually believed that Rob and Laura did get it on.") The typical TV marriage had been more about bickering than affection. And Reiner made sure to give his nimble lead actor physical bits, knowing his gift for pantomime.

The show holds up remarkably well. Michelle Obama said that she liked watching *Dick Van Dyke* reruns better than her husband's debates. (She was joking, right?)

Reiner aimed for an evergreen quality, stressing not the topical, as Lear would later do, but a strong story with characters to care about. This marked a transition from the sketch- and gag-driven world of Sid Caesar. Garry Marshall, a writer on *The Dick Van Dyke Show*, said that what he learned above all from Reiner was the importance of "structure" in comedy; other shows cared about jokes, but Reiner focused on the narrative whole. Reiner was, according to Marshall, "the first genius at doing a show every week." (Marshall's sister, Penny, later married Reiner's son Rob, keeping it all in the family.)

After five seasons, Reiner felt the show had run its course. But much more remained in his career. As a feature film director, he debuted with *Enter Laughing*, an adaptation of his own autobiographical novel, but his breakthrough came with *Oh, God!* in 1977, with George Burns in the title role, decades before fellow Roctogenarian Morgan Freeman became Hollywood's go-to God guy.

It was about that time that Steve Martin, seeking to transition from stand-up to features, asked Reiner to direct his first film, *The Jerk*, now recognized as a comedy classic. Martin credits Reiner as his "greatest mentor, in movies and in life," someone who helped him transform from a zany stand-up and sketch artist to one of the finest comic leading actors of his generation. Much of that had to do with Reiner's approach to storytelling: "Carl's most valuable contribution to the movie was its emotional center, and I suspect it was those heart tugs that made the film a success," said Martin. Other collaborations followed: *Dead Men Don't Wear Plaid*, *The Man with Two Brains*, *All of Me*. Knowing Reiner's influence, it's hard not to see a hint of Dick Van Dyke in Steve Martin's awkward but agile physical comedy.

Hitting his golden years, Reiner remained just as active as Lear and Mel Brooks would. He took a memorable role as a veteran con man in Steven Soderbergh's trio of heist films, *Ocean's Eleven*, *Twelve*, and *Thirteen*. And, a writer at heart, he began setting down his memoirs, penning nearly a book a year in his nineties. He remained engaged in the world, active on Twitter in speaking out against threats to Americans' constitutional freedoms.

Reiner viewed old age as a time of opportunity and productivity. "Every morning before having breakfast," he would say, "I pick up my newspaper, get the obituary section and see if I'm listed. If I'm not, I'll have my breakfast."

That quip provided the title for a 2017 HBO documentary that he hosted, *If You're Not in the Obit, Eat Breakfast*. The film featured nonagenarian friends like Lear, Brooks, Van Dyke, Betty White, Kirk Douglas, and Iris Apfel doing all kinds of creative things. Tony Bennett, then ninety, opened the film singing "The Best Is Yet to Come."

Reiner was frequently asked about his secret to a long and happy life. Family and friends were a key for him. "The key to longevity is to interact with other people," he says in the film. At another point, Brooks asks him, "Is laughter what's keeping us alive?" "While you're alive, you can laugh," Reiner deadpans. "When you're dead, the laughter is so difficult. *So* difficult."

But for all the range and versatility of his comic talents, when Reiner passed away, during the height of the Covid pandemic, his friends remembered him for his kindness even more than his talents and accomplishments. "A mensch," said Dick Van Dyke. "The greatest human being I ever met in my life." Steve Martin addressed his departed friend, saying, "For me, one of your qualities stands out that is not often cited in the legacies of the famous: decency. All along, it was your decency that infused and invigorated your incredible gifts." And Norman Lear told me, "He was rare in that I can't remember him being in a bad mood or him telling me about a bad mood." He added, "He was a great hugger. There was never a better friend."

Mel Brooks of course paid tribute, saying, "I loved him." But Brooks's real tribute followed. For a year after Reiner's death, he would drive every night to Reiner's house on Rodeo Drive and have dinner in front of the television.

Mel Brooks

gleefully offending and delighting audiences into his tenth decade

Of all the talented writers and comedians who came out of the New York variety show scene, one stood out to Norman Lear. "Mel was clearly the most hilarious, north, south, east, and west," he said. "He was as funny as anyone I ever met, just naturally." Whether in front of a camera, in a writers' room, or at a cocktail party, the self-described ham (Brooks did not keep kosher) never stopped performing. "He's Mel Brooks all the time," said Lear. Carl Reiner agreed, noting simply, "He was always the funniest one."

Brooks was born Melvin Kaminsky in Brooklyn in 1926. His father died when he was two, and Brooks has suggested that his comedy grew out of anger at that loss. (His style always seemed more sharp-edged than Lear's or Reiner's.) Yet he also remembers that he was well loved. In the wintertime, his mother would warm his clothes on the tenement's radiator before dressing him for school.

The passion for show business struck early. As he told an interviewer for *Billboard*, "My uncle Joe was a cab driver and he took me to see this brand-new show that just opened—it was 1935—and it was called *Anything Goes*, a beautiful Cole Porter show. . . . We sat in the last seat of the last row of the last balcony, and even then I thought Ethel Merman was too loud." At that point he resolved to make a career in entertainment. "Years later," he wrote in his autobiography, "when I discovered to my amazement that Cole Porter wasn't Jewish, I was taken aback for a moment but then quickly forgave him."

Music was just as important as jokes for young Mel, who soon changed his last name—not to sound less Jewish but to avoid being confused with the jazz trumpeter Max Kaminsky. He learned to play piano and drums, stealing an occasional lesson from his neighbor Buddy Rich, the older brother of a classmate, who played with the bandleader Artie Shaw.

Four years younger than Reiner and Lear, Brooks enlisted in the army in 1944, after his brother Leonard was shot down flying a mission over Austria. After training at Virginia Military Institute and Fort Sill, Oklahoma, he shipped out to Normandy, where he served mainly as a combat engineer, helping to rebuild roads and bridges for the Allied advance. Contrary to Wikipedia, he didn't fight in the Battle of the Bulge, arriving in France two months after the Allies beat back that final German offensive. But that lack of combat experience didn't stop Brooks from joking about his good fortune in escaping injury. "I'm short. I lived. They shot over me," he said to Conan O'Brien years later.

After V-E Day, Brooks stayed on as an entertainment specialist, making the Allied troops in Europe laugh while Carl Reiner was doing the same thing in the Pacific. His talent began to emerge, and he was promoted to corporal, tasked with organizing large events. Onstage, he did Hitler impressions—a bit of shtick that would never leave his repertoire—and song parodies. Biographer Patrick McGilligan quotes Brooks's version of the Cole Porter standard "Begin the Beguine," which he adapted for army life: "When you begin / To clean the latrine . . ."

After his discharge, Brooks worked at various borscht belt gigs before being hired by Sid Caesar, whom he'd known since the mid-1930s when they met at a summer camp in Sullivan County, New York. Soon he was writing for *Your Show of Shows*. There, as you know by now, he and Reiner cooked up the 2000 Year Old Man routine. At this point, Brooks was young, but the role of an aged, experienced, and nutty alte kaker came effortlessly. When Reiner asked him how he stayed healthy, he replied that his diet consisted solely of pristine mountain spring water. "Only mountain spring water?" Reiner asked. "That, and a stuffed cabbage," Brooks answered. "What am I gonna live for, a little mountain water? You think I'm going to stay alive?"

Like Lear and Reiner, Brooks kept busy with different kinds of work in the early 1960s—albums with Reiner, TV sketches for his friend Zero Mostel, an Oscar-winning animated short called *The Critic*, a musical called *All American*. But the sitcom was the form then emerging as the comedy writer's path to financial stability. Brooks's opportunity came in 1964, when a producer teamed him with writer Buck Henry to develop a spy parody series. It was the height of the Cold War, and espionage was in. Ian Fleming and John le Carré were writing their great spy novels; NBC was airing *The Man from U.N.C.L.E.*; Peter Sellers, with his brilliant Inspector Clouseau, was making it all funny. Brooks and Henry were ready, in the words of *Time* magazine, to get on the "Bondwagon."

Your Show of Shows had traded in parodies like Sid Caesar and Imogene Coca playing Stanley Kowalski and Blanche DuBois from *A Streetcar Named Desire*, and so a genre spoof was the perfect fit for Brooks. "I was sick of looking at all those nice sensible situation comedies," Brooks said. "I wanted to do a crazy, unreal comic-strip kind of thing about something besides a family." Snappy writing, gags like the shoe phone, and the deadpan nasal delivery of Don Adams as Agent 86 made *Get Smart* a classic.

Then came the breakout. Brooks's first movie, *The Producers*, began as a quip. In 1962, during a press conference for *All American*, Brooks had been asked what was next. "Springtime for Hitler!" he blurted out, a reference to a now obscure 1931 play, *Springtime for Henry*. That quip became an idea, then an unpublished novel, then an unproduced play, then a thirty-page film treatment. At its core is what Larry David called "possibly the greatest comedic premise that anyone has ever dreamed up": two corrupt producers want to get rich by producing a flop and so put on a Broadway musical about Hitler. Needless to say, the big studios wouldn't touch "a gay romp with Adolf and Eva at Berchtesgaden," so Brooks rounded up independent funding, persuaded Zero Mostel to star, then recruited Gene Wilder, who had been performing on Broadway opposite Brooks's future wife, Anne Bancroft, in Brecht's *Mother Courage*.

The critics didn't get it. Pauline Kael, the reigning doyenne of the art cinema world, found it in bad taste and too Jewish (Kael herself was Jewish), suggesting that John Barrymore would have played the role of Max Bialystock better than Mostel. But when Peter Sellers happened to screen the film for a private party, he was so thrilled that he took out ads in *Variety* and the *New York Times* touting its transgressive brilliance. Brooks won the Oscar for Best Original Screenplay and his film career was launched.

The follow-up, *The Twelve Chairs*, had a reasonably favorable reception. Then came *Blazing Saddles*, which Brooks wrote with a team of collaborators including Richard Pryor. Instead of taking on the Nazis (Nazis do make a cameo appearance), it spotlights America's history of racism. It does so, however, through the unlikely vehicle of a western parody. The combination of edgy racial humor, cowboys, borscht belt shtick, fart jokes, Nietzsche references, and a postmodern ending—in which a western brawl spills over onto a Hollywood backlot and the sheriff himself rides into a theater showing the conclusion of *Blazing Saddles*—established the Brooks formula: high and low, zany and brainy, music and spectacle, disdain for good taste, and a loving but pointed send-up of film history. In *The Producers*, Gene Wilder's Leo shouts, "I want everything I've ever seen in the movies!," and that's what *Blazing Saddles*—and really all of Brooks's films—provides.

Blazing Saddles paved the way for Brooks's run of great comic films, most of them genre parodies, through the 1970s and '80s, as he remade monster movies, silent comedies, Hitchcock, Roman epics, *Star Wars*, and more. (He continued to take his shots at Hitler, remaking Ernst Lubitsch's 1942 Jack Benny vehicle, *To Be or Not to Be*.) He also branched out beyond comedy as a producer, overseeing critically acclaimed films such as David Lynch's *The Elephant Man* and David Cronenberg's *The Fly*.

Then, when Brooks was in his seventies, came the remarkable next act—it's hard to say at this point whether it was his third, fourth, or fifth act. He returned to *The Producers*, coming full circle. Teaming with *Annie* book writer Thomas

Meehan, he adapted his own movie about a musical into a stunningly successful musical (which four years later was adapted back into a film). Since Brooks's introduction to Cole Porter at age nine, musical theater had been dear to his heart, and there's hardly a film he made that doesn't feature a glorious showstopper. In a 2002 interview, choreographer and longtime collaborator Alan Johnson describes "a Mel Brooks theory of filmmaking" in which "three-quarters of the way through the film you need to give the audience a *zetz.*" That *zetz* (Yiddish for a smack in the head) is a song-and-dance spectacle, like the revolving human swastika of "Springtime for Hitler," or Madeline Kahn channeling Marlene Dietrich in *Blazing Saddles* with "I'm Tired" (itself a master class in comedy; not a single moment of that performance is unconsidered), or the Busby Berkeley–style treatment of the Spanish Inquisition in *History of the World, Part I.*

Just before the musical version of *The Producers* opened on Broadway, Brooks was profiled on *60 Minutes* and told Roctogenarian Mike Wallace why Hitler had played such a recurring role in his comedy:

> *Hitler was part of this incredible idea that you could put Jews in concentration camps and kill them. And how do you get even? How do you get even with the man? How do you get even with him? There's only one way to get even. You have to bring him down with ridicule. Because if you stand on a soapbox and you match him with rhetoric, you're just as bad as he is. But if you can make people laugh at him, then you're one up on him. And it's been one of my lifelong jobs to make the world laugh at Adolf Hitler.*

By the time the show opened, reviewers like the longtime *Village Voice* film critic J. Hoberman had come to understand that it was a completely fitting project for a Jewish comedian, "far less redolent of self-hatred than self-love."

In 2005, when *The Producers* was turned into a second movie, Brooks chose Susan Stroman, the director of the stage musical, to direct the film as well. It was in keeping with a lesser-known cause of his, advocacy for opportunities for female directors. The director Rachel Feldman relates that years before, "during a heated industry meeting regarding the fight to increase employment for women directors," Brooks stood up and cried, "You are nit-picking and pettifogging these women into the shithouse!" The outburst helped sway the group, and the directors won their vote. In 2019, Geena Davis made the documentary *This Changes Everything*, about bias in the profession, and highlighted Brooks's work in this regard.

Anne Bancroft's death in 2005, after forty-one years of marriage, was naturally a terrible blow to Brooks, but he fell back on friends, Lear and especially Reiner, who were in the same stage of life. (Reiner lost his wife, Estelle, in 2008, after sixty-five years of marriage.) Like them, Brooks remained creatively active and engaged with the world. Laughter, once again, was his secret. "Laughter is a protest scream against death, against the long goodbye. It's a defense against unhappiness and depression," he wrote in his autobiography. In 2023, interviewed by *Variety* on the release of his new series *History of the World, Part II*, he said much the same thing: "There's no greater payment for somebody in comedy than the audience breaking up. It's just thrilling. There's nothing like comedy. You don't think about the time or throwing up or falling off the horse. You don't think about bad things. You think about whether something is really funny and if it makes you laugh. It's a bit of a miracle. I love it."

But maybe the best advice on long life came from years earlier, from the world-weary character he got famous portraying. As Brooks relates a bit of his old routine: "Carl says, 'What's the secret to your longevity?' I say, 'Don't die.' That's it. 'Don't die.' And it gets the laugh."

Brooks's ninth and tenth decades have kept him busy receiving honors. He had both Lear and Reiner at his side in 2014 when he added his handprints and foot-prints to the walk in front of Grauman's Chinese Theater on Hollywood Boulevard. Brooks brought along a prosthetic pinkie and gave the handprint a disconcerting sixth digit, just so that a tourist from Idaho would someday scream, "Look at this! Mel Brooks has six fingers."

Two years later, he was welcomed at the Obama White House to receive the National Medal of Arts, one of the highest civilian honors the country awards. As the nation's first Black president bestowed a medal upon a Jewish nonagenarian famous for fart jokes and Nazi humor, the United States Marine Band played a rousing version of "Springtime for Hitler." It was a heartwarming yet surreal scene that felt like something out of one of Brooks's own movies, in its own way as all-American as you can get.

Norman Lear

the master of the sitcom and a civic leader until 101

Norman Lear may not have invented the situation comedy, but more than anyone else, he made sure that it said something important. So of course I jumped at the chance to profile him for *CBS Sunday Morning* back in 2015.

At the time, Norman was workshopping a pilot script for what he hoped would be yet another hit sitcom. *Guess Who Died* was about a group of residents of a Palm Springs senior community. On our first day together, I sat next to him as the actors onstage read through the script. Norman was laser-focused. He mouthed the words, sometimes getting testy if the actors didn't land the jokes. ("No, no, that's not it," he said at least a few times, exasperated. "Pacing, pacing.") A couple of times he left his seat to get up onstage to coach the actors. He wanted to get this right. He *needed* to get this right.

Did I mention he was ninety-three?

It had been forty-four years since *All in the Family* debuted on CBS, marking a sea change in what television could be. Archie Bunker, a cabbie from Queens, was an inexhaustible source of racist, sexist, and homophobic remarks, locked in a continuous battle with a world that was rapidly changing all around him.

When I asked for the word that best described Archie, Norman answered: "Fearful. Fearful of progress, fearful of tomorrow . . . never able to admit that he isn't good enough for what's coming." (Norman didn't like when Archie was simply labeled a "bigot." Indeed, Archie could be lovable, certainly in his love for his own family.)

Thanks to Carroll O'Connor's portrayal and the writing and direction overseen by Lear, Archie's warts-and-all realness proved irresistible to the prime-time television audience, which might be 40 or 50 million strong on any given Saturday night in the early seventies. America was able to laugh both *at* Archie and *with* him—often at the same time. His feuds with his son-in-law, Michael (played by Reiner's son, Rob), his wife Edith's feminist cousin Maude (Bea Arthur), his Black neighbor George Jefferson (Sherman Hemsley), and many others were uproarious versions of arguments happening in real families across the nation, but which television had mostly ignored. Yet for all the tension and anger let loose when the Bunkers aired their political differences, *All in the Family* staged these arguments in a way that was, in the end, comforting. Archie and Edith reassured us that our families and our country would manage to hold together.

To fully understand Norman Lear's impact on TV, you need to know what the TV world was like in the sixties. These were the days when *The Beverly Hillbillies* was the number one show, and tens of millions of people gathered around the set (housed in a big wooden cabinet, with enormous built-in speakers and lots of knobs and an antenna) to watch Granny do battle with a kangaroo that she mistakes for a giant jackrabbit and intends to make into a stew for the family dinner. (That episode was watched by over sixty million people. Really.) The TV universe was dominated by rural characters and rural settings, and it blotted out the decade's political assassinations, the sexual revolution, the civil rights movement, and the Vietnam War. (For background, I recommend the episode "The Rural Purge" from Season 2 of *Mobituaries*, my podcast.) The sitcom in particular was an escapist genre; even the best-written programs, like *The Andy Griffith Show*, hardly registered the upheaval that was wracking the nation. As a southern sheriff in the 1960s, the amiable Andy was as far away from the racist Bull Connor as you could imagine.

But *All in the Family*, along with other CBS shows like *The Mary Tyler Moore Show* (featuring the female lead from Reiner's *The Dick Van Dyke Show*) and Larry Gelbart's *M*A*S*H*, turned all that upside down. With his longtime creative partner, Bud Yorkin, Lear used the truculent Archie to tackle volatile issues being discussed on front pages and at kitchen tables across America. Lear encouraged his writers to read the newspapers daily—and not only the liberal ones, since he wanted them "to get a broadening of attitudes." His writers penned stories about interracial marriage, gun control, the Vietnam War, immigration. Sexuality became a topic for open discussion as rarely seen before on TV. In one hilarious episode—which would have gone completely over my head had I been allowed to watch at the time—Edith unwittingly invites over some swingers (played by Rue McClanahan and Vincent Gardenia), who are expecting a lot more than a slice of pie. But the show also dealt with deadly serious issues. In one episode, Edith fights off a rapist.

Finding the funny in the serious began early for Lear. Born in New Haven, Connecticut, he was nine when his father was sent to prison for three years for selling fake bonds. As Norman told me in 2015, he never forgot a neighbor's "words of wisdom" at the time: "Puts his hand on my shoulder and says, 'Well, you're the man of the house now, Norman. There, there, a man doesn't cry.' Nine years old, I'm hearing that!" Humor became a way to cope with pain. "Ultimately it taught me there's—there's humor everywhere, in every situation."

After serving in the military (more on that below), Lear enjoyed a reasonably accomplished career writing for variety shows in New York. He found some success as a feature film writer, winning an Oscar nomination for *Divorce, American Style*, a comedy adapted from a Neil Simon play and starring Dick Van Dyke. But it remained Lear's ambition to create his own sitcom—in part because he had learned, in going through an expensive divorce, the financial value of owning your own show. When Yorkin suggested adapting a British show called *Till Death Us Do Part*, about a conservative working-class father in London's East End, Lear saw the potential to do something special.

The success of *All in the Family* was just the beginning. Over the next decade Lear would become the most important writer-producer-showrunner in television, maybe in TV history. Extending his formula of mixing political and social issues with everyday family dynamics, he spun off show after show. Together these hit shows made up a Lear Sitcom Universe as rich and textured as anything created by George Lucas or Stan Lee.

In *Maude*, Lear created a committed feminist who could be just as strident as Archie Bunker. In his memoir, he wrote that "of all the characters I've created in a cast, the one who resembles me most is Maude."

Personal experience also played a role when he helped bring *The Jeffersons*, *Good Times*, and *Sanford and Son*—the first all-Black comedy series since the demise of *The Amos 'n Andy Show* in the early 1950s—to TV. Norman had never forgotten traveling from Connecticut to New York in his boyhood and peering into Harlem apartment buildings from the train, which passed close enough for him to glimpse scenes of different families, most of them Black. As he told me, "I used to wonder about them. Who were these families, what were they thinking, what were their problems?" Today, prominent Black film and TV writers including Tyler Perry and Kenya Barris credit Lear as the first to air stories about complex, three-dimensional African American families, whether wealthy or working-class. The writer and podcast host Larry Wilmore says that it was completely thrilling for him as a kid to see George Jefferson talking back to a white man like Archie Bunker—and getting the last word.

Buoyed by his success, Lear was fearless in breaking taboos. *All in the Family* gave TV its first openly gay character in Steve, Archie's drinking buddy; in *The Jeffersons*, George's fellow Korean War veteran, Edie, is often cited as TV's first sympathetic portrayal of a trans character. In a famous episode of *Maude* (written by

Golden Girls creator Susan Harris), the title character finds herself pregnant at forty-seven and has an abortion. In an episode of *Good Times*, eleven-year-old Michael is suspended from school for pointing out that George Washington owned slaves.

As Lear's dominance of the Nielsen ratings began to wane in the late 1970s, his concern about the rise of intolerance in the country began to grow. He especially worried about the emerging political power of the religious right. (He wrote that he was alarmed by televangelist Jimmy Swaggart asking his congregation to pray for the "removal" of a liberal Supreme Court justice. This was before Swaggart's prostitution scandal.) In 1981, Lear cofounded Citizens for Constitutional Concerns (the name was changed four years later to People for the American Way) to promote the values that he called "religious liberty and pluralism and diversity." Lear's old-style liberalism, which included causes like reproductive rights and gay rights, was one that in his view had a conservative side, and he embraced the principles of the Constitution and the Declaration of Independence. (In 1978, he defended the right of neo-Nazis to march in Skokie, Illinois, a position for which someone defaced his front door with a swastika.) And his patriotism had deep roots. A war hero, he quit college to enlist in the army when Pearl Harbor was attacked, and ended up flying more than fifty bombing missions over Germany and Italy in the fight against fascism.

In his sixties, Lear was often busier as an entrepreneur than as a writer, creating and selling production companies, and watching his bank account swell. To escape the grind of the Hollywood business world, he and his wife would invite a select group of friends—the Reiners, the Brookses, the Gelbarts, and actor Dom DeLuise and his wife, Carol Arthur—for weekends away in Palm Springs or La Costa. They called their group the "Yenem Velt," Yiddish for "the other world," since it represented a complete and total escape. "Once or twice a year maybe for six or eight years we went away for a weekend," Lear related. They would stay in their pajamas all weekend, joking, singing, eating and drinking, and trying to make each other laugh. Gelbart wrote a "Yenem Velt" anthem to the tune of "O Tannenbaum" that they sang before meals. In Brooks's recollection, Reiner would rouse his guests by singing the song over the house intercom first thing in the morning, like a comic Old Country version of reveille. "In the history of fun," said Lear, "no group ever had more."

Now this is the point in the story—when Norman is in his seventies—when he might have been expected to start winding down. He'd made his mark in pop culture and public affairs. He was more than set financially. Instead, after turning eighty, he struck up a relationship with the writers of *South Park*. He saw them as inheritors of his creative spirit. (Trey Parker and Matt Stone have cited Archie Bunker as an influence on the foul-mouthed Eric Cartman.) He contributed to the show as a guest writer and consultant, and played the voice of Roctogenarian Ben Franklin in one episode. He even officiated at Parker's wedding.

Guess Who Died—the sitcom Norman was trying to sell to a network when I met him—never went to series. It died after a pilot was filmed. But just two years later, Lear presided over a 2017 reboot of *One Day at a Time* in which the Romanos of the original series are reimagined as the Alvarezes, a Cuban American family. Another Roctogenarian, Rita Moreno, then in her mideighties, played the grandmother. And in 2019, he teamed with Jimmy Kimmel to produce *Live in Front of a Studio Audience*, which recreated memorable episodes from Lear's sitcoms, and made Lear, at ninety-seven, the oldest Emmy winner in history.

Lear always insisted that his continued vitality was nothing special, and that it was the predominant cultural view of aging that was wrong. "It's all there for us," he told me. If cultural expectations were different, he said, "people turning seventy and eighty would turn seventy and eighty with a different attitude, like they're coming into another phase of life as opposed to opening a door to go out of it. You know, age is not an exit door." His daughter Kate attributed his vitality to his optimism and interest in other people. "Because of this," she wrote, "as he grew older, his world expanded rather than contracted."

That engagement with the world included distress at recent attacks on American freedom and the rule of law. On his one hundredth birthday, alarmed at the

insurrection of January 6, 2021, he wrote an op-ed for the *New York Times*. In it, he noted his advanced age, then quipped, "To be honest, I'm a bit worried that I may be in better shape than our democracy is."

When he won the Carol Burnett Award at the 2021 Golden Globes, he spoke gratefully and optimistically about the power of laughter in his life. "I could not be more blessed," he said in his acceptance remarks. "I am convinced that laughter adds time to one's life. . . . At close to ninety-nine, I can tell you I've never lived alone. I've never laughed alone. And that has as much to do with my being here today as anything else I know." Ultimately, he saw the target of his laughter not as any particular political opponent; his comedy was never so much progressive as it was *humane*, poking fun at, as he called it, "the foolishness of the human condition." He was still that nine-year-old boy, watching his father get hauled off, being told by a neighbor that he was now "the man of the house." And he was laughing.

———————

On a personal note, the last time I was with Norman in person was on New Year's Eve 2019. My partner, Alberto, and I were guests at a party to ring in the new year thrown by Norman's daughter Kate and her husband, Jon LaPook. A group of us, including Norman, stood around the piano singing songs like Rodgers and Hart's "I Could Write a Book" and "Where or When." We sang the World War II classic "I'll Be Seeing You." (One of my favorite discoveries when I interviewed Norman was that he had Jimmy Cagney singing "Give My Regards to Broadway" as his cellphone ringtone.) Toward the end of the evening, after I'd texted my mother to wish her a Happy New Year, Norman asked, "How old is she?" "Ninety-one," I answered. Norman waved his hand, unimpressed. "She's just a kid."

opposite page: Ninety-three-year-old Norman Lear showing me and the CBS News crew his workout in 2015.
Jay Kernis

The Norman Lear Players

Norman Lear's shows didn't just break ground in subject matter, they defied conventional casting. As the columnist Rhonda Garelick has pointed out, in the decade of Farrah Fawcett and Lynda Carter, Lear gave starring roles to middle-aged actresses with typical bodies, even acknowledging that in middle age they might still enjoy sex. Many of his lead actors, female and male, came not from other TV shows but from the stage. "As a kid, I fell in love with the theater," Norman told me back in 2015. "I saw Bill Macy chokin' on a chicken bone in a play off-off-off-Broadway and never forgot him, and he became Maude's husband. So all those performances through the years, that's where I drew the talent to bring to California." These were actors with experience . . . and experience comes with age. Not one of these stars was "old" in the normal world. But in Hollywood? Out there they'd be diplomatically known as "veterans."

Bea Arthur as Maude Findlay
Bea Arthur always had a commanding presence. So it made perfect sense she served as a staff sergeant in the marines during World War II. (Back then she was Bernice Frankel.) From her earliest days as a stage actress in New York, her imposing stature (5'10") and voice (imagine if a smokestack could sing) set her apart. Her first big role on Broadway was as Yente the Matchmaker in *Fiddler on the Roof*. Two years later she won a Tony as Angela Lansbury's bosom buddy Vera Charles in the 1966 musical *Mame*. (Check out YouTube for the two of them singing it years later. Now *that's* a match made in Broadway heaven.) But it was *off*-Broadway, way back in 1955, where Lear heard Arthur singing the comedic novelty song "Garbage" in a revue, which incidentally included a then-unknown Chita Rivera. (In her memoir, Rivera called Arthur "as brash and bold as New York" but also a master of precision, a "comic scientist" who taught her how to be funny.) Arthur made a lasting impression on Lear, who in 1971 put her on *All in the Family* as Edith's cousin, the outspoken feminist Maude Findlay. She proved herself a worthy adversary to Archie, and it was decided that this comic gold needed her own series—another Lear milestone. Arthur, then fifty, took the starring role on *Maude*. Women's issues were now part of the prime-time landscape.

Bea Arthur would return to television again at the age of sixty-three in another wildly successful sitcom, *The Golden Girls*.

Carroll O'Connor as Archie Bunker
It's a little bit jarring to watch Carroll O'Connor as an ancient Roman senator—played with a British accent, natch—conspiring against

Julius Caesar in the 1963 movie *Cleopatra*. (Oh, what I wouldn't have given to hear him call Brutus "Meathead.") Four years later, in the movie *Point Blank*, a much gruffer O'Connor, shoulders tensed, faces off with Lee Marvin. When he barks, "You're a very bad man, Walker!" you can see and hear someone much closer to the character that would make him famous a couple of years later. O'Connor had begun kicking around off-Broadway in the late 1950s, costarring in one show with Zero Mostel, being directed in another by a twenty-year-old Peter Bogdanovich. But when it came time to cast *All in the Family*, Norman Lear wanted Mickey Rooney for the role of the never-afraid-to-offend Archie Bunker. Rooney said no thanks, though. "He thought it was ridiculous that I was thinking of doing a show about a bigot. 'You're going to get killed in the streets,' Norman told me. 'They're going to shoot you dead.'" And so at forty-six, Carroll O'Connor got his biggest break. A character as unforgettable as Archie usually means the actor never gets to play anyone else. But at sixty-three O'Connor returned to series TV for seven seasons of *In the Heat of the Night*—doubly impressive, since he was playing the role that won Rod Steiger an Oscar in the original film version. That's how good an actor he was.

Jean Stapleton as Edith Bunker

If, like me, you're a fan of both *All in the Family and* classic American musical theater, then growing up you too loved hearing Jean Stapleton's voice pop up on the cast recordings of *Damn Yankees* (listen to her bray her way through a reprise of the hit song "Heart"), *Bells Are Ringing*, and *Funny Girl* (listen to her explain to Barbra Streisand's Fanny what happens "If a Girl Isn't Pretty"). She'd begun her theatrical career years before, doing summer stock as a teenager and making sporadic appearances on the live television drama programs that were a vital part of television's infancy. A Christian Scientist, Stapleton credited her faith with lifting her despair when she could not find work—and curing her of "blind ambition." Her optimistic disposition plus a whole lot of talent made her a perfect fit for the always sunny, if scatterbrained, Edith Bunker, a role that she began playing at age forty-seven. She won three Emmy Awards before leaving the series at the end of her contract. Stapleton admired her character's humanity and "native wisdom" but also felt there was nothing left to mine from the role.

She went on to play Eleanor Roosevelt in a TV movie, a role she loved. (Stapleton was an ardent supporter of the Equal Rights Amendment.) She turned down a lead part in another series that "didn't seem to be the kind of role I could get my teeth into." So *Murder, She Wrote* went on to star Angela Lansbury in her place.

Esther Rolle as Florida Evans

Esther Rolle's stage work ranged from playing Lady Macbeth—in a 1977 remounting of Orson Welles's famous 1936 Voodoo *Macbeth*—to appearing in the Broadway musical *Don't Play Us Cheap* (alongside Mabel King, who would go on to play the mom on TV's *What's Happening!!*). But it was playing Maude's housekeeper, Florida Evans, that would make Rolle famous. Soon enough, Florida got her own series. *Good Times* took place in the projects of Chicago, where Florida lived with her husband, James, and their three young children. That the show featured a two-parent African American family made it a rarity for the time. There was never any mention of Maude, and only a cursory reference to Florida's previous life as a domestic was made, in one episode. (This was not unlike the situation with Charlotte Rae's Edna Garrett. As housemother at the prestigious Eastland Academy on *Facts of Life*—and later the proprietress of Edna's Edibles—Mrs. Garrett's past as a housekeeper for the Drummond family on *Diff'rent Strokes* was never mentioned after the pilot episode.) While Rolle and her on-screen husband, played by John Amos, appeared to be roughly the same age, in real life she was fifty-three, and nineteen years his senior. Jimmie Walker, who played their misfit teenage son J.J., was only eight years younger than John Amos.

Good Times was another huge Norman Lear hit for CBS. But both Esther Rolle and John Amos grew unhappy as the series became less about Black themes and family issues . . . and more about the clowning antics of J.J. and his catchphrase "DYN-O-MITE." John Amos left at the beginning of the fourth season; his character was killed in an off-screen car accident. Rolle left the show for a year before returning for the sixth and final season.

Isabel Sanford as Louise "Weezy" Jefferson

Isabel Sanford was in her fifties when Louise Jefferson—aka "Weezy"—was introduced late in the first season of *All in the Family*. A neighbor and a good friend to Edith Bunker, Louise was likewise bighearted and benevolent. Isabel Sanford was the youngest and only child of seven to survive past infancy, which very well may have fostered her drive to succeed. Despite her religious mother's wish that she not pursue acting, Isabel would not be deterred. As a teenager, she competed in the famous Apollo Theatre Amateur Night, winning third place. After leaving a bad marriage, she boarded a bus for Hollywood with her three kids. Her film debut came in the landmark *Guess Who's Coming to Dinner* in 1967. Sanford found steady work in small roles on shows ranging from *Bewitched* to *The Mod Squad* and caught the attention of Norman Lear, who cast her in her signature role. By the time *The Jeffersons* debuted in January 1975, she was fifty-seven—and twenty-one years older than her on-screen husband, the temperamental and opinionated George, played hilariously by Sherman Hemsley. In 1981, Isabel Sanford became the first Black woman to win an Emmy award in a prime-time leading role. In her speech, she said, "I'm only going to name two names . . . I want to thank God and thank Norman Lear for hiring me."

LaWanda Page as Aunt Esther
How has there not been a movie made about the life of LaWanda Page? Born Alberta Richmond in 1920, she was raised in St. Louis, where she became grade school friends with future costar and fellow comedy legend Redd Foxx. LaWanda knew early she wanted to be a star. (Lena Horne in *Cabin in the Sky* was an inspiration, though one gets the sense that Page would have found her way without any role models at all.) It helped that she was a knockout. But real life didn't make it any easier. Married and pregnant at fourteen, she was a widow by nineteen. By that time she was working the Chitlin' Circuit as the scantily clad "Bronze Goddess of Fire." A drag queen named Taboo had taught her to swallow fire. She added a snake to her act, because why not? She didn't even try stand-up until she was in her thirties. "When I got too old to dance, I turned to comedy." Her act was funny—and gloriously raunchy. Perfect for the era of the party record. (Party records were comedy acts on vinyl that propelled the careers of many Black comics who otherwise had trouble booking mainstream venues.) Redd Foxx had blazed the trail, releasing comedy albums *before* Bob Newhart and Mort Sahl. LaWanda released five of her own with bits that still kill. (The one about the psychiatric nurse and the patient screaming out for a particular remedy—from her 1977 album *Watch It, Sucker*—is a favorite of mine. Listen to LaWanda ride the waves of screaming laughter.) She was fifty-two when a producer called her to costar with her old friend Redd Foxx. The role was Aunt Esther, the Bible-toting, self-righteous, sassy adversary of Fred Sanford on *Sanford and Son*. So unfamiliar with TV was Page that at her first rehearsal, she read the stage directions out loud, along with her actual lines. The producers were ready to fire her, but Redd Foxx gave them the "if she goes, I go" ultimatum, and she quickly found her groove. When Aunt Esther (who most certainly would not have approved of Page's stand-up material) and Fred Sanford went at it, it was ferociously hilarious. *Sanford and Son* made LaWanda Page a star, and she became a familiar face on other television shows, including *The Dean Martin Celebrity Roasts*, where she dinged everyone from Betty White to Frank Sinatra. Was she ever scared? Unlikely. The woman had swallowed fire and danced with snakes. (For more on her life and the history of party records, check out the Season 4 LaWanda Page episode of the *Mobituaries* podcast.)

Eddy Goldfarb

Whatis it about a plastic set of disembodied chattering teeth skittering across a table that is so funny? Is it that they move at all? The sound they make?

If you ask Eddy Goldfarb, the inventor of chattering teeth (originally called Yakity-Yak Talking Teeth), he'll tell you that the idea came to him in the 1940s, when he saw an ad for something called a "tooth garage" that was used to store dentures. "I was young. I thought false teeth were funny. I went to my dentist and asked for an old pair," Goldfarb once explained. After attaching a wind-up motor to those dentures, he created the toy that "Never runs out of talk. Good for a million laughs," as the ads would later tout. He sold the rights to novelty king Irving Fishlove (a man famous for selling fake vomit), coming out of the deal with nine hundred dollars—hardly worthy of a toy that would become legendary with comedians, magicians, and schoolkids, but enough to buy a warm coat for a cold Chicago winter. (Presumably this stopped his actual teeth from chattering.) When the teeth went on sale in 1950, they were a "hit right from the start," according to Goldfarb.

Toys and gag gifts were Goldfarb's destiny. As a child, when an inventor friend of his father's came to dinner, young Eddy decided that it was the life he wanted. While serving aboard a submarine during World War II, he would jot down toy ideas in his spare time. "I realized that the toy industry needed new toys every year," Goldfarb later told *USA Today*.

Today he has eight hundred toys to his name. KerPlunk, Bubble Guns, Stompers, and Spin-Art are all his brainchildren. At 102, Goldfarb continues to invent, delighting in coming up with toys that will keep children of all ages entertained. As he told *CBS Sunday Morning* in 2023, "I believe if you do creative work of any kind, if you start with nothing and end with something, it stimulates your brain, and I think that's very good for your body."

Unfinished Business

Diana Nyad

& Brian May

Diana Nyad: Swimming with Sharks
swam from Cuba to Florida at sixty-four

The New York City of the 1970s is still famous for its energy and its anarchy. A place of supersize personalities and garish tabloid headlines, it overflowed with crisis, chaos, and culture all at once. It was the home of Billy Martin's dysfunctional Yankees; *Saturday Night Live* and *Saturday Night Fever*; early punk, rap, and disco; the blackout of 1977; the Son of Sam murders; "Warriors, come out and pla-ay"; "Ford to City: Drop Dead."

In 1975, a twenty-six-year-old graduate student in comparative literature shouldered her way into this jostling, dirty, colorful scene by swimming around Manhattan, through the legendarily filthy East, Harlem, and Hudson Rivers, in a record-breaking 7 hours and 57 minutes. With that triumph, Diana Nyad became an overnight celebrity, scoring appearances on Johnny Carson's *The Tonight Show* and *SNL* and going on a date with Woody Allen, despite the fact that she was a lesbian. ("I presented myself as straight, because I was such a fan," she explained.) But for Nyad, eight hours in the slime and sludge of New York's waterways would turn out to be merely a prelude to the real quest—a 110-mile swim from Cuba to Florida.

Nyad, a New York native raised in Fort Lauderdale, had been a high school state champion in the backstroke. Her father had given her his auspicious last name: in Greek mythology, a naiad is a water nymph. (Less noted but equally auspicious is the fact that "Diana" is an anagram of "naiad.") Aristotle Nyad impressed upon his daughter the idea that her name was her fate—although years later she would learn that he was not her biological father, and that his name was not actually Nyad. Aris Notaras was in fact a con man whose schemes created an unstable life for Diana, her mother, and her siblings. Worse, when Diana was eleven, he sexually assaulted her. This trauma, at least in part, led to her ambitions as a swimmer. As Nyad told Ariel Levy of *The New Yorker*, after the assault, the water became a kind of refuge;

there, wrote Levy, "She felt safest and most free." In her teens, Nyad has claimed, she suffered additional, repeated, and more severe abuse, from a coach named Jack Nelson; though she was never able to have him prosecuted, she continues to this day to speak out for victims of sexual abuse.

Despite her enormous talent as a swimmer, Diana missed out on a shot at the Olympics due to a heart infection. She recovered from the infection but never again attained the speed necessary to qualify for the 1968 Games in Mexico City. Seeking an outlet for her uncontainable ambition, she turned to marathon swimming, in which her powerful will could more than compensate for the speed she had lost. At age twenty, she swam across Lake Ontario.

Cuba held a special allure in the later years of the Cold War. Nyad had grown up reading news stories of "hundreds of Cubans" who, fleeing communism, attempted to swim to freedom—none of them of course making it the distance. For Nyad, Cuba was a "forbidden land we're not allowed to go to." The swim itself, through shark-infested and potentially rough waters, was a daunting task on a purely physical level, but the idea of a passage from Cuba to the U.S. lent the challenge an air of romance.

When Nyad first attempted the swim, in 1978, she was twenty-eight, at her athletic peak. Yet almost as soon as she set out, just about everything that could go wrong did. She was stung by jellyfish, battered by thunderstorms, and pushed off course to the west by the powerful and fickle currents of the Gulf Stream. After forty-two hours of swimming, she was hauled into the boat that had accompanied her, nowhere near the Florida coast. Heartbroken, she consoled herself by completing a 102-mile swim from the Bahamas to Florida just about a year later, on her thirtieth birthday—in the process breaking the distance record for an open water swim by anyone, male or female. (For my thirtieth birthday, a group of friends took me out for margaritas. I could barely *walk* home.) But even that remarkable achievement could not soothe the sting of failure.

For thirty years, Nyad put her dream aside. She became a successful writer and broadcaster, regularly appearing on ABC's *Wide World of Sports*, among other prominent TV and radio programs. In the 1990s, she became an advocate for gays and lesbians in the professional sports world, sharing the story of how executives at ABC prohibited her from bringing her partner to company social events. But neither her courage nor her professional success could quench the desire to complete the challenge that had bested her in 1978.

Like writer Laura Ingalls Wilder, Nyad found herself confronting mortality when her mother died. Diana was fifty-nine at the time. As she told Levy, "I don't care how healthy I am—it's not like I'm going to live another sixty years." She became aware of a "speeding up of the clock" and asked herself what she wanted from life. "This one-way street is hurtling toward the end now," she continued, "and you better be the person you admire."

The person she admired was the one who could swim across the Florida Straits. And so she decided to try it again—this time at age sixty. As she told *Time*, "It's not like I was fixated on doing that swim all those years, but I guess somehow, I was, and that I always did have Cuba in the back of my brain."

The 2023 Netflix film *Nyad*, starring Annette Bening as Nyad and Jodie Foster as Bonnie Stoll, her best friend and trainer, gives something of a sense of the obstacles Nyad faced, which were not only physical but also logistical. Nyad would need to put together a team of twenty-five to thirty people that included not only Stoll but also a crew for the boat that would accompany her, a medical team, divers who could fend off sharks—she would be swimming without a protective cage—and, finally, enough funding to get the whole gang to St. Maarten, where she would be training, and then to Cuba to make the actual attempt. (Two other swimmers claimed to have completed the swim before that point: Walter Poenisch in 1978 and Susie Maroney in 1997, but both of them swam inside a protective shark cage.)

The physical task itself wasn't going to be any easier than it had been in 1978. Whether swimming, running, or biking, the human body does not lose its capacity for endurance as quickly as it loses its capacity for top speeds; nonetheless, by age sixty there is inevitably a tailing-off. Nyad would be crossing more than one hundred miles of open water over the course of three days, swimming night and day without rest. She would be fed periodically from the accompanying boat, but her support team could not physically touch her, lest the record she was aiming for be invalidated. Divers and kayakers equipped with electronic repellent devices would keep away the sharks. A greater threat were the box jellyfish, tentacled warmwater monsters that Levy describes as "the most venomous creatures in the ocean." The amount of salt water swallowed in the rough seas would be enough to defeat most swimmers, and the unpredictable currents and weather were constant perils. Seasickness, hypothermia, and exhaustion would be unavoidable.

Getting in shape was the least of Nyad's worries. She knew how to push herself. As Bonnie Stoll said, "Diana is the least lazy person I have ever met in my life." Indeed, Nyad considered herself in better physical condition at sixty than she had been in her twenties, and she gradually built her endurance as she progressed from swims of eight hours to fourteen to twenty. And her mental toughness was nothing short of awesome. As the Diana of the movie says, "My mind has never been clearer. Don't you get it? The mind. This is what I was missing when I was younger. I've got it now." But the first summer she set out to make the swim, in 2010, the weather conditions were never right, and she returned to her home in California without even having made an attempt.

The next summer, she returned to the Gulf to train again and to wait for the perfect weather conditions. She set out on August 7, but a combination of excruciating shoulder pain, dehydration, and a bad attack of asthma cut the swim short after twenty-nine hours. She was undeterred. Only six weeks later, with the prospect of what looked like ideal water conditions, she tried again. This time she was twice stung by box jellyfish, and by the time she got the needed medical attention, she was miles off course, once again due to the unpredictable currents of the Gulf. Again, the swim had to be halted. This time, Nyad was lucky to be alive.

By now it seemed that the iron-willed super athlete had crossed a fine line from indomitable spirit to downright nuts. "I sort of thought, Oh, she's crazy," said Karen Sauvigne, a friend, adding, "And she *is* on some level crazy." Sauvigne is a triathlete who completed a four-hundred-mile bike ride at age sixty, so she has a pretty high standard when it comes to what's too much.

A fourth attempt in August 2012 failed after Nyad had spent fifty-one hours in the ocean. Once again, it was a result of jellyfish stings—Nyad wore a protective suit and mask but was stung on the mouth—plus a tropical storm.

At this point, Nyad later related, pretty much everyone involved, whether friends, doctors, scientists, or the members of the support team, figured that the swim just couldn't be done. Only she herself wanted to try again.

On her fifth attempt, beginning August 31, 2013, she encountered what were by now familiar challenges. The mask she wore as protection against jellyfish was rough on her skin and made every moment painful. Pushing herself to her physical limits, she began to hallucinate. Looming in front of her, improbably, she saw both the Taj Mahal and the Yellow Brick Road from *The Wizard of Oz*. (This scene is animated memorably in the 2023 film.) Stoll told her not to worry—just to swim around the colossal mausoleum.

And this time, those powerful Gulf currents were working in Nyad's favor for a change, pushing her northward. Toward the end of her second night in the water, she thought she saw the beginnings of a sunrise on the horizon. She was mistaken. It was the lights of Key West. She was nearing Florida, ahead of schedule. "I still had fourteen or fifteen hours to go," she recollected. "But for me that's a training swim."

Of course, Nyad made it to shore, stumbling to her feet, sunburned and sick, her face puffy and blotchy, as crowds cheered her on. On the beach, colorful Pride flags waved alongside the Stars and Stripes. The sixty-four-year-old woman had triumphed where the twenty-eight-year-old had failed.

(Some in the open water swimming community have questioned Nyad's accomplishment, citing among other things a lack of verifying data logs from Nyad's team. Not a single member of Nyad's forty-person crew has cast doubt on her achievement, though.)

Among Nyad's most ardent and passionate fans was another breaker of glass ceilings, Hillary Rodham Clinton, who had been tracking the swim online. The former secretary of state tweeted, "Flying to 112 countries is a lot until you consider swimming between 2. Feels like I swim with sharks—but you actually did it! Congrats!"

Clinton had first learned of Nyad's quest in 2010, when the swimmer was seeking State Department clearance to travel to Cuba. Nyad was encountering the usual bureaucratic delays, which were dragging on so long that the trip was in jeopardy. Feeling herself "getting desperate," she reached out to a CNN pundit named Hilary Rosen, saying, "I know there are more important things in the world than my swim, like foreign affairs, but what's going on here?" Rosen got the request to Clinton, Clinton wrote to advisor Jake Sullivan, and within a day Nyad and her team were cleared.

From that moment, Clinton became a fan and admirer, following Nyad's efforts until she completed her swim. Three years after Nyad's triumph, Clinton was slugging it out in the grueling 2016 presidential election. A reporter asked the candidate how she managed to persevere. Clinton responded that she was reading Nyad's *Find a Way*, her account of the successful swim. "When you're facing big challenges in your life, you can think about Diana Nyad getting attacked by the lethal sting of box jellyfishes," Clinton commented. "And nearly anything else seems doable in comparison." And when it came time for Clinton to write *The Book of Gutsy Women* (with her daughter, Chelsea), she included a chapter on Nyad, writing:

> *There are lessons in Diana's story for any woman—any person, really—who is navigating uncharted waters. Lessons about the power of taking risks and refusing to be defined by failure. Lessons about the incredible strength each of us possesses, even those of us who aren't world-class athletes. Lessons not just about sports but*

Sixty-four-year-old Diana Nyad making landfall in Florida after swimming from Cuba on September 2, 2013.

Andrew Innerarity/Reuters/Redux

about life—about the importance of not simply trying to reach the finish line but learning to enjoy the journey, with all its disappointments, setbacks, and suffering.

Finally, there is another older woman who took inspiration from Nyad's perseverance. That was Annette Bening, who played her in the 2023 movie.

Bening is a five-time Oscar nominee with a long list of standout performances to her name. Yet playing the role of Diana Nyad was a special challenge. At the time of the filming, Bening was sixty-four, the same age that Nyad was when she made her historic swim. But Bening didn't just have to play a woman in her midsixties. She had to play a woman in her midsixties who was in extraordinary physical condition and who would be filmed for most of the two-hour movie in a swimsuit. The actress didn't want to rely too much on body doubles. As she later said, she "wanted to do Diana justice . . . to do real swimmers justice." She put everything she had into the role.

To transform herself into Diana Nyad, Bening hired Rada Owen, a coach and former top-level swimmer who had competed for the United States in the 2000 Summer Olympics. She trained with Owen for a year, sometimes swimming as much as eight hours a day. At times the task was so daunting that Bening broke down crying in the pool. As she later said, "I didn't cry in front of Jodie Foster because I was so intimidated. . . . But I cried in the pool, by myself."

Yet when all was said and done, Bening had indeed transformed herself. Nyad was utterly convinced. As she told an audience at a screening of the film, "We professional swimmers watched [Annette] in the footage and said, 'You can't tell that that isn't a professional swimmer.' You did it, girlfriend."

Another remarkable aspect of Bening's performance: she resisted the Hollywood biopic tendency (more powerful than any tide) to make her heroine overly likable. As depicted by Bening, Nyad's monomaniacal drive makes everyone around her admire her . . . and want to strangle her at times. "Do you have any idea how exhausting you are as a friend?" Foster's Bonnie says at one point.

It was such a thorough transformation that Bening remains a swimmer to this day. She became addicted to her routine and, despite the physical demands, finds it emotionally therapeutic. "It relaxes the central nervous system," she told an interviewer, adding, "That's why people who are on the water tend to be kind of mellow."

Then the actress paused and added one important qualification: "Except Diana Nyad, she's not mellow. She's the one person who's never mellow."

Brian May: Back to School

rock star who earned a PhD in astrophysics at sixty

When you start to hear the life story of Queen guitarist Brian May, it sounds like a familiar tale. An ordinary English boy gets his first guitar at age seven, grows up listening to American blues and folk and R&B and then, as he gets older, British skiffle. (Skiffle—a hybrid of jazz, country, and bluegrass originating in America in the 1920s and played on improvised instruments like the washboard and jugs— became a craze in Britain in the late 1950s.) Buddy Holly is a particular favorite. He gets a band together, with the aim of becoming the next Lonnie Donegan (aka the King of Skiffle) or, better yet, the next John Lennon. As the sixties roll on, the music that kids are playing and listening to gets more complex. Hendrix and Clapton are doing amazing things with the electric guitar; songwriters and producers are growing ever more experimental. The boy, now a young man, drops out of school to chase his dream of becoming a rock star.

But here's where the story of Brian May, who is really more of a "ROCKtogenarian," is different. May didn't quit high school or even college to become a rock star. He quit *graduate school*. And not just any graduate school—he quit a PhD program in astrophysics at Imperial College London. You see, May was the kind of kid who not only built his own guitar as a teenager but also built his own telescope. He was an aspiring guitar god *and* an aspiring cosmologist. (Not to be confused with a cosmetologist, which other future glam rockers may very well have aspired to.) De-cades later, after he had compiled a legendary catalog of hit records, he took a look in the rearview at his abandoned astronomy career. With little left to accomplish as a guitar hero, he channeled his inner Rodney Dangerfield and went back to school. (*Back to School*: still hilarious after all these years). And at age sixty, he earned his PhD in astrophysics.

As a boy, Brian equally enjoyed staring into the night sky and being carried away by the new music that was revolutionizing youth culture. His father, an elec-tronics engineer, taught him to play the ukulele, but he also let his son stay up late to watch the astronomer Sir Patrick Moore explain the nature of the universe on the BBC's *The Sky at Night*. "You talk to any astronomer in the UK and they'll say their first inspiration was Patrick Moore," May later said. "This wonderful music would come on, and you'd have these glimpses of the cosmos. I was completely enthralled by the whole thing. I wanted to be a musician and astronomer at the same time."

In fact, for May, there was really no conflict between these two sides of himself—the introverted, brainy stargazer and the shaggy-haired, guitar-wielding rock and roller. "I think the things tend to go together," he told an interviewer in 2012. "Maybe it's a kind of a romantic spirit to making music that spills over into curiosity about the universe. I would say the majority of musicians I know have a bit of passion for the night sky." As he got older, he remained a studious teen whose parents expected him to do well in school, but at the same time he was drawn to the London music scene. The breakthrough bands of the British Invasion had shown what might be possible for ordinary kids if they could score a hit record.

It was while studying physics at Imperial College that he first heard Hendrix play live. "Jimi Hendrix really opened up the heavens," May says. "It's really hard to imagine the world without Jimi because he changed it so much. All of us thought we knew what guitar playing was. Jimi tore asunder all the limitations that none of us really knew were there." Before long, his band was playing on the same bill as the Jimi Hendrix Experience at Royal Albert Hall.

In 1968, May was just a few months past his twenty-first birthday when he received his bachelor of science degree with honors. Two days later, his prog-rock band Smile opened for Pink Floyd, who were playing at Imperial College in the midst of an eleven-month tour of Europe and North America. By now, May was definitely living in two different worlds. You have to wonder if he had many opportunities to discuss the nature of the space-time continuum with the roadies and groupies who hung out backstage at the concerts he played.

He continued to lead his double life. In 1970, he and bandmate Roger Taylor met an aspiring singer, a young man of Indian Parsi heritage from Zanzibar named Farrokh "Freddie" Bulsara, the future Freddie Mercury. (I always wanted to be from a place as exotic-sounding as Zanzibar. Instead I'm from Maryland.) Along with bassist John Deacon, they formed the band Queen. During these years, May was periodically flying off to Tenerife for his astronomical research—his thesis topic was zodiacal dust, which seems just about right for the age of psychedelia and glam rock. He would occasionally play guitar for his professors. He recalls them as being mildly amused, but skeptical about his odds of success in the music world.

But as Queen began to get real attention, May had to make a choice. Would he be a rock star, or would he study interstellar rocks? There simply wasn't enough time in his life anymore to do both. What made up his mind, he says, was not the excitement of life on the road playing sold-out arenas. It was the fear that he might not have what it took to excel as a scientist: "My choice was made on the assumption that I wasn't very good at physics and I might be quite good at music."

May probably underestimated his scientific abilities, but he was spot-on about being quite good at music. Queen released its first album in 1973, and by 1975's *A Night at the Opera* (they were Marx Brothers fans), with its genre-breaking anthem "Bohemian Rhapsody," they were stars. You probably know the hits that followed— "We Are the Champions," "We Will Rock You," "Crazy Little Thing Called Love," "Another One Bites the Dust," "Under Pressure" (cowritten by David Bowie), and many more. By the 1980s, Queen was one of the world's most celebrated bands, their megastardom dimming only with the tragic death of Mercury from AIDS in 1991. (In later years, at different times, the singers Paul Rodgers of Bad Company and Adam Lambert from *American Idol* joined the group.) Today May is regularly ranked among the greatest rock guitarists in history, even besting the cosmos-shattering Jimi himself in a *Guitar World* reader's poll.

The hit records and the honors piled up. In 2005, May was named CBE, Commander of the Most Excellent Order of the British Empire, the highest honor in the United Kingdom shy of knighthood, given for contribution to the arts, sciences, or public service. He stood atop the music world, with virtually no peaks left to scale.

But May apparently had never quite satisfied that itch to understand the universe. His old doctoral thesis remained what he called "unfinished business." "It was always in my mind," he said. "All that work that I did from 1970 to 1974 . . . I packed it all away into suitcases and it [was] sitting there ever since." And so he dug up the suitcases, unpacked them, and brought his old notebooks on tour with him. Perhaps he believed, as the writer George Eliot once wrote, that "it's never too late to be what you might have been." (Okay, there's no evidence Eliot ever wrote that. In the 1990s, this quote was displayed in the subway car I was riding and attributed to her. This was in the days before everyone just stared at their cellphones on the way to work.) As May tells it, "I mentioned on my website that I was looking at my thesis again. Who should read the website but the head of the astronomy department at Imperial College, Michael Robinson." Robinson, only a few years older than May, had become in the intervening years a prominent scholar and the president of the Royal Astronomical Society. He wrote to May and invited him back to Imperial College to resume his studies. As May put it, "That's something you can't say no to."

And so, in 2006, Brian May returned to Imperial College to finish his thesis on interplanetary dust clouds, "A Survey of Radial Velocities in the Zodiacal Dust Cloud." And while it may sound esoteric, it's actually fundamental to the existence of everyone reading this book. As Dr. Tim Naylor of the University of Exeter explains, the study of interstellar dust "has its roots in a very important problem—the problem of how the planet that you're sitting on today coagulated from dust around the early sun." What was it that Joni Mitchell said? We are stardust.

As May relates, he was also fortunate that his decades-old thesis topic had come back into academic fashion:

When I began, it was a hot topic, but in that 30 years it kind of lapsed. What happened very luckily for me, however, [was that] people began discovering dust clouds around other suns, in other solar systems. And suddenly my subject became very in-demand again. I started talking about astronomy again to people who said, "Why don't you still do it?" I put everything, and I mean everything, on hold for a year. And they put me in a little office in Imperial College and I got down to it.

He completed his thesis the next year, at age sixty. He was now Dr. Brian May, CBE, PhD.

In the years since he earned his doctorate, May has returned to life as a modern-day Renaissance man. He went on to work with NASA on several projects, including the OSIRIS-REx mission, launched in 2016, to collect samples from an asteroid. May helped to analyze images of the asteroid's surface using a technique known as stereoscopy.

Rock star and astrophysicist Brian May, standing in between his guitar and his telescope, both of which he built when he was a teenager, in 2009.
Max Alexander/Science Photo Library

His expertise in stereoscopy also came in handy to scientists analyzing data from NASA's New Horizons probe, sent into space to help us understand the nature of Pluto, its moon Charon, and the Kuiper Belt, a massive band of frozen gaseous objects at the outskirts of our solar system. May, of course, continued to play music— including at the 2022 Platinum Jubilee for the late Queen Elizabeth II—while also becoming a leading advocate for animal welfare and the elimination of fox hunting in England. And, oh yeah, he cowrote a history of the universe for laymen with two other astronomers—one of whom was Sir Patrick Moore, the man he grew up watching on the BBC in the late 1950s and early '60s. (Talk about a Roctogenarian: Moore hosted *The Sky at Night* for almost fifty-six years. And he was eighty-eight when the book he coauthored with Brian May was published.)

May has no regrets for having chosen the path of rock star rather than astronomer. "I'm sure it was the right decision," he says. "I think you have to go where your heart tells you."

During a commencement address at the University of Exeter, May mentioned that "as an old guy, none of us can resist giving a little advice." And what he told the graduates is worth repeating, since it speaks to both the wisdom of recognizing that life will always be beyond our control and the risk one takes in trying something new: "It seems to me the secret is to always just play the cards that are in your hand to the best of your ability . . . accept what comes to you, find joy in what comes to you, and make it into something great. I have to say that most of the great things in life are very scary, and this is included."

When asked if he could have been a famous astronomer, May is both humble and sanguine: "It's funny . . . my conclusion is that you have to take big steps, not small steps, 'cause if I hadn't wholeheartedly plunged into music and made a success of that, then I am sure I wouldn't be here now."

OLD SMOKY: Tootsie Tomanetz

In the world of barbecue, one woman is queen—Norma Frances Tomanetz, better known as Miss Tootsie. But this queen's reign began relatively late in life.

Tootsie's career started by chance. Her husband was working as a butcher at City Meat Market in Giddings, Texas, when the market's owner found himself shorthanded at the barbecue pit one day in 1966. Tootsie, then a thirty-one-year-old housewife, was asked to fill in, later remembering, "I told them I didn't know anything about it, but I was willing to learn and do my best." She would go on to work that barbecue pit for a decade, eventually buying City Meat Market outright with her husband, running the place for twenty years. There was pleasure in barbecuing, but little recognition.

When her husband had a stroke, they were forced to sell the business. Tootsie took a job as a custodian at the local middle school. But barbecue came back into her life in a big way in 2003, when, at sixty-eight, she took on the role as pitmaster at a brand-new joint, Snow's BBQ. Within five years, *Texas Monthly* was calling Snow's "the best barbecue in Texas," thanks in large part to Tootsie's pitmaster prowess. Tootsie was receiving accolades she never dreamed of, with people making pilgrimages to taste her brisket, pork, and chicken.

So what makes Tootsie's barbecue so delicious? Aside from years of honing her technique, which includes a mop sauce—where she literally applies sauce onto her meats with a cotton mop—Tootsie insists there's no secret recipe, just "salt and pepper, tender loving care."

The job of pitmaster is not always pleasant, particularly for someone who's eighty-nine. The day starts at 2:00 a.m. each Saturday and is subject to Texas weather extremes. But Tootsie believes barbecue keeps her young. And it's been her salvation, particularly after the deaths of her husband in 2015 and her son, who died from brain cancer in 2016. "It was the Lord's work to call them home because these opportunities were ahead for me. God knew what my achievements would be, so he took them home."

It's About Time

Tyrus Wong,

Carmen Herrera

& John Goodenough

Most of the stories in this book are about people who have done remarkable things later in life. But there are other ways in which old age can be a time of unexpected blessings. Many people work their whole lives at a particular trade or career but for various reasons fail to get the public recognition they seek or deserve. Sometimes this is just a matter of bad luck. Other times, it might be that a society's prejudices prevent it from seeing their accomplishments. And still other times, it might be a person's own character—a humility, an aversion to promoting oneself, or simply an indifference to fame and recognition—that keeps their story from making headlines.

How wonderful, then, when the public stands up and cheers *before* the person has exited the stage? In the stories below, three exceptional people achieved recognition very late in life, thus avoiding the fate of, say, Van Gogh, who died largely unheralded at thirty-seven. Of course it helps that all three of these artists reached the triple-digit stage of life. (Two of them lived till 106.)

There's another significant connection among these three very different lives. In each case, a long and healthy marriage—of fifty-eight years, sixty-one years, and sixty-five years, respectively—provided the sustenance and support that fame and fortune did not.

Tyrus Wong: The Wilderness No More

animator recognized as Disney Legend at ninety

The cruel and criminal mastermind Dr. Fu Manchu bent on infiltrating the Western world. The sexually predatory dragon lady corrupting morally upright white men. The amiable, subservient detective Charlie Chan, speaking a ludicrous pidgin English. Offensive stereotypes like this were the dominant images of East Asians in the Hollywood of the 1930s. Indeed, for decades Asian characters were usually played by white actors in yellowface, whether it was Mary Pickford in *Madame Butterfly* or, infamously, Mickey Rooney in *Breakfast at Tiffany's*. And the world of animation was no better—maybe worse. Amid a sadly familiar collection of African cannibals, Mexican banditos, and murderous Native Americans, you find alarmingly crude Chinese characters who, in the words of animation historian Charles Solomon, "jabber incomprehensible syllables and run laundries."

Golden Age Hollywood's default denigration of Asian people and Asian cultures makes it all the more remarkable that one of the foundational films in the history of animation owes its visual design to the Chinese American artist Tyrus Wong. Though credited merely as a background painter when the film was released, Wong is now recognized as the artistic visionary behind the classic film *Bambi*. Yet in spite of a remarkable career as both a commercial and fine artist, it was not until he was in his nineties that Wong began to get his due.

Wong Gen Yeo was born in 1910 in Guangdong Province, China. Maybe our names really do contain our destiny, because Wong's Chinese name translates into English, rather amazingly, as "beautiful scenery," which is exactly what he spent his life painting. Wong, who passed away in 2016 at 106, liked to point out that the same phrase in Spanish would be *buena vista*, which happens to be the name of the Burbank, California, street on which the Walt Disney Studio is located and was, until recently, the name of Disney's film distribution company.

Wong grew up in poverty. He told the writer Lisa See that the family shared their home in China with their pigs and chickens. They kept their food suspended on ropes to keep it away from the rats. No wonder that when Tyrus was nine, his father took him to America to seek a better life. They left China in 1920. That was the last time that the boy, who took the American name Tyrus, saw his mother or sister.

Xenophobia was a fact of everyday life in California in the 1920s. When Tyrus and his father arrived at Angel Island, in the San Francisco Bay, they were separated. The immigration regime was brutal, thanks to the Chinese Exclusion Act of 1882, which virtually banned Chinese immigration to the U.S. (Tyrus and his father had to adopt false names and pretend to be relatives of existing Chinese residents to gain entry.) Tyrus was detained for a month at Angel Island without family or friends. In *Tyrus*, Pamela Tom's award-winning 2015 documentary, he recalled the experience. "I just suffered," he said. "Every day was just miserable. . . . I hated that place." Others suffered too, as the American immigration and naturalization services deliberately sought reasons to turn away Chinese people. Wong remembered that there were immigrants who died by suicide while he was held there.

Tyrus recalled seeing the tears in his father's eyes when he was released to him. Once they were settled, it was a tough life. The father found work as a cobbler's assistant in Sacramento, coming home at night with his hands scraped up. The boy, meanwhile, learned about racism. He recalled a trip to see a movie at Sacramento's Godard Theater with a white friend; the usher insisted that Tyrus sit up in the balcony while the white boy sat up front. (For more on the California of Tyrus's youth, check out the *Mobituaries* podcast episode on film star Anna May Wong.)

Tyrus and his father moved south to Pasadena in search of a better situation. The boy struggled to pay attention in school. But on the bright side, his doodles were astonishingly precocious. (One time he built an entire model symphony orchestra out of matchsticks.) A junior high school teacher saw his drawings and, rather than scolding him, recommended him for Pasadena's Otis Art Institute.

Tyrus's father borrowed money so that the boy could attend. This was a risky move. At that time, they were living in a men's boardinghouse in an impoverished neighborhood—a butcher shop on one side of them, a brothel on the other. Under such conditions, how many fathers would go into debt so their son could learn to paint? "Son," Tyrus recalled his father saying, "promise me one thing. Really study hard and make me feel it was worthwhile." For his part, the adolescent Tyrus—the youngest student at the school—remembered his first time painting a nude female model, a memory vivid eighty years later. "That was really a lot of fun," he recalled with a grin. As he told my colleague Tracy Smith on *CBS Sunday Morning*, he "didn't know whether to draw or just look."

But Tyrus took his pledge to his father seriously. Art became his entire world. Baseball, the beloved pastime of most American boys, was forbidden, since a broken finger or hand could end Tyrus's career before it began. He drew and painted all the time, studying the European masters. At the same time, he deepened his knowledge of his native culture. At his father's insistence, he mastered the brushwork necessary for Chinese calligraphy. He visited art libraries to study reproductions of traditional Chinese art. Indeed, it was from the Chinese tradition that he came to appreciate the importance of landscape and scale, rejecting excessive detail in favor of mood and impression. This would be crucial for his future career.

Tyrus was still studying at the Otis Institute when his father died, probably from diabetes. "I was completely on my own," Tyrus recalled, remembering how much his father had sacrificed to give him a better life. He found a mentor, however, in the artist Stanton Macdonald-Wright, director of the Art Students League of Los Angeles. Macdonald-Wright encouraged Tyrus to combine his interest in cutting-edge modernist painting with the traditions of Chinese art, particularly the monumental landscapes of the Song dynasty (960–1279). "I learned that nature is always greater than man," Tyrus later told Lisa See. "It is the balance and harmony between man and nature that is important." By the age of twenty-two, after only twelve years in the U.S., Tyrus was featured by the Art Institute of Chicago in an exhibition that also included works by Picasso, Matisse, and Klee. "Tyrus Wong should have a great future," judged one reviewer.

In Pamela Tom's documentary, Sonia Mak, a museum curator, notes that "it was an exciting time" for young Chinese immigrants "to be gaining visibility" despite the discrimination, official and unofficial, that they faced. In the 1930s, there were restrictions not only on immigration but on the right to testify in court, the right to buy property, even the right to marry: marriage between Asians and whites was forbidden in California until 1948, when a court struck down the statute. In spite of these barriers, Tyrus and other Asian artists would gather at an antiques shop owned by a mixed-race businessman named Eddy See (grandfather to the writer Lisa mentioned above). As a group, they promoted Asian American art, turning the upper floor of the shop into a gallery. When business slowed during the

Depression, the basement became a Chinese restaurant, Dragon's Den, that drew Hollywood stars including Anna May Wong. The artists decorated the walls with murals; Tyrus created matchbooks and menus to suit the decor.

Since money was tight, Tyrus started waiting tables, and while there, he began dating fellow employee Ruth Kim, a first-generation American from Bakersfield who attended UCLA. Their first date was an evening at the movies; they saw George Cukor's *David Copperfield*. During these years, Tyrus also found work with the Federal Art Project, a New Deal program that helped support thousands of unemployed or underemployed artists. By sustaining the careers of painters like Jacob Lawrence and Jackson Pollock, it laid the groundwork for decades of American excellence in the arts.

Soon Tyrus and Ruth married. In Tom's documentary, the artist is asked what moment in life gave him the most joy. He breaks into a smile. The answer is easy. "When I got married," he says, before shedding a tear for his late wife.

Before long, a baby arrived, and Tyrus needed consistent and lucrative work. Ruth suggested he try Walt Disney Pictures. Tyrus was hired to work on Mickey Mouse cartoons, making what are called "in-between" sketches—the transitional drawings that filled in the gaps between the animated characters' different poses. The work was tedious. But Tyrus heard that the studio was beginning work on a film adaptation of *Bambi*, a 1923 novel by the Austrian Jewish writer Felix Salten (translated into English, oddly enough, by Whittaker Chambers, who testified in the 1950 trial of Soviet spy Alger Hiss). Disney had recently released its first feature-length animated film, *Snow White and the Seven Dwarfs*, and it was a blockbuster. To this day it remains (in inflation-adjusted dollars) the highest-grossing animated film in history. In the wake of this success, Disney launched several other feature film projects, including *Pinocchio*, *Fantasia*, and *Bambi*.

Tyrus worked up some rough paintings and showed them to Tom Codrick, the film's art director. The paintings, in the style Tyrus had been cultivating, emphasized color and composition over realistic detail, creating a soft atmospheric mood influenced by both Song dynasty landscapes and the French Impressionists' play with color and light. They were unlike anything the Disney studio had done, a far cry from the heavily detailed style of *Snow White*. Codrick brought them to Walt Disney, who, according to one animation historian, "went crazy over them." He was won over by their beauty and simplicity. Michael Labrie, who later curated an exhibit of Wong's work for the Walt Disney Family Museum, told Tracy Smith, "So here was this vision that Tyrus had created with his Asian influence, sort of like Chinese scroll paintings. He did these forests [where] you could feel the moisture in the forest. He was an amazing visual storyteller in these little sketches."

While nominally credited as a background painter, Tyrus's visual concepts became the keynote for the entire film. He was the visionary behind the film's color palette, the tone, the mood. Every aesthetic aspect of the film referred back to the evocative atmospheric paintings he created. As Labrie put it, "The other artists were trained to draw like Tyrus for that film. The morning mist in the forest . . . the deer going in and out of the shadows, all of those things were something that Tyrus had worked out."

In the documentary, veteran animation director Eric Goldberg emphasizes how Wong "was using color to raise the emotional stakes of what was going on in the story." It was one of many times Tyrus would find a way to move his art in an experimental direction yet appeal to ordinary viewers, enabling a film's commercial success.

Remarkably, despite his groundbreaking work on *Bambi*, Wong was never introduced to Walt Disney. There were few Asian artists at Disney in those days, and Tyrus's ethnicity almost certainly was part of the reason for his neglect. And so, despite the brilliant work that is revered by animators today, Tyrus's tenure at Disney was brief. In 1941, the animators went on strike. The Screen Cartoonists Guild had been formed in 1938, and across Hollywood artists were unionizing. Of the major animation studios, Disney was the lone holdout, refusing to negotiate. When the artists complained that Walt Disney himself was behind the unequal distribution of rewards and privileges, he responded with anger: "My first recommendation to the lot of you is this: put your own house in order, you can't accomplish a damn thing by sitting around and waiting to be told everything. If you're not progressing as you should, instead of grumbling and growling, do something about it." Eventually Disney, pressured by the National Labor Relations Board, signed an agreement, but he exacted revenge by laying off hundreds of artists. Among the layoffs was Wong, who, in a terrible irony, was not himself one of the striking workers.

If Tyrus Wong's work on *Bambi* is little known, the rest of his career is even more neglected. Yet for the next eight decades—yes, *eight decades*—he worked in a variety of mediums while supporting his wife and three daughters. A Disney veteran named Dick Kelsey got him work creating Christmas cards for Hallmark; one gorgeous 1954 card, which depicts a tiny shepherd under a pink-blossomed cherry tree staring up at a star, sold over a million copies. A classmate from Tyrus's days at the Otis Institute invited him to paint pottery for Winfield Pottery, also in Pasadena. The "Chinese modern" style that he developed possesses, in the words of one expert, "a grace and an ease that made his work really accessible to a large part of the American public." But his steadiest source of work was from the movies. Another former Disney colleague, Travis Johnson, brought Tyrus into the art department at Warner Bros., and over the next twenty-six years he designed sets and drew storyboards for dozens of films, including *The Sands of Iwo Jima*, *Rebel Without a Cause*, *The Music Man*, and *The Wild Bunch*. Most of this work was uncredited.

By the late 1960s, independent production was on the rise and the studios were downsizing. In 1966, Jack Warner, then in his seventies, sold the controlling interest in Warner Bros., and in 1968 Tyrus was let go. In the years after his involuntary retirement from Hollywood, Tyrus—who had mastered drawing and painting, art design, pottery, and greeting cards—took up a new art form: kite making.

Now in his sixties, Tyrus checked out books from the library on kite making just as he had checked out books on Song dynasty art fifty years earlier, turning his

A young Tyrus Wong in the art department at Warner Bros.

Estate of Tyrus Wong

new hobby into a new art form. He held himself to an exacting standard, insisting, for example, that a butterfly kite catch the wind in just the right way so that it would move like a real butterfly. His colorful kites—centipedes, cranes, owls, butterflies—became a familiar sight on the beach in Santa Monica. Wong had always enjoyed fishing; of kite flying he said, "This is just like fishing, except in fishing you look down. Kite flying, you look up." For museum curator Sonia Mak, the kites are both engineering marvels and fully realized works of art: "He thought about the mechanics of what he was making and how they would look when they're animated by the wind, how they would look against a blue sky."

Ruth, Tyrus's wife, suffered a series of strokes as she aged, and dementia set in. For more than forty years she had supported Tyrus not only by raising their daughters but by handling correspondence and bookkeeping for his various business endeavors. Tyrus now put aside his art to devote himself to her care. It was a long illness; Ruth died in 1995, at the age of eighty-five. Tyrus's daughters feared that he would be unable to carry on. But after her death, Tyrus returned to kite making, the creative work that sustained him.

No doubt he would have lived out the rest of his life contentedly. But then something remarkable happened: public recognition. It's not clear what exactly spurred the rediscovery, but in 2000, Tyrus was honored by the Pacific Asia Museum, and the following year Disney recognized him as a "Disney Legend," an honor reserved for the most significant contributors to the Disney corporation. Soon retrospective exhibitions began. L.A.'s Chinese American Museum put up the show *Tyrus Wong: A Retrospective*. The Craft & Folk Art Museum ran *Mid-Century Mandarin: The Clay Canvases of Tyrus Wong*. The Academy of Motion Picture Arts and Sciences hosted *The Art of the Motion Picture Illustrator: William B. Major, Harold Michelson and Tyrus Wong*, and San Francisco's Walt Disney Family Museum put together the comprehensive *Water to Paper, Paint to Sky: The Art of Tyrus Wong*. Even Malibu's city hall took part, exhibiting an ambitious display of Tyrus's kites.

We *do* know what inspired Pamela Tom's 2015 documentary, which PBS

A young-at-heart Tyrus Wong, many decades later, still making art.

Irene Poon Anderson

included in their prestigious American Masters series. Tom had been watching *Bambi* with her young daughter back in 1997 when she saw Wong's name in the credits. "My first thought was, 'Chinese American? Working at Disney in the 1930s?' I just had to find out who he was." In the final fifteen years of his 106-year life, Tyrus received lifetime achievement awards from—and this is just a partial list—the Otis Institute, the Art Directors Guild, the Angel Island Immigration Station Foundation, and the International Animated Film Association.

None of this went to Tyrus's head. As Pamela Tom said, "This is somebody who teaches us how to live the life of an artist, and how to lead such a meaningful life, with humility, with humor, with generosity. I don't know if it's because of his roots in a village in China or if it's just Tyrus. But there's just something so genuine about him and so humble. It's kind of mind-blowing." Maybe when accolades like this come so late in life, the artist is long past the age when he craves fame or public recognition. Or maybe Tyrus was just the sort of artist who cared more about his work than the rewards it might bring. When asked about his "greatest achievement," his answer was not *Bambi*, or his ceramics, or showing with Picasso and Matisse as a twenty-two-year-old. It was, he said, the three "wonderful" daughters he raised with his beloved Ruth.

Carmen Herrera: The Bus Finally Came

first solo show at a major museum at 101

In 2015, a big change came to the New York art world. The Whitney Museum of American Art, an essential stop on any art lover's tour of the city, relocated from its weighty granite fortress of a home on Madison Avenue to an edgier downtown location at the south end of the High Line in the Meatpacking District. First Lady Michelle Obama offered dedicatory remarks at a ceremony attended by prominent artists, curators, critics, and donors. An inaugural exhibition called *America Is*

Hard to See displayed artworks that drew from the full range of the Whitney's vast holdings. And among the dozens of famous American painters whose works were on show—Marsden Hartley, Edward Hopper, Jasper Johns, Ellsworth Kelly—was a newcomer, the Cuban American artist Carmen Herrera.

There were other newcomers also included in this ambitious show, but what made the inclusion of Herrera especially notable is that when she earned this landmark honor, she was just a few weeks away from her one hundredth birthday. Herrera had been creating art for eight decades, working doggedly, even obsessively, in almost total obscurity. Now, suddenly, her work was being displayed at one of the most important museums in the world. Even better, she was getting a loud, proud shout-out from the First Lady. Talk about making up for lost time.

"It's about time," Herrera told a reporter from the *New York Times*. "There's a saying that you wait for the bus and it will come. I waited almost a hundred years."

Herrera was born eight years before Ellsworth Kelly, fifteen years before Jasper Johns. Both of those men were celebrated at the peak of their careers, during the middle decades of the twentieth century. In those days, American abstract art became an international phenomenon. Thanks to the work of Jackson Pollock, Mark Rothko, and Robert Rauschenberg, among others, and to new museums like MoMA, the Guggenheim, and the Whitney itself, New York City had overtaken Paris as the capital of the global art scene. The leaders of the new movements were featured on the cover of *Life* magazine. Traveling exhibits exported a taste for the new style to Europe and beyond.

But although Herrera was a contemporary of these men, living and working in New York just as they were, doing cutting-edge work just as they were, she was entirely overlooked by the critics and collectors, let alone the general public. Undoubtedly, this neglect occurred at least in part because she was a Cuban American woman working in a world dominated by . . . shall we say . . . prominent male egos. In a late-life interview with the *Guardian*, Herrera recalled being rejected by a gallery owner—a female gallery owner, no less: "She said, 'You know, Carmen, you can paint rings around the men artists I have, but I'm not going to give you a show because you're a woman.' I felt as if someone had slapped me on the face. I felt for the first time what discrimination was."

But now, with the opening of the new Whitney building, a vigorous Herrera was, at ninety-nine, finally getting the accolades that had eluded her. The next year, 2016, brought further recognition, as the Whitney honored her with a solo show, *Carmen Herrera: Lines of Sight*. Curator Dana Miller had determined that a solo exhibit was necessary because "the more of [Herrera's] work that you see, the more you appreciate it. . . . Seeing just one work was not enough." The exhibition focused on the emergence of what Miller called Herrera's "trademark style," a stark, colorful, geometric minimalism. These striking, confident, and flat-out gorgeous canvases pull the viewer to them as if by magnetic force. After first viewing Herrera's work, the British art critic Laura Cumming seemed to speak for the entire art world when she asked, "How can we have missed these brilliant compositions?"

Herrera was born in Havana in 1915 to well-off parents, both journalists. Her father was the founding editor of the Cuban newspaper *El Mundo*; her mother worked there as a reporter. Their friends included writers, artists, and intellectuals. Her childhood was one of seemingly benign neglect, as her parents had their hands full with the newspaper—not to mention six other children. Still, in such an environment, culture must have seemed a birthright to the young Carmen, and she showed a penchant for drawing at a young age. As a teenager, she was sent to Paris for school. She returned home to Cuba to pursue a degree in architecture. Then, in 1937, while still a student, she met a visitor from New York, an English teacher named Jesse Loewenthal. The couple fell in love and were married two years later. Over the course of a sixty-one-year marriage, they built a life together, mainly on the Lower East Side of New York.

Jesse supported them working as an English teacher at New York's Stuyvesant High, where, years later, he would be joined on the faculty by author and

Roctogenarian Frank McCourt. (McCourt recalled Loewenthal as a dignified scholar dressed in an "elegant three-piece suit, the gold watch chain looping across his waistcoat front.") Carmen studied at the Art Students League in midtown. After the war, Jesse secured a sabbatical and the couple moved to Paris, finding an apartment in the bohemian neighborhood of Montparnasse. Jesse found work teaching, while Carmen cultivated her painting, absorbing the influence of abstract European artists like the Dutchman Piet Mondrian and the Russian Kazimir Malevich. (Jesse, meanwhile, extended his sabbatical.) For five years, Carmen revised, refined, and honed her style, emphasizing weighty geometric shapes, bold colors and contrasts, and strong straight lines. "There is nothing I love more than to make a straight line," she later said. "How can I explain it? It's the beginning of all structures, really."

By 1953, financial realities demanded that the couple return to New York, where Carmen continued painting. Yet despite the obvious talent that radiates from her canvases, public recognition remained fitful at best. The artist Tony Bechara, a close friend and, in Herrera's later years, an assistant in the studio, is convinced that being a woman worked against Herrera. If you were a woman in those years, he recalls, "you were supposed to do maternity scenes or watercolors"—certainly not the "tough and decisive" geometric forms that Herrera painted. Herrera herself commented tersely that in those postwar years, "Everything was controlled by men, not just art."

Through the 1960s, '70s, '80s, and '90s, the New York art world saw movements, fads, trends, booms, and changes of taste. New superstars shot suddenly into the firmament, sometimes burning out just as fast. Throughout it all, Herrera continued to do her work, painting on a rigorous schedule, occasionally showing at a gallery here or there, but remaining largely overlooked.

In 2000, her beloved husband Jesse, whose belief in her talent had never wavered, died at the age of ninety-eight. Carmen was holding his hand when he took his last breath. "Jesse was a saint," she said to one interviewer, recalling their life together. "I'm thinking back and I never even thanked him for all he did for me.

He was the only one I ever spoke to about my paintings. He understood what I was doing and he was always supportive." Despite the lack of wealth and fame, Carmen felt that they had "a very good life" together. Over their six decades of marriage, she said, "We became closer and closer, and by the end we were one person. We could think without talking."

Jesse was not there in 2004, when, at age eighty-nine, Carmen's professional fortunes suddenly turned. Like much of society, the art world was belatedly starting to change, paying new attention to female artists and artists of color. Frederico Sève, a Brazilian gallery owner, was putting together a show featuring Latin American women artists at his space on Hudson Street in TriBeCa. One of the artists had dropped out, and Sève needed a replacement. One night, he was having dinner with Tony Bechara, and Bechara recommended Carmen.

Frederico Sève was bowled over by Herrera's work and put her in the show. Holland Cotter of the *New York Times* gave the exhibit a very brief review; almost as minimalist as the art itself, the two sentences he wrote about Herrera were actually more of a notice. Still, the show began to generate buzz. Three major collectors, all women, snapped up over a dozen of Herrera's paintings. One was donated to MoMA. Soon major museums in the U.S. and the UK were acquiring Herrera's work. Prices on her canvases jumped into the five figures, then six.

No one was more surprised at this meteoric rise than the artist herself. She had labored for decades, having long ago relinquished any hope for fame. Fortune was even further from her mind. She told an interviewer that it was "compulsion" that drove her to create art. "I do it because I have to do it," she said. And although she sometimes seemed inconvenienced by the sudden attention, in her candid moments she confessed that she enjoyed it.

In her nineties and hundreds, Herrera continued to paint, even though she was often confined to a wheelchair and reliant on assistants. (Critics and curators have made comparisons to Matisse—an artist Herrera loved and considered superior to Picasso.) The money she welcomed, mainly because it paid for medical expenses and aides. She died at the age of 106, finally having taken her place among the masters of American abstract art.

As she told the *New York Times* in 2009, when she was a lass of ninety-four: "I never in my life had any idea of money, and I thought fame was a very vulgar thing. So I just worked and waited. And at the end of my life, I'm getting a lot of recognition, to my amazement and my pleasure, actually."

John B. Goodenough: An Extraordinary Life Span

won the Nobel Prize in Chemistry at ninety-seven

When the future father of the lithium-ion battery arrived at the University of Chicago as a graduate student in 1946, he was dismayed to learn that he was already over the hill.

Back in 1943, John Goodenough had interrupted his undergraduate studies at Yale (where he joked he had done "good enough") to aid the wartime effort as an army meteorologist. He served on active duty in Newfoundland and the Azores. During his service, he managed to complete his Yale degree, but the years in the military delayed his matriculation at graduate school. By the time he got to Chicago to begin a master's degree in physics, the twenty-four-year-old was older than most of his classmates—by a whopping two years. It was at that point that one of his professors, Dr. John A. Simpson, told Goodenough that he had no future in the field. He was too old. It was that simple.

"I don't understand you veterans," Simpson told Goodenough. "Don't you know that anyone who has ever done anything significant in physics had already done it by the time he was your age—and you want to *begin*?" (Jeez, who knew physicists could be so catty?)

Simpson was far from alone in holding this view of "older" scientists. (Simpson, who had spent the war years working on the Manhattan Project, was himself only six years older than his student.) STEM disciplines, especially the most abstract and theoretical ones—mathematics, particle physics—are notoriously areas where genius emerges early if it emerges at all. These fields are intellectual playgrounds for whiz kids, savants, and prodigies. Marie Curie was not yet thirty when she began her research on radiation, and only thirty-six when she won the Nobel Prize in Physics. James Watson was a mere lad of twenty-five when he co-discovered the molecular structure of DNA; his Nobel Prize, in Physiology or Medicine, followed at age thirty-four. And the great physicist Werner Heisenberg was just twenty-six when he published his revolutionary paper on the uncertainty principle. (I would explain uncertainty, but I'm just not sure I can.) He was made a laureate at the precocious age of thirty-one. You can see why Simpson thought that his new student Goodenough was not quite, well . . . up to par.

Defying the actuaries, however, Goodenough did go on to win a Nobel Prize—in Chemistry. When his recognition came, he was a robust ninety-seven. Knocking on the door of his eleventh decade, he traveled to Stockholm. Photos show a fit and trim Goodenough, in tuxedo and white tie, with a full head of white hair, seated in his wheelchair, shaking hands with the king of Sweden, Carl XVI Gustaf, while members of the Royal Swedish Academy of Sciences stand and applaud. He was the oldest person ever to win a Nobel Prize. (The youngest was seventeen-year-old Malala Yousafzai, who won the Nobel Peace Prize in 2014 for her efforts on behalf of children's right to education.) As the *Guardian* put it, "Only his remarkable longevity saved the Swedish committee from an embarrassing injustice."

Goodenough's extraordinary persistence and longevity may have owed something to his early academic struggles. Born to American parents in Germany in 1922, Goodenough grew up in Woodbridge, Connecticut, where the family moved after his father was hired as a professor of religion at Yale. Both parents were emotionally aloof, and Goodenough grew up a lonely boy, finding companionship mainly in his siblings and the family dog. He was dyslexic, and because the condition was undiagnosed, this enormously intelligent child struggled throughout elementary school. But thanks to hard work and wise counseling, Goodenough persevered. When he was shipped off to the Groton School in Massachusetts, he mastered Latin and Greek and graduated first in his class. At Yale he continued to excel academically. Even with an interruption for military service, he graduated summa cum laude, with a degree in mathematics.

After his years in the military, Goodenough was surprised to discover that a Yale professor had recommended him for funding that would allow him to study physics at the University of Chicago. At the time, Chicago's world-class program boasted famous scientists such as Clarence Zener, Edward Teller, and Enrico Fermi (the last a Nobel laureate). Despite Simpson's skepticism about his late start, Goodenough completed his master's, and then, two years later, his PhD. Snappily titled "A Theory of the Deviation from Close Packing in Hexagonal Metal Crystals," this page-turner of a dissertation proposes a mechanism to explain "how the Fermi surface interacts with Brillouin zone boundaries," all in a brisk sixty-three typewritten pages. While at Chicago, Goodenough also met his wife, Irene Wiseman, a history graduate student from Canada to whom he remained married for sixty-five years, until her death in 2016. In a Valentine's Day message posted on Twitter a few years later, Goodenough celebrated their love, concluding on a poignant and characteristically understated note. "I'm afraid I miss my wife quite a bit," he wrote. "She was very special."

After Chicago, Goodenough embarked on an impressive career. He was hired at MIT and after more than a decade there was offered a position at Oxford. At Oxford he began the work in electrochemistry that would lead to his Nobel Prize more than fifty years later. This was the 1970s, when, in the wake of the OPEC oil embargo and worsening smog in cities across the globe, policymakers and scientists were beginning to seek cleaner alternatives to fossil fuels. Goodenough turned his research to renewable batteries.

His work in this area has been described as central to the development of the lithium-ion battery that is widely in use today. This once-experimental technology now powers many of our most prized technological devices, including smartphones, laptops, and tablets—not to mention cardiac defibrillators and, lest we forget, hoverboards. Portable low-maintenance lithium batteries were a new technology in the 1970s. But not even Goodenough himself fully grasped how essential they would become for our current moment, in which our future as a species depends upon the efficient use of energy.

In developing the lithium-ion battery, Goodenough improved upon the work of M. Stanley Whittingham, one of the scientists with whom he shared the Nobel, making a lithium-cobalt-oxide cathode that gave the battery higher voltage and greater stability than anything that had come before. These batteries are increasingly small and light, with high energy density, which makes them ideal for, among other things, electric vehicles.

At Oxford in the 1980s, ageism was still part of the academic profession, and as he hit sixty, Goodenough was peering down the road at compulsory retirement. But instead of waiting to be retired, in 1986 he took a new position at the University of Texas, where he was able to continue his research for three more decades. In his late years, he was acutely aware of the climate crisis pressing down on the planet, and he felt an urgency to accomplish even more. His goal became to eradicate petroleum emissions from the world's highways. "We have to, in the near future, make a transition from our dependence on fossil fuels to a dependence on clean energy," he told an interviewer for the University of Chicago alumni magazine. "So that's what I'm currently trying to do before I die."

That kind of selflessness characterized John Goodenough for his entire life. He seemed to care little for money, and signed away rights to many of his intellectual discoveries. He received no revenue from the corporate production of the lithium-ion battery that he played an essential role in creating. Yet without his inventions, Apple stock would be worthless.

Three years after winning his Nobel Prize, John Goodenough—the man who helped pioneer the long-lasting battery—died at the age of one hundred, in June of 2023. His *New York Times* obituary reports that he shared revenues from patents with his collaborators and often donated his prizes and award money to scholarships, or used them to fund additional research. In the wake of his Nobel, Goodenough was asked about the work that scientists do. "They want to understand nature so they can serve it," he said. "And they want to understand nature so they can, in conformity with nature, do something for their fellow man."

OLD-FASHIONED: Ann Roth

If you saw the movie *Barbie*, you probably remember when Margot Robbie sits down at a bus stop next to an older woman. Barbie is overcome by emotion and tells her, "You're so beautiful." To which the woman confidently replies, "I know it."

Studio executives lobbied director Greta Gerwig to cut this scene for time, but Gerwig pushed back. She would later call the moment a "transaction of grace," acknowledging it's a "little cul-de-sac that doesn't lead anywhere—except for, it's the heart of the movie." And the beautiful woman at the bus stop? A nonagenarian costume designer named Ann Roth.

Roth has been putting her stamp on Hollywood and Broadway for decades. She gave us Jon Voight's fringed suede jacket in *Midnight Cowboy* and the lingerie ensemble with pink handprints worn by Barbra Streisand in *The Owl and the Pussycat*. Roth also gets credit for Nicole Kidman's fake nose in *The Hours* and John Lithgow's breasts in *The World According to Garp*.

She got her start in costumes in the 1950s apprenticing with legendary designer Irene Sharaff. She worked on the movie musicals *Brigadoon*, *The King and I*, and *A Star Is Born*. Her first solo gig was on 1964's *The World of Henry Orient*, starring Peter Sellers. Since then, Roth has designed the costumes for over one hundred films and over one hundred Broadway shows and squeezed in some television productions as well. With her Oscar for 2021's *Ma Rainey's Black Bottom*, Roth, then eighty-nine, became history's oldest female Oscar winner.

Roth understands how clothes shape and reveal character. As one of her favorite collaborators, Meryl Streep, told the *New York Times*'s Maureen Dowd, "You don't come away from her work saying, 'Oh, weren't the costumes gorgeous?' You just remember the people she has clarified for you through what they chose to put on their bodies in the morning."

Roth is both exacting and empathetic. As she told my colleague Rita Braver, "I am very very kind and understanding with actors. When they take their clothes off in the fitting room, they are at the most vulnerable anybody could possibly be."

As for her own definition of a successful design, Ann Roth once said, "If you don't notice it, it's a success. It should go unnoticed." Ninety-three in 2023, Roth is rightfully getting noticed more than ever.

Misspent Old Age

This book celebrates late-in-life debuts, comebacks, and capstones. Now let's take a moment to acknowledge those luminaries who, at the eleventh hour, could taste victory—who really just had to do *nothing* to secure their place in history—but for some godforsaken reason decided to self-destruct.

Rudy Giuliani

Giuliani had controversies as mayor of New York City. But by most measures, he left the city in much better shape—certainly safer—than he found it. When *Time* magazine named him Person of the Year in 2001, it was for his leadership after the devastating terrorist attacks of 9/11. His legacy as "America's mayor" seemed cemented. Cut to 2020, when he was filmed lying on a bed, his hands down his pants, after a reporter (actually an actress in a Sacha Baron Cohen movie) invited him to her hotel room. Far worse were his efforts to overturn that year's presidential election. In 2023, a day after he was ordered to pay $148 million in damages for defamation of Georgia election workers, he filed for bankruptcy. The former prosecutor who once brought down the Mafia now faces calls for disbarment. Giuliani is a lifelong opera fan. Perhaps he should have modeled himself on the heroic Radamès from *Aida*, or the romantic Rodolfo from *La Bohème*, instead of the despicable Scarpia from *Tosca*, or the pathetic, miserable court jester Rigoletto. (Ask Alexa!)

Phil Spector

Every time I listen to Tina Turner sing 1966's "River Deep—Mountain High," I get chills. The epically talented Turner is backed by twenty-one musicians and an equal number of backup vocalists. It's the single greatest musical monument to producer Phil Spector's orchestral Wall of Sound. Spector was already a force by this point, dubbed by Tom Wolfe the First Tycoon of Teen, the producer of "Be My Baby," by the Ronettes, and "Unchained Melody," by the Righteous Brothers. When Spector was recording with Tina, he wisely paid the monstrously abusive Ike Turner to stay out of the session. But after the song failed to hit in the U.S., Spector went into a decades-long decline of erratic behavior, especially troubling in light of his massive handgun collection. "I'm my own worst enemy. I have devils inside that fight me," he told one interviewer in 2003, just weeks before he was arrested for murdering actress Lana Clarkson with a single gunshot. (Spector may have turned him away, but it turned out he had much more in common with Ike.) Convicted in 2009, Spector died in a prison hospital in 2021.

John Tyler I was kind of liking our tenth president. Over his two marriages, Virginian John Tyler fathered fifteen children. Now that's spunk! I actually interviewed his charming grandson Harrison Tyler in 2012. Yup, the former president, born in 1790, has a grandson still living in 2023. Tyler was the first vice president to succeed a president upon his death—in his case, ninth president William Henry Harrison. (He's the one who died a month into office in 1841, after delivering an hours-long inaugural address in bitterly cold weather without a hat.) By stepping into the role forcefully, Tyler averted what could have been a constitutional crisis, and set a crucial precedent. But then, sixteen years after leaving office, as the Civil War began, he sided with the people trying to destroy the country he had once led. He won election to the Confederate House of Representatives but died before taking his seat. His *New York Times* obit described him as "the most unpopular public man that had ever held any office in the United States." This is one guy who needed to quit earlier to spend more time with his family.

Ezra Pound The brash and talented Pound did as much as anyone to transform American poetry in the early twentieth century. After losing a teaching job at Wabash College, Indiana, for the infraction of having a young woman in his room, Pound sailed for Europe at age twenty-two. He eventually landed in London, where he set out to shake up the literary world. Scorning the dreamy lyrics of the Victorian era, he favored a poetry based on hard, radiant images, free of what he called "emotional slither." As an editor and impresario, he helped to launch the careers of T. S. Eliot, William Carlos Williams, James Joyce, Hilda Doolittle (H. D.), and Ernest Hemingway. But Pound's radicalism extended beyond literature, and his crackpot theories about economics led him to espouse anti-Semitic views and embrace Mussolini's fascism. By World War II he was living in Italy and broadcasting anti-American propaganda, which led to his arrest for treason. Declared mentally unfit to stand trial, he was committed to St. Elizabeths, a psychiatric hospital in Washington, DC, where he spent the next thirteen years. His reputation has never recovered.

OLD FOGEY: John Fogerty

In 1969, John Fogerty wrote the song "Bad Moon Rising," with the lyric "I see the bad moon a-risin' / I see trouble on the way." The words were prophetic.

Fogerty and his band Creedence Clearwater Revival had it very good during their brief life span, 1968–1972. CCR had seven albums and hit after hit penned by Fogerty: "Proud Mary," "Fortunate Son," and my personal favorite, "Have You Ever Seen The Rain." The band outsold even the Beatles in 1969. Many of the songs certainly seemed political, but Fogerty told *Rolling Stone*, "Our music has a specific aim: to make you want to jump up and dance. Later on, we may want people to reflect on our words. . . . But right now, we just want our music to make people feel."

The problems arose even while the band was flying high. At Woodstock in 1969, they went on after 1:00 a.m., when the crowd was dead. (In fact, he blamed the Grateful Dead for putting them to sleep.) Fogerty was so frustrated with the audience and his own band's sound that he vetoed their inclusion in the subsequent Woodstock movie and soundtrack. Many would forget that Creedence had even been there.

Creative differences and infighting between Fogerty, who was described as autocratic, and his fellow bandmates (which included his brother, Tom) eventually led to Creedence breaking up. Fogerty also fought a decades-long legal battle with a record label after signing away the publishing rights to his songs.

So the music stopped for a bit. But eventually, Fogerty returned. *Centerfield*, his 1985 album, went to No. 1. In 1987, he performed "Proud Mary"—a song that had become a much bigger hit for Ike and Tina Turner—for the first time in years. He's put out ten studio albums. But perhaps Fogerty's happiest moment was in 2023, when, after fifty-plus years, he got worldwide control of the publishing rights to his Creedence Clearwater Revival songs.

"A lot of rain has fallen on my raincoat," said Fogerty, who at seventy-nine is still touring. "And at some point there's a certain humility about anything going right."

An Old Story

Ebenezer Scrooge

Ebenezer Scrooge

became a better person before it was too late

Hopefully by this point in the book, we've convinced you that whatever your age, it's not too late to learn a new hobby, write a first book, or maybe even win a Nobel. But if you're aiming even higher and hoping to become a better human being, then look no further than Ebenezer Scrooge, the famous miser at the center of Charles Dickens's beloved holiday classic, *A Christmas Carol.* True, Scrooge is a fictional character, but that's not a problem. One of the wonderful things about fictional characters is that they can illustrate for us, in particularly memorable ways, aspects of the human experience that we might otherwise fail to appreciate. In fact, you could say the whole reason Scrooge exists is to help us understand this simple, straightforward point: that it's *never* too late to change. After all, the old Victorian skinflint didn't just take up ceramics or join an Aquacise class. No, after years of cold, bitter misanthropy, he reconsidered the entire meaning of life, finding spiritual redemption by opening his heart to help out the less fortunate. As a result, he has become a vivid example of the Christmas message that love is the most powerful force of all.

But *why* does Scrooge have this sudden and dramatic change of heart? What would cause an old man as set in his ways as an epitaph on a tombstone to rethink the entire course of his life? It's said that no one changes their ways unless they truly want to change, and when we read *A Christmas Carol*, we believe that Scrooge's change of heart is real. The question that bedevils Scrooge that fateful night before Christmas is a question that surely everyone asks if they live long enough: *How will the world remember me after I'm gone?*

A Christmas Carol is Dickens's spooky, sentimental, and thoroughly heartwarming 1843 novella about a mean-tempered old man who discovers, through his encounters with the Ghosts of Christmas Past, Present, and Future, that the holiday spirit really isn't such a humbug after all. If you haven't read the book, that's okay; you've almost certainly seen some kind of stage or screen adaptation, since there are dozens, maybe hundreds, out there. They range from a pretty cool-looking six-minute silent film shot in 1901 to modern versions featuring George C. Scott, Bill Murray, Jim Carrey, and the Muppets. In fact, during my visit to London's Charles Dickens Museum, the curator proclaimed 1992's *The Muppet Christmas Carol* her favorite adaptation. I don't disagree. Kermit the Frog gave an Oscar-worthy (pun intended) turn as Scrooge's hardworking, ill-used clerk Bob Cratchit. A flesh-and-blood Michael Caine did the honors as Scrooge. It works so well because Caine plays it so real. As director Brian (son of the late Jim) Henson told the *Guardian* years later about Caine's approach: "He said, 'I'm going to play it like I'm playing opposite the Royal Shakespeare Company. . . . I'm going to play it completely straight and completely committed, and that, I think, will make the right Scrooge.'"

The man who actually created Scrooge was born in 1812. Charles Dickens was Victorian England's most prominent and popular novelist. Having begun his career as a journalist and writer of humorous sketches, he went on to create some of the most memorable characters in all of English literature. He had a unique ability to cultivate, through pathos and humor, a special bond between his characters and his readers. Those readers were so devoted that in 1841 his American fans (at least according to legend) thronged the docks in New York City to await the arrival of the final installment of his multipart novel *The Old Curiosity Shop*, whose heroine, the beloved orphan Little Nell, was teetering on the brink of death. (I don't want to give anything away. Let's just say that there was no sequel about a twentysomething Nell opening up an adorbs boutique in Soho.) Books like *Oliver Twist*, *A Tale of Two Cities*, *David Copperfield*, and *Great Expectations* remain cultural touchstones that high school kids still pretend to read even today. But probably none of Dickens's novels or other stories has lodged itself in the popular imagination as deeply as *A Christmas Carol*.

The story is pretty straightforward. We are introduced to the miser Scrooge, whose name, biographer Michael Slater points out, squeezes together "screw" and "gouge." Ebenezer, meanwhile, rhymes with "geezer." (Scrooge's age is never mentioned in the book, but adaptations generally place him in his late fifties. I know, he usually looks like he's eighty, but that's what a nineteenth-century London winter will do to you. Hair conditioner wasn't invented for another fifty years.) Dickens introduces his hero with some lavish language:

> *Oh! But he was a tight-fisted hand at the grindstone, Scrooge! a squeezing, wrenching, grasping, scraping, clutching, covetous old sinner! Hard and sharp as flint, from which no steel had ever struck out generous fire; secret, and self-contained, and solitary as an oyster. The cold within him froze his old features, nipped his pointed nose, shrivelled his cheek, stiffened his gait; made his eyes red, his thin lips blue; and spoke out shrewdly in his grating voice. A frosty rime was on his head, and on his eyebrows, and his wiry chin.*

One Christmas Eve, readying for bed, this coldhearted "old sinner" is visited by the ghost of his dead partner, Jacob Marley, who announces imminent visits from three other spirits, the Ghosts of Christmas Past, Christmas Present, and Christmas Yet to Come.

Sidebar: In the Muppets version, Statler and Waldorf play Jacob and Robert Marley, the latter of whom does not appear in the book. But you can't have Statler without Waldorf. They're great in the roles, shackled in chains from a lifetime of avarice. In their big number they sing about evicting an entire orphanage, and it's funny. But then it's equally powerful when they warn in song, "As freedom comes from giving love, so prison comes with hate." The Muppets at their best.

Each of the three Ghosts, through the magic possible only in fiction, reveals to Scrooge scenes that move his heart.

First come poignant scenes from the past, including Scrooge's lonely childhood, which move the old man to take pity on his young, tender self; we also see the young man Scrooge being dumped by a beautiful fiancée who explains that *he* has stopped loving *her* because of his obsession with acquiring wealth. Next come scenes from the present, as Scrooge witnesses the joyous Christmas celebrations of others, including Scrooge's own underpaid clerk, Kermit—I mean Bob Cratchit—whose frail, disabled little son Tim famously declares at the dinner table, "God bless us every one!" Finally, Scrooge sees a vision of his own demise; he dies virtually alone, unloved and unmourned. The few servants who take note of his passing are, if anything, relieved.

But the morning after these dreamlike visitations, Scrooge wakes to discover that it is Christmas Day and he is still alive. This is essential: there *is* time to change his ways. He's overjoyed, unshackled from the metaphorical chains that had weighed him down for so long. "I am as light as a feather, I am as happy as an angel, I am as merry as a schoolboy," he cries. "I am as giddy as a drunken man. A merry Christmas to everybody! A happy New Year to all the world. Hallo here! Whoop! Hallo!" With a new lease on life, he sends an enormous turkey to the Cratchit family, gives a generous donation to the charity seekers he rejected the day before, and joins his nephew and his wife for dinner, games, and general conviviality. Back in the office the next morning, he gives Bob Cratchit a long overdue raise.

This simple narrative makes a perfect moral fable. The neat, symmetrical series of ghosts—Past, Present, Future—provides the sturdy architecture of a fairy tale, and each visit is called a "stave," or staff, as if it were the verse of a Christmas song. The narrator's tone is just playful enough to take the edge off any real terror that these ghosts or dream visions might induce. (*Really* playful, with the Muppets' Gonzo as the narrator.) With artful irony, all of Scrooge's cold and unfeeling gestures from the story's opening—mocking charity seekers, dismissing Christmas carolers, rejecting his own nephew's goodwill—come back to haunt him. And while Scrooge's overnight conversion to kindness and generosity may seem sudden, total realism is no more the point here than it is in *Snow White*. What matters is the affecting power of the scenes that he witnesses and the dramatic turnaround in his own emotional state.

There is a broader context here too. As Dickens's story makes clear, the

It's never too late: Reginald Owen as Ebenezer Scrooge in the 1938 motion picture *A Christmas Carol.*
Bettmann/Getty Images

Victorian era in England was a time of both burgeoning wealth and miserable poverty. The nineteenth century witnessed the explosion of modern industrial capitalism, which generated unimagined new inventions and luxuries, ranging from the automobile to the zipper. But the new economy also made exhausting demands on laborers—on coal miners, factory workers, even office clerks like the long-suffering Bob Cratchit. For these workers, Christmas, with its conviviality and good cheer, its homey comforts, represented a break from the merciless demands of economic survival.

And the poverty and suffering spawned by industrialism affected Dickens in a very personal way. He had experienced these ills himself in childhood. Although he was born into a middle-class family, his father, John Dickens, fell into debt. Two days before Charles's twelfth birthday, the boy was sent to work in what was called a blacking warehouse, a factory that bottled liquid shoe polish, where he applied labels to bottles for six shillings a week. John Dickens, meanwhile, was arrested for bankruptcy—yes, you could be arrested for bankruptcy in England in 1824—and sent to debtors' prison. The ensuing loneliness and shame, and the indignation of having suffered poverty, never left Charles. Roughly twenty years later, he had established himself as a writer, but as he looked around himself, he saw a society that was still failing to address the struggles of the poor. In 1843, the government issued a shocking report, detailing the brutal conditions of children laboring in coal mines and factories. Dickens was, in the words of his biographer Claire Tomalin, "fired with anger and horror at the indifference of the rich to the fate of the poor."

In October of that year he decided to take action. For the accomplished author, this meant writing what he described as "something that would come down with sledgehammer force"—a story that would move people's hearts by dramatizing the gulf between the haves and the have-nots.

Dickens claimed to have written *A Christmas Carol* in a kind of possession, composing in his head as he walked the streets of London at night, laughing and crying to himself. He wanted the book to be beautiful and commissioned a leading illustrator, John Leech, to draw highly expensive full-color illustrations. The gamble seemed to pay off, as the book was an instant success, selling six thousand copies in the first week. But because it was expensive to produce, and because theater owners could easily pirate the story for stage productions, Dickens saw little in the way of profits. Widely read and widely praised, it helped make Dickens's name forever associated with Christmas. In 1903 a critic named Frederick George Kitton dubbed Dickens "the man who invented Christmas."

To say that Dickens *invented* Christmas is definitely a stretch; the holiday had to be already meaningful if Dickens was writing stories about it. But Richard Jones, a forty-year veteran tour guide of Dickens's London, calls *A Christmas Carol* the second most famous Christmas story ever told. "It's about any one of us. No matter what, we can reform," he told me. "We can become better people. And I think that's its strength."

Dickens helped to make Christmas a celebration about family and caring for the poor. (He also helped popularize turkey as a Christmas mainstay. Before then it was seen as an exotic bird.) Of course, the holiday was also an occasion for religious observance, but for Victorian England its primary purpose became to gather with loved ones around a roaring fire, to amuse each other playing parlor games, and to partake of a great feast of the sort that we see the Cratchit family enjoying in *A Christmas Carol*. Dickens's son Harry later described their own family celebrations as "a great time, a really jovial time." He added, "My father was always at his best, a splendid host, bright and jolly as a boy and throwing his heart and soul into everything that was going on."

So what is it that actually moves Scrooge to change his ways? Notably, Dickens's story is *not* a traditional religious account of moral repentance. Scrooge is not shown visions of hellfire and damnation, and he does not worry about the eternal torment of his soul over a pit of sulfurous flame. The spirits that visit him are ghosts from pagan folklore, not figures from the Bible or Christian iconography. Instead of threatening Scrooge with damnation, Dickens offers an emotional appeal designed to address the masses of middle-class readers who bought his books every year. As biographer Tomalin writes, "From his own deep self he drew the understanding that a grown man may pity the child he had been, and learn from that pity, as Scrooge does."

In other words, Scrooge, after his encounters with the ghosts, is moved by compassion and love—for his younger self as well as for others—that has long lain dormant in his soul. He regrets that in his ruthless pursuit of gain, he has lost the woman he once loved. He worries for fragile Tiny Tim, and fears that the boy will not live to celebrate another Christmas. As he contemplates his remaining years, he fears that he will continue to miss out on the irreplaceable pleasures of enjoying Christmas festivities with loved ones.

But to my mind, what is the most haunting realization is his insight that when his own death comes, nobody will care. That will be his legacy, to be remembered as a man whose death was greeted with indifference or even gratitude by the world of the living. In his final vision, courtesy of Christmas Yet to Come, Scrooge initially witnesses some men discussing a recent death; he doesn't know yet that it's his own. "It's likely to be a very cheap funeral," says one of the men, "for upon my life I don't know of anybody to go to it." Another suggests with a laugh that he might be persuaded to attend by a good lunch.

Then Scrooge sees some servants, discussing the minor possessions they have stolen from the deceased. They're unafraid of being caught because the dead man had "frightened everyone away from him when he was alive." And, just to hammer home the point, one of the servants wonders, "Why wasn't he natural in his lifetime?" She is suggesting that there's something perverse and cruel about Scrooge's greed and selfishness. "If he had been, he'd have had somebody to look after him when he was struck with Death, instead of lying gasping out his last there, alone by himself." This is the most chilling vision of all for Scrooge, as he realizes that he is the dead man.

But of course the story doesn't end with this dark vision. Instead, the thought that he will die alone and unloved becomes the final spur to a real, heartfelt change. Scrooge does not want to be remembered as a selfish old miser; nor does he want to be forgotten entirely. Like all of us, he wants to matter in the world, and he comes to understand, belatedly but authentically, that he can only matter by making a difference in the lives of others.

Or, as Gonzo the narrator put it: "But the thing that made Scrooge happiest of all was that his life lay before him. And it could be changed."

AN APPRECIATION: Maria Luisa Rocca

Ask questions, get answers. There's no better way of getting to know who your parents are while you still have them. In the just the last year, I've learned the following about my mother:

- In 1875, there was a massive earthquake in the Colombian town of Cúcuta. Up to 10,000 people died. In the aftermath, a doctor rescued a young woman from the wreckage. The two would marry and become grandparents to my mother. Pretty dramatic stuff.

- In the fall of 1928, when my mother was just three months old, her father moved the whole family (three kids at that point) by boat from Colombia to New York. America was the promised land. His timing could not have been worse. A year later the stock market crashed. Three years after that—broke, and with two more mouths to feed—the family returned to Colombia. "We came up in a cabin next to the captain's," my grandmother supposedly said. "We returned in a room next to the boiler." My grandfather never recovered from the humiliation.

- My mother's grandmother (the one pulled from the rubble) taught her to read from an old-fashioned primer. "I learned really fast!" my mother tells me, with more than a hint of self-congratulation. It's well deserved. My mother never finished high school. She never got the validation that comes with graduation or a diploma.

- In the late 1950s, she got a job in the secretarial pool (she could type at lightning speed) at the Organization of American States in Washington, DC. She was eventually assigned to the statistics journal, where she did such a good job, they put her on the masthead: assistant to the editor.

- She was on her way to see the cherry blossoms, walking along 17th Street, when a mutual friend introduced her to a handsome young man. That man offered to teach her English. When she asked what he charged, he said, for her, nothing. She said no thanks. (She was and is very old-fashioned.) Lucky for me, the two would meet again and eventually marry.

Five things I didn't know before. I'm thinking of that old game show *Concentration*. Alex Trebek hosted a version of it for a few years starting in the late 1980s. On the show, the game board was covered by thirty numbered rectangles. Gradually the rectangles revealed a series of clues underneath. The object was to uncover enough of the puzzle to solve it.

That's how I've come to think of my mother and time. As the years go by (if you did the math above, you'd know she's now four years shy of a *very big birthday*), I'm uncovering more pieces of the puzzle. I don't know that I'll ever *solve* it—I'm not even sure what that would mean—but at least I'm seeing more of the picture.

When I was growing up, my mother was many things: the person who cut the crust off the sandwich for my bag lunch, just the way I liked it; who marveled over the board game I created about geography, with game pieces cut in the shapes of different countries; and who, one day after school, showed me how to plant the seeds of a grapefruit I was eating. (More than forty years later, that plant has grown into a tree that she still takes care of.)

But I didn't know much about my mother's past. I knew she came from a place very far away. Everything she described, I imagined in black-and-white, through a kind of mist or fog. (Maybe that's because she told me how cold and rainy Bogotá is most of the time.) There was one crazy story about her sister Julita mouthing off to some nuns at the convent school they were sent to. As punishment, Julita was put into solitary confinement, a white handkerchief tied over her mouth, in a room where drunks outside the window catcalled her all night. That one haunted me. "I thought the devil took her," my mother said. I must have had her tell me that story twenty times.

I knew my mother got her nickname Tini (that's what everyone calls her) because she was such a tiny baby. I knew she was one of seven children—her parents had two more after they returned to Colombia—and I gathered they didn't have much. I would ask about the house she grew up in, but she could never describe it. Now I know it's because they were constantly moving, often looking for cheaper places to live.

Growing up, I always felt that my mother needed to be protected, partly because English wasn't her native language, but maybe also because she was so protective about her own past. (I think, like Frank McCourt, she was embarrassed by the scarcity of her upbringing.) But as I got older it occurred to me that she didn't need special protection, that in fact she did something bolder than I've ever done.

As a young woman, she didn't see much of a future for herself in Colombia. And so in February 1956, with money she'd been saving since she was a teenager, she went to New York. She spoke no English and she had no real plan. (When it snowed on day three, she realized she didn't have the right shoes, either.) After a month, she made her way to Washington, DC, where a friend of hers was staying.

At first, she was homesick and called her mother back in Bogotá. Her mother told her to come home. But something made my mother stay. "I didn't want to be defeated," she says now, almost as if this hadn't occurred to her before. "I said at least I have to learn English."

And so she stayed. She got a job as a hatcheck girl at the Mayflower Hotel. Then she got that job at the OAS. And she learned English. When I ask her if she can appreciate her own boldness, she seems genuinely in awe of her younger self:

"Sometimes I think it's amazing. And in a way I was very timid, that's the funny thing. Because I was shy. Whenever they asked me to do something in school, I would start trembling. But here I got strong." In the United States, she says, she was less afraid. "I didn't have to care about anything. I didn't have any person to judge me."

That makes sense. She came from a rigidly class-conscious society. "They are very critical. You have no idea," she says with a laugh. "You have to be so proper. Otherwise, they will destroy you. In Bogotá I would be most of the time quiet. Most of the time I was just listening." That may explain why my mother is probably the best listener I know. She really does not miss a thing.

After my parents married, my mother helped my father build his business—one

Two fabulous women: Maria Luisa Rocca and Chita Rivera, December 2013.
Mo Rocca

329

successful enough to give their three children the formal education she was unable to get. (My father's business included an English language school for foreign students. My mother was the registrar. She loved interacting with the students who came from all over the world. I think she saw herself in them.)

In other words, she built a successful life for herself in the United States, something her father was unable to do.

Time with my mother is a gift, even without daily disclosures. I have great access to her, since she lives just upstairs in the same building. I like doing laundry with her (she insists on line-drying about half of her clothes), and it's fun introducing her to people in the neighborhood. Isaac Mizrahi complimented her eyewear. She's got impossibly chic tortoiseshell glasses from the 1950s. They're not a fashion statement; she just didn't want to throw away perfectly good frames. I took her to see the late, great Chita Rivera's nightclub act and afterward introduced them. That was special. She had seen Chita in the original production of *West Side Story*, in the pre-Broadway DC tryouts.

Another gift: that my mother allowed me to write about her at all. (You can damn well bet she had approval over this.) Until recently, she seemed to dismiss her own story. "Too long and complicated," she said at one point. She may still be very private, but she's come to recognize that her story *is* worth telling.

"It's amazing, no?" she mused again, during one of our chats. I'd say so.

Acknowledgments

Mo Rocca

For much of my career I've gravitated toward older interview subjects, largely because of what I can learn from them. (If the audience learns something, too, all the better.) Plus we like the same kind of music. So first and foremost I thank the people profiled in this book, living and dead, some of whom I was able to interview.

Getting back in the sandbox with Jon Greenberg, not long after our *Mobituaries* book, has been a joy. Anyone who can see how Henri Matisse and Clara Peller belong in the same book? That's my kind of collaborator. If every professor were as smart and sensitive, and had his sense of play, America's campuses would be a lot less grumpy.

I thank Jon Karp for his confidence and our conversations as this project took shape—and for his support in once again turning my name into a book title. Mindy Marques's unflagging enthusiasm and authentic wonder at the life stories contained here kept us going when we couldn't afford to slow down. Thanks also to the rest of the top-notch team at Simon & Schuster—Ruth Lee-Mui, Hana Park, Yvette Grant, copyeditor (or is it "copy editor"?) Janet Byrne, and Larry Hughes—and to photo editor Crary Pullen.

For decades now, Don Epstein and Peter Grant have protected and guided me through the business side of this business, allowing me to pursue my creative ambitions as freely and comfortably as possible. Rand Morrison at *CBS Sunday Morning* encouraged me and gave me the space to see this book through. A master of mix, his influence pervades these pages.

On the research side, Zoë Marcus's instincts for who might make a good Roctogenarian were invaluable. I hope she doesn't forget us as her career continues to soar. Likewise, Roger Raines and Michelle Kessel provided essential editorial support. Among those who generously shared their insights: Michael Blowen, Frank Bruni, General Wesley Clark, Scott Ehrlich, Steve Hartman, Kate Lear, Kay Lim, Rita Moreno, Theresa Pierno, and Sybil Sage.

For ten seasons I had the honor of hosting a show out of The Henry Ford Museum of American Innovation in Dearborn, Michigan. The series may have ended, but the staff there did not hesitate to answer my call for help on this project. They include Wendy Metros and curators Matt Anderson, Katherine White, Charles Sable, and Jeanine Miller.

Although their stories are not contained in these pages, I am grateful for all the grandparents across America I cooked with on *My Grandmother's Ravioli*. They (along with my two actual grandmothers) taught me how rich a third act can be.

Finally, my deepest thanks to Alberto Robaina. He pulled quadruple duty as editorial adviser, proofreader, fact-checker, and cheerleader. (I'm so grateful he doesn't charge by the hour.) Oh, and he made sure I ate. I look forward to our own eighties together.

Jonathan Greenberg

One of the many pleasures of writing this book was brainstorming with friends and family for names of potential Roctogenarians whom Mo and I might write about. Some of these suggestions made the final cut and others didn't, but the abundance of great ideas surely helped to make this a better book. Among those who suggested people or topics were Lee Behlman, Megan Blumenreich, Suzanne Farkas, Hank Greenberg, Tony Ianuale, John Lasiter, Dan Lawson, Harry Moskowitz, and

Acknowledgments

Scott Stevenson. (I know I've forgotten some people; forgive me!) After a spirited pickleball game one fall morning, Frank and Laurie Albanese batted around titles and subtitles with me and Megan.

Once the heavy work of writing began, Zoe Marcus, Hank Greenberg, and Alexis Grainger provided essential research assistance; Oscar Alcantara stood at the ready as my go-to source for all questions musical; Naomi Liebler read and commented on a thick packet of early drafts. Mo Rocca's creative talents speak for themselves, but his generosity as a friend and collaborator is a quality you can only appreciate by working on two books with him (as well as a musical comedy drag show thirty-seven years ago).

I am grateful for Jonathan Karp's vision, for Mindy Marques's scrupulous attention (as well as her oenological expertise), and for the efforts of everyone at Simon & Schuster who helped bring this project to fruition in record time . . . or at least a personal best for me. My agent, Andrew Stuart, again handled all the agency stuff with the cool mastery of Tom Brady running a two-minute drill.

Megan, Maggie, and Hank remain, collectively, my North Star; I never get lost when I have them in my sights. Finally, my father, Robert Greenberg, did not get to read this book but I know that his nine wonderful, extraordinary decades have, in one way or another, found their way into its pages.

Bibliography

Fast-Food Legends

Armstrong, Jack. "The Life of Peanut: Inside the Story of the World's Oldest Living Chicken." *Great Lakes Echo*, July 25, 2023. greatlakesecho.org/2023/07/25/the-life-of-peanut-inside-the-story-of-the-worlds-oldest-living-chicken/

"Clara Peller of Wendy's 'Where's the Beef?' Fame Meets NYC Mayor Ed Koch." Jan. 9, 2018. *PIX 11 News*. YouTube. www.youtube.com/watch?v=WXAD5Xwon9c

"Clara Peller of 'Where's the Beef?' Fame Messes Up Her Line: WrestleMania 2." *WWE.com*. Jan. 7, 2019. www.wwe.com/videos/clara-peller-of-where-s-the-beef-fame-messes-up-her-line-wrestle mania-2

"Clara Peller, the Actress in 'Where's the Beef?' TV Ad." *New York Times*. Aug. 12, 1987. www.nytimes.com/1987/08/12/obituaries/clara-peller-the-actress-in-where-s-the-beef-tv-ad.html

Dawson, Victoria. "How Colonel Sanders Made Kentucky Fried Chicken an American Success Story." *Smithsonian Magazine*. July 6, 2015. www.smithsonianmag.com/smithsonian-institution/how-colonel-sanders-made-kentucky-fried-chicken-american-success-story-180955806/

Evans Asbury, Edith. "Col. Harland Sanders, Founder of Kentucky Fried Chicken, Dies." *New York Times*. Dec. 17, 1989. www.nytimes.com/1980/12/17/archives/col-harland-sanders-founder-of-kentucky-fried-chicken-dies-cooked.html

Folkart, Burt A. "Clara Peller (Where's the Beef?) Dies at 86." *Los Angeles Times*. Aug. 12, 1987. https://www.latimes.com/archives/la-xpm-1987-08-12-mn-440-story.html

Harrington, Richard. "Clara Peller: A Stake in the Beef." *Washington Post*. Mar. 28, 1984. www.washingtonpost.com/archive/lifestyle/1984/03/28/clara-peller-a-stake-in-the-beef/d4d109d9-4572-45fc-a474-810366fa991e/

"Hey! Here's (Where's the Beef?) Clara." *Los Angeles Times*. Mar. 11, 1984. ProQuest.

"History." *Kentucky Colonels*. Oct. 15, 2021. www.kycolonels.org/history

Hunter, Marjorie. "A Kentucky Colonel Advises Aging to Work at Staying Young." *New York Times*. Nov. 4, 1971. www.nytimes.com/1971/11/04/archives/a-kentucky-colonel-advises-aging-to-work-at-staying-young.html

"Joe Sedelmaier: Art and Design in Chicago." *WTTW Chicago*. Nov. 2, 2018. interactive.wttw.com/art-design-chicago/joe-sedelmaier

Konheim, Orrin. "One-Man Brand." *American History Magazine*. Oct. 19, 2021.

Kuczka, Susan. "Clara Peller of 'Where's the Beef?' Fame Dies." UPI. Aug. 12, 1987. www.upi.com/archives/1987/08/12/Clara-Peller-of-Wheres-the-beef-fame-dies/9995555739200

Lawrence, Jodi. "Chicken Big and the Citizen Senior." *Washington Post*. Nov. 9, 1969. ProQuest.

Bibliography

Maier, Frank. "Clara Peller Has No Beef with Success." *Atlanta Journal-Constitution*. Mar. 29, 1984. *Newspapers.com*. www.newspapers.com/article/the-atlanta-constitution/37010732/

Nemetz, Dave. "The Inside Story of Wendy's 'Where's the Beef?' Ad." *Tumblr*. Feb. 1, 2017. davenemetz.tumblr.com/post/156670534234/the-inside-story-of-wendys-wheres-the-beef-ad

"NBC Interview with Clara Peller." Mar. 31, 2011. NBC. YouTube. www.youtube.com/watch?v=NKZ2rr4XMTA

OVP—Retro Wrestling Podcast [@ovppodcast]. "Clara Peller: Great Wrestlemania Celebrity, or GREATEST Wrestlemania celebrity?" *Twitter*. Jan. 9, 2021. https://twitter.com/ovppodcast/status/1347912307528097796

Ozerky, Josh. "KFC's Colonel Sanders: He Was Real, Not Just an Icon." *Time*. Sept. 15, 2010. archive.ph/20120913184609/http://www.time.com/time/printout/0,8816,2019218,00.html#selection-127.356-127.593

Pearce, John Ed. *The Colonel: The Captivating Biography of the Dynamic Founder of a Fast-Food Empire*. Doubleday, 1982.

"Prego Plus Commercial (Clara Peller), 1985." *Hugo Faces*. Apr. 20, 2017. YouTube. www.youtube.com/watch?v=3kZejc2-h_s

Price, Mark. "World's Oldest Living Chicken Dies in Michigan." *Charlotte Observer*. Dec. 30, 2023. www.charlotteobserver.com/news/nation-world/national/article283646398.html

"Prime Ribbing." *Time*. Mar. 26, 1984. content.time.com/time/subscriber/article/0,33009,921646-1,00.html

Sanders, Harland. *Life as I Have Known It Has Been Finger Lickin' Good*. Creation House, 1974.

Sheraton, Mimi. "For the Colonel, It Was Finger-Lickin' Bad." *New York Times*, Sept. 9, 1976. www.nytimes.com/1976/09/09/archives/for-the-colonel-it-was-fingerlickin-bad.html

Shister, Gail. "Where's the Beef Takes Her to the Big Time." *Philadelphia Inquirer*. Mar. 10, 1984. ProQuest.

Smith, J. Y. "Col. Sanders, the Fried-Chicken Gentleman, Dies." *Washington Post*. Dec. 17, 1980. www.washingtonpost.com/archive/local/1980/12/17/col-sanders-the-fried-chicken-gentleman-dies/64925eb3-3a20-4851-afbc-ba4fe16e9770/

"The Vault: A Brief History of Colonel Sanders." Dec. 19, 2021. WHAS11. YouTube. www.youtube.com/watch?v=W-UkcM9Eo9g

Vrabel, Brendan, and Emily Van de Riet. "Peanut, the World's Oldest Chicken, Dies at Age 21." WBTV.com. Dec. 29, 2023. www.wbtv.com/2023/12/29/peanut-worlds-oldest-chicken-dies-age-21/

Whitworth, William. "Kentucky-Fried." *The New Yorker*. Feb. 14, 1970. https://www.newyorker.com/magazine/1970/02/14/kentucky-fried

Yoshihara, Nancy. "Hamburger Job Lost After Spaghetti Sauce Commercial: Wendy's Has a Beef with Clara." *Los Angeles Times*. Mar. 23, 1985. www.latimes.com/archives/la-xpm-1985-03-23-fi-21253-story.html

Old Money

Clifford, Catherine. "Warren Buffett Bought $114.75 in Stock at Age 11." CNBC. Feb. 25, 2019. www.cnbc.com/2019/02/25/warren-buffett-bought-114point75-in-stock-at-11what-itd-be-worth-now.html

Bibliography

Guzman, Zack, and Mary Stevens. "Here's How Warren Buffett Hustled to Make $53,00 as a Teenager." CNBC. Jan. 31, 2017. www.cnbc.com/2017/01/31/heres-how-warren-buffett-hustled-to-make -53000-as-a-teenager.html

Housel, Morgan. *The Psychology of Money: Timeless Lessons on Wealth Greed and Happiness*. Harriman House, 2021.

LaFranco, Rob, and Chase Peterson-Withorn, eds. "World's Billionaires List: The Richest in 2023." *Forbes*. www.forbes.com/billionaires/

Morris, Chris. "Legendary Investor Warren Buffett Is Turning 93." *Fortune*. Aug. 30, 2023. fortune .com/2023/08/30/how-old-warren-buffett-birthday-billionaire-berkshire-hathaway-ceo/

Zweig, Jason. "Warren Buffett and the $300,000 Haircut." *Wall Street Journal*. Aug. 28, 2020. www.wsj .com/articles/warren-buffett-and-the-300-000-haircut-11598626805

LIke Fine Wine

"1973 Chateau Montelena Chardonnay Crafted by Miljenko 'Mike' Grgich Named to Smithsonian's '101 Objects That Made America.'" PR Newswire. Apr. 9, 2014. www.prnewswire.com/news -releases/1973-chateau-montelena-chardonnay-crafted-by-miljenko-mike-grgich-named-to -smithsonians-101-objects-that-made-america-254527321.html

Asimov, Eric. "Mike Grgich Dies at 100; His Wine Stunned the French by Besting Theirs." *New York Times*. Dec. 15, 2023. www.nytimes.com/2023/12/15/dining/drinks/mike-grgich-dead.html

Boutte, Coy. "About Our Barrels." Tabasco.com. Aug. 29, 2019. www.tabasco.com/blog/about-our -barrels

Ciprietti, Elena. "Foods of Italy: A Tale of Culinary Heritage and Top-Notch Quality." *Walks of Italy*. July 6, 2023. www.walksofitaly.com/blog/food-and-wine/dop-foods-from-italy

Davis, Tim. "Bitto Storico: The Oldest Edible Cheese in the World." *Luxe Adventure Traveler*. Feb. 3, 2023. luxeadventuretraveler.com/bitto-storico-cheese/

Gane, Tamara. "Does Honey Expire? The Answer Might Surprise You." *Southern Living*. Jan. 31, 2023. www.southernliving.com/food/sweeteners/honey/does-honey-expire

Geiling, Natasha. "The Science Behind Honey's Eternal Shelf Life." *Smithsonian Magazine*. Aug. 22, 2013. www.smithsonianmag.com/science-nature/the-science-behind-honeys-eternal-shelf-life -1218690

Grace, Roger M. "Was Col. Maunsel White the True Originator of Tabasco Sauce?" *Metropolitan News-Enterprise*. July 15, 2004. www.metnews.com/articles/2004/reminiscing071504.htm

Gray, W. Blake. "The Vintner Who Did It His Way: Mike Grgich's Storied Journey from Yugoslavian Bookkeeper to Napa Valley Legend." *San Francisco Chronicle*. May 11, 2007. www.sfgate.com /wine/article/The-vintner-who-did-it-his-way-Mike-Grgich-s-2574567.php

Grgich Hills Estate. "Honoring a Legend: In Memoriam, Miljenko Grgich." Grgich.com. www.grgich .com/miljenko-grgich-in-memoriam/

Krebiehl, Anne. "What Really Happens as Wine Ages?" *Wine Enthusiast*. May 4, 2023. www.wine enthusiast.com/culture/wine/what-happens-wine-ages/

Lieu, Lynn. "Wine Legend Miljenko Grgich Retells Past." *The Desert Sun*. June 4, 2014. www.desert sun.com/story/life/food/2014/06/03/miljenko-grgich-wine-country-napa-valley/9938777/

Bibliography

Matulich, Nada Pritisanac. "100th Birthday of Legendary Croatian-American Winemaker Miljenko 'Mike' Grgich." *Croatia Week.* Mar. 29, 2023. www.croatiaweek.com/100th-birthday-of-legendary -croatian-american-winemaker-miljenko-mike-grgich/

"May-24-1976: Judgment of Paris." *Today Past.* May 24, 2020. todaypast.wordpress.com/2016/05/24 /may-24-1976-judgment-of-paris/

Montagne, Renee. "Tabasco's Hot History." NPR. Nov. 29, 2002. www.npr.org/2002/11/29/861201 /tabascos-hot-history

"Napa Wineries: Grgich Hills Estate: Our Story." Grgich Hills Estate. Apr. 28, 2023. www.grgich.com /our-story

"The Origin of Zinfandel and Primitivo." *Vivino.* Oct. 20, 2020. www.vivino.com/wine-news/the -origin-of-zinfandel-and-primitivo

"Orson Welles for Paul Masson Wine (1978)." Mar. 15, 2017. YouTube. www.youtube.com/watch ?v=5C6EwLTAvHc

"The Paris Tasting." Grgich Hills Estate. Jan. 24, 2023. www.grgich.com/the-paris-tasting/

Peterson, Thane. "The Day California Wines Came of Age." *Business Week Online.* May 8, 2001.

Riddle, Sharla. "The Chemistry of Honey." *Bee Culture.* July 25, 2016. www.beeculture.com/the -chemistry-of-honey/

Smith, Rod. "Solved: The Great Zinfandel Mystery." *Los Angeles Times.* July 10, 2002. www.latimes .com/archives/la-xpm-2002-jul-10-fo-wine10-story.html

Stanz, Carissa. "The Untold Truth of Tabasco." *Mashed.* Jan. 31, 2023. www.mashed.com/106443 /untold-truth-tabasco/

"The Story of Mike Grgich." Oct. 10, 2011. YouTube. www.youtube.com/watch?v=E41NYBXobw8

Sullivan, Michael. "Soup's On! And On! Thai Beef Noodle Brew Has Been Simmering for 45 Years." NPR. Nov. 3, 2019. www.npr.org/sections/thesalt/2019/11/03/772030934/soups-on-and-on-thai -beef-noodle- brew-has-been-simmering-for-45-years

Taber, George M. *Judgment of Paris: California vs. France and the Historic 1976 Paris Tasting That Revolutionized Wine.* Scribner, 2005.

Old Country

Flippo, Chet. "Matthew, Mark, Luke, and Willie." *Texas Monthly.* Sept. 1975. www.texasmonthly.com /articles/matthew-mark-luke-and-willie/

Hann, Michael. "Willie Nelson: 'I've Bought a Lot of Pot, and Now I'm Selling Some Back.'" *The Guardian.* May 17, 2012. www.theguardian.com/music/2012/may/17/30-minutes-with-willie -nelson

Light, Alan. "Why Willie Nelson Is America's Favorite Outlaw." *Wall Street Journal.* June 2, 2021. www .wsj.com/articles/willie-nelson-interview-profile-11622635975

Rosen, Jody. "Willie Nelson's Long Encore." *New York Times Magazine.* Aug. 21, 2022. www.nytimes .com/2022/08/17/magazine/willie-nelson.html

Bibliography

The Players

Anderson, Tre'vell. "Q&A: 'You've Got to Make Hay While the Sun Is Shining,' the Ever-Active Morgan Freeman Says." *Los Angeles Times*. Mar. 31, 2017. www.latimes.com/entertainment/movies /la-et-mn-morgan-freeman-going-in-style-20170330-story.html

Bernstein, Adam. "Estelle Getty, 84; 'Golden Girl' Actress Won an Emmy Award." *Washington Post*. July 23, 2008. archive.ph/20131013122134/articles.washingtonpost.com/2008-07-23/news /36768221_1_barry-gettleman-arthur-gettleman-comedy-series#selection-3367.0-3367.58

Deeyn, June. "17 Unbelievable Facts about Estelle Getty." *Facts.net*. Oct. 10, 2023. facts.net /celebrity/17-unbelievable-facts-about-estelle-getty/

Dudar, Helen. "For Morgan Freeman, Stardom Wasn't Sudden." *New York Times*. Dec. 10, 1989. www .nytimes.com/1989/12/10/arts/film-for-morgan-freeman-stardom-wasnt-sudden.html

"Estelle Getty." *The Telegraph*. July 24, 2008. www.telegraph.co.uk/news/obituaries/2450286/Estelle -Getty.html

"Estelle Getty 2000 Intimate Portrait." Sept. 9, 2015. YouTube. www.youtube.com/watch?v=CT 7vq2ZnF0I

"Estelle Getty and Cybill Shepherd Wins Best Golden Globes 1986." Jan. 21, 2012. YouTube. www .youtube.com/watch?v=cxqP62SbYiQ

"Estelle Getty at the Emmy Awards 1988." Jan. 21, 2012. YouTube. www.youtube.com/watch ?v=CLQfpbvLwu8

"Estelle Getty Interview—ROD Show Season 1, Episode 48, 1996." June 23, 2021. YouTube. www .youtube.com/watch?v=_vCZs3cbH1A

"Estelle Getty Interview 2—ROD Show Season 1, Episode 155, 1997." Dec. 27, 2021. YouTube. www .youtube.com/watch?v=oa7z5fu_n1E

"Estelle Getty on Joan Rivers' Show in 1986." Jan, 26, 2012. YouTube. www.youtube.com/watch ?v=ow4hIvkEv9M

Fink, Jenny. "A Career Defined by Kids: Stars of Children's Show Finds Time to Perform," *Las Vegas Sun*. Sept. 30, 2008. lasvegassun.com/news/2008/sep/30/career-dened-kids/

Finkle, David. "Q-Ratings: The Popularity Contest of the Stars." *New York Times*. June 7, 1992. www .nytimes.com/1992/06/07/arts/television-q-ratings-the-popularity-contest-of-the-stars.html

Gaber, C. L. "*Shawshank Redemption* Line Still Inspires Morgan Freeman." *Las Vegas Review- Journal*. Sept. 28, 2023. www.reviewjournal.com/livewell/shawshank-redemption-line-still-in spires-morgan-freeman-2912436/amp/

Getty, Estelle, and Steve Delsohn. *If I Knew Then What I Know Now . . . So What?*, Contemporary Books, 1988.

"'Golden Girls' Good Morning America—1987 Betty White, Estelle Getty, Bea Arthur, Rue McClana-han." Jan. 23. 2021. YouTube. www.youtube.com/watch?v=Tl957ccDwgc

Harrington, Richard. "Morgan Freeman Meets His Match." *Washington Post*. Mar. 3, 1989. www .washingtonpost.com/archive/lifestyle/1989/03/03/morgan-freeman-meets-his-match/36993ac7 -bf73-4d9f-99ab-1c6dec929558/

"How Morgan Freeman Developed His Voice. Late Night with Conan O'Brien." Oct. 17, 2007. NBC. www.youtube.com/watch?v=RIiNuLgUInk

Bibliography

Hueso, Noela. "A Look Back with Morgan Freeman." *Hollywood Reporter.* June 8, 2011. www.holly woodreporter.com/movies/movie-news/a-look-back-morgan-freeman-195215/

Kael, Pauline. "Manypeeplia Upsidownia." *The New Yorker.* Apr. 12, 1987. www.newyorker.com /magazine/1987/04/20/manypeeplia-upsidownia

Keck, William. "Rita Moreno Recalls Her Electric Company Years with Morgan Freeman." *TV Guide Magazine.* June 16, 2011. www.tvguide.com/news/kecks-exclusives-rita-moreno-1034283 /#google_vignette

Kennedy, Mark. "Morgan Freeman's Had It with Mr. Gravitas," *Seattle Times.* May 11, 2008. www .seattletimes.com/entertainment/morgan-freemans-had-it-with-mr-gravitas/

Luther, Claudia. "Estelle Getty, 84; 'Golden Girls' Actress Brought Humor, Depth to Mother Roles." *Los Angeles Times.* July 23, 2008. www.latimes.com/entertainment/la-me-getty23-2008jul23-story.html

"Meet the Golden Girls: Sophia (1992) Estelle Getty Interview." Mar. 3, 2012. YouTube. www.youtube .com/watch?v=bGouqSr0eBE

Moreno, Rita. Interview with Mo Rocca. Jan. 22, 2024. "Morgan Freeman—Receives Lifetime Achievement SAG Awards (2018)." Jan. 21, 2018. YouTube. www.youtube.com/watch?v=_QufBstcsrc

"Morgan Freeman Reveals the Secret of His Amazing Voice." Oct. 7, 2011. YouTube. www.youtube .com/watch?v=aFxKt1sexVc

Miller, Stephen. "Estelle Getty, 84, 'Golden Girl' Had Avant-Garde Career." *New York Sun.* July 22, 2008. www.nysun.com/article/obituaries-estelle-getty-84-golden-girl-had-avant-garde

Nicholson, Amy. "SAG Life Achievement Honoree Morgan Freeman Proves Life Can Begin at 50." *Variety.* Jan. 18, 2018. variety.com/2018/film/awards/sag-honoree-morgan-freeman-1202665616/

Oaklander, Mandy. "Science Explains Why You Love Morgan Freeman's Voice." *Time.* Feb. 23, 2016. time.com/4233926/morgan-freeman-voice-waze-science/

Rocca, Mo. "Rita Moreno: Still Sizzling." *CBS Sunday Morning.* Aug. 18, 2013. www.cbsnews.com /news/rita-moreno-still-sizzling/

Schulman, Michael. "Rita Moreno Has Time Only for the Truth." *The New Yorker.* June 17, 2021. www .newyorker.com/culture/the-new-yorker-interview/rita-moreno-has-time-only-for-the-truth

Silverman, Stephen M. " 'Golden Girls' Star Estelle Getty Dies at 84." *People.* Dec. 1, 2020. people.com /celebrity/golden-girls-star-estelle-getty-dies-at-84/

Syken, Bill. "Remembering the Historic All-Black 'Hello, Dolly!' from 1967." *Life.* Jan. 18, 2023. www .life.com/arts-entertainment/remembering-the-historic-all-black-hello-dolly-from-1967/

Toomey, Alyssa. "Rita Moreno Drops F-Bomb, Cozies Up to Morgan Freeman While Accepting Lifetime Achievement Honor at SAG Awards." *E! Online.* Jan. 19, 2014. www.eonline.com /news/501230/rita-moreno-drops-f-bomb-cozies-up-to-morgan-freeman-while-accepting-life time-achievement-honor-at-sag-awards

Trescott, Jacqueline. "Actor Morgan Freeman Can Take His Pick of Roles. And He Has." *Washington Post.* Dec. 10, 1997. www.washingtonpost.com/archive/lifestyle/1997/12/10/actor-morgan -freeman-can-take-his-pick-of-roles-and-he-has/d3a7eda2-3701-408c-aca5-94770bcf8bfc/

Weber, Bruce. "Estelle Getty, 'Golden Girls' Matriarch, Dies at 84." *New York Times.* July 23, 2008. www.nytimes.com/2008/07/23/arts/television/23getty.html

Bibliography

"Why Morgan Freeman Was 'Terrified' to Work on the Kids Show 'The Electric Company.'" *Rich Eisen Show*. Dec. 6, 2017. YouTube. www.youtube.com/watch?v=CzPyHU4jMpY

Old Spice

Abrams, Simon. "Sophia Loren Makes Her Return to Film: 'I'm a Perfectionist.'" *New York Times*. Nov. 13, 2020. www.nytimes.com/2020/11/13/movies/sophia-loren-the-life-ahead-netflix.html

"Awards Watch: Cinematographers Roundtable." *Hollywood Reporter*. Nov. 18, 2009. www.hollywoodreporter.com/business/business-news/awards-watch-cinematographers-roundtable-91521/

Clarke, Henry. "People Are Talking About . . . Sophia Loren." *Vogue*. Sept. 15, 1958. ProQuest. www.proquest.com/docview/911891574/citation/7949239A64C14193PQ/3?

Fremont-Smith, Eliot. "*Lady L*, a Disturbing Film." *New York Times*. May 19, 1966. www.nytimes.com/1966/05/19/archives/screen-lady-l-a-disturbing-filmsophia-loren-vehicle-shown-in-2.html

Hornady, Ann. "Netflix's *The Life Ahead* Proves that Sophia Loren's Still Got It." *Washington Post*. Nov. 10, 2020. www.washingtonpost.com/goingoutguide/movies/the-life-ahead-movie-review/2020/11/10/882ded6c-212d-11eb-b532-05c751cd5dc2_story.html

Meares, Hadley Hall. "Bellissima: Sophia Loren's Love-Filled Life." *Vanity Fair*. Aug. 31, 2022. www.vanityfair.com/hollywood/2022/08/sophia-loren-memoir-cary-grant

"Movies Abroad: Much Woman." *Time*. Apr. 6, 1962. content.time.com/time/subscriber/article/0,33009,896055,00.html

Playing for Herself

H. T. "8-Year-Old Pianist Is Hailed at Debut." *New York Times*. Nov. 14, 1933. timesmachine.nytimes.com/timesmachine/1933/11/14/90652985.pdf

Rocca, Mo. "Pianist Ruth Slencyznska on Her Life in Music." *CBS Sunday Morning*. Apr. 3, 2022. YouTube. www.youtube.com/watch?v=Z1CKfnmkvks&t=61s

Old Chestnut

Bernstein, Jonathan. "Inside the Life of Brenda Lee, the Pop Heroine Next Door." *Rolling Stone*. Feb. 20, 2018. www.rollingstone.com/music/music-features/inside-the-life-of-brenda-lee-the-pop-heroine-next-door-205175/

Carrollton, Betty. "Brenda Lee Is an Incurable Prankster." *Atlanta Journal-Constitution*. Oct. 5, 1958. ProQuest.

Lee, Brenda, with Robert Oermann and Julie Clay. *Little Miss Dynamite: The Life and Times of Brenda Lee*. Hyperion, 2002.

Thanki, Juli. "Rockin' for 57 Years." *The Tennessean*. Dec. 14, 2015. ProQuest.

Trust, Gary. "New Old-Fashioned No. 1: Brenda Lee's 'Rockin' Around the Christmas Tree' Tops Hot 100, 65 Years After Its Release." *Billboard*. Dec. 4, 2023. www.billboard.com/lists/brenda-lee-rockin-around-the-christmas-tree-number-one-hot-100/longest-span-of-no-1s-2/

Bibliography

The Writers

Barry, Dan. "McCourt Tells Students the Storytelling Power of a Life." *New York Times*. www.nytimes
  .com/1997/04/10/nyregion/mccourt-tells-students-the-storytelling-power-of-a-life.html

Beswick-Jones, Hana, et al. "Peter Mark Roget." *The Physiological Society*, School of Life Sciences,
  University of Nottingham. Dec. 14, 2022. www.physoc.org/magazine-articles/peter-mark-roget/

Blades, John. "McCourt's Memoir Awash in Tales of Ireland, Booze." *Chicago Tribune*. Oct. 22, 1996.
  www.chicagotribune.com/news/ct-xpm-1996-10-22-9610220081-story.html

Carbery, Genevieve. "UL Chair Named in Honour of McCourt." *Irish Times*. Mar. 11, 2011. www
  .irishtimes.com/news/ul-chair-named-in-honour-of-mccourt-1.568739

Chaffee, Keith. "A Week to Remember: Laura Ingalls Wilder." Los Angeles Public Library. Feb. 6, 2018.
  www.lapl.org/collections-resources/blogs/lapl/week-remember-laura-ingalls-wilder

Clifford, Naomi. "The Premature Death of Samuel Romilly." *Naomi Clifford*. Aug. 2, 2015. www
  .naomiclifford.com/the-premature-and-lamented-death-of-sir-samuel-romilly/

Donoghue, Steve. "The Selected Letters of Laura Ingalls Wilder Shows a Devotion to Readers." *Christian Science Monitor*. Mar. 30, 2016. www.csmonitor.com/Books/Book-Reviews/2016/0330/The
  -Selected-Letters-of-Laura-Ingalls-Wilder-shows-a-devotion-to-readers

Eaton, Anne T. "Books for Children: The Eagle's Gift. Alaska Eskimo Tales." *New York Times*. Apr. 24,
  1932. www.nytimes.com/1932/04/24/archives/books-for-children-the-eagles-gift-alaska-eskimo
  -tales-by-knud.html

Fatzinger, Amy S. "Learning from Laura Ingalls Wilder." *The Atlantic*. Sept. 10, 2018. www.theatlantic
  .com/entertainment/archive/2018/09/laura-ingalls-wilders-little-house/569629/

Fields, Liz. "Eight Interesting Facts about Laura Ingalls Wilder." PBS. Jan. 7, 2021. www.pbs.org/wnet
  /americanmasters/8-interesting-facts-about-laura-ingalls-wilder/16581/

Fraser, Caroline. *Prairie Fires: The American Dreams of Laura Ingalls Wilder*. Metropolitan Books, 2017.

Goddu, Krystyna Poray. "The 'Pioneer Girl' Project: The Long Road to Bringing Laura Ingalls Wilder's
  1930 Autobiography into Print." *Publishers Weekly*. Aug. 21, 2014. https://www.publishersweekly
  .com/pw/by-topic/childrens/childrens-book-news/article/63738-the-pioneer-girl-project-the
  -long-road-to-bringing-laura-ingalls-wilder-s-1930-autobiography-into-print.html

Grimes, William. "Frank McCourt, Whose Irish Childhood Illuminated His Prose, Is Dead at 78."
  New York Times. July 19, 2009. www.nytimes.com/2009/07/20/books/20mccourt.html

Italie, Hillel. "Author Frank McCourt's Brilliant 'Second Act' Comes to a Close." *Seattle Times*. July 20,
  2009. www.seattletimes.com/entertainment/books/author-frank-mccourts-brilliant-second-act
  -comes-to-a-close/

Kendall, Joshua C. *The Man Who Made Lists: Love, Death, Madness, and the Creation of Roget's Thesaurus*. Berkley Books, 2008.

Kendall, Joshua. "The Remarkable Roget's Thesaurus." *Merriam-Webster*. www.merriam-webster
  .com/wordplay/rogets-thesaurus

Krug, Nora. "Laura Ingalls Wilder Finds New Stardom in an Old-Fashioned Way." *Washington Post*.
  Apr. 22, 2015. www.washingtonpost.com/entertainment/books/laura-ingalls-wilder-finds-new-star
  dom-in-an-old-fashioned-way/2015/04/22/78776db2-e75e-11e4-9767-6276fc9b0ada_story.html

"Laura I. Wilder, Author, Dies at 90; Writer of the 'Little House' Series for Children Was an

Bibliography

Ex-Newspaper Editor Wrote First Book at 65." *New York Times*. Feb. 12, 1957. www.nytimes
.com/1957/02/12/archives/laura-i-wilder-author-dies-at-90-writer-of-the-little-house-series.html

Liebenthal, Ryann. "Our Lady of the Plains." *New Republic*. Mar. 2, 2016. newrepublic.com/article
/129021/laura-ingalls-wilder

Lifson, Amy. "Reading Laura Ingalls Wilder Is Not the Same When You're a Parent." National Endow-
ment for the Humanities. 2014. www.neh.gov/humanities/2014/julyaugust/feature/reading-laura
-ingalls-wilder-not-the-same-when-youre-parent

Limerick, Patricia Nelson. "*Little House on the Prairie* and the Truth About the American West."
New York Times. Nov. 20, 2017. www.nytimes.com/2017/11/20/books/review/prairie-fires-laura
-ingalls-wilder-biography-caroline-fraser.html

Mallon, Thomas. "Obsessed (Agog, Beset, Consumed, Driven, Etc.)." *New York Times*. Mar. 16, 2008.
www.nytimes.com/2008/03/16/books/review/Mallon-t.html

"The Master Muses on the Making of a Memoir." *Hartford Courant*. Apr. 6, 2003. www.courant
.com/2003/04/06/the-master-muses-on-the-making-of-a-memoir/

McCourt, Frank. "81st Commencement Address." Digital Commons @ Connecticut College. May
1999. digitalcommons.conncoll.edu/commence/5

McCourt, Frank. *Angela's Ashes: A Memoir*. Scribner, 2003.

McCourt, Frank. "How I Wrote Angela's Ashes." *Slate*. Mar. 27, 2007. slate.com/news-and-politics
/2007/03/how-i-wrote-angela-sashes.html

McCourt, Frank. *Teacher Man*. Scribner, 2005.

McCourt, Frank. *'Tis: A Memoir*. Scribner, 1999.

McCourt's Ashes Still Divides Limerick." CBC News. CBC/Radio Canada. July 20, 2009. www.cbc.ca
/news/entertainment/mccourt-s-ashes-still-divides-limerick-1.802201

McGrath, Charles. "The Keeper (See: Steward, Caretaker) of Synonyms." *New York Times*. Apr. 18,
2008. www.nytimes.com/2008/04/18/books/18book.html

McLellan, Dennis. "Frank McCourt Dies at 78; Late-Blooming Author of *Angela's Ashes*.'" *Los Angeles
Times*. July 20, 2009. www.latimes.com/local/obituaries/la-me-frank-mccourt20-2009jul20-story
.html

Mitgang, Herbert. "Thesaurus at 200 Still Looks for (Seeks) Words." *New York Times*. Jan. 18, 1979.
www.nytimes.com/1979/01/18/archives/thesaurus-at-200-still-looks-for-seeks-words-first-us
-edition-in.html

"Obituary: Dr. Roget." *Medical Times and Gazette*, Volume 2. London: John Churchill and Sons,
p. 395. Sept. 25, 1869. Google Books.

Rutten, Tim. "Frank McCourt's Career Rose from Ashes." *Los Angeles Times*. July 20, 2009. www
.latimes.com/entertainment/la-et-mccourt-appreciation20-2009jul20-story.html

Sheridan, Anne. "Scatter My Ashes on the Shannon When I Go, Says Frank McCourt." *www.limerick
city.ie*. Nov. 17, 2007. https://www.limerickcity.ie/media/mccourt,%20frank%20095.pdf

"The Master Muses on the Making of a Memoir." *Hartford Courant*. Apr. 6, 2003. www.courant
.com/2003/04/06/the-master-muses-on-the-making-of-a-memoir/

Thurman, Judith. "*Little House on the Prairie*'s Wilder Women." NPR. Aug. 18, 2009. www.npr
.org/2009/08/18/111992555/little-house-on-the-prairies-wilder-women

Bibliography

———. "The *Little House* Memoir." *The New Yorker*. Feb. 18, 2015. www.newyorker.com/culture /cultural-comment/pioneer-girl-memoir-little-house-prairie

———. "The Women Behind the *Little House* Stories." *The New Yorker*. Aug. 3, 2009. www.newyorker .com/magazine/2009/08/10/wilder-women

Walls, Jeannette. "Introduction." *Angela's Ashes*. Scribner, 1999.

Wilder, Laura Ingalls. "Speech to the Detroit Book Fair." 1937. Detroit, Michigan.

———. *Pioneer Girl: The Annotated Autobiography*. Edited by Pamela Smith Hill. South Dakota Historical Society Press. 2014.

Wilder, Mrs. A. J. [Laura Ingalls]. "Columns from *The Missouri Ruralist*, 1911–1931." Transcribed from originals by Nansie Cleaveland. Sept. 2007. http://www.pioneergirl.com/missouri_ruralist.pdf

Winchester, Simon. "Word Imperfect." *The Atlantic*. May 2001. www.theatlantic.com/past/docs /issues/2001/05/winchester.htm

The Readers

"About Mary Walker." *Mary Walker Foundation*. marywalkerfoundation.org/about/

"Adult Literacy in the United States." National Center for Education Services. July 2019. nces.ed.gov /pubs2019/2019179/index.asp

"Bray Named to Centenarians of Oklahoma Hall of Fame." *Tahlequah Daily Press*. Mar. 22, 2023. www.tahlequahdailypress.com/news/bray-named-to-centenarians-of-oklahoma-hall-of-fame /article_10d1e8e2-c2a3-5e9b-8973-d6347c8db7c1.html

Graham, Ginnie. "Karaoke Keeps Up New-Found Literacy Skills for World War II Veteran." *Tulsa World*. Aug. 13, 2014. tulsaworld.com/news/local/karaoke-keeps-up-new-found-literacy-skills -for-world-war-ii-veteran/article_2f18632f-e129-5f47-b910-fd50070454c3.html

Hartman, Steve. "WWII Veteran Refuses to Close the Book on His Life." Nov. 8, 2013. CBS. www .youtube.com/watch?v=MczEU0QAJ-E

Hill, Selena. "Born into Slavery, This Centenarian Learned to Read at 116, Becoming the Nation's Oldest Student." *Black Enterprise*. Jan. 3, 2020. www.blackenterprise.com/meet-former-slave-learned -to-read-116-mary-walker/

"Kenya OAP School Pupil Flies High." BBC News | Africa. Sep. 8, 2005. news.bbc.co.uk/2/hi /africa/4225824.stm

Martin, John. "A Chattanooga Icon: The Life of Mary Walker." *Local3News.com*. Dec. 1, 2021. www .local3news.com/local-news/local-3-in-your-town/a-chattanooga-icon-the-life-of-mary-walker /article_dbacae98-8c31-52b4-854d-853a53c0978f.html

"Oldest Person to Begin Primary School." *Guinness World Records*. www.guinnessworldrecords.com /world-records/oldest-person-to-begin-primary-school

Old Testament

McKie, Robin. "Discovery of 'Methuselah Gene' Unlocks Secret of Long Life." *The Guardian*. Feb. 3, 2002. www.theguardian.com/science/2002/feb/03/genetics.medicalscience

"Methuselah a Youngster." *Cincinnati Enquirer*. Apr. 30, 1913. *Newspapers.com*. www.newspapers .com/newspage/33361705/

Bibliography

"Methuselah's Age Given as Only 192 Years." *New York Times.* Aug. 26, 1940. www.nytimes.com/1940/08/26/archives/methuselahs-age-given-as-only-192-years-ancient-code-misread-yale.html

Pennisi, Elizabeth. "Single Gene Controls Fruit Fly Life-Span." *Science* 282, no. 5390, Oct. 30, 1998, p. 856. DOI: 10.1126/science.282.5390.856a

The Changemaker

Appleton, Sarah. "Jane Goodall." *National Geographic.* Feb. 5, 2024. education.nationalgeographic.org/resource/jane-goodall/

"Because of Her Story: Activist and Suffragist Mary Church Terrell." National Museum of African American History and Culture. nmaahc.si.edu/explore/stories/because-her-story-activist-and-suffragist-mary-church-terrell

Brulliard, Nicolas. "These Ten National Parks Wouldn't Exist without Women." National Parks Conservation Association. Mar. 1, 2020. www.npca.org/articles/1478-these-10-national-parks-wouldn-t-exist-without-women

Caplan, Marvin. "Eat Anywhere!" *Washington History* 1, no. 1 (1989), pp. 24–39. *JSTOR.* www.jstor.org/stable/40072980

Carson. Tom. "The Awakening of Norman Rockwell." *Vox.* Feb. 26, 2020. www.vox.com/the-highlight/2020/2/19/21052356/norman-rockwell-the-problem-we-all-live-with-saturday-evening-post

District of Columbia v. John R. Thompson Co., Inc. 346 U.S. Supreme Court 100. 1953. supreme.justia.com/cases/federal/us/346/100

Doyle, Eva. "Eye on History: Mary Church Terrell, Daughter of Slaves, Civil Rights Leader, Fought for Rights of Blacks." *Buffalo News.* Feb. 12, 2022. buffalonews.com/opinion/columnists/eye-on-history-mary-church-terrell-daughter-of-slaves-civil-rights-leader-fought-for-rights/article_1e039924-8b66-11ec-8c09-6f5a0c93442e.html

Frisken, Amanda K. "'A Song without Words': Anti-Lynching Imagery in the African American Press, 1889–1898." *Journal of African American History* 97, no. 3 (Summer 2012), pp. 240–69. www.jstor.org/stable/10.5323/jafriamerhist.97.3.0240

Henderson v. United States, 339 U.S. Supreme Court 816. 1950. supreme.justia.com/cases/federal/us/339/816/

Jane Goodall Institute. "About Jane." *JaneGoodall.org.* janegoodall.org/our-story/about-jane/

Leone, Janice. "Integrating the American Association of University Women, 1946–1949." *The Historian* 51, no. 3 (1989), pp. 423–45. *JSTOR.* www.jstor.org/stable/24447356

Little, Becky. "How Woodrow Wilson Tried to Reverse Black American Progress." *History.com*, A&E Television Networks. July 24, 2020. www.history.com/news/woodrow-wilson-racial-segregation-jim-crow-ku-klux-klan

Mansky, Jackie. "How One Woman Helped End Lunch Counter Segregation in the Nation's Capital." *Smithsonian Magazine,* June 8, 2016. www.smithsonianmag.com/history/how-one-woman-helped-end-lunch-counter-segregation-nations-capital-180959345

"Mary Church Terrell." National Women's Hall of Fame. www.womenofthehall.org/inductee/mary-church-terrell

Bibliography

Michals, Debra. "Biography: Mary Church Terrell." National Women's History Museum. 2017. www
.womenshistory.org/education-resources/biographies/mary-church-terrell

Mitchell, Damon. "The People's Grocery Lynching, Memphis, Tennessee." *JSTOR Daily*. Jan. 24, 2018.
daily.jstor.org/peoples-grocery-lynching

Nakagawa, Martha. "Sue Kunitomi Embrey." *Densho Encyclopedia*. Oct. 16., 2020. encyclopedia
.densho.org/Sue%20Kunitomi%20Embrey

"One Camp, Ten Thousand Lives; One Camp, Ten Thousand Stories." Manzanar National Historic
Site: National Park Service. www.nps.gov/manz/index.htm

Powell, Patricia Hruby. *Josephine: The Dazzling Life of Josephine Baker*. Chronicle Books, 2014.

Quigley, Joan. *Just Another Southern Town: Mary Church Terrell and the Struggle for Racial Justice in
the Nation's Capital*. Oxford University Press, 2016.

Sheehan, Charles J. "'Lost Laws' to 'Eat Anywhere': *D.C. v. Thompson* and the Road to *Brown*." *Journal
of Supreme Court History* 47 (2022), pp. 284–304. doi.org/10.1111/jsch.12307

Sinkler, George. "Benjamin Harrison and the Matter of Race." *Indiana Magazine of History*. Aug. 1969.
scholarworks.iu.edu/journals/index.php/imh/article/view/9444

Steptoe, Tyina. "Mary Church Terrell (1863–1954)." *BlackPast.org*. Jan. 19, 2007. www.blackpast.org
/african-american-history/terrell-mary-church-1863-1954/

Terrell, Mary Church. "Lynching from a Negro's Point of View." *North American Review* 178, no. 571
(June 1904), pp. 853–868. *JSTOR*. www.jstor.org/stable/pdf/25150991

Williamson, Joel. "Wounds Not Scars: Lynching, the National Conscience, and the American Historian." *Journal of American History* 83, no. 4 (1997), pp. 1221–1253. *JSTOR*. doi.org/10.2307/2952899

"Woodrow Wilson: Federal Segregation." National Postal Museum. postalmuseum.si.edu/research
-articles/the-history-and-experience-of-african-americans-in-america's-postal-service-3

Old Navy

"Carter Extolls Old Navy Boss Rickover." UPI. July 9, 1986. www.upi.com/Archives/1986/07/09
/Carter-extolls-old-Navy-boss-Rickover/3885521265600/

Old Soldiers Never Die, They Just Reenlist

Balestrieri, Steve. "Samuel Whittemore, the American Revolution's Oldest Lion." *SOFREP*. July 4,
2021. sofrep.com/news/samuel-whittemore-the-american-revolutions-oldest-lion/

Brady's National Photographic Portrait Galleries, photographer. Gettysburg, Pennsylvania. John L.
Burns cottage. Burns seated in the doorway. July 1863. www.loc.gov/item/2018670711/

"A Brit Looks at Sam Whittemore." *YourArlington*. Oct. 23, 2012. www.yourarlington.com/arlington
-archives/town-school/local-history/5161-whittemore-102312.html

Brown, Charles Brockden, and Robert Walsh. *The American Register; or, General Repository of History, Politics and Science*. C. & A. Conrad, 1808.

Chachowski, Richard. "Yoda's Complete Chronological History in Star Wars." *Wealth of Geeks*.
June 13, 2023. wealthofgeeks.com/yoda-complete-chronological-history-in-star-wars/

Crane, Gregory R., ed. "Benjamin Cutter, William R. Cutter, History of the Town of Arlington, Massachusetts, Formerly the Second Precinct in Cambridge, or District of Menotomy, Afterward the

Bibliography

Town of West Cambridge. 1635–1879, with a Genealogical Register of the Inhabitants of the Precinct." Tufts University. www.perseus.tufts.edu/hopper/text?doc=Perseus%3Atext%3A2001.05.0320%3Achapter%3D4%3Apage%3D76

Crane, Gregory R., editor-in-chief. "Lucius R. Paige, History of Cambridge, Massachusetts, 1630–1877, with a Genealogical Register." Tufts University. www.perseus.tufts.edu/hopper/text?doc=Perseus%3Atext%3A2001.05.0228%3Achapter%3D22&force=y

"Fortress of Louisbourg National Historic Site: Tourism Nova Scotia, Canada." Tourism Nova Scotia. www.novascotia.com/see-do/attractions/fortress-of-louisbourg-national-historic-site/1583

Fulks, Sonny. "If You Want to Go: What John Burns Did, and What He Didn't Do." *Gettysburg Magazine* 53, July 2015, pp. 77–82. muse.jhu.edu/pub/17/article/586335/pdf

Gallucci, Maria. "Two Adorable, Newly Discovered Yoda-like Creatures Will Make Your Star Wars Day Even Better." *Mashable*. May 4, 2017. mashable.com/article/may-the-fourth-star-wars-yoda-tarsiers

"George Lucas Explains Where Yoda Comes From: Empire Strikes Back." Jan. 20, 2021. YouTube. www.youtube.com/watch?v=a2gVkGCq2GE

Getty, Katie Turner. "Before the Bayonetting: The Untold Story of Capt. Samuel Whittemore." *Journal of the American Revolution*. June 6, 2017. allthingsliberty.com/2017/06/bayonetting-untold-story-capt-samuel-whittemore/

Harkin, Chris. "Star Wars: 7 Things You Didn't Know About Yoda." *Game Rant*. Jan. 2, 2023. gamerant.com/star-wars-facts-trivia-yoda/

Harte, Bret. "John Burns of Gettysburg." *Theotherpages.org*. Poets' Corner. www.theotherpages.org/poems/2001/harte0101.html

Hill, Amelia. "Who Is Jedi Master Yoda?" *LiveAbout*. Feb. 18, 2019. www.liveabout.com/yoda-in-star-wars-2957947

"How Yoda Became a Jedi [Full Story]—Star Wars Canon and Legends." Nov. 20, 2019. YouTube. www.youtube.com/watch?v=uE9XhRBFZNs

James, Jessica. "Old John Burns of Gettysburg: A War of 1812 Veteran Fighter." *Past Lane Travels*. Jan. 20, 2023. pastlanetravels.com/john-burns-defends-gettysburg/

"Jean Thurel: The Oldest Soldier in History?" *HistoryExtra*. Aug. 15, 2023. www.historyextra.com/period/modern/jean-thurel-who-french-oldest-soldier-history/

"John Burns, Gettysburg, Fights Confederates, 1863." *American History Central*. June 23, 2023. www.americanhistorycentral.com/john-burns-gettysburg-1863/

"John Burns Memorial." *Gettysburg Battlefield Tours*. May 18, 2015. www.gettysburgbattlefieldtours.com/john-burns-memorial/

Mandresh, Jason. "Samuel Whittemore—the Oldest Revolutionary, the Most Courage." *Founder of the Day*. June 8, 2021. www.founderoftheday.com/founder-of-the-day/samuel-whittemore

"Monument at Gettysburg to Civil War Hero, Civilian John Burns." *The Battle of Gettysburg*. Dec. 21, 2019. gettysburg.stonesentinels.com/monuments-to-individuals/john-burns/

Morrison, Sara. "He Joined the Revolution as an Old Man, Was Shot in the Face—And Lived Another 18 Years." *Boston.com*. July 2, 2015. www.boston.com/news/local-news/2015/07/02/he-joined-the-revolution-as-an-old-man-was-shot-in-the-face-and-lived-another-18-years/

Bibliography

"Samuel Whittemore, the Oldest, Bravest and Maybe Craziest American Revolutionary." New England Historical Society. Apr. 13, 2023. newenglandhistoricalsociety.com/samuel-whittemore-the-oldest-bravest-and-maybe-craziest-american-revolutionary/

Schneider, Caitlin. "How Einstein Influenced the Look of Yoda." *Mental Floss*. Dec. 1, 2015. www.mentalfloss.com/article/71795/how-einstein-influenced-look-yoda

Smith, Timothy H. *John Burns: The Hero of Gettysburg*. Thomas Publications, 2000.

"Star Wars Episode II 0 – Attack of the Clones – Yoda vs Count Dooku – 4K Ultra HD." July 25, 2020. YouTube. www.youtube.com/watch?v=wg1ydN42ukY

Taylor, Maureen A. "John L. Burns: Civil War Sharpshooter at Age 69." *Family Tree Magazine*. Yankee Publishing. familytreemagazine.com/history/john-l-burns-civil-war-sharpshooter-at-age-69/

"To George Washington from Samuel Whittemore, 1 March 1790." *Founders Online*. National Archives. founders.archives.gov/documents/Washington/05-05-02-0122. *The Papers of George Washington*, Presidential Series, vol. 5, *16 January 1790–30 June 1790*, ed. Dorothy Twohig, Mark A. Mastromarino, and Jack D. Warren. Charlottesville: University Press of Virginia, 1996, pp. 195–196.

"The True Power of Yoda – Yoda's Greatest Force Feats [Legends] – Star Wars Explained." Sept. 12, 2018. YouTube. www.youtube.com/watch?v=Uq2cpaVAXg8

"Yoda." *Wookieepedia*. Fandom, Inc. starwars.fandom.com/wiki/Yoda

"Yoda's Death [HD]." Dec. 3, 2016. YouTube. www.youtube.com/watch?v=5ZK57xBaGwM

Old Glory

Clague, Mark. "Separating Fact from Fiction About 'The Star-Spangled Banner.'" National Constitution Center. Sept. 14, 2016. constitutioncenter.org/blog/separating-fact-from-fiction-about-the-star-spangled-banner

Gelb, Norman. "Francis Scott Key, the Reluctant Patriot." *Smithsonian Magazine*. Sept. 2004. www.smithsonianmag.com/history/francis-scott-key-the-reluctant-patriot-180937178/

"Honors to the Flag: The Bands Will Play, and the Men Will." *Washington Post*. July 30, 1889. ProQuest.

"Not One National Song." *New York Times*. Aug. 25, 1889. www.nytimes.com/1889/08/25/archives/not-one-national-song-a-chance-for-patriotic-american-composers-the.html

"Red Sox Beat Cubs in Initial Battle of World Series." *New York Times*. Sept. 6, 1918. www.nytimes.com/1918/09/06/archives/red-sox-beat-cubs-in-initial-battle-of-worlds-series-one-run-gives.html

"Song Bears Plea of 6 Million to House for National Anthem." *New York Herald Tribune*. Feb. 1, 1930. ProQuest.

"Star-Scrambled Banner." *Newsweek*. Dec. 2, 1968. ProQuest.

"'Star-Spangled Banner'" Is Now Official Anthem." *Washington Post*. Mar. 5, 1931. ProQuest.

"The Star-Spangled Banner: Some Over-Fussy People Object to Its Provocative Words and to the Bacchanalian Origin of Its Music." *San Francisco Chronicle*. Aug. 25, 1918. ProQuest.

Bibliography

It Could Happen to You

Archerd, Army. "Tom Poston Farewell." *Variety*. May 7, 2007. variety.com/2007/voices/columns/tom _poston_fare-919.

Bark, Ed. "Late Bloomers: Suzanne Pleshette, Tom Poston Married Late, Met Their Fates." *Unclebarky. com*. Jan. 22, 2008. unclebarky.com/back_files/4d899cb879a2b1f7670eee8fe082ed29-18.html

Barnes, Mike. "Harry Kullijian, Carol Channing's Husband, Dies." *Hollywood Reporter*. Dec. 28, 2011. www.hollywoodreporter.com/movies/movie-news/harry-kullijian-carol-channings-husband -276501

Berinstein, Dori, director. *Carol Channing: Larger Than Life*. Written by Dori Berinstein and Adam Zucker. *Dramatic Forces and Entertainment One*. 2012.

"Dream Comes True for Carol Channing." CBS News. May 12, 2003. www.cbsnews.com/news /dream-comes-true-for-carol-channing/

"Golden Fleecing (Broadway, Stephen Sondheim Theatre, 1959)." *Playbill*. Oct. 15, 1959. playbill.com /productions/golden-fleecingbroadway-stephen-sondheim-theatre-1959#carousel-cell237160

Jones, Kenneth. "Harry Kullijian, Arts Advocate and Husband of Carol Channing, Dies at 91." *Playbill*. Dec. 27, 2011. www.playbill.com/article/harry-kullijian-arts-advocate-and-husband-of-carol -channing-dies-at-91-com-185891

"Kenneth Felts on Coming Out at 90 Years Old." Studio 10. YouTube. www.youtube.com/watch ?v=TpDxX-T_Beg

Kindon, Frances. "'I Had Twins at 73, Then My Husband Died,' Says Devastated 'World's Oldest Mum.'" *The Mirror*. Mar. 15, 2021. www.mirror.co.uk/news/world-news/i-twins-73-husband -died-23721639

LaGorce, Tammy. "A Happiness That Took 90 Years to Achieve." *New York Times*. Aug. 11, 2023. www .nytimes.com/2023/08/11/style/kenneth-felts-johnny-hau-wedding.html

Nemy, Enid. "Carol Channing Dies at 97: A Larger-Than-Life Broadway Star." *New York Times*. Jan. 15, 2019. www.nytimes.com/2019/01/15/obituaries/carol-channing-dead.html

"Oh Sweet Baby Pickles." Houston Zoo. Mar. 16, 2023. www.houstonzoo.org/blog/oh-sweet-baby -pickles/

Oxenden, McKenna. "A 90-Year-Old Tortoise Named Mr. Pickles Is a New Dad of Three." *New York Times*. Mar. 22, 2023. www.nytimes.com/2023/03/22/us/houston-zoo-tortoise-babies.html

Richards, David. "Carol Channing, Unhappily Ever After End to 41-Year Marriage Stuns Friends." *Washington Post*. May 22, 1998. www.washingtonpost.com/archive/lifestyle/1998/05/22/carol -channing-unhappily-ever-after-end-to-41-year-marriage-stuns-friends/787396bc-a0ba -4592-ad98-9cead3620072/

"Sarah." *Jewish Virtual Library*. www.jewishvirtuallibrary.org/sarah-2

"Suzanne Pleshette Interview Part 1 of 5: Television Academy.com/Interviews." *Foundation Interviews*. Feb. 8, 2019. *Television Academy*. www.youtube.com/watch?v=ME4HH5WXsM8&t=1620s

"Suzanne Pleshette Interview Part 2 of 5: EmmyTVLegends.org." *Foundation Interviews*. July 12, 2012. YouTube. www.youtube.com/watch?v=ArXCBMjYhF4

"Suzanne Pleshette on Meeting Tom Poston: EmmyTVLegends.org." *Foundation Interviews*. Oct. 2, 2012. YouTube. www.youtube.com/watch?v=-mni8LJj2aU

Bibliography

"The Theater: New Plays on Broadway, Oct. 26, 1959." *Time*. Oct. 26, 1959. content.time.com/time /subscriber/article/0,33009,865018,00.html

"Upworthy Voice: Kenneth Felts on Coming Out at Age 90." Upworthy. YouTube. www.youtube.com /watch?v=ykoa3dtPbyY

Young, Olivia. "Arvada Man Comes Out as Gay—at 90 Years Old: 'It's Never Too Late.'" CBS News Colorado. Oct. 12, 2022. www.cbsnews.com/colorado/news/kenneth-felts-coming-out-colorado -gay-90-years-old-arvada-man-comes-out/

Old Yeller

Hammond, Percy. "The Theaters." *New York Herald Tribune*. Nov. 2, 1930. ProQuest.

Merman, Ethel, with Pete Martin. *Who Could Ask for Anything More, by Ethel Merman, as Told to Pete Martin*. Doubleday, 1955.

Smith, J. Y. "Broadway Singing Star Ethel Merman Dies." *Washington Post*. Feb. 15, 1984. www .washingtonpost.com/archive/local/1984/02/16/broadway-singing-star-ethel-merman-dies /7e7a0ce1-acb6-4294-bb64-55819fc90b4f/

Wallach, Allan. "Ethel Merman 1909–1984: Broadway Heard Her Loud and Clear." *Newsday*. Feb. 16, 1984. ProQuest.

Wilson, John S. "Ethel Merman at Carnegie Hall." *New York Times*. May 12, 1982. www.nytimes .com/1982/05/12/arts/pop-ethel-merman-at-carnegie-hall.html

The Widows

Battersby, Eileen. "An Eye for a Bloom." *Irish Times*. Feb. 6, 2010. www.irishtimes.com/life-and-style /people/an-eye-for-a-bloom-1.618641

Blakemore, Erin. "How Medgar Evers' Widow Fought 30 Years for His Killer's Conviction." *History .com*. A&E Television Networks. June 9, 2023. www.history.com/news/medgar-evers-widow -justice

Campsie, Philippa. "The Veuve Barbe-Nicole Clicquot and Other Widowed Women Entrepreneurs." *A Woman's Paris*. June 4, 2010. awomansparis.wordpress.com/2010/06/04/how-to-succeed-in -business-circa-1805/

Delany, Mary. *The Autobiography and Correspondence of Mary Granville, Mrs. Delany: With Interesting Reminiscences of King George the Third and Queen Charlotte*. R. Bentley, 1861. archive.org /details/autobiographycor03delauoft/page/n7/mode/2up

Dreifus, Claudia. "The Widow Gets Her Verdict." *New York Times Magazine*. Nov. 27, 1994. www .nytimes.com/1994/11/27/magazine/the-widow-gets-her-verdict.html

Geiling, Natasha. "The Widow Who Created the Champagne Industry." *Smithsonian Magazine*. Nov. 5, 2013. www.smithsonianmag.com/arts-culture/the-widow-who-created-the-champagne-industry -180947570/

Harrison, Eric. "Beckwith Is Convicted of Killing Medgar Evers: Verdict: The Avowed White Supremacist, Now 73, Had Been Tried Twice Before. He Is Sentenced to Life in Prison." *Los Angeles Times*. Feb. 6, 1994. www.latimes.com/archives/la-xpm-1994-02-06-mn-19819-story.html

Bibliography

"Mary Delany." The British Museum. www.britishmuseum.org/about-us/british-museum-story/people-behind-collection/mary-delany

"Mary Delany (1700–88): A Stem of Stock." Royal Collection Trust. www.rct.uk/collection/452388/a-stem-of-stock

Mazzeo, Tilar J. *The Widow Clicquot: The Story of a Champagne Empire and the Woman Who Ruled It.* Harper, 2009.

"Medgar Evers Murdered." *SNCC Digital Gateway.* Sept. 24 2021. snccdigital.org/events/medgar-evers-murdered/

Rosenberg, Karen. "A Shower of Tiny Petals in a Marriage of Art and Botany." *New York Times.* Oct. 22, 2009. www.nytimes.com/2009/10/23/arts/design/23delany.html

Stern, Jane, and Michael Stern. "A Kick from Champagne." *New York Times.* Dec. 25, 2008. www.nytimes.com/2008/12/28/books/review/Stern-t.html

"Veuve Clicquot: The First International Businesswoman." *Medium.* May 18, 2020. arenaissancewriter.medium.com/madame-clicquot-the-first-international-businesswoman-3436a3411f4a

Old News

Mike Wallace wouldn't reveal his sources, but here are ours:

"79-Year-Old Wallace Signs 4-Year Contract with CBS." *Deseret News.* Sept. 11, 1997. www.deseret.com/1997/9/11/19333436/79-year-old-wallace-signs-4-year-contract-with-cbs

Mifflin, Lawrie. "The Stopwatch Ticks On." *New York Times.* May 19, 1997. www.nytimes.com/1997/05/19/arts/as-television-changes-60-minutes-holds-its-own.html

Nelson, Valerie J. "The Tough Guy of '60 Minutes.'" *Los Angeles Times.* Apr. 9, 2012. www.latimes.com/archives/la-xpm-2012-apr-09-la-me-mike-wallace-20120409-story.html

Reed, Christopher. "Mike Wallace Obituary." *The Guardian.* Apr. 8, 2012. www.theguardian.com/world/2012/apr/08/mike-wallace

Steinberg, Jacques. "Mike Wallace of '60 Minutes' to Retire." *New York Times.* Mar. 6, 2006. www.nytimes.com/2006/03/15/world/americas/15iht-wallace.html

Weiner, Tim. "Mike Wallace, CBS Pioneer of '60 Minutes,' Dies at 93." *New York Times.* Apr. 8, 2012. www.nytimes.com/2012/04/09/business/media/mike-wallace-cbs-pioneer-of-60-minutes-dead-at-93.html

Turning Loss into Gain

"21 Facts about Henri Matisse." Sotheby's. June 28, 2019. www.sothebys.com/en/articles/21-facts-about-henri-matisse

Albino, Donna, ed. "Through the Horn-Rimmed Looking Glass: Junior Show, Class of 1960." *A Postcard Collection of Mt. Holyoke College.* mtholyoke.com/dalbino/recordings/glass/index.html

Borges, Jorge Luis. "Autobiographical Notes." *The New Yorker.* Sept. 11, 1970. www.newyorker.com/magazine/1970/09/19/jorge-luis-borges-profile-autobiographical-notes

Borges, Jorge Luis. "In Praise of Darkness." *Borges: Selected Poems.* Edited by Alexander Coleman. Translated by Hoyt Rogers. Penguin, 1999.

Bibliography

Borges, Jorge Luis. *The Maker: Prose Pieces 1934–1960*. Translated by Norman Thomas DiGiovanni. Edited by Jonathan Basile. libraryofbabel.info/Borges/themaker.pdf

Borges, Jorge Luis. *The Sonnets*. Edited and introduced by Stephen Kessler. Translated by Willis Barnstone et al. Penguin, 2010.

Buchberg, Karl., et al., editors. *Henri Matisse: The Cut-Outs*. Tate Publishing, 2014.

Buchberg, Karl, et al. "Henri Matisse: The Cut-Outs." Museum of Modern Art. www.moma.org/calendar/exhibitions/1429

Butler, Karen K. *Matisse in the Barnes Foundation: 3 Volume Set*. Thames & Hudson, Jan. 25, 2016.

Carelli, Francesco. "Painting with Scissors: Matisse and Creativity in Illness." *London Journal of Primary Care* 6, no. 4 (2014), p. 93. doi.org/10.1080/17571472.2014.11493424

Carmody, Tim. "Borges on Homer, Milton, and Blindness." *Kottke*. Oct. 27, 2017. kottke.org/17/10/borges-on-homer-milton-and-blindness

Cortínez, Carlos, editor. *Borges the Poet*. University of Arkansas Press, 1986.

Cotter, Holland. "Wisps from an Old Man's Dreams." *New York Times*. Oct. 10, 2014. www.nytimes.com/2014/10/10/arts/design/henri-matisse-the-cut-outs-a-victory-lap-at-moma.html

Cullinan, Nicholas. "His Brilliant Final Chapter." *Tate*. Mar. 10, 2014. www.tate.org.uk/tate-etc/issue-30-spring-2014/his-brilliant-final-chapter

"Davin Stowell on 35 Years of Smart Design." *Smart Design*. Oct. 13, 2021. smartdesignworldwide.com/news/davin-stowell-fast-company-35-years/

"Designs for Aging: New Takes on Old Forms." *The Henry Ford*. Nov. 18, 2022. www.thehenryford.org/explore/blog/tag/design/

Eder, Richard. "Not the Untroubled Man They Said He Was." *Los Angeles Times*. Sept. 25, 2005. www.latimes.com/archives/la-xpm-2005-sep-25-bk-eder25-story.html

Fox, Margalit. "Sam Farber, Creator of Oxo Utensils, Dies at 88." *New York Times*. June 21, 2013. www.nytimes.com/2013/06/22/business/sam-farber-creator-of-oxo-utensils-dies-at-88.html

Gargan, Edward A. "Jorge Luis Borges, a Master of Fantasy and Fable, Is Dead." *New York Times*. June 15, 1986. archive.nytimes.com/www.nytimes.com/books/97/08/31/reviews/borges-dead.html

Gutierrez, Iliana. "Henri Matisse: Drawing with Scissors, Part II." *Noble Oceans*. Aug. 18, 2017. www.nobleoceans.com/artists/2017/8/18/henri-matisse-drawing-with-scissors-part-ii

"Henri Matisse." Sotheby's. 2015. www.sothebys.com/en/auctions/ecatalogue/2015/impressionist-modern-art-evening-sale-l15002/lot.7.html

"Henri Matisse and the Chapelle Du Rosaire." Musée Matisse de Nice. www.musee-matisse-nice.org/en/the-artist/matisse-and-the-rosary-chapel/

"Henri Matisse: The Dance." Barnes Collection Online. collection.barnesfoundation.org/objects/6967/The-Dance/

"Henri Matisse: The Swimming Pool." Museum of Modern Art. 2014. www.moma.org/interactives/exhibitions/2014/matisse/the-swimming-pool.html

Herwig, Malte. *The Woman Who Says No: Françoise Gilot on Her Life with and without Picasso*. Greystone Books, 2020.

Hirsch, Edward. "I Am Going Blind, and I Now Find It Strangely Exhilarating." *New York Times*. Mar. 28, 2023. www.nytimes.com/2023/03/28/opinion/embracing-blindness-disability.html

Bibliography

Jackson, Liz. "We Are the Original Lifehackers." *New York Times*. May 30, 2018. www.nytimes
.com/2018/05/30/opinion/disability-design-lifehacks.html

Kazin, Alfred. "Meeting Borges." *New York Times*. May 2, 1971. archive.nytimes.com/www.nytimes
.com/books/97/08/31/reviews/borges-meeting.html

Koenenn, Connie. "Form and Function Meet in the Kitchen." *Los Angeles Times*. Sept. 14, 2000. www
.latimes.com/archives/la-xpm-2000-sep-14-cl-20664-story.html

Koenenn, Connie. "Practical View: Gadget Mania: Aging Baby Boomers Demand Products That
Make Life Easier." *Los Angeles Times*. Jan. 21, 1993. www.latimes.com/archives/la-xpm-1993-01
-21-vw-1948-story.html

Lacayo, Richard. "Review: Henri Matisse: The Cut-Outs at Moma." *Time*. Oct. 23, 2014. time
.com/3533573/matisses-great-paper-chase/

Levy, Adam Harrison. "Henri Matisse: The Lost Interview." *Design Observer*. Jan. 21, 2015. design
observer.com/feature/henri-matisse-the-lost-interview/38738/

Liston, Valerie. "Behind the Design: Oxo's Iconic Good Grips Handles." *OXO*. Jan. 31, 2017. www.oxo
.com/blog/behind-the-scenes/behind-design-oxos-iconic-good-grips-handles

Matis, Marylin E., and Sylvie Ryckesbusch. "OXO International." Harvard Business School. Jan. 1997.
store.hbr.org/product/oxo-international/697007

May, Matt. "The Same, but Different: Breaking Down Accessibility, Universality, and Inclusion in
Design." *Medium*. Thinking Design. Apr. 3, 2018. medium.com/thinking-design/the-same-but
-different-breaking-down-accessibility-universality- and-inclusion-in-design-80ebc42cc24d

"Mrs. Kriegsman, Architect, Is Wed." *New York Times*. Mar. 17, 1985. www.nytimes.com/1985/03/17
/style/mrs-kriegsmanarchitect-is-wed.html

Petroski, Henry. "Everyday Design." *American Scientist*, Nov. 2001, pp. 495–499.

Riggle, Nick. "How Henri Matisse (and I) Got a 'Beautiful Body.'" *New York Times*. Dec. 25, 2022.
www.nytimes.com/2022/12/25/opinion/matisse-disability-beauty-body.html

Rodriguez Monegal, Emir. *Jorge Luis Borges: A Literary Biography*. E. P. Dutton, 1978.

Rolfes, Ellen. "New Exhibit of Matisse's Cut-Outs Shows How Artist Began 'Painting with Scissors.'"
PBS. Apr. 14, 2014. www.pbs.org/newshour/arts/new-exhibit-matisses-cut-outs-shows-artist
-began-painting-scissors

"Sam Farber." Industrial Designers Society of America. May 8, 2023. www.idsa.org/profile/sam
-farber/

"Samuel Farber, Founder of Oxo Utensils, Dies at 88." UPI. June 22, 2013. www.upi.com/Business_
News/2013/06/22/Samuel-Farber-developer-of-kitchen-utensils-dies- at-88/UPI-69701371918952/

"Santoprene Offers the Performance Industries Demand." *Kent Elastomer Products*, Oct. 25, 2022.
www.kentelastomer.com/santoprene-offers-the-performance-industries-demand/

Spurling, Hilary. "Matisse and His Models." *Smithsonian Magazine*. Oct. 1, 2005. www.smithsonian
mag.com/arts-culture/matisse-and-his-models-70195044/

Spurling, Hilary. *Matisse the Master: A Life of Henri Matisse: The Conquest of Color, 1909–1954*.
Knopf, 2005.

Stirling, George. "The Impact of Surgery on Fine Art." *Perspectives in Biology and Medicine* 37, no. 1
(Autumn 1993), pp. 67–73. muse.jhu.edu/article/400976/pdf

Bibliography

Tóibín, Colm. "Don't Abandon Me: Borges and the Maids." *London Review of Books*. May 11, 2006. www.lrb.co.uk/the-paper/v28/n09/colm-toibin/don-t-abandon-me

Torres, Dani. "Blindness by Jorge Luis Borges." *A Work in Progress: Essay & Short Story Reading Projects*. Apr. 9, 2010. danitorres.typepad.com/workinprogress/essay-short-story-reading-projects .html

Weeks, John. "Borges: The Blind Librarian." *CLT Journal*. Oct. 26, 2020. blog.cltexam.com/borges -the-blind-librarian/

"What Is Santoprene?" U.S. Plastic Corp. Mar. 12, 2015. www.usplastic.com/knowledgebase/article .aspx?contentkey=996

Wilson, Jason. *The Cambridge Companion to Jorge Luis Borges*. Edited by Edwin Williamson. Cambridge University Press, 2013, pp. 186–200. doi.org/10.1017/CCO9780511978869.018

Wilson, Mark. "A History of the Oxo Good Grips Peeler." *Fast Company*. Sept. 24, 2018. www.fast company.com/90239156/the-untold-story-of-the-vegetable-peeler-that-changed-the-world

Wolff, Benjamin. "A Second Life: Renewing Ourselves in a Time of Constraints and Isolation." *Forbes*. July 19, 2020. www.forbes.com/sites/benjaminwolff/2020/07/19/a-second-life-renewing-our selves-in-a-time-of-constraints-and-isolation/

Wood, Michael. "Productive Mischief: Borges and Borges and I." *London Review of Books*. Feb. 1999. www.lrb.co.uk/the-paper/v21/n03/michael-wood/productive-mischief

Yates, Donald. A. "Jorge Guillermo Borges (1874–1938): Two Notes." *Variaciones Borges* 32 (2011), pp. 215–220. www.jstor.org/stable/24881535

Old English

Dowd, Maureen. "Queen! Bow Down to Tattoo-Flashing Octogenarian Dame Dench." *New York Times*. Sept. 21, 2017. www.nytimes.com/2017/09/21/style/dame-judi-dench.html

"Judi Dench Interview: 'Retirement Is a Rude Word,'" *Telegraph*. Feb. 22, 2015. ProQuest.

St. Martin, Emily. "Judi Dench Says Her Deteriorating Eyesight Has Made It 'Impossible' to Read Scripts." *Los Angeles Times*. Feb. 17, 2023. www.latimes.com/entertainment-arts/story/2023-02 -17/judi-dench-degenerative-eye-condition

Walter, Simon. "Despite Everything, the Queen Is Still the Most Respected Figure in Britain—Even If the Person We REALLY Like Best Is Dame Judi." *Mail on Sunday*. June 2, 2002. ProQuest.

Ageless Architects

Albert, Calvin, et al. "Callous Disregard: An Open Letter on Frank Lloyd Wright's Guggenheim Design." Received by Mr. James Johnson Sweeney, Director, and the Trustees, the Solomon R. Guggenheim Museum, 1956. *Lapham's Quarterly* 3, no. 2, 2010. www.laphamsquarterly.org/arts -letters/callous-disregard

Allsop, Laura. "At 93, Louvre Pyramid Architect I. M. Pei Is Still Going Strong." CNN. July 28, 2010. www.cnn.com/2010/WORLD/europe/07/28/im.pei.paris/index.html

Barnes, Sara. "Guggenheim Museum: How Frank Lloyd Wright Brought His Masterpiece to Life in New York." *My Modern Met*. Jan. 28, 2022. mymodernmet.com/guggenheim-museum-new-york -architecture/

Bibliography

Bernstein, Richard. "I.M. Pei's Pyramid: A Provocative Plan for the Louvre." *New York Times*. Nov. 24, 1985. www.nytimes.com/1985/11/24/magazine/im-pei-s-pyramid-a-provative-plan-for-the-lou vre.html

Bigar, Sylvie. "Originally Controversial, Glass Pyramid at Paris Louvre Museum Celebrates 30th Anniversary." *Forbes*. Apr. 11, 2019. www.forbes.com/sites/sylviebigar/2019/04/11/originally -controversial-glass-pyramid-at-paris-louvre-museum-celebrates-30th-anniversary/

Black, Nicolas, and Jackson Hodges. "Price Tower." *Clio: Your Guide to History*. May 3, 2022. theclio .com/entry/1864

Brook, Mitch. "You Can Now Follow a Beyoncé and Jay Z Tour through the Louvre." *AWOL*. July 9, 2018. awol.com.au/beyonce-and-jay-z-tour-the-louvre/63572

Chu, Henry. "He's Still Shaping a Legend." *Los Angeles Times*. Mar. 29, 2005. www.latimes.com /archives/la-xpm-2005-mar-29-fg-niemeyer29-story.html

Donadio, Rachel. "How I. M. Pei Shaped a Change-Resistant Paris." *The Atlantic*. May 17, 2019. www .theatlantic.com/international/archive/2019/05/im-pei-louvre-pyramid-changed-paris/589735/

Farzan, Antonia Noori. "Kevin Roche, Leading Corporate Architect of Postwar Boom Years, Dies at 96." *Washington Post*. Mar. 4, 2019. www.washingtonpost.com/local/obituaries/kevin-roche -leading-corporate-architect-of-postwar-boom-years-dies-at-96/2019/03/02/6f4f5860-3d33 -11e9-a2cd-307b06d0257b_story.html

"Frank Lloyd Wright." Nov. 10, 1998. PBS. www.pbs.org/kenburns/frank-lloyd-wright/

"The Frank Lloyd Wright Building." The Guggenheim Museums and Foundation. www.guggenheim .org/about-us/architecture/frank-lloyd-wright-and-the-guggenheim

"The Frank Lloyd Wright Building Timeline." The Guggenheim Museums and Foundation. https:// www.guggenheim.org/about-us/architecture/timeline

"Frank Lloyd Wright Dies. Famed Architect Was 89." *New York Times*. Apr. 10, 1959. timesmachine .nytimes.com/timesmachine/1959/04/10/83679525.pdf

"Frank Lloyd Wright's Beth Sholom Synagogue." *Slate Magazine*. Jan. 26, 2006. www.slate.com /articles/arts/architecture/2006/01/wright-revisited.html

Giovannini, Joseph. "Arata Isozaki, Prolific Japanese Architect, Dies at 91." *New York Times*. Dec. 29, 2022. www.nytimes.com/2022/12/29/arts/design/arata-isozaki-dead.html

Goldberger, Paul. "I. M. Pei, Master Architect Whose Buildings Dazzled the World, Dies at 102." *New York Times*. May 16. 2018. www.nytimes.com/2019/05/16/obituaries/im-pei-dead.html

Goldberger, Paul. "Kevin Roche, Architect Who Melded Bold with Elegant, Dies at 96." *New York Times*. Mar. 3, 2019. www.nytimes.com/2019/03/02/arts/kevin-roche-dead-architect.html

Gorman, Sophie. "The Louvre Pyramid That Shocked Paris Turns 30." *France 24*. Mar. 29, 2019. www .france24.com/en/20190329-paris-france-louvre-pei-pyramid-30

Hodes, Laura. "In Frank Lloyd Wright's Only Synagogue, a Masterful Blending of Color and Light." *Forward*. Nov. 4, 2021. forward.com/culture/art/477591/frank-lloyd-wright-synagogue-elkins -park-pennsylvania-beth-sholom/

Hurst, Will. "From Banks to Bamboo: Pakistan's First Female Architect Yasmeen Lari." *Architects' Journal*. Apr. 27, 2023. www.architectsjournal.co.uk/news/from-banks-to-bamboo-pakistans -first-female-architect-yasmeen-lari

Bibliography

"I. M. Pei, Architect." JFK Library. www.jfklibrary.org/about-us/about-the-jfk-library/history/im-pei-architect

"I. M. Pei. Buildings, House & Louvre: Biography." *Biography.com*. May 20, 2021. www.biography.com/artist/im-pei

Lehmann, Megan. "Bruce Beresford to Direct Frank Lloyd Wright Biopic 'Taliesin' (Exclusive)." *Hollywood Reporter*. Dec. 5, 2011. www.hollywoodreporter.com/news/general-news/bruce-beresford-frank-lloyd-wright-taliesin-269721/

Levy, Natasha. "Stove by Yasmeen Lari Lets Pakistani Women Do Eco-Friendly Cooking." *Dezeen*. Nov. 5, 2021. www.dezeen.com/2021/11/05/stove-design-eco-cooking-yasmeen-lari/

Katsikopoulou, Myrto. "'I Believe in the Democratization of Architecture.' Yasmeen Lari on Self-Sufficient Communities." *Designboom*. July 10, 2023. www.designboom.com/architecture/architecture-decolonization-democratization-yasmeen-lari-self-sufficient-communities-uia-world-congress-07-10-2023/

Moore, Rowan. "Architect Yasmeen Lari: 'The International Colonial Charity Model Will Never Work'." *The Guardian*. May 7, 2023. www.theguardian.com/artanddesign/2023/may/07/architect-yasmeen-lari-royal-gold-medal-2023-interview-pakistan-barefoot-social-architecture-floods-earthquake-what-a-terror-i-was-when-i-designed-those-mammoth-buildings

O'Malley, Eric., et al. Issue 155. Wright Society. June 26, 2019. wrightsociety.com/issues/155

Oriaku, Ali. "Kevin Roche, the Quiet but Bold Modernist Architect, Dies at Age 96." *The Architect's Newspaper*. Mar. 6, 2019. www.archpaper.com/2019/03/kevin-roche-obit/

Pearsons-Freedland, Mark, and Mike Parsons, hosts. "Frank Lloyd Wright." *Moonshots Podcast*. Apr. 3, 2019. www.moonshots.io/blog/2018/franklloydwright

Pimlott, Mark. "Grand Louvre & I. M. Pei (2007)." *Artdesigncafé*. Feb. 4, 2011. www.artdesigncafe.com/louvre-paris-i-m-pei

Plitt, Amy. "The History of the Guggenheim Museum's Iconic New York City Building." *Curbed*. Oct. 7, 2019. ny.curbed.com/2017/6/8/15758978/guggenheim-museum-new-york-frank-lloyd-wright-history

Ramzi, Shanaz. "Retrospective: Yasmeen Lari." *Architectural Review*. Sept. 9, 2019. www.architectural-review.com/buildings/retrospective-yasmeen-lari

Reinberger, Mark. "Architecture in Motion: The Gordon Strong Automobile Objective." Frank Lloyd Wright Foundation. Nov. 4, 2019. franklloydwright.org/architecture-in-motion-the-gordon-strong-automobile-objective/

"Remembering I. M. Pei, Renowned Architect and Friend to Asia Society." Asia Society. May 17, 2019. asiasociety.org/remembering-im-pei-renowned-architect-and-friend-asia-society

Rockwell, John. "A Grand Opening for the 'Grand Louvre.'" *New York Times*. Nov. 18, 1993. www.nytimes.com/1993/11/18/arts/a-grand-opening-for-the-grand-louvre.html

School of Architecture and Planning. "Renowned Architect I. M. Pei '40 Dies at 102." *MIT News: Massachusetts Institute of Technology*. May 17, 2019. news.mit.edu/2019/renowned-architect-mit-alumnus-im-pei-dies-0517

Stephan, Von Carmen. "'People Need Beauty': Architect Oscar Niemeyer Turns 100." *Der Spiegel*.

Bibliography

Dec. 14, 2007. www.spiegel.de/international/zeitgeist/people-need-beauty-architect-oscar-nie meyer-turns-100-a-523409.html

van Huyssteen, Justin. "Who Was Frank Lloyd Wright, the Architect?" *Art in Context*. Sept. 25, 2023. artincontext.org/frank-lloyd-wright/

Wang, Lucy. "Automobile Objective by Frank Lloyd Wright." *Dwell*. Dec. 18, 2018. www.dwell.com /article/gordon-strong-automobile-objective-frank-lloyd-wright-393c4802

Wilk, Christopher. "Letter: Wright's Defence." *The Independent*. July 30, 1992. www.independent .co.uk/voices/letter-wrights-defence-1536547.html

"Wright Architecture, Bio, Ideas." *The Art Story*. www.theartstory.org/artist/wright-frank-lloyd/

"Usonian Architecture." Rosenbaum House, www.wrightinalabama.com/usonian-architecture

"Yasmeen Lari." UIA World Congress of Architects, 2023. uia2023cph.org/speaker/yasmeen-lari/

"Yasmeen Lari." Fukuoka Prize, 2016. fukuoka-prize.org/en/laureates/detail/6e1c328d-3184-45ca -bff2-ae91fbd07611

"Yasmeen Lari: Barefoot Social Architecture Benefitting People and the Planet." Architectural League of New York. Dec. 14, 2021. archleague.org/event/yasmeen-lari-current-work/

Old Town

Koenig, H. P. "Relics of St. Augustine's Golden Age." *New York Times*. Nov. 24, 1957. www.nytimes .com/1957/11/24/archives/relics-of-st-augustines-golden-age-occasional-rolls.html

"The Land of Flowers." *New York Times*, Jan. 4, 1903. timesmachine.nytimes.com/timesmachine /1903/01/04/118490761.html

Landphair, Ted. "America Is Aging, but Youth Will Be Served." *VOA News*. Mar. 18, 2009. www .voanews.com/a/a-13-2009-03-18-voa35-68728187/409838.html

Muther, Christopher. "A Florida City that Has Something for Everyone." *Boston Globe.com*. Jan. 29, 2020. www.bostonglobe.com/2020/01/29/lifestyle/florida-city-that-has-something-everyone/

"Ripley Curios to Be Shown." *Miami Herald*. Dec. 8, 1950. ProQuest.

No Signs of Slowing Down

Brean, Henry. "Team Leader's Death Doesn't End Quest for Land Speed Record in Nevada." *Las Vegas Review-Journal*. Sept. 17, 2018. www.reviewjournal.com/local/local-nevada/team-leaders-death -doesnt-end-quest-for-land-speed-record-in-nevada/

Hochman, David. "This 75-Year-Old Is Getting Set to Break the Land Speed Record of 763 Mph." *Speed*. Nov. 30, 2016. nymag.com/speed/2016/11/this-75-year-old-is-set-to-break-the-land -speed-record.html

Middleton, Marc, and Bill Shafer, hosts. "Ed Shadle 3." *Growing Bolder TV and Radio*. Oct. 20, 2020. growingbolder.com/radio-podcast/ed-shadle-3/

"North American Eagle Land Speed Car." *South Bay Riders*. Mar. 19, 2018. www.southbayriders.com /forums/threads/159561/

"North American Eagle." Mar. 5, 2012. YouTube. www.youtube.com/@Landspeed/videos

"North American Eagle." *North American Eagle*. 2022. landspeed.com/

Bibliography

"The North American Eagle." Sept. 30, 2016. KBTC Public Television. YouTube. www.youtube.com/watch?v=lHs9o8FZdlE

Strohl, Daniel. "After a Hairy 477 MPH Ride, North American Eagle Land-Speed Racing Team Heads Home Empty-Handed." *Hemmings.com.* Oct. 10, 2016. www.hemmings.com/stories/2016/10/10/after-a-hairy-477-mph-ride-north-american-eagle-land-speed-racing-team-heads-home-empty-handed

Wapling, Greg. "North American Eagle." *North American Eagle: Land Speed Racing History.* 2012. www.gregwapling.com/hotrod/land-speed-racing-history/land-speed-racing-north-american-eagle.html

"When Should You Take Away the Car Keys?" *Comfort Keepers.* www.comfortkeepers.com/articles/info-center/senior-independent-living/when-should-you-take-away-the-car-keys/

Old Ironsides

"Going Strong: Nearing 80, Jack Lalanne Is Still Pumped Up About Physical Fitness." *Chicago Tribune.* Sept. 19, 1994. www.chicagotribune.com/1994/09/19/going-strong-6/

Goldman, Tom. "Jack LaLanne: Founding Father of Fitness." NPR. Jan. 24, 2011. www.npr.org/2011/01/24/133175583/jack-lalanne-founding-father-of-fitness

Goldstein, Richard. "Jack LaLanne, Founder of Modern Fitness Movement, Dies at 96." *New York Times.* Jan. 23, 2011. www.nytimes.com/2011/01/24/sports/24lalanne.html

Horn, Houston. "LaLanne, a Treat and a Treatment." *Sports Illustrated.* Dec. 19, 1960. vault.si.com/vault/1960/12/19/lalanne-a-treat-and-a-treatment

"LaLanne Eulogized by Schwarzenegger at Memorial Service." CBS News Bay Area. Feb. 1, 2011. www.cbsnews.com/sanfrancisco/news/lalanne-eulogized-by-schwarzenegger-at-memorial-service/

A Trifecta of Horse Stories

"Arlington Park (1927–2021)." *Medium.* Aug. 17, 2021. medium.com/@illinitoffee/arlington-park-1927-2021-7195ec1c02ac

Corrigan, Ed. "Snowman Returns for Final Accolade." *New York Times.* Nov. 9, 1969. www.nytimes.com/1969/11/09/archives/snowman-returns-for-final-accolade.html

Davis, Ron, director. *Harry and Snowman.* FilmRise, 2015. Amazon Prime Video. www.amazon.com/Harry-Snowman-DeLeyer/dp/B01MTOY7JT

Donohue, Gwyn. "Rating the 2008 Internationals." *The Equiery.* July 16, 2018. equiery.com/rating-the-2008-internationals/

Ehalt, Bob. "John Henry: An Undersized $1,100 Purchase Who Became the People's Champion." *America's Best Racing.* Aug. 8, 2023. www.americasbestracing.net/the-sport/2023-john-henry-undersized-1100-purchase-who-became-the-peoples-champion

Ferry, Tom. "Against All Odds Statue." *All About The Race.* allabouttherace.com/againstallodds

"Frequently Asked Questions About the Overpopulation of Wild Horses and Burros on Federal Lands." American Veterinary Medical Association. www.avma.org/wild-horses-burros-faq

Harry and Snowman. "We Found a 1964 Bulova Watch Ad with Snowman at the Farm in Long Island." Facebook. June 29, 2014. www.facebook.com/harryandsnowman/photos/we

Bibliography

-found-a-1964-bulova-watch-ad-with-snowman-at-the-farm-in-long-island/1522116391
339694/

Henry, Miles. "The World's Fastest Horses: Top Speeds and Common Traits." *Horseracingsense.com*. Nov. 27, 2023. horseracingsense.com/speed-worlds-fastest-horses/

Hersh, Marcus. "How Old Is Too Old for a Racehorse?" *Daily Racing Form*. Dec. 9. 2010. www.drf .com/news/how-old-too-old-racehorse

"John Henry." johnhenryhorse.blogspot.com

"John Henry: Part 1 of 2." Oct. 18, 2011. ESPN. www.youtube.com/watch?v=llm8HgC5lrE

"John Henry: Part 2 of 2." Oct. 18, 2011. ESPN. www.youtube.com/watch?v=hyevJDwBaHg

Johnson, Keeler. "Flashback: John Henry Rallies to Win Inaugural Arlington Million." *Horse Racing Nation*. Aug. 6, 2019. www.horseracingnation.com/news/Flashback_John_Henry_rallies_to _win_inaugural_Arlington_Million_123

Kinnish, Mary Kay. "What Made John Henry Run?" *Equus Magazine*. May 1985. equusmagazine .com/horse-world/johnhenryrun_101107

Lee, April. "Life After Racing: What Happens to Racehorses When They Retire?" *Helpful Horse Hints*. Oct. 18, 2023. www.helpfulhorsehints.com/what-happens-to-racehorses-when-they-retire

Letts, Elizabeth. *The Eighty-Dollar Champion: Snowman, the Horse That Inspired a Nation*. Ballantine Books, 2012.

Letts, Nicole. "Meet the Man Giving Former Racehorses the Ultimate Retirement." *Southern Living*. May 3, 2023. www.southernliving.com/old-friends-racehorse-retirement-farm-kentucky-7488681

Majendie, Matt. "Snowman: 'The Cinderella Horse' Who Rode into a Nation's Hearts." CNN. Nov. 3, 2016. www.cnn.com/2016/10/24/sport/snowman-harry-de-leyer/index.html

Murthi, Vikram. "'Harry and Snowman' Exclusive Clip: Documentary Chronicles Friendship Between Champion Horse and Owner." *IndieWire*. Sept. 22, 2016. www.indiewire.com/features /general/harry-and-snowman-clip-documentary-horse-harry-deleyer-ron-davis-1201729815/

Nack, William. "John Henry Was the One in the Million." *Sports Illustrated*. Sept. 3, 1984. vault .si.com/vault/1984/09/03/john-henry-was-the-one-in-the-million

Paulick, Ray. "Death of a Derby Winner: Slaughterhouse Likely Fate for Ferdinand." *BloodHorse. com*. July 25, 2003. www.bloodhorse.com/horse-racing/articles/180859/death-of-a-derby-winner -slaughterhouse-likely-fate-for-ferdinand

Pedulla, Tom. "Old Friends Farm a Decades-Long Journey for Michael Blowen." *America's Best Racing*. June 26, 2023. www.americasbestracing.net/the-sport/2023-old-friends-farm-decades-long -journey-michael-blowen

Rendel, John. "German Riders Score in Horse Show; Atoll First in $28,650 Remsen." *New York Times*. Nov. 12, 1958. timesmachine.nytimes.com/timesmachine/1958/11/12/82216657.html

Risen, Clay. "Harry Deleyer, 93, Dies; He Saved a Horse and Made Him a Legend." *New York Times*. July 22, 2022. www.nytimes.com/2021/07/22/sports/harry-deleyer-dead.html

Rocca, Mo. "A Kentucky Home for Retired Racehorses." CBS News. May 16, 2021. www.cbsnews.com /news/old-friends-kentucky-home-for-retired-racehorses/

Sellnow, Les. "Leg Conformation." *The Horse*. June 11, 2014. thehorse.com/14455/leg-conformation/

Shoemaker, Bill, and Barney Nagler. "Secrets of the Amazing Shoe: In His Own Words, Bill Shoemaker

Bibliography

Sets the Record Straight About His Legendary Racing Career." *Los Angeles Times*. Feb. 7, 1988. www.latimes.com/archives/la-xpm-1988-02-07-tm-41360-story.html

"Show Jumping Hall of Fame." *Showjumpinghalloffame.net*. Jan. 18, 2012. showjumpinghalloffame .net/pdf/1992%20Snowman.pdf

"Snowman Flies High." Nov. 1, 1961. Photograph. www.loc.gov/item/2013650118

"Snowman Scores at L. I. Horse Show." *New York Times*. June 9, 1958. timesmachine.nytimes.com /timesmachine/1958/06/09/81863484.html

"Snowman." *Snowman: Horse Stars Hall of Fame*. www.horsestarshalloffame.org/inductees/82/snowman

"A Sticky Situation: The History of Glue and Horses." *Horse Rookie*. Aug. 9, 2023. horserookie.com /is-glue-made-from-horses/

Swinney, Nicola Jane. "Sixteen Common Conformation Terms You Should Know, but Probably Don't." *Horse and Hound*. July 19, 2023. www.horseandhound.co.uk/features/common-conformation -terms-explained-311580

"Two-Time Horse of the Year John Henry Euthanized." ESPN. Oct. 8, 2007. www.espn.com/sports /horse/news/story?id=3055036

Old Faithful

"At 103, Sister Jean Publishes Memoir of Faith and Basketball." AP. Feb. 16, 2023. apnews.com/article /sports-parasports-jean-dolores-schmidt-chicago-06b8d438408e6abe08b395e3cd13d7

Beaton, Andrew. "Sister Jean Has Outrun Two Pandemics." *Wall Street Journal*. Mar. 16, 2021. www .wsj.com/articles/sister-jean-loyola-ncaa-tournament-101-years-old-11615855459

Drape, Joe. "Loyola-Chicago Is in the Final Four After a Rout of Kansas State. *New York Times*. Mar. 24, 2018. www.nytimes.com/2018/03/24/sports/ncaabasketball/loyola-chicago-kansas-state -ncaa-tournament.html

Schmidt, Jean Dolores. "Sister Jean: How I Became a Basketball Star at 98." *Newsweek*. Feb. 23, 2023. www.newsweek.com/college-basketball-sister-jean-loyola-march-madness-final-four-chicago -1782675

Schmidt, Jean Dolores, with Seth Davis. *Wake Up with Purpose!: What I've Learned in My First Hundred Years*. Harper, 2023.

Founding Fathers of Comedy

Acken, Lori. "HBO's *If You're Not in the Obit, Eat Breakfast*: We Talk with Carl Reiner!" *Channel Guide Mag.* May 27, 2017. www.channelguidemag.com/tv-news/2017/05/27/if-youre-not-in-obit -eat-breakfast-hbo-carl-reiner-interview/not-in-obit-reiner-white/

"ACLU SoCal Statement on Death of Norman Lear." ACLU of Southern California. Dec. 6, 2023. www.aclusocal.org/en/press-releases/aclu-socal-statement-death-norman-lear

"Act iii." *NormanLear.com*. 2023. www.normanlear.com/act-iii

"All in the Family. Archie Reconciles Lionel and George." Jan. 30, 2023. YouTube. www.youtube.com /watch?v=h65i0vfBa7A

"All in the Family. The Bunkers Have Some Weird Guests." Mar. 29, 2021. YouTube. www.youtube .com/watch?v=RWV9dUCIERo

Bibliography

"All in the Family. George Jefferson Has a Fight with Archie." May 16, 2022. YouTube. www.youtube
   .com/watch?v=tPkgTwf5P4c

Alter, Rebecca. "Rob Reiner, Mel Brooks, Alan Alda, and More Celebs Share Tributes to Carl Reiner."
   Vulture. June 30, 2020. www.vulture.com/2020/06/carl-reiner-rob-reiner-celebrity-tributes.html

Apatow, Judd. "The Immortal Mel Brooks." *The Atlantic*. June 9, 2023. www.theatlantic.com
   /magazine/archive/2023/07/mel-brooks-judd-apatow-interview/674167/

Axelrod, Jim. "The Art of Funnyman Carl Reiner." *CBS Sunday Morning*. Jan. 22, 2023. YouTube.
   www.youtube.com/watch?v=hdUqA-Sf62M

Beard, Alison. "Life's Work: An Interview with Norman Lear." *Harvard Business Review*. Nov. 2014.
   hbr.org/2014/11/norman-lear

Berkvist, Robert, and Peter Keepnews. "Carl Reiner, Multifaceted Master of Comedy, Is Dead at 98."
   New York Times. July 9, 2020. www.nytimes.com/2020/06/30/arts/television/carl-reiner-dead.html

Blackwelder, Carson. "Norman Lear Dead at 101: Jimmy Kimmel, Tyler Perry and More React to
   TV Icon's Death." ABC News. Dec. 6, 2023. abcnews.go.com/GMA/Culture/norman-lear-dead
   -101-jimmy-kimmel-tyler-perry- others-react/story?id=105421042

"Book Excerpt: An Army Tale by Carl Reiner." *Military Times*. Aug. 17, 2022. www.militarytimes
   .com/military-honor/salute-veterans/2016/11/30/book-excerpt-an-army-tale-by-carl-reiner/

Bonanos, Christopher. "Carl Reiner Taught the World What a Comedy Writer Does." *Vulture*. June 30,
   2020. www.vulture.com/2020/06/a-tribute-to-carl-reiner-comic-legend-dead-at-98.html

Bouzereau, Laurent, director. *The Making of The Producers*. 2002. MGM Home Entertainment. DVD.

Brooks, Mel. *All About Me: My Remarkable Life in Show Business*. Ballantine, 2021.

Brooks, Mel, director. *The Producers*. Written by Mel Brooks. 1967. MGM Home Entertainment.
   DVD.

"Caesar's Writers: Mel Brooks Is Late." Nov. 17, 2011. YouTube. www.youtube.com/watch?v=91RK
   gxUUGvw

Campbell, Alastair. "Why Mel Brooks Can Save the Human Race." *The Guardian*. Nov. 2, 2006. www
   .theguardian.com/film/2006/nov/03/comedy

Capretto, Lisa. "Norman Lear Says There's One Big Secret to His Longevity." *HuffPost*. July 27, 2016.
   www.huffpost.com/entry/norman-lear-longevity_n_5797ebe9e4b01180b530c36a

"Carl Reiner." *GI Jews: Jewish Americans in World War II*. June 14, 2017. www.gijewsfilm.com
   /interviews/carl-reiner.php

"Carl Reiner: Keep Laughing." National Comedy Center. Sept. 19, 2023. comedycenter.org/carl
   -reiner-keep-laughing-exhibit/

"Carl Reiner Was Almost the Star of the Dick Van Dyke Show." MeTV. Aug. 31, 2023. www.metv.com
   /stories/carl-reiner-was-almost-the-star-of-the-dick-van-dyke-show

"Carl Reiner's Documentary Explores Life After 90." KPCC. June 5, 2017. www.kpcc.org/news
   /2017/06/05/72566/carl-reiner-s-documentary-explores-life-after-90/

"Carl Reiner's Final Interview." June 22, 2020. YouTube. www.youtube.com/watch?v=mhju_o9FStY

"Celeb Vet: Mel Brooks and Carl Reiner, WWII War Buddies Until the End." *Veterans Advantage*.
   July 13, 2020. www.veteransadvantage.com/blog/veterans-advantage-awards/celebvet-mel-brooks
   -carl-reiner-wwii-war-buddies-until-end

Bibliography

Chawkins, Steve, and Dennis McLellan. "Carl Reiner, Prolific Comedy Legend Who Created 'The Dick Van Dyke Show,' Dead at 98." *Los Angeles Times*. June 30, 2020. www.latimes.com/obituaries /story/2020-06-30/carl-reiner-dead

Cohen, Sandy. "Brooks, Reiner, Lear, Van Dyke Discuss Living Well After 90." AP. May 18, 2017. apnews.com/article/5c06bfa8a2f546c29c349202ff31e6c7

Copeland, Donna. "This Changes Everything." *Texas Art & Film*. July 26, 2019. www.texasartfilm.net /this-changes-everything/

Coyle, Jake. "Q&A: Mel Brooks, 95, Is Still Riffing." AP. Nov. 30, 2021. apnews.com/article/entertain ment-lifestyle-new-york-brooklyn-billy-crystal498d176f828f9b76953f0efe1af4038c

Davis, Ivor. "Mel Brooks Still Rocks in His 90s." 15 Minutes Forever. Dec. 15, 2021. 15minutesforever .com/2021/12/15/mel-brooks-still-rocks-in-his-90s/

Deggans, Eric. "The Legacy of Visionary TV Producer Norman Lear, Dead at 101." NPR. Dec. 6, 2023. www.npr.org/2023/12/06/1217663356/the-legacy-of-visionary-tv-producer-norman-lear -dead-at-101

Dennis, Helen. "These Entertainers in their 90s Offer Suggestions for Good Health and a Long Life." *Los Angeles Daily News*. Dec. 27, 2020. www.dailynews.com/2020/12/27/these-entertainers-in -their-90s-offer-suggestions-for-good-health-and-a-long-life/

Dowd, Maureen. "Mel Brooks Isn't Done Punching Up the History of the World." *New York Times*. Mar. 15, 2023. www.nytimes.com/2023/03/11/style/mel-brooks-comedian.html

Elber, Lynn. "Comedy Legend Carl Reiner Turns Emmy Shot into Punchline." AP. Aug. 22, 2018. apnews.com/article/1e826fe3ef5140e5a09dc3197c351a01

Feldman, Rachel. "Guest Post: Hollywood's Dirty Little Secret." Women and Hollywood. Oct. 4, 2012. www.womenandhollywood.com/guest-post-hollywoods-dirty-little-secret-fb67a2e000d5/

Feloni, Richard. "8 Powerful Life Lessons from 93-Year-Old Norman Lear, One of the Most Influential People in TV History." *Business Insider*. July 7, 2016. www.businessinsider.com/norman-lear-life -lessons-2016-7#you-cant-predict-how-things-

Freeman, Hadley. "Mel Brooks on Losing the Loves of His Life: 'People Know How Good Carl Reiner Was but Not How Great." *The Guardian*. Dec. 4, 2021. https://www.theguardian.com/film/2021 /dec/04/mel-brooks-on-losing-the-loves-of-his-life-people-know-how-good-carl-reiner-was-but -not-how-great

Garelick, Rhonda. "The Quiet Feminism of Norman Lear's Middle-Aged Women." *New York Times*. Dec. 7, 2023. www.nytimes.com/2023/12/07/style/norman-lear-tv-women-feminism.html

Goodman, Amy. "TV Legend Norman Lear on the Black Panthers, Nixon's Enemies List and What Gives Him Hope." *Democracy Now!* Oct. 25, 2016. www.democracynow.org/2016/10/25/norman _lear_on_nixons_enemies_list

Greenberg, Jonathan. "Springtime for Ulysses." *PMLA* 136, no. 5 (October 2021): 728–745.

Halliday, Ayun. "Carl Reiner & Mel Brooks' Timeless Comedy Sketch: The 2000-Year-Old-Man." *Open Culture*. July 3, 2020. www.openculture.com/2020/07/carl-reiner-mel-brooks-timeless -comedy-sketch-the-2000-year-old-man.html

Heimann, Rachel. "#Veteran of the Day: Marine Veteran Bea Arthur." VA: U.S. Department of Veterans Affairs. Mar. 3, 2020. news.va.gov/72168/veteranoftheday-marine-veteran-bea-arthur/

Bibliography

Honeycutt, Kirk. "'We Ran Out of Controversy': Bea Arthur Says Farewell to 'Maude.'" *New York Times*. Apr. 16, 1978. www.nytimes.com/1978/04/16/archives/we-ran-out-of-controversy-bea -arthur-says-farewell-to-maude.html

Hughes, Mike. "Reiner Mastered the Modern Sitcom." June 30, 2020. www.mikehughes.tv/2020/06/30 /reiner-mastered-the-modern-sitcom/

Hyman, Dan. "For Carl Reiner and His Fellow Nonagenarians, Death Can Wait." *New York Times*. June 2, 2017. www.nytimes.com/2017/06/02/arts/television/carl-reiner-if-youre-not-in-the-obit -eat-breakfast-hbo.html

Ibrahim, Samantha. "101-Year-Old Norman Lear Reflects on His Birthday: 'Living in the Moment.'" *New York Post*. July 28, 2023. nypost.com/2023/07/28/101-year-old-norman-lear-reflects-on-his -birthday/

"If You're Not in the Obit, Eat Breakfast." HBO. May 12, 2017. YouTube. www.youtube.com /watch?v=yr85aIIrDHU

Italie, Hillel. "Carl Reiner, Comedy's Rare Untortured Genius, Dies at 98." AP. June 30, 2020. apnews .com/article/ab0308881d262c03587e24c656afc81e

Ivry, Benjamin. "Why Comedy Was the Perfect Career for a Bronx Bred Jewish Boy like Carl Reiner." *Forward*. June 30, 2020. forward.com/culture/449938/why-comedy-was-the-perfect-career-for-a -bronx-bred-jewish-boy-like-carl/

Johnson, Ross. "15 Norman Lear Episodes That Changed TV History." *Lifehacker*. Dec. 6, 2023. life hacker.com/15-norman-lear-episodes-that-changed-tv-history-1849337456

Jonathan LaPook, M.D. [@DrLaPook] "Today, #NormanLear turned 100 & told me this," Twitter, July 27, 2022. twitter.com/DrLaPook/status/1552357143663230977

Kashner, Sam. "Producing *The Producers*." *Vanity Fair*. Jan. 6, 2004. archive.vanityfair.com/article /2004/1/producing-the-producers

Keveney, Bill. "Remembering Carl Reiner: His Best Quotes on Show Business, Eulogies, Friend Mel Brooks." *USA Today*. June 30, 2020. www.usatoday.com/story/entertainment/celebrities /2020/06/30/carl-reiner-death-best-interview-quotes-usa-today/5348869002/

Kilday, Gregg. "Norman Lear on Old Age: 'There's a Good Time to Be Had.'" *Hollywood Reporter*. July 5, 2016. www.hollywoodreporter.com/news/politics-news/norman-lear-confronts-old-age -908636/

"A King of Comedy: An Interview with Carl Reiner." *Los Angeles Review of Books*. Oct. 25, 2020. You-Tube. www.youtube.com/watch?v=YQb_vQUNWho

King, Susan. "Carl Reiner, Mel Brooks, Dick Van Dyke Wow Crowd at *If You're Not in the Obit, Eat Breakfast* Premiere." *Variety*. May 18, 2017. variety.com/2017/scene/news/carl-reiner-mel-brooks -dick-van-dyke-if-youre-not-in-the-obit-eat-breakfast-premiere-1202433968/#!

King, Susan. "Classic Hollywood: Bea Arthur Took 'Maude' out of 'Family's' Shadow. *Los Angeles Times*. Mar. 14, 2015. www.latimes.com/entertainment/classichollywood/la-et-st-ca-bea-arthur -classic-hollywood-20150315-story.html

Kinnard, Judith. "Brooks, Reiner Revive 2,000-Year,-Old Man, Now 2,013." *New York Times*. Aug. 27, 1973. www.nytimes.com/1973/08/27/archives/brooks-reiner-revive-2000yearold-man-now-2013 -appreciative-audience.html

Bibliography

LaMotte, Sandee. "At 99, Iconic Producer Norman Lear Doesn't Want to Quit Working. Can Work Help Us All Live Longer?" CNN. June 3, 2022. www.cnn.com/2022/06/02/health/work-and-aging -life-itself-wellness/index.html

Lear, Kate. "Norman Lear's Daughter Shares His Secret to Longevity on His 100th Birthday." PBS. July 27, 2022. www.pbs.org/wnet/americanmasters/norman-lears-daughter-secret-to-longevity -on-100th-birthday/23044/

Lear, Norman. "On My 100th Birthday, Reflections on Archie Bunker and Donald Trump." *New York Times*. July 27, 2022. www.nytimes.com/2022/07/27/opinion/archie-bunker-donald-trump-nor man-lear.html

Levine, Ken. "Yet Another Reason Why Mel Brooks Was an Inspiration." Dec. 1, 2021. kenlevine .blogspot.com/2021/12/yet-another-reason-why-mel-brooks-was.html

Lloyd, Robert. "Why 'All in the Family' Would Be All but Impossible to Pull Off Today." *Los Angeles Times*. Sept. 22, 2022. www.latimes.com/entertainment-arts/tv/story/2022-09-22/norman-lear -100-all-in-the-family-maude-sanford-son-jeffersons

Locker, Melissa. "Here's What Carl Reiner Had to Say About Life, Family, and Comedy in His Last Interview During Quarantine." *Time*. June 30, 2020. time.com/5861678/carl-reiner-interview/

Luna, Brooke. "Mel Brooks: A Life of Laughter." *Culture Sonar*. Apr. 16, 2022. www.culturesonar.com /mel-brooks-a-life-of-laughter/

Malanowski, Jamie, and Joey Nolfi. "Norman Lear, Legendary 'All in the Family' and 'Jeffersons' Producer, Dies at 101." *Entertainment Weekly*. Dec. 6, 2023. ew.com/norman-lear-dead-age-101 -8411302

Mance, Henry. "Mel Brooks: 'I Should Feel Something Like 91 But I Don't.'" *Financial Times*. Feb. 16, 2018. www.ft.com/content/01fbf2c2-123d-11e8-940e-08320fc2a277

Martin, Steve. "Carl Reiner, Perfect." *New York Times*. July 9, 2020. www.nytimes.com/2020/07/09 /movies/steve-martin-carl-reiner.html

Martinez, Gina. "Norman Lear Credits 'Love and Laughter' for His Longevity on 100th Birthday." CBS News. July 27, 2022. www.cbsnews.com/news/norman-lear-100th-birthday-credits-love -and-laughter/

Mason, Connie. "Wisdom from Betty and Norman." *Cowley Courier Traveler*. Mar. 18, 2022. www .ctnewsonline.com/news/article_dcbbbc4a-a635-11ec-8232-d39a466201d7.html

"Mel Brooks and Carl Reiner Interview (1997)." July 24, 2016. YouTube. www.youtube.com /watch?v=ovKJbf5dWBg

"Mel Brooks, Carl Reiner, and Jerry Seinfeld." June 29, 2020. YouTube. www.youtube.com /watch?v=ZJu7oqiBXcg

"Mel Brooks, Steve Martin, Son Rob Pay Tribute to Carl Reiner." AP. June 30, 2020. apnews.com /article/rob-reiner-dick-van-dyke-sid-caesar-mel-brooks-steve-martin-fddf60cd85313f3d ca8112e9f71cf8be

McGilligan, Patrick. *Funny Man: Mel Brooks*. Harper, 2020.

Nashawaty, Chris. "95 Things We Love About Mel Brooks on His 95th Birthday." AARP. June 24, 2021. www.aarp.org/entertainment/celebrities/info-2021/95-things-we-love-about-mel-brooks.html

Nordyke, Kimberly. "Mel Brooks: 'I Was the Quentin Tarantino of My Day' (Video)." *Hollywood*

Reporter. Apr. 23, 2023. www.hollywoodreporter.com/news/general-news/mel-brooks-i-was
-quentin-444125/

"Norman Lear." The Kennedy Center. 2017. www.kennedy-center.org/artists/l/la-ln/norman-lear/

"Norman Lear Receives the Carol Burnett Award—Golden Globes 2021." NBC. Feb. 28, 2021. You-
Tube. www.youtube.com/watch?v=VG58uqZPWsU

O'Brien, Conan. "Carl Reiner Recites Queen Gertrude's Monologue from 'Hamlet.'" *TBS.* Aug. 18,
2017. YouTube. www.youtube.com/watch?v=RdvwoIFAegg

O'Brien, Conan. "Carl Reiner Tells a Dirty Joke." *TBS.* Mar. 14, 2017. YouTube. www.youtube.com
/watch?v=RcGeOQCNuMo

O'Brien, Conan. "Carl Reiner's WWII Service." *TBS.* Feb. 12, 2016. YouTube. www.youtube.com
/watch?v=b7cbkm07IWs

Odman, Sidney. "Carl Reiner: 8 of His Most Memorable Works." *The Hollywood Reporter.* June 30,
2020. www.hollywoodreporter.com/lists/carl-reiner-dead-8-his-memorable-works-1025615/

Otterson, Joe. "Mel Brooks Talks Working on 'History of the World, Part II' at 96: 'I'm the Jewish Advisor.'" *Variety.* Mar. 6, 2023. variety.com/2023/tv/news/mel-brooks-history-of-the-world-part-ii
-interview-hulu-1235544371/

Poniewozik, James. "Carl Reiner Knew TV Like the Back of His Head." *New York Times.* July 9, 2020.
www.nytimes.com/2020/06/30/arts/television/carl-reiner.html

"Q&A: Mel Brooks." *Billboard.* Dec. 8, 2005. www.billboard.com/music/music-news/qa-mel-brooks
-60417/

Rocca, Mo. "Carl Reiner, a Founding Father of TV Comedy." *CBS Sunday Morning.* July 5, 2020. You-
Tube. www.youtube.com/watch?v=5he62h6GFSU

Rocca, Mo. "LaWanda Page: Death of a Comedy Queen." Mobituaries with Mo Rocca. Podcast. Jan. 3,
2024. mobituaries.com/news/the-podcast/lawanda-page-death-of-a-comedy-queen/

Hoberman, J. "When the Nazis Became Nudniks." *New York Times.* Apr. 15, 2001. www.nytimes
.com/2001/04/15/movies/film-when-the-nazis-became-nudniks.html

Sander, Brice. "Exclusive: Hollywood Icons Norman Lear, Jane Fonda, and Lily Tomlin on
Aging." *Kare11.* May 8, 2017. www.kare11.com/article/entertainment/entertainment-tonight
/exclusive-hollywood-icons-norman-lear-jane-fonda-and-lily-tomlin-on-aging-and-opting-out
-of/89-437779995

Schleier, Curt. "Carl Reiner, 95, Dishes His Secrets to Longevity." *Times of Israel.* May 25, 2017. www
.timesofisrael.com/carl-reiner-95-dishes-his-secrets-to-longevity/

Schulman, Michael. "Mel Brooks Writes It All Down." *The New Yorker.* Nov. 28, 2021. www.new
yorker.com/culture/the-new-yorker-interview/mel-brooks-writes-it-all-down

Seegert, Liz. "Norman Lear on Aging, Comedy, and a Happy Life." Association of Health Care Journalists. Oct. 18, 2017. healthjournalism.org/blog/2017/10/norman-lear-on-aging-comedy-and-a
-happy-life/

"Siskel & Ebert: Take 2—Mel Brooks or Woody Allen." July 6, 2021. YouTube. www.youtube.com
/watch?v=iK8l7TMhziE

Smith, Tracy. "Golden Boys." CBS News. June 4, 2017. www.cbsnews.com/news/golden-boys-dick
-van-dyke-carl-reiner-norman-lear/

Snelling, Sherri. "Norman Lear on Laughter, Longevity, and Love for the USA." *Next Avenue*. Aug. 5, 2015. www.nextavenue.org/norman-lear-on-laughter-longevity-and-love-for-america/

Stamberg, Susan. "Carl Reiner, Who Turns 97 Soon, Is Still Working on Projects." NPR. Jan. 21, 2019. www.npr.org/2019/01/21/687085948/carl-reiner-who-turns-97-soon-is-still-working- on-projects

Starr, Michael. "Carl Reiner's Life Advice for Senior Citizens: 'Get Off Your Ass.'" *New York Post*. June 1, 2017. nypost.com/2017/06/01/carl-reiners-life-advice-for-senior-citizens-get-off-your-ass/

Stuever, Hank. "Carl Reiner's Key to Living a Long, Funny Life? Never Stop Having Something to Say." *Washington Post*. June 30, 2020. www.washingtonpost.com/entertainment/tv/carl-reiners-key-to -living-a-long-funny-life-never-stop-having-something-to-say/2020/06/30/b7c4a75c-baec-11ea -8cf5-9c1b8d7f84c6_story.html

Stuever, Hank. "Norman Lear Put His Foot Down and Trump's White House Flinched." *Washington Post*. Nov. 26, 2017. www.washingtonpost.com/entertainment/tv/norman-lear-put-his-foot-down --and-trumps-white-house-flinched/2017/11/26/1b08527a-c5b1-11e7-84bc-5e285c7f4512_story .html

"The Very Best of Mel Brooks with Gene Wilder, Anne Bancroft, & Carl Reiner." June 14, 2019. YouTube. www.youtube.com/watch?v=XTujWe175Ts

Walsh, David. "American Comic Writer and Performer Carl Reiner, 1922–2020." *World Socialist Web Site*. July 2, 2020. www.wsws.org/en/articles/2020/07/02/rein-j02.html

Wilmore, Larry, host. "Remembering Norman Lear." *Black on the Air*. Spotify. Dec. 8, 2023. podcasts .apple.com/us/podcast/larry-wilmore-black-on-the-air/id1234429850

"Witness to History." Georgetown University et al. Carl Reiner Collection. 1943. Personal Narrative. Retrieved from the Library of Congress. www.loc.gov/item/afc2001001.76156/

Wojciechowski, Michael. "Carl Reiner on Being Vital After 90." *Next Avenue*. June 2, 2017. www.next avenue.org/carl-reiner-vital-after-90/

Old Jokes

Burbank, Luke. "Toying Around with Toymaker Eddy Goldfarb." *CBS Sunday Morning*. Dec. 17, 2023. www.cbsnews.coam/video/toying-around-with-toymaker-eddy-goldfarb/

Kisken, Tom. "Thousand Oaks Inventor Who Produced Talking Teeth, 800 Other Toys Still Working at 100." *Ventura County Star*. Dec. 23, 2021. www.vcstar.com/story/news/local/2021/12/23 /legendary-inventor-kerplunk-yakity-yak-wind-up-teeth-800-other-baby-boomer-toys-works -age-100/8918832002/

Jensen, Erin. "102-Year-Old Toy Inventor, Star of 'Eddy's World' Documentary, Attributes Longevity to This." *USA Today*. Dec. 1, 2023. www.usatoday.com/story/entertainment/tv/2023/12/01/eddys -world-documentary-toy-inventor-eddy-goldfarb/71731103007/

"The Man Who Invented 800 Iconic Toys." *New Yorker Video*. Dec. 14, 2020. www.newyorker.com /video/watch/the-man-who-invented-more-than-eight-hundred-iconic-toys

Unfinished Business

Alvarez, Lizette. "Sharks Absent, Swimmer, 64, Strokes from Cuba to Florida." *New York Times*. Sept. 2, 2013. www.nytimes.com/2013/09/03/sports/nyad-completes-cuba-to-florida-swim.html

Bibliography

Boyle, Alan. "Five Years After Pluto Encounter, New Horizons Probe Does a Far-out Parallax Experiment." *GeekWire*. June 12, 2020. www.geekwire.com/2020/five-years-pluto-mission-new-horizons-probe-far-parallax-experiment/

Brathwaite, Lester Fabian. "How Nyad Star Annette Bening and the Filmmakers Weathered a Storm for Inspiring Long-Distance Swim." *Entertainment Weekly*. Sept. 29, 2023. ew.com/movies/nyad-director-annette-bening-swim-scenes-preparation/

"Brian May News24 Interview from La Palma." July 24, 2007. YouTube. www.youtube.com/watch?v=79tZ36noVeo

Brockes, Emma. "Diana Nyad's Epic Swim from Cuba to Florida Isn't Even the Most Astounding Part of the Story." *The Guardian*. Nov. 9, 2023. www.theguardian.com/commentisfree/2023/nov/09/diana-nyad-cuba-us-netflix-annette-bening-jodie-foster

Clinton, Hillary Rodham, and Chelsea Clinton. *The Book of Gutsy Women: Favorite Stories of Courage and Resilience*. Simon & Schuster, 2020.

Drake, Nadia. "Meet the Rock Guitarist Who Helped NASA Land on an Asteroid." *National Geographic*. Oct. 4, 2023. www.nationalgeographic.com/science/article/brian-may-guitarist-astrophysicist

Eames, Tom. "Brian May Interview: Queen Legend Reveals How Buddy Holly and Lonnie Donegan Influenced Him." *Gold*. Apr. 26, 2022. www.goldradiouk.com/artists/queen/brian-may-interview-another-world-buddy-holly/

Eicher, David J. "Brian May: A Life in Science and Music: The Full Story." *Astronomy Magazine*. July 23, 2012. www.astronomy.com/science/brian-may-a-life-in-science-and-music-the-full-story/

Gajewski, Ryan. "*Nyad* Star Annette Bening on Swimming Eight Hours a Day for Netflix Biopic: 'It Has Changed My Life.'" *Hollywood Reporter*. Nov. 17, 2023. www.hollywoodreporter.com/movies/movie-news/nyad-star-annette-bening-swimming-eight-hours-netflix-1235662998/

Johnson, John. "Brian May: From Queen to Cosmos." *Los Angeles Times*. June 7, 2008. www.latimes.com/archives/la-xpm-2008-jun-07-sci-queen7-story.html

Kaufman, Michelle. "Inside Hillary Clinton's Email, How Swimmer Diana Nyad Got a Clearance to Cuba." *Miami Herald*. Sept. 2, 2015. www.miamiherald.com/news/politics-government/article33212961.html

Kluger, Jeffrey. "Queen Guitarist (and Astrophysicist) Brian May on His Work with NASA and His New Song about Ultima Thule." *Time*. Jan. 2, 2019. time.com/5492147/brian-may-ultima-thule/

Lea, Robert. "Queen Guitar Legend Brian May Helps Analyze NASA's OSIRIS-Rex Asteroid Samples." *Space.com*. Oct. 18, 2023. www.space.com/nasa-osiris-rex-brian-may-queen-guitarist-helps-analyze-asteroid-sample

Levy, Ariel. "Diana Nyad Breaks the Waves." *The New Yorker*. Feb. 2, 2014. www.newyorker.com/magazine/2014/02/10/diana-nyad-profile-cuba-florida-swim

Lewis, Danny. "Queen Guitarist Brian May Is Now a New Horizons Science Collaborator." *Smithsonian.com*, July 29, 2015. www.smithsonianmag.com/smart-news/new-horizons-team-got-little-help-queen-guitarist-brian-may-180956073/

Lipsyte, Robert. "Reflections on a Secret Life in Professional Sports." *New York Times*. Sept. 12, 1999. www.nytimes.com/1999/09/12/sports/reflections-on-a-secret-life-in-professional-sports.html

Bibliography

May, Brian. "Brian May in Exeter Today: Citation and Acceptance Speech." *BrianMay.com*. July 10, 2007. brianmay.com/brian-news/2007/07/brian-may-in-exeter-today-citation-and-acceptance-speech/

Meek, Andy. "Diana Nyad Completes Cuba-to-Florida Swim on Fifth Try." *Time*. Sept. 2, 2013. keepingscore.blogs.time.com/2013/09/02/diana-nyad-becomes-the-first-to-complete-cuba-to-florida-swim/

Nyad, Diana. "My Life After Sexual Assault." *New York Times*. Nov. 9, 2017. www.nytimes.com/2017/11/09/opinion/diana-nyad-sexual-assault.html

"Oct News Bits 2: Judy Davis, Tony Roberts, Diana Nyad, Phil Rosenthal, Mr Robot and More." *The Woody Allen Pages*. Oct. 31, 2015. www.woodyallenpages.com/2015/10/oct-news-bits-2-judy-davis-tony-roberts-diana-nyad-phil-rosenthal-mr-robot-and-more/

"Orders and Medals." *UK Honours System*. May 11, 2023. honours.cabinetoffice.gov.uk/about/orders-and-medals/

Park, Alice. "The Deeper Story Behind Netflix's *Nyad*." *Time*. Nov. 3, 2023. time.com/6330894/nyad-movie-true-story-netflix/

Petit, Stephanie. "Hillary Clinton Talks About the Inspiration That Will Get Her Through the General Election." *People*. June 9, 2016. people.com/celebrity/hillary-clinton-says-mother-and-diana-nyad-book-are-her-inspiration/

Prial, Frank J. "Woman Swimmer Circles Manhattan on Her Second Attempt." *New York Times*. Oct. 7, 1975. www.nytimes.com/1975/10/07/archives/woman-swimmer-circles-manhattan-on-her-2d-attempt-woman-swims.html

Sanderson, Frank. "Dr Brian May CBE." Liverpool John Moores University. 2007. www.ljmu.ac.uk/about-us/fellows/honorary-fellows-2007/brian-may

Sloop, Hope. "Annette Bening Recalls Crying in the Pool While Training for Demanding Diana Nyad Movie." *ET Online*. Nov. 14, 2023. www.etonline.com/annette-bening-recalls-crying-in-the-pool-while-training-for-demanding-diana-nyad-movie-exclusive

"Tim Naylor." *Tim Naylor's Home Page*, University of Exeter. www.astro.ex.ac.uk/people/timn/. Accessed Nov. 29, 2023.

Vasarhaelyi, Elizabeth Chai, and Jimmy Chin, directors. *Nyad*, 2023. Black Bear Pictures/Mad Chance Productions, Netflix.

Walsh, Savannah. "Diana Nyad's Swimming-World Controversy Meets Oscar-Season Scrutiny." *Vanity Fair*. Oct. 18, 2023. www.vanityfair.com/hollywood/2023/10/diana-nyads-swimming-world-controversy-meets-oscar-season-scrutiny

Wolk, Douglas. "The 250 Greatest Guitarists of All Time." *Rolling Stone*. Oct. 10, 2023. www.rollingstone.com/music/music-lists/best-guitarists-1234814010/

Old Smoky

Disbrowe, Paula. "Southern Makers: Tootsie Tomanetz." *The Local Palate: Food Culture of the South*. June–July 2019. thelocalpalate.com/articles/southern-makers-tootsie-tomanetz/

"Lexington: Snow's Barbecue." *Texas Monthly*. June 2008. www.texasmonthly.com/food/lexington-snows-bbq/

Bibliography

Pennell, Julie. "Meet the 83-Year-Old Texas BBQ Pitmaster Shaking Up the Culinary World." *Today*. Oct. 14, 2018. www.today.com/food/meet-83-year-old-pitmaster-shaking-culinary-world-t13 9751

Vaughn, Daniel. "Snow's Queen." *Texas Monthly*. Oct. 2016. www.texasmonthly.com/food/meet -legendary-snows-bbq-pitmaster-tootsie-tomanetz

It's About Time

America Is Hard to See. Whitney Museum of American Art. 2015. whitney.org/exhibitions/america -is-hard-to-see

Ball, Phillip. "John Goodenough Obituary." *The Guardian*. July 10, 2023. www.theguardian.com /science/2023/jul/10/john-goodenough-obituary

Binlot, Ann. "'Lines of Sight': Carmen Herrera's Minimal Abstraction Takes Over the Whitney Museum of American Art." *Wallpaper*. Sept. 19, 2016. www.wallpaper.com/art/cuban-artist-carmen -herreras-minimal-abstraction-takes-over-ny-whitney-museum-of-american-art

Boyers, Sara Jane, et al. "Painting the Sky: The Kites of Tyrus Wong." *CODAworx*. Apr. 1, 2020. www .codaworx.com/projects/painting-the-sky-the-kites-of-tyrus-wong-city-of-malibu/

"Carmen Herrera." *Carmen Herrera: Whitney Museum of American Art*. whitney.org/artists/15319

Cotter, Holland. "Concrete Realities: The Art of Carmen Herrera, Fanny Sanin and Mira Schendel." *New York Times*. May 14, 2004. www.nytimes.com/2004/05/14/arts/art-review-concrete-realities -art-carmen-herrera-fanny-sanin-mira-schendel.html

"Dana Miller on Carmen Herrera: Lines of Sight." Whitney Museum of Art. Nov. 10, 2016. YouTube. www.youtube.com/watch?v=IfTAh6L-GHg

De Bertodano, Helena. "Carmen Herrera: 'Is It a Dream?'" *The Telegraph*, Dec. 20, 2010. www .telegraph.co.uk/culture/art/art-features/8207018/Carmen-Herrera-Is-it-a-dream.html

Emma. "Animators' Strike 1941." *Once Upon a Disney Blog*. Aug. 10, 2017. onceuponadisneyblog .wordpress.com/2017/06/25/animators-strike-1941/

Espinel, Mónica. "Carmen Herrera's Chronology for Lines of Sight." Whitney Museum of American Art. *MonicaEspinel.com*. Sept. 16, 2016. monicaespinel.com/wp-content/uploads/2020/03 /Carmen-Herrera-Lines-of-Sight-%E2%80%93-Chronology.pdf

Fang, Karen. "Commercial Design and Midcentury Asian American Art: The Greeting Cards of Tyrus Wong." *Panorama*. Spring 2021. journalpanorama.org/article/asian-american-art/the-greeting -cards-of-tyrus-wong/

Fox, Margalit. "Tyrus Wong, *Bambi* Artist Thwarted by Racial Bias, Dies at 106." *New York Times*. Dec. 30, 2016. www.nytimes.com/2016/12/30/movies/tyrus-wong-dies-bambi-disney.html

Goodenough, John B. "A Theory of the Deviation from Close Packing in Hexagonal Metal Crystals." *Physical Review* 89, no. 1 (1953), pp. 282–294. doi.org/10.1103/physrev.89.282

Gregg, Helen. "From UChicago to Nobel: How John Goodenough Sparked the Wireless Revolution." *University of Chicago News*. Dec. 3, 2019. news.uchicago.edu/story/how-john-goodenough -sparked-wireless-revolution

Gregg, Helen. "His Current Quest." *University of Chicago Magazine*. Summer 2016. mag.uchicago .edu/science-medicine/his-current-quest

Bibliography

Gyorody, Andrea. "Tyrus Wong." *Now Dig This! Art in Black Los Angeles, 1960–1980.* Digital Archive. Los Angeles. Hammer Museum. 2016. hammer.ucla.edu/now-dig-this/artists/tyrus-wong

Hattenstone, Simon. "Carmen Herrera: 'Men Controlled Everything, Not Just Art.'" *The Guardian.* Dec. 31, 2016. www.theguardian.com/artanddesign/2016/dec/31/carmen-herrera-men-controlled -everything-art

Lee, Adrienne. "UT Mourns Lithium-Ion Battery Inventor and Nobel Prize Recipient John Good-enough." *UT News.* June 26, 2023. news.utexas.edu/2023/06/26/ut-mourns-lithium-ion-battery -inventor-and-nobel-prize-recipient-john-goodenough/

"Lithium-Ion Battery: Clean Energy Institute." Clean Energy Institute, University of Washington. Aug. 16, 2023. www.cei.washington.edu/education/science-of-solar/lithium-ion-battery/

Loos, Ted. "An Artist at 100, Thinking Big but Starting Small." *New York Times.* Apr. 15, 2016. www .nytimes.com/2016/04/17/arts/design/an-artist-at-100-thinking-big-but-starting-small.html

McFadden, Robert D. "Carmen Herrera, Cuban-Born Artist Who Won Fame at 89, Dies at 106." *New York Times.* Feb. 13, 2022. www.nytimes.com/2022/02/13/arts/design/carmen-herrera-dead.html

McFadden, Robert D. "John B. Goodenough, 100, Dies; Nobel-Winning Creator of the Lithium-Ion Battery." *New York Times.* June 26, 2023. www.nytimes.com/2023/06/26/science/john-good enough-dead.html

Morgan, Thaddeus. "How Hollywood Cast White Actors in Caricatured Asian Roles." *History.com.* A&E Television Networks. Aug. 20, 2018. www.history.com/news/yellowface-whitewashing-in -film-america

The Nobel Prize [@NobelPrize]. "Love Has to Do with Friendship." *Twitter.* Feb. 14, 2023. twitter. com/NobelPrize/status/1625573659078189074

Obama, Michelle. "Remarks by the First Lady at Opening of the Whitney Museum." National Archives and Records Administration. Apr. 30, 2015. obamawhitehouse.archives.gov/the-press -office/2015/04/30/remarks-first-lady-opening-whitney-museum

"Otis Legacy Project: Tyrus Wong, 1935: Otis College of Art and Design." Nov. 2007. Otis College of Art and Design. www.otis.edu/video/tyrus-wong

"Remembering *Bambi* Artist Tyrus Wong." Jan. 8, 2017. YouTube. www.youtube.com/watch?v=fx FAQZdnXQU

Salisbury, Katie Gee. "We Need to Talk about Yellowface." *Medium.* ZORA. May 23, 2023, zora .medium.com/we-need-to-talk-about-yellowface-b4fdcb858b51

Sontag, Deborah. "At 94, She's the Hot New Thing in Painting." *New York Times.* Dec. 19, 2009. www .nytimes.com/2009/12/20/arts/design/20herrera.html

See, Lisa. *On Gold Mountain: The One-Hundred-Year Odyssey of My Chinese-American Family.* Vintage Books, 2012.

Tom, Pamela, director. *Tyrus.* Written by Pamela Tom, featuring Tyrus Wong, 2015. PBS. American Masters. DVD.

Wagstaff, Steel. "The Lives." The *"Objectivists."* Sept. 15, 2018. theobjectivists.org/the-lives/

"Water to Paper, Paint to Sky: The Art of Tyrus Wong." *Water to Paper, Paint to Sky: The Art of Tyrus Wong.* The Walt Disney Family Museum. 2013. www.waltdisney.org/exhibitions/water-paper -paint-sky-art-tyrus-wong

Wong, Tyrus, and Bill Stern. *Mid-Century Mandarin: The Clay Canvases of Tyrus Wong*. Museum of California Design, 2004.

Woo, Byelaine. "Tyrus Wong, Artist Whose Paintings Inspired Disney's *Bambi* and Other Films, Dies at 106." *Los Angeles Times*. Dec. 31, 2017. www.latimes.com/local/lanow/la-me-ln-tyrus-wong -obit-20161230-story.html

Old-Fashioned

Dowd, Maureen. "Ann Roth Is Hollywood's Secret Weapon." *New York Times*. July 23, 2023. www .nytimes.com/2023/07/23/style/ann-roth-costume-designer.html

Hiatt, Brian. "The Brain Behind *Barbie*: Inside the Brilliant Mind of Greta Gerwig." *Rolling Stone*. July 3, 2023. www.rollingstone.com/tv-movies/tv-movie-features/barbie-greta-gerwig-interview -margot-robbie-ryan-gosling-superhero-movie-1234769344/

Longsdorf, Amy. "It's the Clothes That Make This Woman." *The Morning Call*. Mar. 23, 2003. www .mcall.com/2003/03/23/its-the-clothes-that-make-this-woman-costume-designer-ann-roth -could-again-be-draped-in-oscar-glory/

Paskin, Willa. "Greta Gerwig's *Barbie* Dream Job." *New York Times Magazine*. July 11, 2023. www .nytimes.com/2023/07/11/magazine/greta-gerwig-barbie.html

Misspent Old Age

"Ezra Pound." *Poetry Foundation*. www.poetryfoundation.org/poets/ezra-pound

Grimes, William. "Phil Spector, Famed Music Producer and Convicted Murderer, Dies at 81." *New York Times*. Jan. 17, 2021. www.nytimes.com/2021/01/17/arts/music/phil-spector-dead.html

Klein, Christopher. "Why John Tyler May Be the Most Reviled U.S. President Ever." *History.com*. Jan. 16, 2020. www.history.com/news/john-tyler-most-unpopular-president

Pound, Ezra. *Literary Essays of Ezra Pound*, edited by T. S. Eliot. New Directions, 1968.

Thrush, Glenn, and Neil Vigdor. "Rudy Giuliani Denies He Did Anything Wrong in New *Borat* Movie." *New York Times*. Oct. 21, 2020. www.nytimes.com/2020/10/21/us/politics/rudy-giuliani -borat.html

"Tycoon of Teen Wrestles with Dark Demons." *The Age*. Feb. 5, 2003. www.theage.com.au/entertain ment/music/tycoon-of-teen-wrestles-with-dark-demons-20030205-gdv6bv.html

Old Fogey

Cantwell, David. "The Creedence Clearwater Revival." *The New Yorker*. Aug. 17, 2022. www.new yorker.com/culture/cultural-comment/the-creedence-clearwater-revival-revival

"Creedence Clearwater Revival." *Billboard*. www.billboard.com/artist/creedence-clearwater-revival/

Fogerty, John, with Jimmy McDonough. *Fortunate Son: My Life, My Music*. Little, Brown, 2015.

Fong-Torres, Ben. "Creedence C'water at the Hop." *Rolling Stone*. Apr. 5, 1969. www.rollingstone.com /music/music-features/creedence-cwater-at-the-hop-186659/

Rogers, Nate. "After Decades of Legal Battles, John Fogerty Is Finally Free." *Los Angeles Times*. Oct. 8, 2023. www.latimes.com/entertainment-arts/music/story/2023-10-05/john-fogerty-creedence -clearwater-revival-contract

Bibliography

An Old Story

Allingham, Philip V. "Dickens: 'The Man Who Invented Christmas.'" *The Victorian Web: Literature History and Culture in the Age of Victoria*. Dec. 14, 2009. victorianweb.org/authors/dickens/xmas/pva63.html

Davis, Paul B. *Critical Companion to Charles Dickens: A Literary Reference to His Life and Work*. Facts on File, 2007.

Dickens, Charles. *A Christmas Carol*. Edited by Richard Kelly. Broadview Press, 2003.

"Did Dickens Really 'Invent' Christmas?" The Dickens Project. University of California, Santa Cruz. Mar. 18, 2012. https://dickens.ucsc.edu/resources/faq/christmas.html

Dotio, Crucible. "A Dickensian Christmas." Trinity Hall, Cambridge. Dec. 5, 2014. www.trinhall.cam.ac.uk/library/a-dickensian-christmas/

Dowd, Maureen. "Why Dickens Haunts Us." *New York Times*. Dec. 24, 2022. www.nytimes.com/2022/12/24/opinion/why-dickens-haunts-us.html

Henson, Brian. "How We Made *The Muppet Christmas Carol*." Interview by Ben Beaumont-Thomas. *The Guardian*. Dec. 21, 2015. www.theguardian.com/culture/2015/dec/21/how-we-made-the-muppet-christmas-carol

John, Juliet. *Dickens and Mass Culture*. Oxford University Press, 2013.

McCarthy, Patrick J. Review of *Christmas and Charles Dickens* by David Parker. *Dickens Quarterly* 23, no. 3 (2006), pp. 192–95. *JSTOR*. www.jstor.org/stable/45292081

"Merry Christmas from the Limited Editions Club, 1934." Salisbury House and Gardens. Dec. 19, 2014. salisburyhouseandgardens.com/2014/12/19/merry-christmas-from-the-limited-editions-club-1934/

Pesca, Mike. "A Brief History of Evil Finger-Tenting." *Slate*. Mar. 24, 2014. slate.com/culture/2014/03/muppets-most-wanted-when-did-finger-tenting-or-steepling-become-a-symbol-of-evil.html

Rocca, Mo. "The Story of *A Christmas Carol*." *CBS Sunday Morning*. Dec. 20, 2015. YouTube. www.youtube.com/watch?v=CGGrnco4hKw

"Scrooge, or Marley's Ghost (1901)." BFI National Archive. Nov. 3, 2009. YouTube. www.youtube.com/watch?v=O9Mk-B7MKP8

Slater, Michael. "The Origins of *A Christmas Carol*." British Library. June 9, 2014. YouTube. www.youtube.com/watch?v=cTHAN3_P7uE

Tomalin, Claire. *Charles Dickens: A Life*. Penguin, 2011.

Tully, Shawn. "Who Is the Real Montgomery Burns?" *Fortune*. Mar. 7, 2015. fortune.com/2015/03/07/who-is-the-real-montgomery-burns/

About the Authors

Mo Rocca is a correspondent for *CBS Sunday Morning*, host of the hit *Mobituaries* podcast, and host of *The Henry Ford's Innovation Nation*. He's also a frequent panelist on NPR's hit weekly quiz show *Wait Wait . . . Don't Tell Me!* and host and creator of Cooking Channel's *My Grandmother's Ravioli*. Rocca is coauthor of the *New York Times* bestselling *Mobituaries: Great Lives Worth Reliving* and author of *All the Presidents' Pets: The Story of One Reporter Who Refused to Roll Over.*

Jonathan Greenberg is a professor of English at Montclair State University and the author of two books of literary criticism along with many articles and essays. He is also an Emmy Award–winning screenwriter who has written for children's shows including *Rugrats*, *Hey Arnold!*, and *Arthur*. Greenberg is the coauthor of *Mobituaries: Great Lives Worth Reliving.*